THE ANCIENT PATHS

GRAHAM ROBB

THE ANCIENT PATHS

Discovering the Lost Map of Celtic Europe

PICADOR

First published 2013 by Picador
an imprint of Pan Macmillan, a division of Macmillan Publishers Limited
Pan Macmillan, 20 New Wharf Road, London N1 9RR
Basingstoke and Oxford
Associated companies throughout the world
www.panmacmillan.com

ISBN 978-0-330-53150-4 HB
ISBN 978-1-4472-2976-6 TPB

3 5 7 9 8 6 4 2

A CIP catalogue record for this book is available from the British Library.

Typeset by Palimpsest Book Production Ltd, Falkirk, Stirlingshire
Printed and bound by CPI Group (UK) Ltd, Croydon, CR0 4YY

Visit www.picador.com to read more about all our books
and to buy them. You will also find features, author interviews and
news of any author events, and you can sign up for e-newsletters
so that you're always first to hear about our new releases.

For my sister Alison

Contents

Protohistory

The idea that became this book arrived one evening like an unwanted visitor. It clearly expected to stay for a long time, and I knew that its presence in my home would be extremely compromising. Treasure maps and secret paths belong to childhood. An adult scholar who sees an undiscovered ancient world reveal itself, complete with charts, instruction manual and guidebook, is bound to question the functioning of his mental equipment.

I was living at the time in a thatched cottage on a hill to the west of Oxford, in the land of Matthew Arnold's Scholar Gypsy. It was the setting of a child's fantasy world, the kind of place where historical secrets seem to offer themselves up like apples from a prolific, untended tree. In the garden, along with the remains of Victorian picnics and the luminous, degraded waste of the twentieth century, there were burnt flints, pieces of smelted metal and crudely fired roof-tile. Under the tangle of a spindle tree, I found a small Iron Age brooch with the corroded remains of its fastening pin and a pattern of three concentric circles. The farmer who lived next door showed me cardboard boxes full of quern stones used for grinding, Samian ware and Roman coins unearthed by his plough.

Though no book mentions it, this quiet place had once been a busy junction. Along one side of the garden, a bridleway was the end of an ancient *straet* that followed the limestone escarpment above the Thames and led to the Berkshire Downs and the Iron Age hill figure known as the Uffington White Horse. On the other side, an unpaved road climbed from a crossing of the Thames called Bablock Hythe, where there is now neither a bridge nor a ford. For many centuries, long before there was a place called Oxford, cattle and sheep had been driven up from the river to the point where the two roads met and broadened into a green with a spring and a pond. The contours of this ancestor of Cumnor village, which lies a twelve-minute walk from the later, medieval centre near the church, were masked by the more recent alignments of garden hedges and parking bays, but it was still possible to make out the form of the earlier village from an upstairs window. These patterns of settlement are too old to appear in documents. An abrupt bank of earth, and the remnant of a circular arrangement that gives the modern road a dangerous curve, are the probable vestiges of an Iron Age hill fort that overlooked the prehistoric settlement on the floodplain of the Thames at Farmoor.

In these conditions, it would not have been surprising if some chronic state of historical hallucination had taken hold. The irresistible visitor in the upstairs room took the form of a diagonal line on a map of western Europe, printed out on two large sheets of paper. I had been planning a cycling expedition along the Via Heraklea, the fabled route of Hercules from the ends of the earth – the 'Sacred Promontory' at the south-western tip of the Iberian Peninsula – across the Pyrenees and the plains of Provence towards the white curtain of the Alps (fig. 1). The hero's journey, with a herd of stolen cattle, is the legendary trace of one of the oldest routes in the Western world. For much of its course, it exists only as an abstraction, an ideal trajectory joining various sites that were associated with Hercules. Where it skirts the Mediterranean in southern France, on certain stretches it turns into a track, sometimes following the trails of transhumant animals, sometimes materialized as the Roman Via Domitia and the modern A9 autoroute. These practical, secular routes run up the eastern coast of Spain, turn north-east in France, and eventually wander off towards Italy. But in its original, mythic incarnation, the Via Heraklea marches in a straight line like the son of a god for whom a mountain was a paltry obstacle.

Two things struck me about this transcontinental diagonal. First, if the surviving sections are projected in both directions, the Heraklean Way follows the same east-north-easterly bearing for a thousand miles, and arrives, precisely, at the Alpine pass of Montgenèvre, which the Celts* called Matrona (the 'Spring of the Mother-Goddesses'). This

---

* The 'Note on Celtic origins' on p. 305 explains that, whatever later interpretations the name acquired, the 'Celts' (with a hard 'c') were not an ethnic group but the inhabitants of Iron Age Europe who shared certain cultural traits and who were

is the pass that Hercules is supposed to have created by smashing his way through the rock. It was as though, when he set off from the Sacred Promontory, he had been carrying some ancient positioning device which told him that he would cross the Alps at that exact point.

The second glimmer of something remarkable was the familiar appearance of the trajectory on the printout. Many ancient cultures – including the Celts, the Etruscans and, occasionally, the Romans – angled their temples, tombs and streets so that they either faced or stood in a geometrical relationship to the rising sun of the solstice. This is one of the two times of the year (around 21 June and 21 December) when the sun rises and sets in almost exactly the same place several days in a row. I consulted the online oracle of astronomical data: two thousand years ago, at a Mediterranean latitude, the trajectory of the Via Heraklea was the angle of the rising sun at the summer solstice – or, if the observer were facing the other way, of the setting sun at the winter solstice.*

This cosmic coincidence has remained entirely undetected. Perhaps its grandeur renders it effectively invisible. Even the least sceptical historian would doubt its existence. Yet it led to so many other verifiable discoveries that it seemed at times to have a mind of its own, a mechanism from another world, accidentally reactivated. The journeys it entailed took several years, but it became apparent within the first few months that the solstice path had been deliberately created. Druids and Druidesses – the priests or scientists of the Celts – standing anywhere on that ancient path, knew that when they looked along it to the west, they were looking towards the ends of the earth, beyond which there was nothing but the monster-haunted ocean and the land of the dead. In the other direction, they were facing the Alps and the Matrona Pass through which the sun returned to the world of the living.

Gradually, a third coincidence added itself to the picture. A few years before, while researching *The Discovery of France*, I had read

---

variously blond, dark-haired, red-haired, curly-haired, tall or short, pale or swarthy, belligerent or pacific. A map of the greatest extent of Celtic lands (sometimes referred to as 'Keltika') is on p. 116. The same map depicts the multiple origins of the Celts according to a Celtic legend.

* For precise details, see p. 14.

about an enigmatic name – Mediolanum – which the ancient Celts
had given to about sixty locations between Britain and the Black Sea.
It meant something like 'sanctuary' or 'sacred enclosure' of 'the centre'
or 'middle'. The word 'Mediolanum' is thought to have been related
to a notion that is also found in other mythologies: the idea that our
world is a Middle Earth whose sacred sites correspond to places in
the upper and lower worlds. In Norse and Germanic mythology, the
word is 'Midgard', from which J. R. R. Tolkien derived the name of
the fictional universe of *The Hobbit* and *The Lord of the Rings*.

In 1974, a professor of literature called Yves Vadé suggested that
the Celts had organized these 'middle places' according to a network,
and that they had been arranged so that each one was equidistant
from two others. The idea was taken up in 1994 by the Professor of
Geography at the Sorbonne, Xavier de Planhol, who concluded that
the network might briefly have served some practical or religious
purpose but that it had been abandoned at an early stage. A random
scattering of dots would produce similar results, and there were other
problems with the idea, which will be mentioned later in this book.
The name was intriguing all the same, especially since, after retracing
the etymologies of all the Gaulish* place names along the route, I
found, on or near the line of the Heraklean Way, six places that had
once been called Mediolanum.

From then on, 'coincidences' cropped up with surprising frequency.
A complex, beautiful pattern of lines emerged, based on solar alignments
and elementary Euclidean geometry. I began to see, as though in some
miraculously preserved document, the ancient birth of modern Europe.
The places called Mediolanum had belonged to an early and comparatively chaotic stage of this mapping of a continent. Out of that fertile
confusion of local systems, a vast network had evolved. The geography
of the Western world had been organized into a grid of 'solstice lines',
based on the original Via Heraklea, with precisely measured parallels
and meridians determining the locations of temples, towns and battles.
At an even later stage, in Gaul, and, more spectacularly, in the British

---

* 'Gaulish' was usually synonymous with 'Celtic' but was also applied – as it is today
and in this book – to the inhabitants of the country known as Gaul (roughly coter-
minous with France). The Gauls spoke a Celtic language known as Gaulish, which
was a branch of Continental Celtic.

Isles, some long-distance roads had been constructed as literal incarnations of the solstice lines. Knowledge of that grid had been lost in the bustle and belligerence of the Roman empire, and it often seemed as though that wonder of the ancient world had never existed at all.

For several months, I followed the Heraklean Way and the other lines on the map, or rather, scrolled along them repeatedly at what must eventually have been the average speed of a real mouse covering the same itinerary on the ground. Ten years ago, without digital maps and mapping software, this would not have been possible – which is one answer to the obvious question, 'Why has no one thought of this before?' Something similar might have been attempted using paper maps, but it would have demanded a team of trained assistants and a desk the size of an aircraft hangar. (It would also have required an aircraft.) The results of this virtual expedition – and of the real expeditions they inspired – form the first part of this book. Readers who have the patience to pursue this journey through its rubble-strewn suburbs will become familiar with the map's peculiarities, and they are hereby invited to 'cheat' by looking ahead at a few examples of its evolution (pp. 154, 244).

The implications were too extraordinary to be ignored or, for that matter, believed: apart from a solar-lunar calendar on a plate of bronze that was found near a lake in the Jura – and which was partially decoded only with the help of computers – this was the first mathematically provable evidence of Druidic science and its achievements. It was, in effect, the earliest accurate map of the world. From somewhere beyond the Alps, this transcontinental masterpiece of sacred geography seemed to extend as far as the British Isles, and perhaps even further, to the remote northern islands seen in the fourth century BC by the explorer Pytheas of Marseille, where the ocean, heaving like a lung, becomes indistinguishable from the sky.

Stare at a series of lines on a map, and eventually a pattern will appear as surely as a human destiny in a fortune-teller's teacup. In any scholarly endeavour, excitement is a false friend: the more thrilling a theory, the more the theorist wants it to be true. For several more months, I tried to disprove it. I forsook the magical shadows of the thatched cottage for the energy-saving gloom of modern libraries. Time spent in another world is never wasted, and so, even if the theory had been hammered into oblivion by historical and archaeological fact, it would still have been a fruitful disappointment. But the more I tried to disprove it, the more evidence emerged. In October 2009, I read about the archaeological discovery, in a cement quarry near Lausanne, of the biggest Celtic sanctuary ever found in Switzerland. It was on a hill called Mormont near a place called Eclépens. I looked at the embryonic map of Druidic paths on which lines of longitude and latitude are bisected by mirror images of the Heraklean Way: Mormont lies on one of the long-distance lines and close to a major intersection.

✻

At this point, I prepared a verbal synopsis and presented the idea to my publishers. Two meetings took place – one in an underground room in a quiet mews near the Portobello Road in London, the other in a venerable gentlemen's club in mid-town Manhattan which the company president assured me had been checked for ear-trumpets and other listening devices. I described the discovery, and swore to secrecy people whose vocation it is to make things public. My thought was not that someone would steal the idea, which, in any case, is not quite as portable as a mathematical equation or a magic spell: I was thinking of friends and acquaintances in various university departments who, if the project were revealed, would be forced to pretend that nothing was amiss.

Anyone who writes about Druids and mysteriously coordinated landscapes, or who claims to have located the intersections of the solar paths of Middle Earth in a particular field, street, railway station or cement quarry, must expect to be treated with suspicion. In its simplest form, the idea was reminiscent of 'ley lines', and I was uncomfortably aware of the fact that a sarcastic trick of fate had sent me to live in a house called Leys Cottage. 'Ley lines' were discovered – some say, invented – in 1921 by an amateur archaeologist, Alfred Watkins. His idea was that alignments of prehistoric and other 'old' sites are remnants of 'the Old Straight Track' followed by Neolithic traders. Watkins believed that they had actually been called 'ley lines' because the word (a common place name meaning 'meadow' or 'pasture') appears on so many of them. His research consisted, in part, of stamping on the ground to detect the hollowness of ancient burial sites. Although he fostered a new sensitivity to ancient configurations of the English landscape, and created the delightful historical pastime of ley-line hunting, his muddling of different eras is anathema to archaeologists and historians. Yet ninety years of increasingly sophisticated prospecting and excavating have shown his original idea to be perfectly plausible: carefully aligned, long-distance paths were well within the capabilities of Neolithic people.

The period covered by this book (roughly 800 BC to AD 600) begins almost a thousand years after the end of the Neolithic Age (c. 1700 BC). The cultures known as Celtic belong to the forbiddingly named Iron Age, which was also the age of precision instruments, high-speed transport, crop rotation and land management, intellectual education of the young and the first European towns. Some archaeologists now place the dawn of the Celtic world a few centuries earlier, in the late Bronze Age. Both ages come under the heading of 'prehistory'. The term is broadly applied to any pre-literate period of humanity; it can also be applied to any period between the first microbial stirrings of the primordial slime and the civilized world that grew up only sixty generations ago. In Britain, the clock of 'history' does not begin to tick until ten o'clock in the morning on a summer's day in 55 BC, when Julius Caesar anchored off the Kentish coast. The following year, he returned with water-clocks, measured the length of the English summer day (longer than on the Continent), and brought prehistory to an end, at least in the south of England.

To a French archaeologist, the ancient Celts are not 'prehistoric' but 'protohistoric'. They are not quite our visible and audible neighbours, but nor are they the nameless, faceless shadows who built Stonehenge. To the Celts, Stonehenge was a mysterious ancient monument. Their writings were not published in Rome and catalogued in the Library of Alexandria, but we know about their lives, customs, beliefs, fashions and diets from Greek and Roman travellers. Some of their myths and legends, preserved in verse and memorized by successive generations of bards, were recorded by foreign writers. The Druids banned all written expression of their wisdom, but their society was certainly literate since writing implements have been found all over the Celtic world. For a dead language, ancient Gaulish is surprisingly lively: inscriptions on plates, pots, coins and curse-tablets are being unearthed all the time, and the lexicon of the language that was practically extinct by the sixth century AD continues to grow like hair on a corpse.

Some of the protohistoric inhabitants of Europe are known to us by name: Vercingetorix, the son of an executed tyrant and leader of the Gaulish resistance; Diviciacus, the Druid scholar and diplomat who stayed in Rome with Cicero and addressed the Roman Senate; Cartimandua, the queen of the British Brigantes who collaborated with the Romans. We know the names of many of their towns and what they looked like. The first time-travelling archaeologist to return to the Iron Age will be sufficiently well equipped to pass for an ancient Celt, albeit a semi-literate Celt with a small, disproportionately obscene vocabulary.

✧

Despite the staggering quantity of information amassed by archaeologists in what must be the greatest collective endeavour in the history of scholarship, the forgotten world of the Celts looks like the land that was never there to be forgotten. In France, the Roman past is everywhere. On some dirt-track sections of the Heraklean Way, it scrunches under the bicycle tyres; on the crumbling perimeters of hill forts, it lies among the litter. In the early morning rush-hour, on the Place Bellecour in the centre of Lyon – formerly known as Lugdunum – I sat down on a concrete bench. The ground had been disturbed by diggers and roughly levelled in preparation for a new surface. Some orange-coloured sherds stood out against the imported red sand. I bent down and picked up five small fragments of Roman pottery, one of which bore the ribbed pattern of a wine-cup similar to those displayed in the nearby Musée de la Civilisation Gallo-Romaine. To my left, through the avenue of lime trees, I could see the basilica of Notre-Dame de Fourvière, high above the river Saône, which readers of Caesar's *Gallic War* can easily distinguish from the neighbouring Rhone: 'There is a river called the Arar', wrote Caesar, 'which flows through the lands of the Aedui and the Sequani and into the Rhodanus with such incredible slowness that the eye cannot tell in which direction it is flowing'. The basilica occupies the presumed site of the Gaulish *oppidum* or hill fort,* but so little survives of the pre-Roman city that no one knows where the first inhabitants of Lugdunum lived.

---

* '*Oppidum*' is the word used by Julius Caesar to refer to the towns of the Gauls. It is now the usual term for the fortified settlements or hill forts of the Celts, which ranged in size from about fifteen to several hundred hectares (see p. 182).

Tribes who used perishable materials where the Romans used stone, and who recorded their histories in nothing more durable than brain tissue, are unlikely to be seen as sophisticated precursors of the modern world. The indifference of present-day Gauls to their Celtic ancestors is understandable. A museum curator in Vienne, whose director had decided not to display the collection of Celtic gold coins, explained it to me thus: 'They lost' (she meant, 'to the Romans'). The fragments that do remain are undervalued. Some of the gold coins kept in museum storerooms are among the most beautiful objects of the pre-Christian world. One day, collectors will stare in disbelief at early twenty-first-century auction catalogues and wish they had been alive when ancient works of art could be bought for the price of a television.

This world is closer than we think, but it takes forms that belong to a very different civilization. The ancient Celts – especially the Gaulish Celts, according to the Greek historian Diodorus Siculus – were not the easiest people to understand: 'They converse with few words and in riddles, hinting darkly at things for the most part and using one word when they mean another.' The curious symbols on Celtic coins, carvings, weapons and utensils are a reminder from artists who worked under Druidic supervision, and who were perhaps Druids themselves, that there was a hidden sense to everything the Celts produced, and that not all their secrets are undiscoverable, because the answers to their riddles lie in the visible universe. Readers who decide to prolong this exploration beyond the borders of this book may find that the world reinvented by the Celts in the image of their gods is not a certain escape from the present: Middle Earth exists, and many of us are living in it now.

PART ONE

1

The Road from the Ends of the Earth

For many centuries, the Celts were a mystery to their neighbours. In the sixth century BC, the Greeks had heard from intrepid merchants following the tin routes or from sailors blown off course of a people called the Keltoi, who lived somewhere along the northern shores of the Mediterranean. In the early fifth century, when the historian Herodotus tried to shine a light on this distant world, he was like a traveller on a starless night holding up a candle to the landscape. Of the Celts, he had been told the following: they live in the land where the Danube has its source near a city called Pyrene, and their country lies to the west of the Pillars of Hercules, on the borders of the Cynesians, 'who dwell at the extreme west of Europe'. This was either fantastically inaccurate (the supposed homelands are nearly two thousand kilometres apart) or an over-condensed version of an amazingly accurate source. Celtic tribes are known to have existed at that time both in the Upper Danube region and in south-western Iberia.

The Pyrenees – confused by Herodotus with a fictitious city called Pyrene – lie almost exactly halfway between the two. They form a great barrier across the western European isthmus, from the Atlantic Ocean to the Mediterranean Sea, dividing France from Spain. Most of the trans-Pyrenean traffic crossed at either end, where the mountains tumble down to the sea, but the central range was surprisingly porous. In the early Middle Ages, the road that leads to the principality of Andorra was used by smugglers, migrant labourers and pilgrims bound for the shrine at Santiago de Compostela. The snowy passes of the Andorran Pyrenees lie on the watershed line, from which the rivers flow either west to the Atlantic or east to the Mediterranean. In the days of the ancient Celts, this

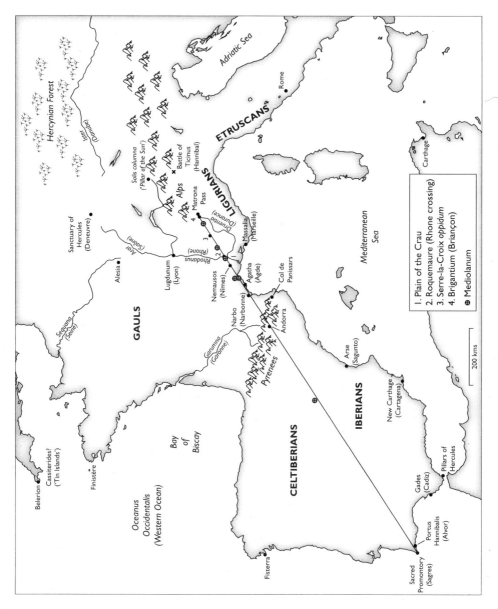

1. The Road from the Ends of the Earth

was the home of a tribe called the Andosini, who entered history when they were defeated by Hannibal in 218 BC during his long march from Spain to Italy. No one knows for certain how the Carthaginian general came to encounter such a remote tribe, but ancient history sometimes hinges on a place that seems desolate beyond significance.

The Celts' own stories of their origins were told over an area so vast that the sun spent an hour and a half each day bringing the dawn to it. Because the Celts were a group of cultures, not a race, they spread rapidly from central Europe, by influence and intermarriage as much as by invasion, until the Celtic world stretched from the islands of the Pritani in the northern sea to the great plains east of the Hercynian Forest, which even the speediest merchant did not expect to cross in under sixty days. As a result, although the tales were told in dialects of the same language, they took many different forms, like trees of the same species rooted in different soils and climates.

One tale in particular was considered pre-eminent and true, since it described what appeared to be a real journey made by a founding father of the Celts. It survived in various fragmented forms; some of the incidents became detached from their original context or were too strange to be part of a coherent narrative; yet they were held together by the geography of half a continent. The journey began at the extreme western tip of Europe – the Sacred Promontory, where a temple to Hercules stood above the roaring sea in a place so holy that no one was allowed to spend the night there. But it was in the mountains between the two seas that the hero entered the country known as Gaul. And since Gaul is the heartland of the first part of this adventure, this is where the story of Middle Earth begins.*

✢

With the mists of the Western Ocean draped over the pine forests, it would have been easy to imagine the scene: the smoke climbing up through the trees, the crackle of branches, and the fire, as red as a lion's mouth. Cattle were stumbling down the riverbeds to the hot plains below. The man knew the route they would take. From the

---

* The places mentioned in this chapter are shown on the map on p. 4.

ends of the earth, where the sun and the souls of the dead plunge into the sea, he had followed rather than driven them, so that it was not entirely true to say that he had stolen the herd. He acted out of desires that were foreign to his mind but not his body. It was in the country of the Bebruces, at the time of year when the sun rises and sets in the northern sky. The daughter of King Bebryx had served him bread, meat and beer in the great wooden hall, and when the sun had returned to the lower world she had taken him to her bed, and he had filled her with the seed of a god's son until the great hall shook and the walls of her chamber were beyond repair.

He had left the hall like a god or a thief. But the part of him that was human was stung by his act of abandonment. He thought of the creature like a snake that was growing inside her; he thought of her shame and of a father's rage. He had stopped where the cork oaks and the olives begin. He strode back up into the green, dark mountains, towards the ridge he had dented and levelled with his feet. Her white limbs lay scattered on the ground as though they had lain together on the pine needles and she had been dismembered by the force of his love. He gathered up the remains of the wolves' feast. Her blood, and the blood of a god's strange grandchild, burned his hands. He thundered her name to the skies that he had once held aloft – the Greek-named daughter of a Celtic king. Her name meant 'fire', 'a gem', or the gold 'grain' of the harvest. He felled a forest, then another. Rivers that had yet to be named began to flow from the bare mountain tops. He built a pyre that the midday sun would light. The smoke would be seen from the Ocean, where sailors hugged the coast in boats of skin; then the wind would carry it across the isthmus to the safe, thronged harbours of the Middle Sea, and even that blazing range of peaks would be unworthy of his Pyrenea.

He caught up with the cattle in the salty plain. He walked behind them in a straight line, carrying his club, the lion skin slung over his shoulder. In his other hand, he carried a wheel, divided into eight sections by its spokes. He paused where the cattle stopped to drink, at a ford or a spring at the foot of a hill. There were rough stones at his feet, shaped only by torrents and volcanoes, but behind them, on the path the man and the animals were trampling out, along with the rich gift of dung, there were sherds of brick and pot, cut stones flushed with cinnabar, ingots of tin and even gold. Keeping the land to his left, he walked beside the lagoons of the Middle Sea. Sometimes, there was a stone watchtower and a sail on the grey horizon. At dawn, by the shivering inlets, the sun rose again in the northern sky and burned a beacon onto his eye. In the warm nights, he angled his stride by the blurry trail of stars where the sun had passed or where his stepmother, tricked while she slept into giving the misbegotten mortal her breast, had wasted her milk in angry ostentation.

Near the mouths of the Rhodanus, birds and merchants came down from the other ocean: this was the region where the midsummer wind was called Buccacircius because it blew so hard that it puffed out a man's cheeks when he tried to speak. The tribes of the region were Ligurians, who belonged to such an ancient time that no one could understand their language. To those wild inhabitants of the hinterland, the road that the man and the animals were creating was something terrible and new. He reached the dry plain called the Crau, which is a desert of silt brought down from the distant Alps to the Rhodanus by the river Druentia. His enemies lurked in the low hills, clutching their quivers; they saw him sleep and watched the cattle that had come from the ends of the earth. The Ligurians had no towns, but if anything had stood on that plain, it would have been smashed like a boat that is splintered and wrecked by the storm. While he dreamt of the circling stars, thunderheads darkened the Crau, the skies cracked, and blazing boulders slashed through the air like a thousand gale-blasts all at once. When he woke, his enemies were gone, and the plain was strewn with stones as far as the horizon. In the dawn's slow light, the cattle were munching the tough green shoots that pushed up between the stones. He had no memory of the battle, but he knew that his prayer had been answered.

For the third time, the sun rose in the same place, as though a god's strong arm were holding its chariot to the same course until the journey was done.

They crossed the Rhodanus where an island divides it into two rushing streams. Beyond the valley, there were blue hills, each one higher than the last, with crests of yellow limestone: they might have been the backs of giants who had been stranded there when he pulled two continents together to prevent the monsters of the Ocean from entering the Middle Sea. He climbed until the air grew thin and the Druentia was just a torrent. At last, he reached a place from where

the rivers flow and the Alps formed an impassable wall. Pausing only
to shift the snow of countless centuries, he piled a forest against the
mountain, set fire to it and waited for the crack of thunder. Then he
cleared away the rubble.

No sooner had the gateway opened in the mountains than people
and animals were passing through it in both directions: soldiers in
bird-crested helmets returning from the east; brides whose braided hair
might have been worked by goldsmiths, travelling in procession to a
new home; merchants with small, stubborn horses carrying salt and
iron, or red wine in leather bags, each one of which was worth a slave.

From then on, guided by the sun, he crossed the land in eight
directions. His club was a feather compared to the weight of Pyrenea's
unbearable generosity, and so he paid his way by performing acts of
public good. He created more roads, set their distances and tolls, and
killed the savage bands who robbed travellers. He diverted rivers,
drained and irrigated fields; he built towns and supplied not only the
building materials – the squared stones, the pointed staves, the mounds
of earth – but also their populations. For wherever he went, he found
fathers more grateful than King Bebryx and virgins curiously skilled
in the art of love.

One town above all received his favour. It lay on a levelled hill
in the fertile land of the northern watershed. This was Alesia, which
became the mother-city of the Celts. The princess of Alesia was a tall
and beautiful girl called Celtine. She served the traveller salted fish
from the distant sea and sides of venison as large as herself; she poured
out the strong wine spiced with cumin. In the mornings, she brought
him strawberries from the woods and the water that was used to
cleanse the honeycombs. She did this out of love and the desire for
a son. But the traveller had grown tired and his head ached with
memories. And so Celtine stole his cattle and – this is the only unbe-
lievable part of the tale – hid them and refused to tell him where they
were until he agreed to rest his heavy limbs on the soft skins of her
bedchamber. Somehow, in that land of tidy fields and gentle hills, a
girl concealed from the son of a god a herd of road-hardened cattle
that had eaten the sharp grass that grows by the Western Ocean . . .
It was the kind of trickery a man of his years could easily excuse. He
accepted his defeat, paid generous tribute to his conqueror, and a son
was born, named Celtus or Galates.

At last, he grew so old that he was recognizable only by his club, his lion skin and his wheel. There was nothing left for him but to tell stories. He never wanted for an audience: as soon as he opened his mouth, the children and grandchildren of Celtine felt his eloquence tug at their ears, and they gathered round like the herd when the shepherd brings the hay. And they knew that everything he said had really happened, because he himself had made the roads on which he travelled, and the roads were as true as the sun that wheels overhead and under-neath the earth, dividing up the heavens and the world below, so that souls are never lost when they journey to the Ocean and the lower world, and from there to the gateway in the east where the sun is reborn.

✿

It is an uncanny characteristic of Celtic myths – including those that recount the adventures of a demi-god – that they often turn out to be true. The bards who preserved tribal memory in verse were not rambling improvisers: they were archivist-poets who knew the dates of battles and migrations. The story that Massalia (Marseille) was founded by Greeks from Phocaea in about 600 BC has been confirmed by archaeological excavations. The legend of a mass resettlement of Gaulish tribes in northern Italy is more accurate than histories written by erudite Romans, who were never sure whether the Celts had come from the east or from the west. In Irish mythology, the great mound called Emain Macha (Navan Fort) was said to have been founded by a certain Queen Macha (identified with a goddess of that name) in 668 BC. This was considered impossibly early until archaeologists dated the oldest features of Emain Macha to c. 680 BC.

The historical truth of Celtic myths was far from obvious to the Greeks and Romans who recorded them. By the time these stories were written down, they no longer made much sense either as legend or as history. Some of them were skewed by Roman propaganda and preju-dice; others had become entangled with local myths from an age before the Celts existed. Cluttered with incomprehensible names and impos-sible events, they spoke of stones hurled down from the heavens and a race of serpents born of human beings. The gods themselves became confused. When the peripatetic writer and raconteur Lucian of Samosata was travelling through Gaul in the second century AD, he was shocked to see a piece of ornamented sculpture which he took to be an insulting depiction of the deified Herakles: the god had the appearance of a grizzled old man with the sun-baked face of a sailor. Lucian was looking at something too exotic to be comprehended: the tongue of the Celtic Herakles was pierced with delicate chains of gold and amber attached to the ears of a happily captive audience. Some of his listeners were so enthralled that the chains had slackened as they surged towards the storyteller. A Greek-speaking Gaul had to explain to Lucian that this was the Gaulish Herakles: his name was Ogmios, and his eloquence was such that his audience literally hung on his every word.

The ear-tugging tales of the Gaulish Herakles were not just a metaphorical expression of the scope and fertility of the Celtic world. They belong to that tantalizing, protohistoric zone between legend and myth. There probably was a tribal chief, some time in the late Bronze Age, who grew rich through cattle rustling, or a warrior-king who pacified the prehistoric tribes that lived along the Mediterranean trade routes. Centuries before the Romans imposed their genocidal peace, the roads had been made safe enough for herders and traders to travel up from Iberia, bringing livestock, salt, amber, iron, tin and gold. The civilizing feats of a heroic figure were celebrated in an Odyssey that was like a storytellers' warehouse of domestic and imported produce. Greeks who founded trading-posts along the Mediterranean recounted the tenth labour of Herakles (the theft of a giant's cattle from Erytheia, the 'red' sunset island on the edge of the world); Phoenician sailors brought tales of the god Melqart, whom the Greeks recognized as their own Herakles. The serpent creature in the womb of Pyrenea was probably the vestige of a snake-god worshipped in the forested foothills long before the Celtic Bebruces occupied the region later known as Gallia Narbonensis. But the passionate gift that she made of herself to a wandering hero from the ends of the earth would have had the sound of recent history to tribes who formed commercial and matrimonial alliances with the Greeks.

The Heraklean Way – the path that adhered wherever possible to the diagonal of the solstice sun – may have required a god-assisted reconfiguration of the landscape in the form of mountain passes, but it was, on the whole, a practical route. It followed the prehistoric trails of transhumant animals which, as Pliny the Elder noted in the first century AD, 'come from remote regions to feed on the thyme that covers the stony plains of Gallia Narbonensis'. It avoided the impossibly rugged coastal route into Italy, which Roman legionaries dreaded and which is an obstacle course even today; instead, it climbed up to the grassy plains of Provence and from there to the only Alpine col that remained passable in winter – the Matrona or Montgenèvre, near the source of the Durance. Beyond the Matrona, a trader or an army could descend to the plains of Etruscan Italy or continue towards the land of the dawn and the salt mines of the eastern Alps.

The people who heard these tales knew that these places existed: the Sacred Promontory, where the journey began; the mist-covered mountains of Pyrenea; the holy spring at Nemausos (Nîmes), which was said to have been founded by a son of Herakles; the rock-strewn desert of the Crau and the Matrona Pass. These tales would have been told in the *oppida* – the Roman name for Celtic hill forts – from which the arrow-straight line of the Heraklean Way can still be seen bisecting the landscape in the form of tracks and field boundaries. The inhabitants of these *oppida* knew that all these sites were joined by a line that had been blessed and ratified by the gods, because it also existed in the upper world.

✿

Now that the sky is just the unreliable backdrop of the daily human drama, and the sky gods' only priests are weathermen, knowledge of celestial trajectories seems almost esoteric. Most people are aware of cardinal points only because of a prevailing wind, a sunny breakfast-room or a damp north-facing wall. Ancient Celts always knew exactly where they stood in relation to the universe. A cognitive psychologist has discovered that speakers of languages in which the same words are used for immediate directions ('right', 'left', 'behind', etc.) and for points of the compass tend to be aware of their orientation, even indoors and in unfamiliar surroundings. Gaulish was one of those languages. '*Are*' meant 'in front of'; it also meant 'in the east'. '*Dexsuo*' was 'behind' and 'in the west'. To head north, one turned to the left ('*teuto*'), and, to head south, to the right ('*dheas*').* In English, 'right' and 'left' are relative to the speaker's position; in Gaulish, directions were absolute and universal. If a Celtic hostess told her guest that the imported Falernian wine was in the *krater* behind him, she meant that

---

* This is the Irish word; the ancient Gaulish equivalent has yet to be rediscovered.

it lay in the same direction as the setting sun. If he went out hunting, he would have known immediately where to point his spear when his host said, 'the boar is coming at you from the south'. And when he left the *oppidum* and rejoined the Heraklean Way, he would have known that he was travelling towards the rising sun of the summer solstice.

The summer and winter solstices were crucial points of reference for ancient civilizations. The complexities of measuring solstice angles will be mentioned later on;* the principle itself is simple. In the course of a year, because of the tilt of the earth's axis, the sun rises and sets in different parts of the sky. Around 21 June, it rises on the north-eastern horizon at what appears to be the same point for several days in a row – hence the term 'solstice' (the 'stand-still of the sun'). The summer solstice itself occurs on the longest day of the year. From then on, the sun rises progressively further south, until the winter solstice, which occurs on the shortest day of the year. Halfway between the two solstices, the sun rises due east and sets due west. These two days are the equinoxes, when the night ('*nox*') is roughly equal ('*aequus*') in length to the day.

According to popular wisdom, the solstice was the object of an absurd superstition. Ancient people are supposed to have seen the sun rising and setting ever further to the north or south and to have concluded that without a good deal of prayer, procession and bloody sacrifice, it would either get stuck in the same place – with disastrous consequences for agriculture – or, worse, continue in the same direction until it disappeared for ever. This would mean that there was once a civilization that was capable of building enormous, astronomically aligned stone temples and yet was otherwise so impervious to experience that it had to renew its knowledge of the universe every six months. The solstice may have been a time of ritual celebration or mourning, but it was also an obvious and useful reality. More accurate bearings can be taken during the solstice than at other times of the year, and since the sun rises and sets at almost exactly the same point for over a week (within a range of 0.04°), a day of cloud and mist is less likely to spoil the operation.

The purpose of those measurements was both scientific and religious. The paths of heavenly bodies revealed the workings of the

---

* See pp. 125 and 227, and 'A Traveller's Guide to Middle Earth', pp. 294–6.

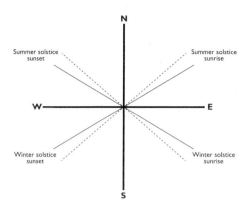

2. Solstice angles

The angles shown here are the solar azimuth angles (see note on p. 14) in 1600 BC at Stonehenge, latitude 51.18° north (dotted lines) and the Pillars of Hercules, latitude 36.00° north (unbroken lines).

universe and the designs of the gods. The Celts' trading partners, the Etruscans, used solstice measurements to align their towns on the cardinal points. In this way, the whole town became a template of the upper world. 'Superstition' lay in the fact that the town's skyscape, too, was divided into quadrants for the interpretation of celestial signs (stars, bolts of lightning and flocks of birds): north-east – the approximate trajectory of the Heraklean Way and the summer solstice dawn – was the most auspicious quadrant; south-east was less auspicious; south-west was unlucky, and north-west extremely ominous. Since north lay to the 'sinister' left, and since the sun's light dies in the west, the system had a certain psychogeographical logic.

These alignments were part of the common fund of knowledge throughout the ancient world. The Celts often built their sanctuaries so that the summer solstice sun would shine through the eastern entrance onto the altar. Though the Romans sneered at superstitious barbarians, their own surveyors used the solstice as a point of reference. No surviving Roman text mentions the astronomical significance of the Heraklean Way, and the secret seems to have been lost for almost two thousand years. But to the ancient Celts, the meaning of its alignment would have been as obvious as though it was explained on a roadside information panel.

The name itself was explanatory. To Celts and Carthaginians, 'Via Heraklea' would have meant, in effect, 'Path of the Sun'. Like his Carthaginian equivalent, Melqart, Herakles was also a sun god. His twelve labours were equated with the twelve constellations of the zodiac through which the sun passes in the course of a year. The face of his Celtic equivalent, Ogmios, had been scorched by the blazing vehicle that carried him across the sky, and the wheel he held in his hand – like the thousands of pocket-sized votive wheels that are still being found in Celtic sanctuaries – was a symbol of the sun. The eight spokes are thought to represent the cardinal points and the rising and setting of the sun at the summer and winter solstices. And because the sun was the ultimate authority in matters of measurement, Melqart or Herakles was also the divine geometer: 'in his devotion to wisdom', said Philostratus the Athenian, 'he measured the whole earth from end to end'.

Herakles' solar wheel evidently served him well as a global positioning device. The solstice line of the Heraklean Way is astonishingly accurate. From Andorra (the cols of Muntaner and Ordino) to the Matrona Pass (almost five hundred kilometres), it has a bearing of 57.53° east of north. This is the angle of the rising sun of the summer solstice at a point roughly halfway from the Sacred Promontory to the Matrona Pass.* Holding to this bearing, it runs through or close to eight tribal centres, including Andorra, Narbonne, Nîmes and Briançon; it also passes by six of the mysterious places once called Mediolanum, of which much more will be said. Over its entire length (almost 1600 kilometres from the Sacred Promontory to the Matrona Pass), the bearing is 56.28°, which, at that enormous distance, is so precise as to be incredible.

Even more surprising, in view of its accuracy, is its great age. One of the earliest surviving references to the Heraklean Way dates from

---

* Since the angle changes with latitude, a local standard would have been chosen in order to produce a straight rather than a curved line. (See p. 227.) Even on a short stretch, standardization would have been necessary since the exact point of sunrise or sunset cannot be observed directly: the sun's light is refracted by the earth's atmosphere, and the horizon is almost never flat and unobstructed. In 600 BC, the angle was 0.5° less than it is today. The angle in question is the solar azimuth angle (the number of degrees, measured clockwise from north, to the point on the horizon where the sun rises).

the third century BC. It was mentioned by the anonymous author –
known as 'the Pseudo-Aristotle' – of *De mirabilibus auscultationibus*
('Wonderful Things I Have Heard'):

> From Italy as far as the country of the Celts, Celtoligurians and
> Iberians, they say there is a road called the 'Road of Herakles', and
> on this road, the traveller, whether native or Greek, is watched by
> the neighbouring tribes so that he may receive no injury; for those
> amongst whom the injury has been done must pay a penalty.

By the time the Pseudo-Aristotle heard of it, the wonderful road
had already seen several generations of travellers. Tracks are hard to
date, but filtering techniques applied to aerial photography have made
the landscapes of ancient Gaul bloom with historical clues. When
Greek traders first sailed towards the setting sun and reached lands
that even Odysseus had never seen, they set up trading posts called
emporia along the coasts of the Gaulish and Iberian Mediterranean.
To supply the new ports, they purchased land from local tribes, and
then divided up the territory into squares of equal size. The process
and its result are known as centuriation. Some of the early Greek
centuriations have been plotted in great detail: on a map, they look
like the gridlines of American cities covering many hundreds of square
kilometres. One of the oldest is the centuriation of Agatha (Agde),
which was a colony of the Greek port of Massalia (Marseille), founded
in the fifth century BC. For a distance of twenty-five kilometres, the
Heraklean Way follows the diagonal line that marks the northern
limit of the Agde centuriation. Since centuriations invariably adopted
the trajectories of existing roads, this section of the Heraklean Way
at least must date back to the very earliest days of Graeco-Celtic
cooperation.

These abstract measurements and trajectories are the comprehensible whisperings of a vanished civilization. For a modern traveller,
the physical inconvenience itself is a sign of ancient mathematical
expertise. The old trail keeps to its cosmic bearing whenever it can.
Later tracks and roads, including some stretches of the Roman Via
Domitia that replaced parts of the Heraklean Way,* are more obse-
quious to the landscape – they curve conveniently around the slopes

---

* The course of the Via Domitia is shown in fig. 46.

and sidle up to villages along the valleys – but the dust-blown Heraklean Way strides over the hills like a heedless athlete. This is the material form of history, the tangible proof that ancient truths are still recoverable. The accuracy of the Heraklean Way is directly related to the accuracy of Celtic legends. Astronomical observations, spanning many years, made it possible not only to project a straight line across the landscape but also (for example, by recording solar eclipses) to attain the kind of chronological accuracy that could date the foundation of an Irish hill fort to 668 BC or the foundation of Massalia to the beginning of the sixth century BC.

Perhaps it was then, in the early 500s, that the tribes of the hinterland encountered the skills and technology that enabled them to trace the sun god's path on earth. Or perhaps a human Herakles from Greece had journeyed to the west as a sailor in search of land and a foreign princess. Even at this great distance in time, myths begin to resolve themselves into legends, and in those legends, historical figures can be glimpsed. The two surviving versions of the story of Massalia's foundation place the day in question – for the convenience of Roman readers – during the reign of the Roman king Tarquinius Priscus (c. 616–579 BC). The original Celtic versions were almost certainly more precise.

On the afternoon in question, a trading fleet from the distant Greek city of Phocaea dropped anchor in what became the harbour of Massalia, the first city in Gaul. The chief of the local tribe, the Segobriges, was about to hold a banquet at which his daughter was to choose a husband. According to tradition, she was to indicate her choice by offering the future bridegroom a cup of pure water. The Greek captains were invited to the ceremony. Seeing the dark-eyed adventurers who had braved the trackless sea, and having perhaps previously inspected their treasures – the painted vases, the bronze flagons and tasting spoons, and the ships like a god's chariots resting in the harbour – she offered the cup of water to one of the fearless navigators.

The couple were married, and, like Herakles and Celtine, a Greek hero and a Celtic princess embodied the happy truth that the origins of a powerful and stable confederation lay, not on the battlefield, but on a long-distance trading route that led unerringly to a woman's bed. A colony was founded at what is now the Vieux Port of Marseille.

Not long after, Greek wares and locally produced Greek wine were being carried up into remote parts of Gaul from the mouth of the Rhone – where a city called Heraklea once stood – and along the Heraklean Way, where Greek pottery of that period is still being dug out of the rubble of hill forts and cemeteries.

✳

The road from the ends of the earth was the beginning of one of the great adventures and inventions of the ancient world. So much about it is improbable – its length, its accuracy, its antiquity: it might all be attributed to the god of chance were it not for the records of a journey made along that trajectory by a real, mortal human being. One of the two accounts – by the Greek historian Polybius – was based on research trips and interviews with people who had witnessed Hannibal's expedition fifty years before; the other, by the Roman historian Livy, used some of the same reports, including a lost account in seven volumes by one of the traveller's companions. Neither historian recognized the transcendent significance of the route.

The journey took place in 218 BC, when the Heraklean Way was already steeped in four centuries of myth and legend – which is partly why it was chosen as the route of the expedition. In the late spring, ninety thousand foot soldiers, twelve thousand cavalry and thirty-seven elephants set off from New Carthage (Cartagena, on the southeast coast of Spain). The Carthaginians' empire had spread from the coasts of North Africa into Iberia, and their only rivals in the Mediterranean were the Romans. The young Carthaginian general, Hannibal, was to march from Iberia, across the Pyrenees and then the Alps, to attack the Romans from the north. Alliances had been formed with Gaulish tribes who had colonized the plains on the Italian side of the Alps; other tribes had been wooed with promises of gold; many of the soldiers on the expedition were Celts from Iberia or Gaul. The city of Rome, according to Livy, was 'on tiptoe in expectation of war'.

At some point, Hannibal – or part of his army – joined the line of the Heraklean Way. It was an obvious route: the origins of Iberian place names suggest an ancient frontier running diagonally between Celtic or Celtiberian tribes to the north-west and the indigenous inhabitants to the south-east. This frontier closely matches the

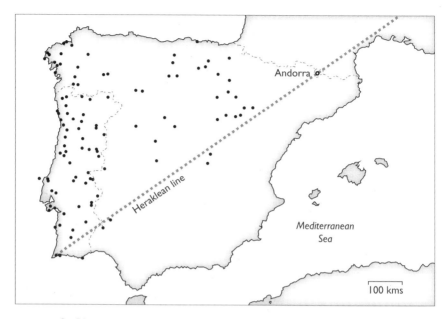

3. Place names and tribal names of Celtic origin in Iberia

Heraklean line, and it leads to what must have seemed an unnecessarily arduous crossing of the Pyrenees. The four tribes that were said by Polybius to have been defeated by Hannibal lived, not on the coast, where a Roman customs post still marks the relatively easy crossing at the Col de Panissars, but in the central Pyrenees, in the region of Andorra, where the Heraklean line crosses the watershed (fig. 1). In warm spring weather, the ascent is not as difficult as it appears on a map, and its remoteness would have had the advantage of delaying news of the Carthaginian invasion.

In the context of the entire expedition, the diagonal route was logical and, more importantly, auspicious. Hannibal had already proved himself a brilliant tactician, and part of his brilliance lay in his ability to assume the role of a god. Before leaving Iberia, he had visited the temple of Melqart-Herakles at Gades (Cadiz), to consult the oracle and to ask for the god's protection. He had wintered part of his army in the harbour of Portus Hannibalis near the Sacred Promontory, where another famous temple of Melqart-Herakles stood on the edge of the inhabited world. Ancient writers who described the Carthaginian invasion knew that Hannibal saw himself and wanted to be seen as the successor of Herakles. He would march across the mountains in the footsteps of the sun god, shining with the aura of divine approval.

Like most of his contemporaries, Polybius had only the vaguest notions of European geography beyond the Mediterranean. He knew about Hannibal's Herculean ambitions but not about the Heraklean Way. According to his source, 'a hero [Herakles] showed Hannibal the way'. Polybius – and Hannibal's later historians – took this to be a rhetorical flourish rather than an indication of the route. Similarly, Livy mistook the key to the whole expedition for a picturesque embellishment and used it in a speech that Hannibal was supposed to have made to his troops when they were quailing at the thought of crossing the Alps: he reminded them that, earlier in the expedition, 'the way had seemed long to no one, though they were pursuing it from the setting to the rising of the sun'. This was not a figure of speech but the cosmological truth.

There were no maps or atlases on which Polybius could have traced a plausible route, and he thought that foreign place names would only confuse his readers with 'unintelligible and meaningless sounds'. Fortunately, the distances that he copied from his source make it possible to calculate the point at which Hannibal and his elephants crossed the Rhone – 'four days' march from the sea', then a further 'two hundred *stadia*' (about thirty-five kilometres) north, to a place where 'the stream is divided by a small island'. Most historians now identify this as Roquemaure, near Châteauneuf-du-Pape, which is certainly correct, since it also happens to be the point at which the line of the Heraklean Way crosses the Rhone.

The next part of the journey is confused and nonsensical in both accounts. The geographical explanations given in the lost source seem to have been treated by Polybius and Livy as a description of Hannibal's actual route. All we know is that the itinerary was somehow related to the distant source of the Rhone. After crossing the river, Hannibal 'marched up the bank away from the sea in an easterly direction [in fact, at this point, the Rhone flows north to south], as though making for the central district of Europe'. Polybius went on to explain, more accurately, that 'the Rhone rises to the north-west of the Adriatic Gulf on the northern slopes of the Alps'.

The details that Polybius and Livy preserved in a muddled form are like barely decipherable remnants of an ancient map. The allusion to the source of the Rhone and 'the central district of Europe' may be the trace of an ancient system of orientation that enabled an army or a merchant to plot a course across half a continent. Parts of this 'map' will be pieced together in the first part of this book. The crucial point is that only a god could have walked in a straight line all the way to the Matrona; even transhumant herds were forced to take a more winding route towards the Alpine pastures and to skirt the north side of Mont Ventoux. But after bypassing the mountainous terrain, it was vital to be able to continue on the same auspicious bearing as before. Whichever route he chose after crossing the Rhone (Livy suggests that Hannibal followed the river Druentia or Durance), he would have rejoined the Heraklean Way as soon as he could – perhaps near the *oppidum* at Serre-la-Croix, where the road once again follows the solstice line for twelve kilometres – and then, climbing towards the source of the Durance, to Brigantium (Briançon) and the final approach to the Matrona Pass.

Since the days of Polybius, historians have wondered where Hannibal and his elephants managed to cross the Alps in early November. Etymologists have analysed place names in search of Carthaginian roots, which are no more likely to be found than the petrified elephant drop-pings that an archaeologist recently hoped to detect along the presumed route of Hannibal. Several expeditions, seeking a suitably heroic crossing, have struggled pointlessly over impossibly high passes, in one case misled by the old 'Elephant' inn on the road to the vertiginous Col Agnel, which, even in the days of motorized snow ploughs, is closed from October to May. In July 1959, a Cambridge engineer drove an Italian circus elephant, which refused to answer to the name Hannibella, over the 2081-metre Mont-Cenis Pass. (The elephant, not having received Carthaginian military training, lost 230 kilograms.) In fact, given a choice of routes, an elephant – or, for that matter, a hiker or a cyclist – would head for Italy over the Col de Montgenèvre, which the Celts called Matrona. Not only is this the lowest crossing of the French Alps (1850 metres), it also marks the Gaulish end of the Heraklean Way. The Matrona had everything a military commander could desire: there was a tribal capital – Brigantium – only eight kilometres away, and a broad plain on which crops ripened and which now supports the lush green lawns of an eighteen-hole golf course.

Twenty-three centuries after the Carthaginian invasion, Mont-genèvre is a defiantly expanding leisure zone of concrete 'chalets' where the Iron Age seems never to have existed. Perhaps its unheroic demeanour explains why it has almost never been identified as the crossing-point. The col itself is now said to lie on the main road through the town, but at the original, unsignposted col, higher up on the narrow road to the Village du Soleil holiday centre, there is something of the electrifying clarity of the high Alpine passes, where distances contract and whole regions suddenly come into view when a bank of cloud disintegrates. At the Matrona Pass, an extraordinary historical vista opens up, though it takes the digital equivalent of a solar wheel to reveal it. If Herakles had stood where the temple of the Mother Goddesses once stood, and turned precisely ninety degrees to the west of the Heraklean trajectory, he would have been looking towards one of the towns he was said to have founded: Semur-en-Auxois, the neighbour of Alesia. If he had followed the setting sun, he would have reached the hill at Lugdunum (Lyon), from where he was said to have looked down on the confluence of the Rhone and the Saône. A bearing of 0° – due north – would have taken him straight to the vast Herculean sanctuary of Deneuvre, where a hundred statues of Hercules (over one-third of all the statues of Hercules ever found in Gaul) were unearthed in 1974. Only a god or a migrating bird returning to its nesting-site could have attained such accuracy.

These hypothetical lines reach far into the depths of ancient tribal Gaul, over ice-bound mountains that had still not been accurately mapped two hundred years ago. Even on a sunny day, it is hard to believe that the precise array of terrestrial solar paths that the Celts would develop is anything other than a beautiful Heraklean coincidence, or some intoxicating piece of false wisdom dispensed by the oracle of the temple, giddy with altitude or Greek wine, conjuring cosmic hallucinations out of the thin air.

When Hannibal stood at the Matrona in the early winter of 218 BC, watching his elephants stumble down to the plains of northern Italy, he knew that he was standing in the rocky footprints of Herakles. His strategists and astrologers, and their Celtic allies and informers, were certain that the sun god had shown them the way. They seem to have known, too, that the source of the Rhone lay in a 'central district of Europe' and that it was somehow related to the Heraklean itinerary.

The computerized oracle agrees: a line projected for two hundred and twenty kilometres from the Matrona at right angles to the summer solstice sunset leads to the region of glaciers where the Rhone rises. At the river's source there was a mountain which, despite its remoteness, was known to the early Iron Age inhabitants of the Mediterranean coast. It was mentioned in a poem of the fourth century AD called *Ora Maritima* ('Sea Coasts'). Using what must have been an excellent scroll-finding service, the Roman proconsul, Rufus Festus Avienus, assembled a collection of ancient *periploi* (descriptions of maritime routes) with the aim of turning them into an unusable but entertaining guide for armchair navigators. One of those ancient texts – of which no other trace remains – was a nine-hundred-year-old handbook for merchants sailing from Massalia to the Sacred Promontory, 'which some people call the Path of Hercules'. In a passage on the Rhone, the author had mentioned the fact that the mountain at the river's source was known to the natives of the region as '*Solis columna*' or 'the Pillar of the Sun'.

When this name was recorded in the sixth century BC, valuable geographical intelligence was already flowing into the busy harbour of Massalia from distant parts, along with works of art from the eastern Mediterranean and precious metals from the enigmatic Cassiterides or 'Tin Islands' – perhaps the islands later known as Britannia – that lay beyond the Carthaginian blockade at the Pillars of Hercules. It might have been common knowledge among the Celts: somewhere in the heart of Europe, many days from the sea routes that were bringing the first trappings of Greek civilization to the barbarous Keltoi, there was a named point of reference, a solar coordinate. The Heraklean Way itself was a wonder of the world, and perhaps there were other wonders, too: Herakles had journeyed throughout Gaul, and his heavenly grasp of the immeasurable earth might have been reflected in other branches and articulations of the Heraklean Way . . . But even four centuries later, in the winter of 218 BC, there was nothing to suggest any such sophistication in the Celtic foot soldiers of Hannibal's army, trudging over the snow-clogged pass in their rough plaid cloaks and hare's-wool boots – nothing, that is, except the glint of an arm-ring or a neck torc, the meticulously coordinated orbits of a compass-drawn brooch, or the geometric spirals of a bronze disc attached to a chariot wheel, performing its mysterious circumvolutions like a microcosm of the turning sky.

2

News of the Iron Age

The guide in the *horreum* was lost in admiration for the Romans. She traced the elegant curve of the vault with a loving gesture, and we peered along a dim passageway at slanting shafts and limestone arches that had braced themselves for centuries against the forum and the market of Roman Narbonne. The buildings above ground had long since crumbled away to form the foundations of later buildings that had disappeared in their turn, but the *horreum* – if it was indeed a warehouse – had survived until it was the only Roman structure in Narbonne.

'You've got to admire those Roman engineers,' said the guide, caressing a nicely pointed section of wall that had required only the lightest of repairs.

The Romans had occasionally copied the beautiful stone-and-timber walls of the natives; they had even built some of their own forts using *muri gallici*; and so it seemed appropriate to put in a word for the guide's Celtic ancestors.

'Or,' I suggested, 'the Gaulish engineers . . .'

The deathly dungeons suddenly came to life with the sound of laughter. Evidently, this was one of the saving graces of a job in the sunless underworld of sunny Narbonne: tourists sometimes said the most amazing things.

'*Oui!*' she almost shrieked. '*Les ingénieurs gaulois!*'

Stepping out of the *horreum* into the light of a first-century-BC afternoon, she might have shared the joke with an ancient Roman. To most Greeks and Romans – especially those who had never left home – the typical Celt was a rampaging drunkard who blundered into battle at the side of his brawny, blue-eyed wife, wearing either animal skins or nothing. At home, the Celts festooned themselves

with gold jewellery and drank undiluted wine – to which the entire
nation was addicted. Their table manners were atrocious: they wore
woollen cloaks and trousers instead of togas, and sat on the hides
of wolves and dogs instead of reclining on couches. This was in the
part of Gaul known as Gallia Bracata ('Trousered Gaul'). Further
north, in Gallia Comata ('Hairy Gaul'), things were even more
exotic. Gaulish aristocrats shaved their cheeks but not their upper
lips, so that their pendulous moustaches trailed in the soup and
served as strainers when they drank. Sometimes, they showed their
appreciation of the meal by fighting to the death over the best cut
of meat.

Ever since the sixth century BC, Greek travellers had been
returning from Gaul with tales of ludicrous and disgusting practices.
Celts who lived by the Rhine tested the legitimacy of their new-born
sons by throwing them into the river. Other Celts waded into the
sea, brandishing their swords until they were swallowed by the waves.
At war councils, punctuality was encouraged by the custom of
torturing the last man to arrive and then putting him to death in
sight of the whole assembly. In their dealings with strangers, the
Gauls were hospitable to the point of insanity: Gaulish men rolled
about in bed with other men, 'raging with outlandish lust', and it
was considered highly offensive if a guest declined to sodomize his
host.

It does not take an anthropologist to suspect that what these
travellers saw or heard about were baptismal rites, the ceremonial
dedication of weapons to gods of the lower world, and the friendly
custom of sharing one's bed with a stranger. The summary execution
of late-comers was presumably a ritualized form of punishment like
those that were meted out to flabby Celtic youths whose bellies had
engulfed their belts, or to people who interrupted a speaker (on the
third offence, the heckler's clothes were slashed to ribbons with a
sword). Some practices that were upsetting to outsiders seemed
entirely acceptable in context. The Greek philosopher Posidonius,
who toured Gaul in the early first century BC, became quite accus-
tomed to seeing human heads preserved in cedar oil nailed to a
doorway or stored in a wooden box. The severed head of an enemy
killed in battle was considered a priceless trophy and was proudly
shown to guests.

These tales from the fringes of the empire are not just a sign of imperial hauteur. The Celts' unfathomable riddles, the faces that appear and disappear in their complex designs, and the geomantic mysteries of the Druids were forms of sophistication to which the Romans were blind. Educated Celts clearly enjoyed bamboozling foreigners. When Caesar was collecting material on the Hercynian Forest for his book on the Gallic War, a native informant told him of a creature called the '*alces*' (elk) which, having no joints in its legs, was forced to spend its entire life standing up. Caesar recorded the information as he heard it: to sleep, the *alces* leant on a tree, so that hunters simply sawed through most of a tree-trunk in a glade where the animal was known to rest, and then returned to collect their prostrate prey.

To the mirthless conqueror of the Gauls, the Celtic mind was a closed book. He knew that the Gauls made fun of the Romans 'because of our short stature compared to their great size', but his attempt to explain the taunts of the Aduatuci tribe when they saw the legionaries building a siege-tower is so clumsy that it takes a while to realize that what the Gauls were shouting from the ramparts was, 'You're so short, you need a tower to see over the wall!' If practical jokes are a sign of civilization, the Celts were one of the most advanced societies of the ancient world. Many years after visiting Gaul in his youth, St Jerome still shuddered to recall the Celts from northern Britain who had assured him that the favourite delicacy of their tribe was shepherd's buttock and breast of shepherd's wife.

It is a shame that so much of what remains of ancient Gaulish is the linguistic equivalent of a spoil heap. Even the dozen words that entered English by various routes seem to confirm the Roman view of a downwardly mobile race of simpletons and trouble-makers: 'bucket', 'car', 'crock', 'crockery', 'dad', 'flannel', 'gaol', 'gob', 'noggin', 'peat', 'slogan' and 'truant'. The only complete sentences of Gaulish to have survived are inscriptions on lead curse-tablets ('May the magic of the infernal gods pursue them!'), phrases in a medical textbook ('Let Marcos take this thing out of my eye!'), graffiti on plates and bottles ('Drink this and you'll be good company!'), and words of endearment etched on spindle-whorls. These circular discs, which were used to weight spindles, were given to girls as love-tokens. The suitor expressed his desire by identifying his principal attribute with the spindle. Some of the phrases are cunningly suggestive, but, as the largest surviving corpus of Gaulish literature, it hardly evokes a civilization to rival Greece or Rome:

> *moni gnatha gabi – budduton imon* ('Come, my girl, take my spindle!')
> *impleme sicuersame* (in Latin) ('Cover me up and spin me round!')
> *marcosior – maternia* ('Ride me like a horse, Materna!')
> *matta dagomota baline enata* ('A girl can get a good fuck from this penis.')
> *nata uimpi – curmi da* ('Pretty girl, give me some beer!')

✿

Even a dispassionate observer might have asked: what evidence is there that the trousered savages were capable of organizing any sort of infrastructure? The only Iron Age road surfaces to have been identified so far are causeways preserved by the bogs they traversed, a rubbish-strewn shopping street in a hill fort and a few sections of rutted limestone. The Gauls are presumed to have transported their precious wine on tracks that wandered about like barbarians returning from a feast. Schoolchildren and museum-visitors are told that the Romans brought with them, not only Latin, bureaucracy and under-floor heating, but also roads, which they rolled out ahead of the invading armies with the speed of a modern paving machine. Since the Roman builders obliterated the traces of earlier carriageways, the Celtic world appears to have been practically roadless. In the view of one archaeologist, the late-Bronze Age wheelwright of Blair Drummond in Perthshire who made a remarkably narrow-rimmed wheel of ash wood for a cart that would have weighed several hundred kilograms might as well have been manufacturing rolling stock for a railway: the vehicles 'would all too easily have become bogged down in mud, and it is unlikely that they travelled very far or very fast' . . .

It might have happened on almost any day in the late Iron Age. A shepherd of the Sequani tribe stands on one of the routes that connect Italy and the Alps to the Oceanus Britannicus. Looking to the south, he sees a billowing cloud of dust, hears the targeted crescendo of hooves and wheels, and hurries his flock to one side as a missile of oak and iron speeds past, piloted by a man with his mind on something distant. Long before the age of steam, Gaulish charioteers had seen the landscape change into a reeling panorama as they travelled far enough north in a short enough space of time to notice the days grow longer, the morning mists thicken and the sky turn a more delicate shade of blue. Before the advent of the Romans, carters employed by Greek merchants were racing by land from Marseille to Boulogne in thirty days. Two thousand years later, in the reign of Louis XV, modern coaches pulled by teams of horses twice the size of Gaulish nags completed the same journey in just a few days less.

Along those trans-Gallic trade routes, in Burgundy, Champagne and the Rhineland, chariots have been found in graves, dismantled and displayed like exploded diagrams. They were delicately sprung and showed an inventor's love of intricate devices: axle-pins with coral discs and enamel inlays, rein-guides and mountings that looked like foliage or the faces of gods. These vehicles assembled by teams of specialists were not designed to be run on rubbly, winding tracks. When the Gauls settled in northern Italy in the fourth century BC, their technology amazed the Romans, whose cumbrous conveyances seemed to belong to an earlier stage of history. Faced with the new machines, the Romans borrowed a whole vocabulary of vehicular transport: *carros* (wagon); *cission* (cabriolet); *couinnos* and *essedon* (two-wheeled chariots); *petruroton* (four-wheeled carriage); *carbanton* (covered carriage); *reda* (four-wheeled coach). Nearly all the Latin words for wheeled vehicles came from Gaulish.

One of those modern chariots was found in the region of Alesia, where Celtine met Herakles. Since the chariot dates from the late sixth century BC, Celtine herself might have owned a similar model. She had a neighbour who lived forty kilometres to the north in a vaulted palace overlooking a valley where the Sequana begins to broaden into a navigable river. The archaeologists who discovered her called her 'la Dame de Vix', which is the name of the local village, near Châtillon-sur-Seine. Her real name might have been Uxouna, Excinga, Rosmerta or, more likely, Elvissa, which means 'very rich'. She had beads of blue glass and amber, bracelets of bronze for her ankles and arms, and a microscopically detailed, twenty-four-carat gold torc that would have been almost too heavy to wear. Objects from all over the known world had been delivered safely to her home: the beads came from the Baltic and the Mediterranean, the torc from the Black Sea; her tableware was

Etruscan and Greek, and she owned a comprehensive range of imported wine paraphernalia.

The largest vessel ever found in the ancient world is her beautiful bronze *krater* (a wine-mixing urn) from southern Italy: it held eleven hundred litres – enough for a week-long banquet or a god's aperitif. When she died in her early thirties, she was laid out on her state-of-the-art chariot. It had wide-angle steering, and the wooden coachwork was suspended above the chassis by tiny, twisted metal colonnettes that seemed to flaunt their gravity-defying frailty. This was a vehicle fit for a journey to another world. It may never have run on the open roads of Middle Earth, but it proves that the technology existed, and that the beauties of mechanical efficiency were appreciated, four hundred years before the Romans brought their civilization to Gaul.

✤

Like a detective story with an unreliable narrator, Caesar's *Gallic War* contains the clues that disprove its self-serving theories. Caesar knew that, in the comfort of their heated villas, his readers would imagine impenetrable, rain-soaked realms ravaged by mudslides and torrents, obstructed by swamps and trackless swathes of tangled oak forest. (Northern oak-woods always looked wild to a Mediterranean eye.) He knew that, as they blessed him for bringing gold and slaves from Gaul, they would marvel at his bridge-building exploits and his lightning marches from one end of the wild land to the other.

Yet Caesar found roads and bridges already in place wherever he went. Otherwise, one would have to believe that the Gauls gave the name '*briva*' to about thirty different towns (Brienne, Brioude, Brive, etc.) and then waited for the Romans to come and build the eponymous bridges. In Gaul, the marching speed of the legions was always well above the average for the Roman empire. An army of several thousand Roman soldiers marched from Sens to Orléans in four days, arriving in time to pitch camp and set fire to the city (twenty Roman miles a day). Caesar himself reached Belgic Gaul from somewhere south of the Alps 'in about fifteen days' (at least twenty-six miles a day). The Gauls were even faster: a battle-weary army of a hundred and thirty thousand marched from Bibracte to the territory of the

Lingones in just four days (thirty miles a day), which gives some idea of the resilience of the road surface.

In the *Astérix* cartoons, road-signs indicating a certain number of leagues to the nearest town are supposed to be humorous anachronisms, yet they certainly existed. In seven years of campaigning, Caesar always knew when he was entering or leaving a tribal territory, and – most telling of all – he always knew the exact distances to be covered. Distances in Gaul were so accurately measured and so comprehensively plotted that even after the conquest, the Romans continued to use a standardized Gaulish league instead of the Roman mile.

There is something almost magically revealing about these simple calculations – something akin to discovering a two-thousand-year-old Gaulish road-atlas in a second-hand bookshop, which is, in effect, what the following operation conjures up.

A pleasant way to while away an afternoon and to make a major contribution to the history of the Western world is to find a perfectly straight section of Roman road on a map, and then to project the line in both directions on exactly the same bearing. Roman roads can usually be distinguished from other straight roads by their medieval names: in Britain, any road in open country called 'Street' is almost certainly Roman, or an ancient road whose alignment was adopted by the Romans; in France, many are conveniently ascribed to 'Jules César' or to a semi-mythical Queen Brunehaut. If the road itself is unnamed, there are always place names such as 'Chaussée', 'Estrées', 'Stone', 'Stratford', 'Stretton' and so on, which indicate settlements that grew up along a Roman road.

Most of these roads take the shortest route between two Roman towns or camps. But sometimes, a 'Roman' road shows a curious attraction to a Celtic site. The road from Amiens to Saint-Quentin heads straight for the Gaulish *oppidum* of Vermand, fifty-eight kilometres to the east. There, in order to reach the Roman town of Saint-Quentin, it turns abruptly nineteen degrees to the south-east. The line to Vermand is so impressively undeviating that this dog-leg at the far end of the road can hardly have been the result of a surveying error.

It may be that the road was built at an early stage of the Roman conquest, before Saint-Quentin existed, and that the Vermand *oppidum*

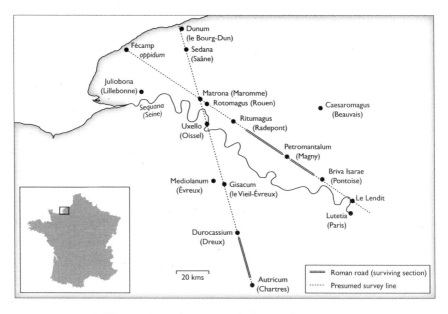

4. 'Roman' roads oriented on pre-Roman sites

was used by the Romans as a marching camp. But many other realignments are harder to explain. The main road to Lutetia (Paris) from the Norman coast, part of which survives as the N14 autoroute, is aimed, not at the Roman centre of Paris on the Left Bank, but at the tribal meeting-place of Le Lendit in the northern suburbs. There, it crosses the Col de la Chapelle, which lay on the prehistoric tin route. In the other direction, it passes through a series of important Celtic sites, including Rotomagus (Rouen), which means 'Wheel-market', and Matrona (Maromme), which shares a name with the pass created by Herakles. After Matrona, the Roman road turns to the west to reach the Roman port of Harfleur, but if the projected line is followed to its logical conclusion, it arrives with what appears to be perfectly engineered precision at the monumental entrance of one of the most important hill fort towns in northern France, the *oppidum* of Fécamp.

A visitor arriving in the Celtic past is bound to wonder sometimes whether the time machine's chronometer has malfunctioned. The trajectories of these 'Roman' roads are a closer match for Celtic Gaul than they are for the Roman province. The line of the road from Chartres to Dreux misses out the Roman town of Évreux and passes instead through the Gaulish sanctuary of Gisacum, before meeting the Paris line at Matrona. The more the puzzle is examined, the less Roman it looks, and the less surprising Caesar's rapid conquest of all the lands between the Alps and Brittany. Either the Gauls already had a coordinated infrastructure worthy of their sleek chariots, or they thoughtfully arranged their settlements and sanctuaries so that once the country had been conquered, the Roman engineers could easily join them all together with straight roads.

✻

At the end of the winter of 53–52 BC, the Romans were given a memorable lesson in Gaulish ingenuity. A victorious Caesar had returned to Italy, secure in the belief that 'the country having been devastated . . . Gaul was now at peace'. Meanwhile, the Gauls were planning one of the biggest allied offensives in European history. The insurrection began at Cenabum (Orléans) when warriors of the Carnutes tribe rose with the sun and massacred the Roman merchants who had settled in the town. At that moment, far to the south, the leader of the Arverni was waiting to hear from Cenabum before coordinating the general revolt that would culminate in the battle of Alesia. Caesar describes the means by which news of the massacre reached the territory of the Arverni:

> The report was conveyed to all the states of Gaul with great speed.
> For whenever anything especially important or remarkable occurs,
> they transmit the news by shouting across the fields and regions;
> others then take it up and pass the news on to the next in line, and
> this is what happened on this occasion. For the things that were
> done in Cenabum at sunrise were heard in the lands of the Arverni
> before the end of the first watch [between 6 pm and 9 pm] – a
> distance of approximately one hundred and sixty miles.

Caesar was often amazed – not just on this occasion – by the 'incredible speed' at which news travelled in Gaul. The Gaulish message system did not rely on the unpredictable spread of rumour: it had to be in a constant state of readiness so that news could be transmitted at any moment. The human transmitters must have been lodged and fed at carefully chosen locations, and relieved at regular intervals. By Caesar's account, which gives almost the exact distance as the crow flies to the chief Arvernian fortress of Gergovia south of Clermont-Ferrand (160 Roman miles or 237 kilometres), it transmitted news at about 24 kph. This is not much slower than the world's first telecommunications system, the Chappe telegraph, which, in 1794, was sending semaphore messages from Paris to Lille at 36 kph.

Anyone who has ever tried to shout across a field will know that transmitting messages in this way is not as simple as it might sound. A long-distance vocal telegraph implies at least as much surveying skill as the pre-Roman road network. If the message follows a straight line over hill and dale, hundreds of transmitters are required. Shouting anything comprehensible from a hilltop, even a few metres downhill, is practically impossible: sound travels far more efficiently along valleys and quiet rivers. But if the line meanders too much around the hills and woodlands, this, too, requires a small army of operators.

Like the road system, the vocal telegraph would have evolved over a long period. At an early stage, perhaps in the sixth century BC, a sound-map of Gaul began to take shape. In areas where settlements were small and isolated, and where shepherds moved their animals over great distances, the acoustic peculiarities of a landscape would have been as familiar as the sounds of neighbours to a modern city-dweller. Using this local knowledge, each tribe would have pieced together a network that joined one hill fort to the next and then, as trade, administration and war demanded, one tribal capital to all its neighbours.

A similar situation arose again in rural France after the end of the Middle Ages. The limits of the tribal or sub-tribal territories that survived as *pays* (from the Latin, *pagus*) were marked by church bells, the size and power of which were directly related to the extent of the *pays*. When news of a threat had to be broadcast more quickly than a messenger could carry it – a foreign invasion or the arrival of a recruiting sergeant, a tax-collector or a pack of ravening wolves – the overlapping circles of sound acted as a crude telegraph system. But this was a system that grew by accident; the Gaulish telegraph was deliberately devised and maintained. Apart from its official purposes, it served what was perceived as a social need. By all accounts, the Gauls had an enormous appetite for news of any sort: they waylaid travellers, mobbed them in market squares and, after feeding them copiously, pumped them for whatever information they might have of distant parts. With the logistical support of the allied tribes of Gaul, such a system could easily have performed the miracles recorded by Caesar.

The whistling language of Pyrenean shepherds, which became extinct in the 1950s, could transmit the contents of the local newspaper up to a distance of three and a half kilometres. The Gauls probably used a monosyllabic code, with repetitions and set phrases to avoid misinterpretations, and the trained lungs of warriors, male and female. Celtic armies famously intimidated their foes by shouting, ululating and blowing their war-trumpets: 'For there were among them such innumerable horns and trumpets, which were being blown simultaneously in all parts of their army, and their cries were so loud and piercing, that the noise seemed to come not merely from trumpets and human voices, but from the whole countryside at once' (Polybius). A bellowing Gaul could certainly have matched the range of a whistling shepherd, in which case fewer than eighty sound transmitters would have been required to send the message all the way from Orléans to Gergovia.

In his deceptively brisk style, Caesar was describing one of the wonders of the ancient world. The message to Gergovia used only one line of the network. While the news from Orléans was racing across the swamps of the Sologne towards the Massif Central, the same message was being 'conveyed to all the states [or tribes] of Gaul' ('ad omnes Galliae civitates'). This simultaneous, mass communication is a significant event in the early history of information technology. To judge by the rapidly assembled confederation of Gaulish tribes in 52 BC, the vocal telegraph served an area of over half a million square kilometres.

It may yet be possible to recover something of this masterpiece of acoustic engineering. New sounds have joined the orchestra of winds, running water and birdsong, but the aural configurations of most landscapes have changed very little in two thousand years. The whisper of Clermont-Ferrand, punctuated by a police siren or a clanging girder, drifts up to the plateau of Gergovia. The metallic glissando of trains speeding along the ancient route from Paris to the Mediterranean can be heard from the hill fort of Alesia.

5. The Gaulish confederation at the battle of Alesia

Sometimes, in the Pyrenean foothills or the mountains of Provence, where walls and rock faces act as sounding-boards, a conversation in a village square can be followed in perfect detail far beyond the village itself.

A hypothetical telegraph line drawn from Orléans to Gergovia and projected in the other direction passes through several tribal centres and the road junction called Matrona. Two-thirds of the way to Gergovia, it crosses a farm on a low ridge above the winding valley of the river Aumance. One kilometre south-east of the farm, on slightly higher ground, are the remains of a small *oppidum*. The farm has become a holiday home with (according to the owners' advertisement) 'long and wide' horizons: 'the only night-time sounds are those of an owl or nightingale'. In the daytime, several other sounds can be heard at a distance of four kilometres, including traffic on the road to Clermont-Ferrand and the lowing of a herd of cattle.

The name of the farm, Les Ingarands, is known to a handful of etymologists as one of the seventy-five place names that can be traced back to a Gaulish word, '*equoranda*' or '*icoranda*': Aigurande, la Délivrande, les Équilandes, Guérande, Ingrandes, Yvrandes, etc.* The *randa* part of the name means 'limit' or 'boundary'. Despite their great antiquity, many of these sites lie on or close to the boundaries of medieval dioceses and modern *départements*, which makes them probably the oldest examples in Europe of the surprising longevity of administrative divisions. The first part of the name – '*equo*' or '*ico*' – is still a mystery. It used to be interpreted as 'water' or 'horse', neither of which is morphologically possible. The '*kw*' sound suggests a word that was already archaic in Caesar's day since, in the Celtic languages that were spoken in Italy, Gaul and Britain, '*kw*' turned into '*p*' at a very early stage, perhaps around 900 BC. Equally mysterious is the distribution of Equorandas: most Celtic place names occur all over the Celtic-speaking world, but, for some reason, Equorandas are found only within the confines of Gaul.

The mystery is not necessarily unsolvable. '*Equo*' or '*ico*' could be related to the Greek '*êchô*' ('sound', 'noise' or 'loud cry') or to the Gaulish verb *eiğ(h)ō*' ('I implore', 'I call'), in which case, an *equoranda*

---

* The complete list, with coordinates, can be found at www.panmacmillan.com/theancientpaths.

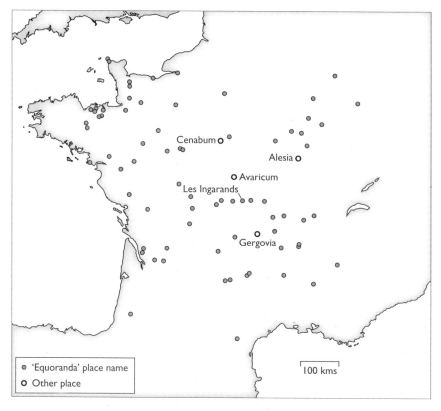

6. Place names derived from 'equoranda'

would be a 'sound-line' or a 'call-line'. Most of them are on low ridges or in shallow valleys, and all the Equorandas that were visited during the writing of this book would have made excellent listening-posts. Practical considerations ruled out the use of a Celtic war-trumpet, and neither member of the expedition was loud or brazen enough to project the message '*Agro Cenabo!*' ('Massacre at Orléans!') very far, but there was usually a convenient sheep, child or car-alarm to give some measure of the location's acoustic potential.

If the places called Equoranda were stations on the vocal telegraph network, this would explain why the name is found only in Gaul, which is the only part of the Celtic world known to have possessed a vocal telegraph network. Though the clue has been erased by mistranslation, the name itself is curiously reminiscent of Caesar's description. The slightly peculiar phrase '*per agros regionesque*' appears to mean 'through fields and regions'. Some translators smooth away the oddness of the expression by turning '*regiones*' into 'villages'. But '*regio*' was also a term used in augury and surveying: a '*regio*' was the line of sight that served as a boundary, either on the earth or in the sky. When Caesar's interpreters were collecting information, '*regio*' would have been the obvious Latin equivalent of the Gaulish '*randa*': 'they transmit the news by shouting across the fields and along boundary lines'.

When the Celts first arrived in Gaul, this may have been the technique that was used to establish frontiers. Until the early nineteenth century, in the French Jura, when a forest was being divided up before felling, two men would stand a certain distance apart and call to one another. A third man would try to position himself in the middle by listening to the shouts and answering them. All three would then call out at regular intervals while a fourth man walked along the path of sound, marking the trees, and when that section of the forest was felled, the result was an astonishingly straight line. The same acoustic surveying technique was used by Persian road-builders, and it was this that gave the prophet Isaiah the image of a voice crying out in the wilderness, 'Make straight in the desert a highway'.

The seventy-five Equorandas that survive as modern place names could only be the scattered remnants of this magnificent network. There are no precise equations for determining the rate at which place names disappear, and so it would be hard to estimate the original number of transmitting stations. The fact that they survive at all suggests that they remained in use for several centuries and that their purpose was generally known and understood.

Two thousand years from now, faced with the near-total erasure of digitized information, an archaeologist working on the late-second millennium AD may notice a recurrence of peculiar place names, attached to moderately high places which appear never to have been inhabited. Their mysterious syllables might eventually be traced back to two Greek words: *tele* and *graphein*. If enough of these names survive, the archaeologist might suggest that once, within the confines of France, there was a 'distance writing' network which involved the use of optical signals. Today, almost one hundred and sixty years after the last message was transmitted to the whole country, announcing the Fall of Sebastopol in the Crimea, there are still enough names on the map, attached to fields, hilltops, mountain passes and some small, inscrutable ruins, to make it

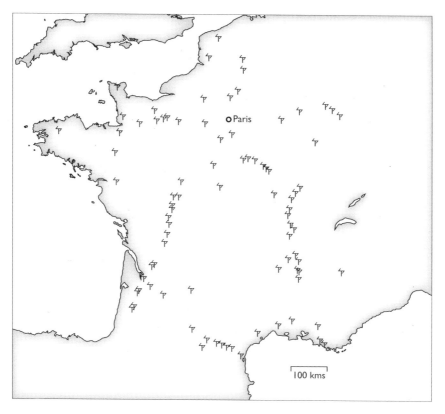

7. 'Télégraphe' place names in 2013

possible to trace the skeletal outline of the Chappe telegraph system. But only eighty-six of the original five hundred and thirty-four stations have left their name on the landscape. Many of the names are no longer commonly used; some are known only to farmers and cartographers. The gaps are growing bigger all the time. Without the zeal of local historical societies, at the current rate of disappearance (about ten per cent of the original total every twenty years), the name 'Télégraphe' would be practically extinct within a generation.

Technological sophistication is no guarantee of survival. Apart from the comparatively gargantuan livestock, the view beyond the computer screen on which these words are appearing is practically unchanged since the Iron Age. A few hundred metres away, at the top of a wooded slope, trains once carried passengers and timber through the borderlands from one former tribal capital (Carlisle) to another (Edinburgh). Although the line was closed less than fifty years ago, practically all that remains in the vicinity is an embankment eroded by cattle, some bricks and lead conduits washed down by the torrents, and a name attached to a pair of cottages. In another two thousand years, the idea that the nineteenth century was an age of empire-spanning transport and communication systems might seem as far-fetched as the concept of a Gaulish engineer.

3

The Mediolanum Mystery, I

Long before the Gauls had long-distance roads and a telegraph system, and even before there was a Lady of Vix living in a palace above the Seine, in an age so remote and poorly documented that it can scarcely be called protohistoric, the lands of the Celts were divided into small tribal enclaves. One of the few signs of inter-regional coordination in this period is a name. 'Mediolanum' was one of the commonest and oldest place names in the Celtic world. It occurred over a vast area, from the Irish Sea to the Black Sea, and from Spain to northern Germany, but principally in Gaul.* Some of the places called Mediolanum eventually became Roman towns; others vanished altogether. Within a few generations of the Roman conquest, 'Mediolanum' was an obscure and baffling term, its meaning known, presumably, only to the Druids who lived in exile or who stayed behind secretly in Gaul. Educated Romans – even those who had a smattering of Gaulish – had no idea what it meant. In the fourth century AD, the citizens of a town in northern Italy called Mediolanum (now the city of Milan) decided that '*medio – lanum*' must be a Latin term signifying 'half wool' and adopted as their coat of arms a weird and impossible creature wearing half a fleece. Not long afterwards, the Gaulish language was extinct, and almost nothing remained to indicate that the Mediolana were relics of the earliest attempts by Celtic tribes to map and organize their territory.

After two hundred years of scholarship, the Gaulish language is better known today than it was at the end of the Roman empire. The

---

* The Greek and, probably, Gaulish, form was 'Mediolanon'. The better-known Latin form, 'Mediolanum', is more commonly used. The plural is 'Mediolana'. '*Lanon*' is unrelated to the Welsh '*llan*' and Breton '*lann*' (an enclosed piece of land, especially the site of a monastery or church). The nearest Welsh equivalent is '*llawn*' ('full' or 'complete').

literal sense of the word 'Mediolanum' is now well established. The Gaulish dictionary compiled by Xavier Delamarre defines it as 'a term of sacred geography': 'a holy centre . . . perhaps a central point of reference on the vertical axis of the three worlds – upper, middle and lower'. For students of the Celts, this is familiar ground. In Celtic mythology, 'middle' was a three-dimensional term. It referred not only to the earth that lies between the upper and the lower worlds, but also to the intersection of lines based on the cardinal points. According to Celtic legend, Ireland was divided in the first century AD into four kingdoms, each of which gave a part of itself to form a fifth, central kingdom called Mide (or Meath), signifying 'middle'. This is the cruciform pattern that can be seen on the ceremonial Celtic bronze spoons which began to appear all over Europe in about 800 BC. It usually takes the form of two perpendicular lines with a circle at the centre. The so-called Celtic cross of the early Christian Church is probably a direct descendant of those designs.

The concept of a geographical and symbolic centre – of a temple, a town, a nation or the entire earth – is common to most Indo-European religions. The Druids, according to Caesar, met at a particular time of the year in 'a region considered to be the centre of the whole of Gaul'. In ancient Greece, the equivalent of a 'holy centre' was the *omphalos* or 'navel' stone, which marked the centre of the world, the most famous being the *omphalos* at Delphi. The exact location was said to have been discovered when Zeus released two eagles or crows at opposite ends of the earth: flying in straight lines at the same speed, the birds met at the place that became Delphi. In Jerusalem, there are two *omphaloi*: the Temple Mount, where Adam was created, and the rock of Golgotha in the Church of the Holy Sepulchre, where Jesus Christ was crucified. On medieval maps of the world, the *omphalos* of Jerusalem is placed at the centre of the earth, with Paradise at the top and the Pillars of Hercules at the bottom.

No such map of the Celtic world has come to light – or nothing that has been recognized as a map – and a glance at the distribution of Mediolana shows why the search for a 'sacred centre' of the Druids has so far proved fruitless. The map of Mediolana printed here is the most detailed yet established, but still no pattern can be seen. The problem is, there are 'sacred centres' or 'middle sanctuaries' all over the Celtic world: Herakles would have passed by six of them on his way to the Matrona Pass, and Caesar's campaigns would have taken him to within a few Roman miles of at least a dozen Mediolana. Some of the Mediolana are now towns or villages, but most of them are so insignificant that they exist only as a small farm or a field. A 'Melaine' in the Compiègne forest was identified as a Mediolanum only when two lead coins of the third century AD were found there inscribed with the abbreviations 'MED L' and 'MEDIOL'. A Mediolanum that was a small island in the Atlantic Ocean near the Île d'Aix was swallowed by the waves some time after 1430. Another Atlantic Mediolanum – a headland near Carnac called the Pointe de Meylant – was never recorded on a map: it turned up during research for this book in a guide for coastal pilots published in 1763.

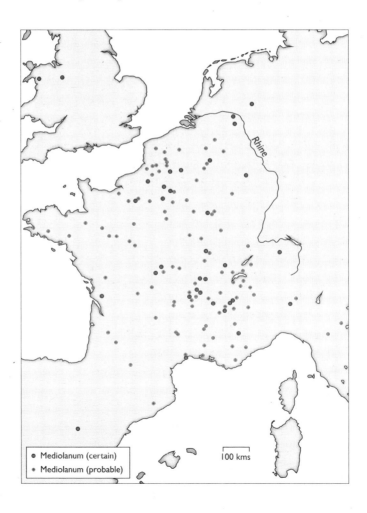

Rhine

• Mediolanum (certain)
⊕ Mediolanum (probable)

100 kms

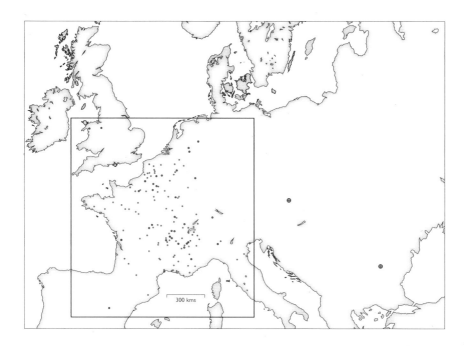

8. Mediolana

The majority of these 'central sanctuaries' were in Gaul, but there were also Mediolana in England, Wales, Belgium, Germany, Switzerland, Italy and Spain. The furthest flung (fig. 43) were in Lower Austria and Bulgaria. The best known – but not the earliest – is the city of Milan. In all, thirty-six places are known for certain to have been called Mediolanum. There are also one hundred and one other places for which no documentary or epigraphic evidence survives but whose names – Meaullens, Miolan, Molliens, etc. – are almost certainly derived from 'Mediolanum'. (For a complete list, with coordinates, see www.panmacmillan.com/theancientpaths.)

Châteaumeillant is a relatively straightforward example. Twenty-three of its earlier forms are recorded: Mediolanum became Mediolens, then Melianum, Millandum, Maiglen and finally, like a pebble tumbled and smoothed by a river, Meillant. The original name is cited by Gregory of Tours (sixth century AD) and on a thirteenth-century map of the world (the Peutinger Map) based on ancient 'itineraries' or lists of staging posts dating from the fourth century AD. The oldest remnant of all can be seen by anyone who cares to stand with a small ladder in the middle of the *route nationale* to Paris in the village of Bruère-Allichamps, where a third-century milestone marks one of the supposed centres of France. Near the top of the column, a Roman inscription indicates that 'MED[IOLANUM]' lies 'L XII' (twelve Gaulish leagues or 32.5 kilometres) from the milestone.

Many of the Mediolana are places that a traveller might well describe as 'the middle of nowhere'. It is extremely hard to tell why these unimportant places bore such a portentous name. For several centuries, Iron Age scholars and the seekers of mystical truths known to French archaeologists as 'Celtomaniacs' puzzled over the meaning of this tantalizing term, which combines geography with religion. Theoretical expeditions returned empty-handed or in disarray. According to some, 'Mediolanum' meant 'middle of the plain' (because Milan is in the middle of a plain): this is disproved by the fact that most Mediolana are on hills or in hilly terrain. Others claimed that the Mediolana were tribal centres: but some Mediolana are only a few kilometres apart and none is in the centre of a Celtic tribal territory.

One of the most persistent attempts to explain the mystery was made by a professor of literature at the University of Bordeaux. Between 1972 and 2000, Yves Vadé developed a theory that these 'middle sanctuaries' had been part of a system of coordinated points. In Vadé's reconstruction of the hypothetical pattern, one of the key points was Châteaumeillant, which lies approximately the same distance from Meilhan-sur-Garonne as from Évreux (formerly Mediolanum). These two places in turn are more or less equidistant from Milan (724 and 728 kilometres). Observing that a few other miscellaneous sites of Celtic and pre-Celtic significance lay close to the lines connecting these points, Vadé drew various combinations of equilateral and isosceles triangles over the Gaulish part of Europe. 'Unless the maps deceive us', he concluded, the places called Mediolanum represented a spectacular application of the principles of sacred geography.

Unfortunately, the maps *do* deceive us. A map is a flat representation of part of a sphere. This translation of a curved surface into two dimensions inevitably produces a certain distortion. For the same reason that a small piece of orange skin can be flattened without tearing its edges, the distortion is insignificant over short distances, but on the scale of Vadé's 'system of equidistances', sizeable discrepancies occur. As a result, some of his triangles are skewed by several degrees and some of his equidistances are out by several kilometres. With the correct equations and projections, it is perfectly possible to replicate the kind of survey that an ancient civilization was capable of producing (p. 147). But even then, no pattern emerges, which is hardly surprising: Vadé assumed that practically all the Mediolana are known, but since relatively few protohistoric place names survive, even the one hundred and thirty-seven Mediolana shown on the map above must be a small minority of the original total.*

Most other Celtic historians who pondered the Mediolanum mystery sensibly added it to all the other unanswerable questions of Iron Age history and hoped that, one day, the mystery would be solved by archaeology.

Surprisingly, archaeology has provided a kind of answer – but an answer so multifarious and unexpected that it took me several months of research even to notice its existence. The stupendous reference work known as the *Carte archéologique de la Gaule* is now at its one-hundred-and-nineteenth undigitized volume. It describes every archaeological find, however small or dubious, made on the territory of modern France. Again and again, it shows that the places once called Mediolanum do indeed have something other than a name in common. The entry for Meylan (Lot-et-Garonne) is fairly representative: 'some iron slag' was found and nothing else. At Molain (Jura), there is a pre-Celtic burial mound, and then the record is blank apart from some Roman coins. In 1873, at the Mediolanum near Pontcharra on the road to Lyon, a subterranean passage was discovered: it led to a small dry-stone chamber; at intervals along the passage, holes for lamps had been carved and there were traces of smoke; but it turned out to belong to a Gallo-Roman dwelling. Despite its Celtic name, Miollan appeared not to have existed until the Roman conquest. For many other Mediolana, there is no entry at all, or just a terse 'nothing to report'.

---

* An additional problem is that the names on maps can be just as deceptive as the maps themselves. Toponymy is like a dream in which familiar faces turn out to belong to strangers. The city of Milan owes its name to 'Mediolanum', but most of the other places called Milan have an entirely different origin. A village that was called 'Moulins' in the eighteenth century (now Molain) is mentioned in an eleventh-century document as 'Villa Mediolanis', but all the other 'Moulins' are mills. The etymological record shows that, of the thirty-nine 'middle sanctuaries' included by Vadé in his calculations, sixteen were never Mediolana. One of the key points in his system is Meilhan-sur-Garonne, which, though it looks like a name derived from 'Mediolanum', was probably the estate of a Roman citizen called Aemilianus.

Bizarrely, the one distinguishing feature of these 'sacred centres', apart from the obviously Celtic name, is the absence of Celtic remains. With a single exception (p. 81), even the few Mediolana that became important towns after the Roman conquest have a void in their history. The Mediolanum which is now the city of Saintes in western France prides itself on its independent Gaulish past, and yet, after several decades of intense excavation, it has not a single museum-worthy object with which to celebrate its pride, not even a Celtic coin, just an undatable potsherd and a small piece of harness that might have come from somewhere else.

Despite this deluge of insignificance, it seemed impossible that the places called Mediolanum had nothing in common but a lack of Celtic evidence and a name – an oddly ineradicable name, attached to nothing in particular, yet as durable as a stone temple – and so, in 2008, remembering the six Mediolana that lie along the Via Heraklea, I decided to include as many 'middle sanctuaries' as possible in each cycling trip to France. The first sign of something out of the ordinary was the fact that it was exceptionally difficult to fit them into long-distance routes. Many of them were in awkward, out-of-the-way locations, and few of them had anything of interest apart from the name on the road sign. To judge by the raised eyebrows of farmers and dog-walkers, no one since the Iron Age had ever asked for directions to Les Miolans or Le Mayollant, and no tourist had ever stopped to photograph the muddy pastures of Maulain or the monolithic grain silos on the otherwise featureless hill of Montmeillant.

In the Burgundian hamlet of Meulin (cited in a ninth-century cartulary as 'Mediolanensis ager'), the GPS unit went blank and never recovered. This was certainly due to the five hours of torrential rain that fell between Paray-le-Monial and Mâcon, but it seemed quite appropriate: even with weeks of advance planning, many of the Mediolana were tricky to find and even harder to leave. On the map, the route looked simple, but on the ground, the 'first left' or 'second right' turned out to be a plausible lane, which ended in an open field. Tracks led off at odd angles and veered in a different direction as soon as they left the village. There was often a choice of two apparently identical onward routes. The church, if there was one, sometimes appeared to belong in a different setting, as though its original village had been lost to another dimension. Yet once the site had been identified, the church spire would remain in view for several kilometres.

By the tenth Mediolanum, this much was obvious: the typical Mediolanum was a tiny place on a hilly site, devoid of Celtic remains, with a disproportionate capacity to bewilder and confuse, set apart from any natural trade route or long-distance road, and inhabited by an agitated dog who knew that any visitor was in the wrong place. None of them looked as though it had ever been a Celtic Jerusalem or Delphi.

It was only later that I learned of a form of cartographic analysis that might have explained the confusion or made it easier to predict. The technique, developed by the archaeologist Éric Vion, is based on the fact that once a route has been created, it almost never disappears completely: thousands of years after it was first tramped out, it might survive as a track, a field boundary or the edge of a wood. It follows that a large-scale modern map is not just a snapshot of the network at a given moment, but a multi-dimensional scan that reveals all the successive strata which make up the present roadscape. Just as an oak tree tells the story of its life in growth-rings and twisted boughs, the whole road system – rather than just the segments that are known to be ancient – is a record of its own evolution.

Even the simplest application of the technique can produce some exciting results. The first step is to identify all the junctions in a given area. Next, one simply counts the number of branches at each junction, including tracks as well as roads. The junctions with the largest number of branches (say, ten or more) are nearly always important places: these are the cities and large towns which remain visible when the map is zoomed out, and which are directly connected to one another over long distances. If the junctions with fewer branches are added, then the small towns and large villages with more local connections appear, and so on, until the whole populated landscape is accounted for.

Sometimes, in this apparently logical system, anomalies appear – a crossroads in open country which turns out to mark the site of an abandoned village or a Roman marching camp; a prehistoric trail that meanders like a sleepwalker, missing out all the villages and cutting across later routes. There may also be some many-branched crossroads that belong to an earlier network. Some of the branches may have lost their original purpose and yet survive in truncated forms. Isolated from the rest of the map, these ancient intersections look like fallen trees with their roots in the air.

Most of the places called Mediolanum fit this description, which explains why it was so easy to get lost in their vicinity. As it entered and left each 'middle sanctuary', the bicycle, unconsciously reading the coded messages of the road system, was slipping in and out of different eras, plunging with a turn of the handlebars into the distant age when Greek sailors were founding trading posts on the Mediterranean and when the solar trajectory of the Heraklean Way was first projected over half a continent.

4

The Mediolanum Mystery, II

I now had the inestimable advantage of knowing in which period I was lost (the very early Iron Age), and it was then that the solution to the Mediolanum mystery appeared. The answer was hardly 'staring me in the face'; it gazed off into the distance like a sphinx, but when I followed its line of sight, this is what emerged.

The Mediolana's apparent absence of significance is typical of survey-points, especially ancient survey-points. In Egypt, Rome and most of the classical world, geometrical surveys were conducted to define the trajectory of a road or the course of a frontier, or to divide a territory into estates. Often, all that remains of the survey – when anything does remain – is a lonely cross or a wordless monolith in a field. Usually, every explanation of the monument's presence has vanished, leaving only a solitary, silent witness to a forgotten event. In rare instances, the monument speaks: in the desert of southern Tunisia, a marker stone was found at the foot of a mountain, inscribed by the Roman surveyor who had failed to place his triangulation point on the highest peak: '*in summum venire non potuit*' ('he couldn't reach the summit'). But without his graven excuse, there would have been nothing but desert.

As coordinates in an early system of land measurements based on astronomical observations, the Mediolana would have been imbued with religious significance. The places themselves, apart from their slight geographical prominence, were of no earthly interest. The closest equivalent today is the online 'Degree Confluence Project', whose adherents, in a peculiarly twenty-first-century spirit of mystical fervour and absurdist irony, visit intersections of whole-number latitude and longitude coordinates (e.g. 55.0, -3.0) with a camera. These mathematically defined sites are, by their nature, nowhere in particular, which is why this admirable application of geekish obsession and physical intrepidity is currently amassing what must be the world's most boring collection of photographs.*

The question is, how can we tell that the Mediolana were coordinates? As Yves Vadé's impossible 'system of equidistances' shows, any network of ancient reference points has long since disappeared. Here, the crucial Celtic term *'medio'* is the guide. It leads, somewhat unpromisingly at first, to the mid-second century AD and to a region so remote that, according to Roman historians, even Herakles had never been there.

In the reign of Emperor Antoninus Pius (AD 138–161), the northernmost frontier of the Roman empire was marked by a sixty-three-kilometre-long embankment of turf and stone. Six days' march north of Hadrian's Wall, the Antonine Wall joined the Firth of Forth to the Firth of Clyde, barricading Caledonia at its narrowest point, *'ubi britania* [sic] *plus angustissima de oceano in oceanum* [*est*]'. Under this heading, the compilation of itineraries known as the Ravenna Cosmography (c. AD 700) lists ten forts along the wall (in all, twenty-four have been found). The sixth fort recorded by the medieval scribe bears the Celtic name 'Medionemeton'.

Medionemeton is now Bar Hill, where the suburbs of Glasgow give way to the Campsie Fells. A path leads through scraggly woodland to the earthworks and some moss-carpeted footings. No one knows why a small Roman fort on the edge of the civilized world bore such an evocative Celtic name. A *'nemeton'* was a sanctuary. There are still about forty place names, most of them in Britain and France, which contain the time-worn phonemes of the word.[†] *'Nemeton'* may have been related to the Greek *'nemos'* ('wood'), because the Celts – so the poet Lucan claimed – made their sanctuaries in sunless groves where the trees dripped with the blood of human sacrifice, and 'altars horrible on massive stones upreared'. A more likely origin is the word *'nem'* – also found in Old Breton and Old Irish – which means 'sky'. This would make a *'nemeton'* a 'celestial place' and 'Medionemeton' a near-synonym of 'Mediolanum'. A *nemeton* was a template of the upper world, a portion of the heavens mapped out on the earth, just

---

* http://confluence.org/

† Nanterre, Nemours, Nîmes, Nempnett Thrubwell, etc. See also pp. 217 and 271 and, for a longer list, www.panmacmillan.com/theancientpaths.

as a Roman *templum* was a space marked out either in the sky or on the ground for the purpose of taking auspices (p. 13).

Apart from the sacred name and the crows in the oak trees, the mysteries of Celtic religion are entirely absent from the Bar Hill fort. The only divine presence unearthed there is a small sandstone altar dedicated to the Roman god Silvanus by the grateful prefect of a cohort of Syrian archers. Perhaps the shrine from which the altar came already existed when the foreign troops arrived with their trenching tools and soil baskets, but there is no evidence of Celtic deities, let alone an 'altar horrible on massive stones upreared'. The '*medio*' has proved just as baffling as it is in 'Mediolanum': Bar Hill is not in the 'middle' of the Antonine Wall; there are twelve forts to the west of it, and eleven to the east; it lies two Roman miles closer to the western terminus than to the eastern. Yet here, on the edge of the Roman empire, the riddle is expressed as the simplest of all designs – a straight line.

The Roman method of planning roads and frontier walls consisted, very roughly, of this. Two terminal points were chosen – in this case, Bishopton, across what was then the fordable Firth of Clyde, and Carriden, ten kilometres west of the Forth Road Bridge. An imaginary line was drawn between the two termini and traced on the ground by a process of triangulation or some other form of geometrical alignment.* Sometimes, the finished road would follow the straight line of the survey. Often, because of a pre-existing route or an obstacle – a marsh, a ravine, a hill too steep for horses – it would deviate from the line, but rarely more than a few Roman miles. The Antonine Wall is a typical example of the art: with the survey line drawn on a map, it resembles a vine entwining itself around a stake. No fort on the Antonine Wall is more than 2.6 kilometres from the survey line, and for its entire length there are conveniently low hills from which the surveyors could take their bearings.

The operation can be recreated on a computer in less time than it takes to lug a dioptra, a sundial and a bundle of wooden posts to

---

* Cartographic triangulation consists of taking three points, measuring the angles of the resulting triangle, and the exact distance on the ground between two of the points. The lengths of the other two sides are provided by basic trigonometry. Another example of a Roman survey line (Watling Street) is shown in fig. 72.

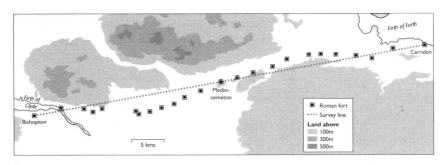

9. Forts of the Antonine Wall

The difference is negligible if the western terminus of the Antonine Wall is taken (as it often is) to be the fort of Old Kilpatrick on the Firth of Clyde, or if Medionemeton is identified with Croy Hill, the eastern neighbour of Bar Hill.

the top of a hill. Something that was known to the original surveyors in AD 142 becomes immediately apparent: the line passes through the shrine at Medionemeton – not just nearby, but bisecting it exactly. This 'middle sanctuary', which occupies one of the highest areas of ground between the two terminal points, was the prime coordinate on a long-distance line and the central pivot of the northern frontier.

To the legionaries who stood guard on the empire's edge, the name 'Medionemeton' probably meant very little. Under the wind-blown beacon, with the black-faced sheep huddled up against the hedges, the sacred geography of a barbarian race would have been a matter of total indifference to a Syrian archer. He was there because Emperor Antoninus had ordered a wall to be built between civilization and the wild tribes of the north. But he was there, too, because a shrine had stood on that spot in days gone by, and because the wall itself, like Hadrian's Wall to the south, followed a route that was already ancient and patrolled by a god more powerful than the imported rustic Silvanus.

✵

Though the Scottish Medionemeton has only now given up its secret, the surveying sense of 'medio' is neither eccentric nor particularly mysterious. Every ancient survey was based on the association of measurement with a mid-point. A 'meridian' (from 'medius' and 'dies') is a line drawn in the direction of the sun's shadow (due north)

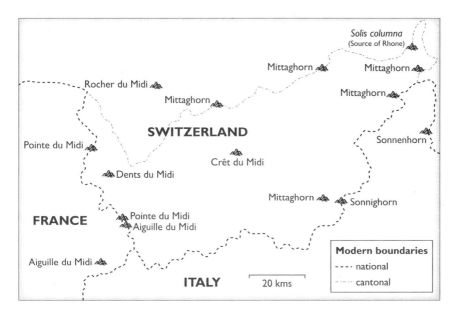

10. 'Midday Mountains' as boundary markers

at the mid-point of its daily course. True midday occurs when the sun lies due south, which is why the 'Midi' is the South of France.

Throughout the Alps and the Pyrenees, for example, there are 'Midday Mountains' (Mittaghorn, Pic du Midi, Punta del Mezzodì, etc.), which are usually said to have indicated, from the point of view of the people who named them, the position of the sun at midday. These convenient peaks are supposed to have been gigantic gnomons on snow-covered sundials. In fact, most of the Midday Mountains are useless as chronometers. A straightforward experiment shows that their practical function was quite different. Plotted on a map, they turn out to mark boundary-lines and frontiers, some of which are at least as old as the Roman empire. Like Medionemeton, these 'midday' points are the surveying poles of territorial divisions that were probably first established in the late Iron Age.

Since many of the commonest place names date back to the Iron Age, it seemed quite possible, when I began to pursue this endless path that led everywhere and nowhere, that these and hundreds of other 'middle' places – some on high ground, others on slopes that scarcely deserve to be called 'hills' – once belonged to the same local networks as the Mediolana.

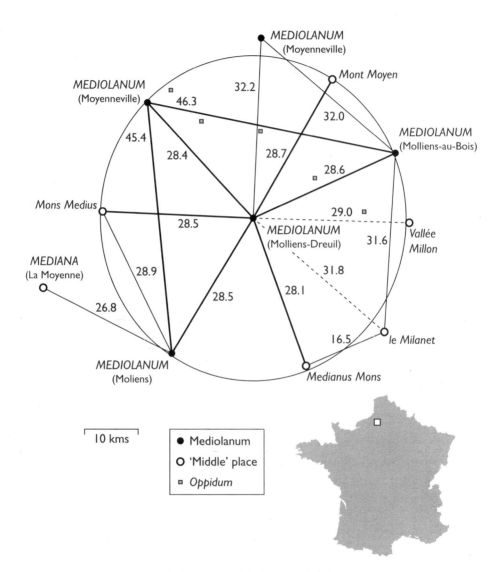

11. Mediolana and 'mid hills' in Picardy

Distances are in kilometres, to the nearest hundred metres. 'Vallée Millon' and 'Le Milanet', on the right of the diagram, may be derived from 'Mediolanum'. They were discovered simply by following the pattern. Coincidentally, perhaps, aerial photographs of the field called 'Le Milanet' – a site unknown to archaeologists – appear to show rectangular ditches or enclosures.

This was not a theory to be tested lightly. In the Middle Ages – which is when most place names were first recorded – there were hundreds of *montes medii* in western Europe. I eventually located almost one thousand 'mid hills' from northern Scotland to the eastern Alps. Some of them occur in the same region as Mediolana and seem to form local groups of 'middle' places. A few had even been Mediolana themselves until the old Celtic name was conflated with the more familiar '*mons medius*'.

When the curiously fascinating operation of finding and plotting every middle place was complete, something quite intriguing appeared. In some regions, where enough place names have survived, even at a distance of more than two and a half thousand years, the patterns are strikingly consistent. Without the Gaulish place names, this map of Mediolana and other 'middle places' in Picardy (fig. 11) would look like one of the triangulation charts produced by the Cassini map-making expeditions of the eighteenth century.

This cartographic pattern deduced from early Iron Age sites may be the oldest detectable sign of large-scale territorial organization in northern Europe. Apart from the stone tablets in the museum of Orange on which roads and rivers are etched across the gridlines of a Roman survey – and ignoring the dubious chiselled stone from 'Caesar's Camp' at Mauchamp on the river Aisne which happens to resemble an outline of France – nothing like a modern map has emerged from the ancient world. But on this evidence, the information needed to create a map existed.

Perhaps the science of long-distance measuring had travelled along the trade routes that opened up at the end of the Hallstatt period, bringing the Aegean to within a few weeks of northern Gaul. Something of Hellenic civilization had already reached the Mediterranean coast of Gaul a generation before Massalia was founded by Phocaean traders. In 650 BC, the natives of Agatha (Agde) were acquiring Greek ideas along with Greek wine and ceramics. When they aligned their necropolis on the rising sun of the summer solstice, they were following a native Bronze Age tradition, but when they divided it up into regular allotments, they used a Greek unit of measurement.

Compared to the precise centuriations of Mediterranean towns, the Mediolanum system in the north of Gaul is patchy and incomplete. The similar distances suggest that an ancestor of the Gaulish *leuca* ('league') was already in use, though, like most units of measurement until the twentieth century, it would have varied from one region to the next. The whole system might even be attributed to chance, were it not for the fact that its regularity is quite distinct from the patterning effects of catchment areas and supply zones. Sanctuaries and hill forts tend to be more or less evenly dispersed: each population required a certain acreage of arable and woodland, and a reasonably convenient centre. Like the five *oppida* shown in the map above (p. 54), which follow the winding course of the river Somme, they usually occur along natural routes. The 'middle places', by contrast, suggest a deliberate application of geodetic science to the landscape.

The urge to map and organize a territory is not completely unexpected in a culture that excelled in the amicable division of land. The inter-tribal roads of the Gauls and their high-speed telegraph system could hardly have been devised without long-distance surveys that would have taken many years to evolve. Nor is it surprising that Celtic tribes wanted to impose an administrative and sacred order on the natural chaos of hills and rivers and on the vagaries of human habitation. Earlier societies had written on the landscape with alignments of ditches and stones. The gigantic prehistoric hieroglyphs of Carnac, Stonehenge and Avebury were known to the Celts. But the organization of middle places implies a collective project almost too ambitious to be credible: it would mean that only a generation or two after a recognizably Celtic civilization arose, the Celts were attempting to survey and measure regions that spanned many tribal territories.

✻

For some time after this ghostly remnant of an ancient map came to light, I thought that the coordinated group of Mediolana in what was later the territory of the Ambiani must be an isolated phenomenon. Only in a few areas do all the other Mediolana and the hundreds of other 'middle' mounds and hills form such coherent patterns. Perhaps only a few local networks ever existed, or perhaps the evidence has vanished beyond recall. The map of Mediolana and middle places presented here (fig. 12) lay on my desk for several weeks as an inscrutable curiosity: was this the threadbare remnant of a continent-sized tapestry of networks or a monument to wasted time? And yet, the map as a whole was strangely eloquent. The concentrations of 'mid hills' are unexpectedly independent of topography: in some of the hilliest regions, there are none at all, while some barely undulating landscapes are full of them. Two lines seem to run from the region of the lower Rhone: one follows the trajectory of the Via Heraklea; another, more ragged line runs up the valley of the river Isère into southern Switzerland. There is no obvious correlation with tribal or linguistic zones, and yet there *is* a pattern, which an archaeologist might recognize at a glance.

The scatter of 'middle places' looks remarkably like a map illustrating the early spread of Celtic civilization from the eighth to the fifth centuries BC. The concentration in the eastern Alps and the middle Danube would correspond to the proto-Celtic Hallstatt culture, which is named after the salt mines of a lakeside settlement south-east of Salzburg. The warrior aristocrats of the Hallstatt owed their wealth to the prehistoric salt routes that joined the European Plain to the Adriatic and the Mediterranean. An unrecorded catastrophe caused the collapse of the Hallstatt aristocracy. With the founding of the Greek trading port of Massalia, new markets opened up, and the rivers Rhone and Saône became important corridors of trade. The centres of power shifted to the west and the north, and to the culture known as La Tène – from an archaeological site on Lake Neuchâtel. This is the culture that produced the characteristic mazy swirls of Celtic art. In Gaul, its main focus was the Marne, though there were also signs of cosmopolitan luxury further south, in the town that was known to the Romans as Avaricum (Bourges).

One of the richest burials of this first period of Celtic expansion is the treasure-filled tomb of the princess of Vix. It lies in a region where a concentration of middle hills begins to fan out towards the Rhineland and the Channel ports. It is not immediately apparent why – five centuries before the planting of the first Gaulish vineyards – a hill in Burgundy should have been the home of such a fabulously wealthy woman, nor, for that matter, why Alesia, the 'mother-city' of the Gauls, should be in the same region. Today, it would be obvious only to a tourist planning a long-distance barge holiday. Vix and Alesia stand at one of the busiest commercial crossroads of the Celtic world: this is the principal watershed zone of western Europe, where merchants coming from north and south unloaded their oak-plank boats and met on the overland route that joined the Rhone–Saône

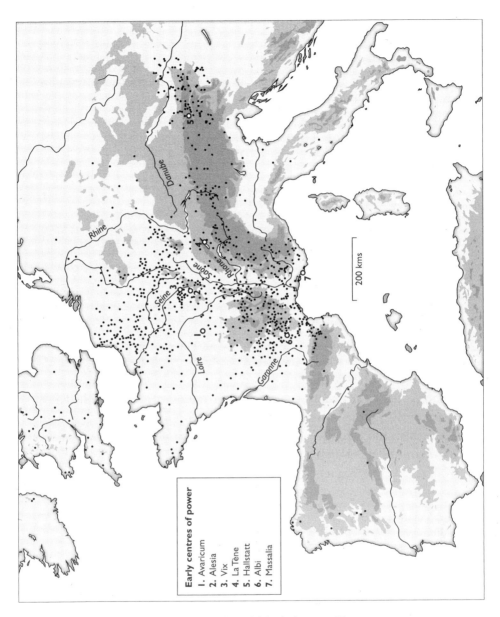

Early centres of power
1. Avaricum
2. Alesia
3. Vix
4. La Tène
5. Hallstatt
6. Albi
7. Massalia

200 kms

12. 'Montes medii' and Mediolana in Europe

From maps, title deeds, topographical dictionaries and various other texts. In France alone, after two thousand years of linguistic change, the term 'medio' takes exactly one hundred different forms, or if the various words for 'hill' and 'mountain' are included, two hundred and eight. Many names will have disappeared before they could be recorded, but the map gives a reasonable impression corridor to the broad and gentle rivers running to the English Channel and the North Sea.

The areas of the map that are either blank or only sparsely covered with 'mid hills' and Mediolana reflect the population patterns of pre-Roman Europe. At this early stage, not all of western Europe was Celtic. The cultural divisions noted by Greek and Roman writers are broadly confirmed by the archaeological record: Ligurians on the coast to the east of Marseille, Etruscans in northern Italy, Germanic tribes in the north-east, and Iberians in the south-west, especially south of the Heraklean diagonal (figs 1 and 3). In Gaul itself, the Atlantic west was a separate zone: relatively few metal objects from the late Bronze Age have been discovered there, and most of those are isolated finds, dissociated from any settlement or cemetery. In south-western Gaul, the river Garonne, which looks like such a useful shortcut from the Mediterranean to the Ocean that it often appears on speculative historical maps as a major trade route, was practically deserted. The reasons are not entirely clear. Perhaps the prehistoric tribes of the Atlantic coast retained a firmer hold there than elsewhere, or perhaps the Celts were reluctant to colonize the last, watery realms before the land of the dead. Even as recently as the nineteenth century, Brittany and the Cotentin Peninsula, the marshes of Vendée and Poitou, and the trackless scrubland of the Landes were culturally and economically separate from the rest of France. The first Celtic settlers probably discovered

---

of the original distribution. The complete list can be found at www.panmacmillan.com/theancientpaths, with latitude and longitude coordinates to four decimal places. This pinpoints the location to within 9.5 and 10 metres, depending on latitude.

Like many apparently banal place names, '*medio*' is a slippery term. In its earliest forms, it occurs most frequently with the word '*mons*', meaning 'hill' or 'mountain'. A 'Mid Hill', a 'Maiden Hill' a 'Meall Meadhonach', a 'Mittelberg' or a 'Montemezzo' can be a hill that lies between two others, a hill of middling height, an upland area where animals are pastured between the lower slopes and the peaks, or a hill shared by two communities; in Britain, it can also be a corruption of 'mickle' or 'muckle', meaning 'very large'. Often, however, its origin is obscure, and toponymists are unable to account for it. In such cases, the Celtic survey provides an explanation.

what ethnologists and administrators found there in the nineteenth century – a stunted, malarial population, clinging feebly to the edge of the inhabited world.

✻

These survey-points of the early Iron Age, and the obscure tales they tell, are certainly Celtic, but they come from an age when the tribes inhabited their own small worlds, each one probably no larger than the *pays* of pre-industrial France. The glorious precision of the Heraklean Way belonged to a relatively cosmopolitan part of Gaul: on the shores of the Mediterranean, where Iron Age hill forts look out over oil refineries and towering cruise-ship cities bound for the Aegean, sophistication of this order still seems quite credible. Further north, on the puddly flats at the foot of Mont Lassois near the hamlet of Vix, there are only a few reminders of a cosmopolitan past – the stickiness of spilled grapes on the tarmac in September and the migrant pickers from what was once the Carthaginian empire. Most foreign visitors follow the same routes as Iron Age traders; they come from the Channel ports and the Low Countries along the 'Route des Anglais' and the 'Route des Hollandais', bringing euros instead of tin and amber, on roads that pass through the northernmost zones of middle mountains.

In rural Burgundy, the protohistoric scene is easy to picture: the maze of hazel hurdles, the granaries on stilts, the sagging, mossy thatch. But if the ancient settlement could be recreated and explored, there would after all be evidence of incongruous inventions and outlandish technology: there, among the hedges and the barns, would be the glowing laboratory of the metallurgist, his threads of gold and his carbon-steel blades, the delicate anvils and directed heating-jets, and all the modern instruments of his magic.

A historian of the Iron Age is often left with nothing but a question mark, like a shepherd clutching his crook when the sheep have run away. Does the microscopic artistry of Celtic smiths imply an equivalent expertise on a larger scale, or was the artist's forge a lonely light in a small, dark world? If some grand measurement and ordering of the Continent was attempted, there must have been a coordinating body or at least an efficient sharing of scientific secrets, and there are few signs of this in the unpromising debris of hill forts and farmsteads.

Archaeologists rightly stress the muddle and diversity of the early Celtic world. The homes and possessions of the living and the dead varied as much as the climate and the vegetation. With each new excavation, it becomes ever more apparent that Celtic civilization was not suddenly imported to western Europe as a flawless operating system of beliefs, aptitudes and techniques. Yet the notion of inter-tribal cooperation is not as fantastic as it seems. The Gaulish tribes still had strong and separate identities four or five centuries later, when the Druids were organizing yearly pan-Gallic conferences and a national education system, and when pale-faced warriors from the Atlantic fringe fought alongside sun-bronzed *oppidum* dwellers from the Lower Rhone.

Even in the sixth century BC, when Latin was an obscure Italic dialect of the lower Tiber, forms of a Celtic language were spoken throughout much of western Europe. No Gaulish warrior would have suffered the fate of the Breton-speaking French soldiers in the First World War who were mistakenly shot as foreigners. The scarcity of the evidence makes it impossible to draw a map of mutual intelligibility in early Iron Age Europe, but there is also the spectacular evidence of that other common language – La Tène art, which was not just a shared taste in décor and personal adornment but a whole world of familiar forms, stories and beliefs.*

✲

When the protohistoric past falls silent, the figures of Celtic legend sometimes appear along the field boundaries, speaking an unexpectedly comprehensible tongue. In Gaul, where the first signs of political cohesion emerged, there was, according to a legend recorded by Livy, a body that might have organized such a grand survey of the Celtic lands. In the sixth or fifth centuries BC, 'supreme power among the Celts lay in the hands of the Bituriges'. The Bituriges were not simply the most powerful tribe; they were the recognized leaders of the Celts: '*Ii regem Celtico dabant.*' The king of Keltika was always a Biturigan.

It was on the southern edge of the Bituriges' homeland that the Mediolanum now called Châteaumeillant existed. This exceptional place is the only Mediolanum that actually contained buildings and people

* See Chapter 8 and the map of Celtic sun-horses, p. 168.

in the days of the ancient Celts (p. 81). It lies towards the west of the principal zones of early expansion, and there are few middle hills in its vicinity. Yet it stands at what appears to be the heart of Gaul, at almost equal distances from the Pyrenees and the Alps, the Mediterranean, the English Channel and the Atlantic Ocean. At the time of the Biturigan hegemony, when a federal Celtic power was first developing in Gaul, and when the old system of 'middle places' was giving way to a wider network, it would have been an obvious *omphalos*, a sacred centre which, like the Hill of Uisneach in Druidic Ireland, stood in a region where several major tribal territories intersected. Châteaumeillant was not noticeably occupied until the second century BC, but perhaps its exceptional status reflects its significance in the earlier network. Perhaps this really was the centre of Gaul when the Bituriges ruled the Celts . . .

The map of the Heraklean diagonal in the thatched cottage now acquired two new lines: a 'midday' line or meridian running north to south, and an equinoctial line from west to east. The two lines formed a cross, centred on Châteaumeillant. This was the common principle of Celtic territorial organization. Celtic tribes in Switzerland, Turkey and south-eastern England divided their lands into four, just as Ireland was divided into four and centred on a fifth province. In Celtic art, the motif first appeared in the early eighth century BC, around the time of the first 'middle places', and then recurred in many different forms. Sometimes, as on the tiny Kermaria obelisk from Finistère, which resembles the *omphalos* stones of Greece, and the countless pocket-sized votive wheels associated with Herakles and the sun god, the centre of the two lines is also bisected by two diagonals. In Celtic iconography, these are thought to represent the rising and setting of the sun at the summer and winter solstices.

When I traced the two lines on the map, something quite simple and logical appeared: the meridian that passes through Châteaumeillant is the longest straight line that can be drawn through the part of the European isthmus known as Gaul. This is the ideal line for a long-distance survey, the uninterrupted axis on which the future map will be based. The cartographer's term is 'line of mid-longitude'. It runs ten kilometres to the west of the Paris Meridian, which is the line of mid-longitude that was chosen in the eighteenth century for the first complete and accurate map of France. The eighteenth-century meridian bisects the centre of the Paris Observatory on the Left Bank;

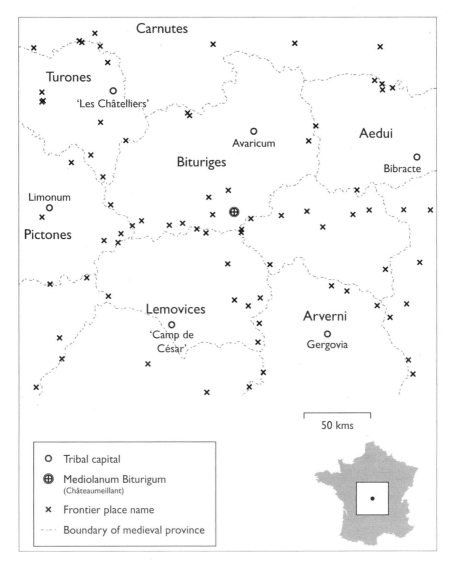

13. The centrality of Mediolanum Biturigum (Châteaumeillant)
Medieval provincial boundaries partially coincide with those of Roman *civitates*,
which were based on Celtic tribal territories. Place names indicating boundaries
give an approximate idea of ancient frontier zones: Bazoches, Feins, Fin(s), Limes,
Limite, Marche, Ouzouer and names including the Gaulish '*randa*'. The band of
frontier places running across the centre of the map follows the much later division of the languages of *oc* and *oïl*.

the Gaulish meridian bisects Nanterre, at the foot of Mont Valérien, which looks down on the Seine beyond the western edge of the Bois de Boulogne. In the days when central Paris was a swamp, Nanterre was a major river port of the Parisii tribe. Its name was Nemetoduron or 'sanctuary of the fortified hill'.

It turns out that the Gaulish meridian was well chosen for other reasons too, but this will require a grounding in Celtic science. A Druidic education could last as long as twenty years, and even the abbreviated curriculum presented in the second part of this book calls for a recreational interlude. A journey along a Druidic pathway towards the centre of Gaul and the midday sun will be a useful preparation for the course, and a chance to meet some of the gods and other ancient creatures who still inhabit Middle Earth. We shall encounter them again when the local grids that were first devised in the distant days of the Mediolana had begun to form a vast network in which the migrations and memories of a civilization would be preserved.

5

Down the Meridian

The expedition set off at dawn from the cathedral city of Amiens and cycled west along the river Samara (the Somme) to join the Gaulish meridian at longitude 2.1958. Three hundred and seventy-six kilometres to the south, the Café de l'Angle on the Avenue de la République in Châteaumeillant stands on the same line of longitude and marks the middle of the Biturigan *oppidum*. This was in September 2009. We had been following the hypothetical line of mid-longitude towards the centre of ancient Gaul for three days – as far as this can be done without actually traversing every field and marsh – and an oddly liberating sense of disbelief had settled in. Although a few stretches of road and track adhere to the line, there is no obvious physical sign that any such meridian ever existed.

The northernmost point of the meridian, five hundred kilometres from Châteaumeillant, lies at a place disconcertingly named Loon Plage. The 'beach' is a desolate zone of wind-bent poplars and container trucks queuing for the cross-Channel ferry. In the late Iron Age, when sea levels were higher than they are today, Loon was an island called Lugdunum, which means 'fortress of Lugh', the Celtic god of light.

Lugdunum shared its name with several other important Celtic towns: Laon, Leiden, Loudun, Lyon and perhaps London. As an island joined to the mainland at low tide, it lay between the worlds of the living and the dead. (Some inhabitants of western shores still believe that the soul of a dying person waits for the tide to go out before leaving the body and beginning its final journey.) Like the tidal island of Ictis off the Cornish coast (probably St Michael's Mount), where, according to Diodorus Siculus in the first century BC, smelted tin was carted out to merchant sailors arriving from the Mediterranean,

14. Gold coin of the Aedui

This coin, which dates from the second or first century bc, was probably discovered at Tayac (Gironde). Medieval Irish legend talks of Lugh 'the long-armed'. The epithet is thought to refer to the god's spear-throwing prowess, but the same god can be seen here, ten centuries earlier, thrashing his sun-chariot across the sky with the long arms of daylight. The prototype of these coins was a gold stater of Philip II of Macedonia.

Lugdunum may also have served as a neutral international trading post. It is better known today as a suburb of Dunkirk, the second largest French harbour on the English Channel. Perhaps the original 'Dune Church', first recorded in 1067, was heir to the ancient holy site, but it would take an enormous leap of faith to see the hand of Lugh in the glare of the halogen security lights that turn the sea beyond the port into a world of darkness.

The next two days were devoted to what seemed, at first, an austere, postmodern form of tourism – visiting sites where there was nothing to see, matching drab places on the ground to their colourful equivalents on the map, pursuing a journey of discovery that would discover nothing but itself. Along the meridian between Loon and the valley of the Somme (120 kilometres), Gaulish sites and places with Gaulish names occur with statistically significant regularity: three possible Mediolana, two Equorandas, two other 'boundary' place names and six medieval sites called 'La Justice' or 'Les Gibets' where criminals were hanged from gibbets. These places of public execution were traditionally located on tribal boundaries, especially those that lay on ancient roads. Places called 'La Justice' are four times as likely to occur along the Gaulish meridian as elsewhere in the region. But statistical significance is not the same as true significance. The Roman fort of Watten, which may once have been a Celtic *oppidum*, two empty fields called 'les Gallois', and a 'Champ de Bataille' named after a forgotten battle or a hoard of Iron Age weapons unearthed by a bemused medieval peasant were probably no more revelatory of a Celtic sun-path than the ruined starting ramps of German V1 rockets that lie on the meridian near a field called 'le Rideau Mollien' (one of the possible Mediolana).

As we cycled past the soggy allotments and fishermen's shacks along the river Somme, the mist rose from the marshes like the charcoal smudge of history book illustrations which serve to mask the areas of ignorance. A few metres from the meridian, we tethered the bicycles and walked along a gravelled path through the woods above the river. At the top of the escarpment, a wide field offered a view of the distant spire of Amiens Cathedral silhouetted against the morning sky. Amiens is usually said to have been the town of Samarobriva ('Bridge on the Somme'), one of the most important tribal capitals in northern Gaul. A general council of all the tribes was held there in 54 BC, and it was at Samarobriva that Caesar spent the winter after his second invasion of Britain. Yet despite the bombs and building projects that have enabled archaeologists to rummage in the foundations of Amiens for the last hundred years, nothing from the pre-Roman period has been found there, and the true location of the Celtic Samarobriva remains in doubt.

In the plains of Picardy, where a traveller's eyes are filled with horizons, it takes some time to notice the intimate corners of the landscape. Just beneath the field, in a leafy hollow, was something resembling the back of a giant mammal slumbering in the woodland: we recognized the water-repellent roof of reed thatch and the tan-coloured daub of an Iron Age house. A path curled down into the hollow, where the tang of a turf fire hung in the air. An ancient Gaul had just completed his morning duties. Inside the house, swirls of smoke were trapped in a shaft of blue-grey sunlight slanting down from the smoke-hole. The man flung the fold of a plaid cloak over his shoulder, stooped under the lintel and the eaves, and disappeared without acknowledging our presence, which was understandable, since he would be spending most of the day trying to convince crowds of texting, tweeting schoolchildren that their Iron Age ancestors were not the unsophisticated brutes they had seen on television.

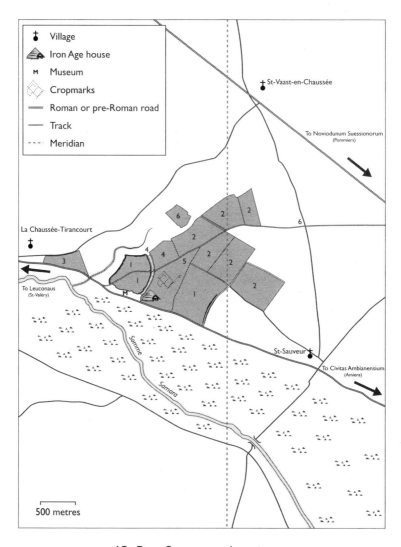

15. Parc Samara and environs

KEY (1–5 are field-names):

1. Camp César or le Grand fort.
2. Les Câtelets or Câttelets (diminutive of 'castellum').
3. Camp Saint-Romain (a Christianized 'Roman') or Champ à Luzet ('Coffin Field').
4. Fossé Sarrasin and Derrière le Fossé Sarrasin ('Behind the Saracen Ditch'): 'Saracen' = 'pagan'.
5. Le Petit fort.
6. Le (sic) Pierre and Chemin de Pierre: probably a paved road.
   (Two modern roads have been omitted.)

There are probably fewer than a dozen reconstructed Iron Age houses in all of France, and the fact that one of them happens to stand on the Gaulish meridian seemed an amazing coincidence. This was supposed to be the first expedition in two thousand years – maybe the first expedition ever – to follow the north–south line from Lugdunum to Mediolanum Biturigum, and now it looked as though someone had not only stumbled on the secret but commemorated it with a fully functioning Iron Age habitat. But if the meridian had been rediscovered, there was no sign of this in the small museum of Parc Samara, 'the nature park of prehistory' (fig. 15). A sequence of illustrated panels guarded by a moustachioed Gaulish warrior on a rearing horse explained that this promontory above the river, which, like many other ancient fortified sites in France, had been known for centuries as 'le Camp de César', was the site of a Roman fort. Despite the unusual preponderance of coins from Massalia and a rampart in the local Gaulish style, the display suggested that 'Caesar's Camp' had never been a Celtic *oppidum*. The Gaulish dwelling was based on an excavation at another site.

Museum displays often have a misleading air of self-confidence. 'Caesar's Camp' has been a mystery from the very beginning. In the spring of 1960, a schoolteacher from Amiens called Roger Agache flew over the site and noticed geometrical patterns in the fields to the east of the fort. From the open window of his biplane, he recognized the ghostly rectangles of a sanctuary complex. Agache, who died in 2011, was also a tireless sleuth on *terra firma*. He interviewed local peasants in the Picard dialect and collected tales of fairies' trysts, vanished churches, and fields where the hand-plough suddenly sank into the ground as though the earth had been recently disturbed.

The Roman fort was excavated between 1983 and 1993, and Parc Samara was opened to the public in 1988. Most of the area beyond the fort is private farmland and has remained unexcavated, but in the silence of the archaeological record, the old field-names are the captions of a treasure map. Stretching either side of the meridian and covering an area ten times the size of the Roman fort are the names that indicate the presence of a ruined Celtic *oppidum*.

Parc Samara may be more important than it thinks. The medieval Peutinger Map, which shows staging posts on Roman itineraries of the fourth century AD (and perhaps also the first century AD), records a distance of ten Gaulish leagues between the previous staging post and Samarobriva, which is supposed to be the city of Amiens. But a traveller following this route – as Caesar and his legions would have done in 57 BC – reaches the future site of Amiens after only about half that distance.* After the full ten leagues, the legions would have come to a Celtic promontory fort on the site of the future Parc Samara. This is the next place after Amiens that might have been called 'Bridge on the Somme', and it is far more likely to have been the tribal capital than the place now called Amiens, where nothing pre-Roman has been discovered.

The siting of roads and bridges changed so little between the days of the Gauls and the French Revolution that the eighteenth-century maps are a useful guide even to this remote age. Here, at the site of Parc Samara, the Cassini map of 1757 shows a road heading south-west across the floodplain. The bridge, which may have been a wooden causeway like the jetties used by local anglers, crossed the Somme a few metres from the meridian, beyond the south-east corner of the settlement. At this level of detail, modern maps which claim to depict 'the Roman road system' are of little use: their convincingly coherent patterns are the effect of a tidying instinct and an overestimation of Roman precision which makes all the roads point directly at the Roman town of Amiens. If the surviving sections of ancient road are plotted precisely, the map looks more like a puzzle of footprints at a crime scene. It shows not one system, but two. The road from Caesaromagus (Beauvais) heads straight for the Roman town of Amiens, but several other roads are distantly attracted, not to Amiens, but to the *oppidum* above the river Somme.

These apparently chaotic lines are evidence of the great upheaval in the late first century BC. The capital that was imposed on each tribe by the Roman conquerors was rarely the same as the original chief *oppidum*. The Roman capitals usually lie several kilometres from the traditional tribal site and in a more convenient, less defensible location (see pp. 76 and 205). Shortly after the Gallic War, Amiens

---

* From Augusta Suessionum (Soissons) in the east, the Peutinger Map shows a logical set of distances between staging posts, but it ceases to be logical if Samarobriva is Amiens. From Rodium to Setucis, the distance is ten leagues (twenty-seven kilometres in a straight line). From Setucis to Samarobriva, the distance is also ten leagues (twenty-seven kilometres to the Parc Samara site, but only fifteen to Amiens).

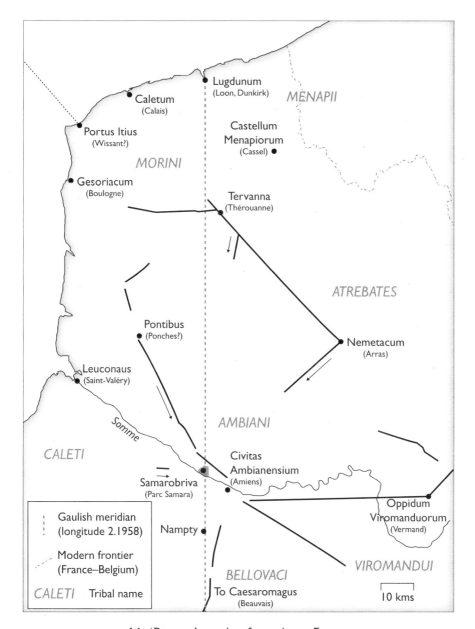

Lugdunum
(Loon, Dunkirk)

MENAPII

Caletum
(Calais)

Portus Itius
(Wissant?)

**Castellum
Menapiorum**
(Cassel) ●

MORINI

Gesoriacum
(Boulogne)

Tervanna
(Thérouanne)

ATREBATES

Pontibus
(Ponches?)

Nemetacum
(Arras)

Leuconaus
(Saint-Valéry)

Somme

AMBIANI

CALETI

**Civitas
Ambianensium**
(Amiens)

Samarobriva
(Parc Samara)

: Gaulish meridian
: (longitude 2.1958)

Nampty

**Oppidum
Viromanduorum**
(Vermand)

Modern frontier
(France–Belgium)

CALETI Tribal name

BELLOVACI

VIROMANDUI

To Caesaromagus
(Beauvais)

10 kms

16. 'Roman' roads of northern France

The surviving sections of road marked with arrows are oriented on the Celtic *oppidum* at Parc Samara (the original Samarobriva?) rather than on the Roman town of Amiens.

became the capital of the defeated Ambiani. The old *oppidum* was left to rot away until nothing remained of it but ditches, coins and boot-nails. Its name, Samarobriva, may then have been transferred to the new Roman town upstream.

Of all the places where Caesar is said to have spent the night, Parc Samara has one of the strongest claims. The *oppidum* of four hundred hectares on the Gaulish meridian would have been one of the largest Celtic sites in Gaul – a worthy setting for the council of the tribes and of Caesar's headquarters. A day's sail downriver was the port of Leuconaus (Saint-Valéry-sur-Somme). A road to the north led to the lands of the Morini and the shortest crossing of the Oceanus Britannicus. The Roman fort was implanted in a corner of the settlement like the fort at the *oppidum* of Hod Hill in Dorset. It was there, in the tribal capital of the Ambiani, that Caesar recovered from his invasion of Britain and waited to hear that his legions had reached their winter quarters.

A fortnight passed before he received news of a tribal uprising in the east – time enough to make preliminary notes for his history of the Gallic War and his account of Celtic customs and religion. 'They worship above all the god Mercury' (to a Roman eye, Mercury was the closest match for Lugh): 'They consider him the inventor of all the arts and the guide of their paths and journeys.' Caesar would not have known that the place in which he spent that long winter was bisected by one of the pathways of the god. Intelligence gathering was hampered by a conspiracy of silence – it had taken the best part of a year to discover the most convenient crossing of the Channel – and in any case, the information would have been of purely ethnological interest. For Caesar, the gods belonged in a separate chapter. He had seen pictures and carvings of Lugh all over Gaul ('*huius sunt plurima simulacra*'), but they mattered little more to him than the face of a farmer or an innkeeper glimpsed from a carriage window. By then (54 BC), a new, secular age had dawned, and military strategy was proving more effective than divinatory wisdom. As the freezing fog rose from the Samara, he settled in to his temporary home and planned his savage response to the uprising, perhaps on the very spot where a fire still burns in a Gaulish house.

✿

After an informative hour with a young archaeologist from Amiens disguised as a Neolithic farmer, the expedition returned to its bicycles, dislodged a cat that had curled up to sleep under the chain-rings, and left the lost city of Samarobriva with the sun standing high in the south. For the next week, the shining road and the light in the sky would be constant reminders that this was, despite appearances, a rational and time-honoured direction of travel. The shadows of rider and wheels raced over the stubble of the wheat fields, first to the west, then to the east; on either side of midday, they contracted into the form of a goblin that ran alongside the bicycle before eventually emaciating itself in the attempt to reach the horizon before sunset. As the days passed, our slightly crooked journey along a straight path seemed increasingly unlike a research trip and more like an unconscious form of pilgrimage.

One hour south of Samarobriva, the meridian bisects the village of Nampty. Nampty was once a *'nemeton'*. Its small white chapel is still a shrine and a place of pilgrimage. When the local monastery closed in 1206, a miracle-working statue of the Virgin was left behind and remained active at least until the First World War, when she persuaded the German army to take a different route to Amiens. Now, the floor of her temple is strewn with petals, and the wooden door, as legend states, is always miraculously open. (The nave itself is barricaded by an unmiraculous iron grille.)

Thousands of people still walk out from Amiens every year to give thanks to Our Lady of the Virtues. Sometimes, pilgrims bound for one of the great shrines of Christendom – Santiago de Compostela – pass through Nampty on their way to Beauvais Cathedral and the Midi. They follow the same guiding light as migrating animals and sun-seeking tourists. Far to the south, beyond the Pyrenees, where one of the Compostela routes crosses the lands that were ravaged by Hannibal, the pilgrims turn west towards the setting sun. Many of them pursue their journey beyond the shrine of St James to the edge of the Continent where a Celtic *'ara solis'* (a sun-altar) stood at Fisterra or Finisterre. The Romans knew the place as Promontorium Celticum. On the site of the *ara solis* at this End of the Earth, modern pilgrims burn the clothes and shoes in which they made the journey, but this is not considered orthodox or even Christian: the Catholic Church warns pilgrims that if they continue to Fisterra, they must do so only as tourists, to bathe in the ocean or to admire the long sunsets over the Atlantic.

It is hard to say exactly when one age of humanity ends and another begins, when Nampty became a shrine instead of a *nemeton*, or when Lugh and other gods replaced the prehistoric deities, and when those gods in turn were supplanted by saints. In the twenty-first century, the Church has no doubt that the incineration of road-soiled garments at Fisterra and the YouTubed commemoration of the offering constitute a form of pagan 'sun-worship'. The same war on paganism was being waged at the end of the Roman empire, when the Church rewrote the histories of Celtic shrines. Along with thousands of other holy sites, Nampty was said to have been a wilderness where outlaws butchered innocent travellers. Like broken pots thrown onto a midden, the old beliefs were relegated to the fields beyond the sacred enclosure. Now, they survive only as names on the meridian nearby: 'le Grez-Qui-Tourne' ('the Turning Stone'), 'Fosse aux Bardes' ('Bards' Grave'), 'le Bosquet du Diable' ('the Devil's Wood').

At Loon, the Iron Age had seemed entirely absent, but after three days of following the meridian, the present was wearing thin and the past becoming ever more populous. South of Nampty, a 'Chaussée Brunehaut' (a medieval name applied to Roman or prehistoric roads) runs along the meridian for four kilometres. Near the village of Cormeilles, the hilltop chapel of St Martin overlooks the stony track. The wooden doors were locked. Kneeling down, I peered through the keyhole and saw, above the altar, what appeared to be the Celtic horse goddess Epona. Magnified on the camera screen, this proved to be a painted image of St Martin, the Roman cavalry officer who met Jesus at the gates of Amiens in AD 334 and devoted the rest of his life to smashing pagan temples and bringing Christianity to Gaul. Many of St Martin's shrines stand by the side of roads on which the new religion arrived. When the Church decreed a more conciliatory approach to pagans, refurbishing temples instead of demolishing them and turning blood sacrifices into Christian feasts, images of Epona were converted into icons of St Martin on his horse.

The goddess and the saint are often almost indistinguishable. Sometimes, all that separates Celtic from Christian religion is a change of clothes and gender. The Three Mother Goddesses of the Celts appear as the three Marys or as Jesus flanked by two angels. In their hasty disguises, the Celtic gods are everywhere. Near the end of the same section of Chaussée Brunehaut, after Cormeilles, where another Christianized Epona stands in a niche, there was a familiar, smiling creature with a large club and a broken nose above the west door of the church at Hardivillers. He looked like a retired peasant on a visit to the farm he had known many years before. It was Ogmios, the Gaulish Hercules, only half-transmuted into his Christian avatar, St Christopher.

Just as Caesar recognized the Roman pantheon in the deities of the Celts, a reincarnated Druid entering certain chapels on the meridian would find himself among familiar figures. He would see a human heart dripping blood and a partially eviscerated man nailed to planks of wood. In the lonely chapel of Condé, he would see cringing sinners impaled by a skeleton and a figure in painted plaster (St Denis) offering its bloodless head to the visitor like a gruesome Sunday roast. In the late Roman empire, when Druids were still guarding some remote rural temples, certain shrines were renamed after saints who were supposed to have wandered all over Gaul, carrying their own severed heads. The original Celtic temples had contained stone pillars carved with niches from which human heads stared out. Sacrificial victims had been hung on the walls so that birds of prey could take their rotting flesh to heaven; others had been left to ferment in 'hollow altars'.

Celtic historians refer to these bloody practices as 'the Cult of the Severed Head'. At Ribemont in Picardy, in the early third century BC, Celtic tribes from the east won a great battle against tribes from the west. After the battle, according to their custom, they raised a gigantic panoply of headless human corpses, exposing victors and vanquished to the elements and the birds of prey. As one observer points out, those gory shrines must have had 'a rather peculiar aesthetic effect'. On the section of the meridian that crosses the swampy forests of the Sologne, the observation was confirmed. At the side of the narrow road, someone had erected a tall wooden structure resembling the front of an open barn or a lychgate at the entrance to a church-yard. Almost every inch of its wooden beams was covered with the nailed skulls of slaughtered animals. To one side, a long wall had been painstakingly adorned with hundreds of leg-bones, exactly reminiscent of the panoply at Ribemont. A hunter who spends whole days in the silence of the forest tracking wild boar and deer had accidentally recreated a Gaulish shrine, as though the old gods had secretly commissioned a new private sanctuary of their own.

❄

The relocation of tribal capitals by the Roman conquerors has an unfortunate consequence for visitors to the Iron Age, who often find themselves forsaking the glories of a Roman and medieval city for a deserted heap of rubble somewhere beyond the suburbs. The expedition crossed the busy roads that converge on Caesaromagus (Beauvais), leaving its Gothic cathedral six kilometres to the west, and arrived instead at the hill called Mont César near Bailleul-sur-Thérain.

'Mount Caesar' was a major *oppidum* of the Bellovaci tribe and almost certainly the tribal capital: its geographical relationship to the nearby Roman capital of Beauvais is typical of a post-conquest tribal resettlement. The meridian passes through the hamlet of Hez on the hill facing the *oppidum* and within a stone's throw of a prehistoric dolmen called 'la Pierre des Fées' ('the Fairies' Stone'), the likely site of a Celtic necropolis. The two plateaux on either side of the river Thérain were joined by a paved 'Chaussée Brunehaut'. They probably belonged to the same settlement, which may be the place mentioned by Caesar: 'The Bellovaci conveyed themselves and all their possessions into the *oppidum* called Bratuspantium.'

It was evidently a cosmopolitan town: hundreds of Celtic coins have been found at Mont César. They came from all over northern Gaul and even Britain, and far more would have been found if the ravages of time had not been accelerated by motocross bikes, metal-detectorists and waste-disposal engineers. The Roman conquest plunged the *oppidum* into insignificance and Mont César was abandoned – except, perhaps, by some of the reclusive pagans referred to in early ecclesiastical documents as Druids – until twelve Christian monks built a hermitage there in 1134. Two years later, they moved into a new building at the foot of the *oppidum* and founded one of the earliest Cistercian abbeys in France. The hermitage became a farm called 'la Vieille Abbaye'. The final degradation of the Bellovacian capital occurred a few years ago, when the Old Abbey was engulfed by the Mont César Sanitary Landfill.

From Mont César, it was a day's ride to what can now be identified as the predecessor of Paris, the capital of the Bellovaci's neighbours, the Parisii. To the west of Paris, beyond the Bois de Boulogne, stood the vast river port of Nemetoduron. The town was divided into residential, industrial and religious quarters. Channels dug through its narrow streets of wattle-and-daub houses brought the rainwater down from Mont Valérien, where a fortress still stands – the nineteenth-century Fort du Mont Valérien. From the summit, one hundred and thirty metres above the Seine, Paris is a distant patch of grey, a vision of its own protohistoric past: there are no signs of Celtic life in the capital of France before the Romans, and archaeologists now believe that the 'island in the river Sequana' where Caesar held an assembly of the Gaulish tribes in 53 BC was not the Île de la Cité. The cathedral of Notre-Dame is part of a comparatively recent development. Its flat little island would have been an odd choice of capital in any case, dominated by surrounding hills and without even a spit of land to connect it to the rest of the world.

Mont Valérien is now considered to be one of the three or four likeliest locations of the Parisii's capital. At that time, the Seine formed a tighter curve and may have given the Romans the impression that the town was on an '*insula*' rather than a peninsula; or perhaps Caesar used the word loosely to refer to the kind of promontory fort or *éperon barré* that was favoured by the Celts – a piece of high ground with natural defences on three sides and an artificial barrier on the fourth. On Mont Valérien, above the boundless sea of urban infrastructure, the sky unfurls itself for the first time since the plains of Picardy, and the solar meridian, which bisects the necropolis under the streets of Nanterre, seemed plausible once again. Until this point in the journey, I had resisted the temptation to use the meridian as an infallible detector of ancient sites, but now its predictive potential was undeniable. Other north–south lines drawn experimentally along randomly chosen degrees of longitude passed through notably fewer places of Celtic significance. At Nemetoduron, above the distant and future city of Paris, the divine pattern seemed as clear as the white clouds sailing for the coast and all the other long-distance arcs and tangents of motorway lighting, power lines and vapour trails.

There was something almost miraculously coherent about these configurations of Celtic locations, occurring conveniently on the same line of longitude like towns on an American interstate. The meridian was not a literal road that carved its way through every accident of topography, yet it led straight to the tribal capitals of the three most powerful tribes of northern Gaul. And on the printout of what had seemed an abstract imposition on the map of Europe, there were signs of the same deliberate coordination with solar pathways stretching far beyond the lands of the Belgic tribes: the equinoctial line from west to east and the transcontinental Via Heraklea are dotted with tribal capitals, and perhaps there are others that have yet to be rediscovered . . .

The more coherent the arrangement, the more mysterious it seems. The Via Heraklea dates back to the earliest days of the Celts in Gaul, while the two lines centred on Châteaumeillant belong to the Biturigan hegemony of the fourth or fifth centuries BC. Yet the tribal capitals that occur on these lines did not exist, or were not inhabited, until the late-second century BC. Until then, there was almost nothing north of the Mediterranean that might be called a town. The locations of these capitals had apparently been established independently of population.

✢

Between Nemetoduron and the Biturigan frontier, the meridian runs through some quiet regions where the archaeological record is almost silent. Châteauneuf-sur-Loire and Mehun-sur-Yèvre (once called Magodunon or 'fortified market') have some of the classic features of *oppida*, but at the time of writing, their Celtic histories are blank. There are other places on the meridian that might once have been *nemetons*: another early Cistercian abbey (la Cour Dieu), another Gallo-Roman shrine (Pithiviers-le-Vieil), and a 'Temple' that was a property of the Knights Templar (the second such site on the meridian). At different points, a roadside cross, a field and a forest track all bear the name 'Merlin', which, like the 'Champ Merlin' at Châteaumeillant, may be remnants of 'Mediolanum' . . . Sooner or later, a traveller on the meridian enters a realm of meditative unease in which either everything or nothing is significant. The sense of being watched by something from the past is heightened by the fact that many of these sites are privately owned and involve a certain amount of tactful trespassing and creeping through undergrowth.

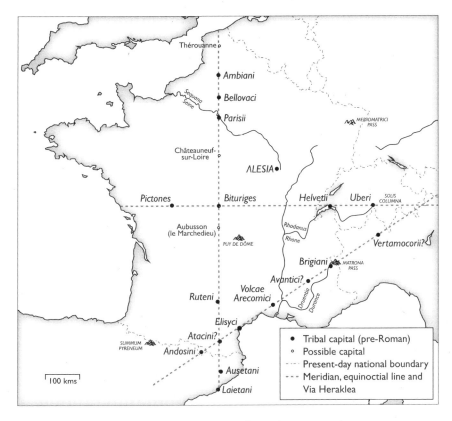

17. Tribal capitals and the solar network
Tribal capitals on the meridian, the equinoctial line and the Via Heraklea.

It was, therefore, with some relief that on the morning of the ninth day after leaving Loon, we crossed the brow of a hill and saw, crouching in the wooded valley of two tiny rivers, the most unlikely *oppidum* in central France. This, the goal of the expedition, was the hypothetical centre of Gaul, and the only Mediolanum with a visible pre-Roman past.

Apart from a musty basilica of the eleventh century which lies on one of the Compostela pilgrim routes, the town of Châteaumeillant (population: 2082) has little to attract a visitor. The antiquated municipal website, which stubbornly indicates '*1 visiteur actuellement sur ce site*', situates the town 'on one of the axes that join Switzerland to the Atlantic Ocean'. This may have been true ten centuries ago, when carts were still trundling along the dilapidated Roman road from

Lyon, but now, the only long-distance travellers are foot-weary pilgrims bound for the Pyrenees and Spain. In cycling twenty-six thousand kilometres in France, I had never once happened to pass through Châteaumeillant. My edition of the *Guide Michelin* ignores it completely. Its only geographical distinction is the fact that it lies 'at the heart of France', though, as the website admits, 'there are already several other "centres of France" in the vicinity'.

Châteaumeillant once belonged to the medieval province of Berry, which, like the nearby city of Bourges, owes its name to the Bituriges tribe. 'Bitu-riges' means 'Kings of the World'. In that self-effacing landscape of pasture and hedgerows, it seems a wonderfully immodest name, another sign that the Celts of that distant age inhabited a parallel universe whose lost majesty could be conjured up only with the aid of computer-generated images. Châteaumeillant no longer has a château: one was demolished in the early twentieth century; the other is unrecognizable as the new gendarmerie. A stone tower, said to have been built by Julius Caesar, once stood near the dismally hygienic 'Merlin's Pond' campground. It was crowned with a gilded statue of the serpent-tailed fairy Mélusine, who was the medieval descendant of a Celtic goddess. The fairy and her tower vanished long ago, but behind almost every gateway there are piles of ivy-strangled rubble and decaying buildings of vastly different eras. Perched on what looks like an unlevelled spoil heap, the lanes of Châteaumeillant seem to have been ravaged by a war of time-zones in which the 1950s won a narrow victory over the late Middle Ages.

Only two events stand out in the modern history of Châteaumeillant. Its frost-haunted vineyards were first planted in the sixth century AD, when the collapse of the Roman empire robbed the Gauls of their red nectar. In 2010, the *vin gris* of Châteaumeillant – a slightly metallic and surprisingly potent rosé – received the accolade of an 'Appellation d'origine contrôlée', and for the first time since the Middle Ages, the name of Châteaumeillant is not entirely unknown beyond its provincial boundaries.

The other notable event occurred in 1972 when a retired postman went out to his back garden to plant some endives and felt the earth give way beneath his feet. When Mme Gallerand came out to inspect the endive trench, she found her husband staring into a void. A hundred years or more before the Roman conquest, a consignment of wine amphorae, each one weighing more than forty kilograms, had been brought by ship and mule from southern Italy. The amphorae had been stored in the home of a wealthy Biturigan merchant which stood on the site of M. Gallerand's vegetable plot. During the Gallic War, when the Gauls were pursuing a scorched-earth policy and burned down more than twenty Biturigan towns in a single day, the house was destroyed by fire. Its contents remained safely buried in the sandy clay until the postman's spade pierced the night of twenty-one centuries.

A few weeks later, the endive trench was large enough to hold a team of excited archaeologists. Wine vessels had been found before in Châteaumeillant, but not in such numbers. Digging continued in the gardens of the Gallerands' neighbours, and eventually three hundred and fifty beautifully turned amphorae were unearthed. One of them still had its seal of cork and pozzolana from Pompeii. Inside, there were traces of the resin that was used as a lining and the sea-water that was added to the wine as a preservative. It was one of the largest stores of amphorae ever found in France. For some unfathomable reason, Châteaumeillant had once been a centre of the Gaulish wine trade.

As so often, an archaeological discovery seemed to make a mockery of historians who paint an orderly and rational picture of the Iron Age. The world in which Châteaumeillant had been a place of such importance must have been governed by criteria that bore no relation to any recognizable form of commerce or town planning. The small *oppidum* where the Kings of the World had sited their international wine warehouse was served only by two small streams, on which a child could barely float a paper boat. Neither river was ever navigable. Unlike most other *oppida*, the town was on relatively low ground and surrounded by higher hills. It had a wall which, according to calculations based on the work of African pool-diggers, would have taken two hundred people almost a year to build. This was not a fortification that had been hastily thrown up when the vocal telegraph brought news of the Roman invasion. Experiments have shown that this type of *murus gallicus*, with its exposed wooden beams and stone facing, was not the best defence against fire and battering-rams. The wall was built that way because it looked nice. If the aesthetically minded Bituriges had remained in charge of Châteaumeillant, the town might never have prospered in an increasingly secular, practical world, but it would certainly have found a place in the *Guide Michelin*.

✻

With its *coiffeurs*, its funeral parlours and its 'Loto' café, modern Châteaumeillant looks like almost any small town in the agricultural heart of France. An anthropologist might conclude that the Castelmeillantais are particularly concerned with hair-dressing, burial practices and a form of divination based on horse racing and ritualized battles. An unassuming museum in a side street displays the hoard of wine amphorae almost exactly as it was found under the postman's vegetable plot. There is little else to attract a casual visitor, and the museum does nothing to counter the impression that Châteaumeillant has always been a backwater. One display features an *Astérix* cartoon in which a rustic Gaulish lass shows off the latest Roman fashion: 'The civilization of the invaders eventually conquers even the remotest corners of the countryside.'

The student at the reception desk was visibly unenthralled by the prospect of spending her summer in an old house full of damaged pottery. Responding to an expression of enthusiastic appreciation, she asked, with a hint of incredulity, '*Ça vous a plu?*' ('You liked it?'). Gaulish exhibits usually suffer from comparison with the dainty products of Roman industry, and, apart from Astérix and his friends, the only protohistoric human presence in the museum is an almost faceless stone bust of a man wearing a torc. Yet some of the original Biturigans can be seen on coins that predate the Roman invasion. One day, perhaps, the *coiffeurs* of Châteaumeillant will be inspired by their sophisticated predecessors to recreate some of the styles that enlivened the streets of Mediolanum Biturigum.

A few hundred metres away, across the river Sinaise, is Châteaumeillant's main attraction: the ungainly Romanesque basilica of St Genès and its amazing collection of one hundred and thirty-one historiated capitals. Though the church is still a temple of the same religion, some of its twelfth-century Christian carvings are now incomprehensible, even to art historians. Their oak-leaf scrolls, labyrinthine entanglements and half-human faces staring almost indistinguishably out of vegetation would probably seem less exotic to a Biturigan Druid.

Inside the church, which had appeared to be empty, two figures were moving slowly through the forest of pillars: one was gazing up at the capitals with the keen eye of a connoisseur; the other man was shuffling about the echoey aisles, apparently lost in inner contemplation. He stopped in front of two antiquated maps that had been hung on a wall of the nave. One map showed the Compostela routes snaking down through Gaul; the other depicted Romanesque churches along the routes. Some of the churches were marked with a symbol signifying '*trésor*'. In this context, 'treasure' means a collection of valuable religious artefacts, especially those that contain the relics of a saint, but the man's intense examination of certain parts of the map seemed to hint at a more romantic interpretation. When he moved away, I inspected the route that passes through the centre of France, and it was faintly disappointing to see that there was no '*trésor*' in Châteaumeillant.

Outside, a small esplanade looks down on the Rue de la Libération. Sounds of sarcastic laughter were coming from the 'Loto' café across the street, where a group of locals were drinking at tables on the pavement. Nothing much happens in Châteaumeillant, and the strangers who wander into town on the Compostela route are evidently cherished as a source of entertainment. When the two men emerged from the church, we struck up a conversation. The man who had been studying the carvings was a modern Christian; he completed a certain section of the route each year on his summer holiday and was about to return home to the Netherlands. His temporary companion, who carried with him the smell of farm buildings and nights under the stars, was walking all the way to Compostela. He had the look of many miles in his eyes and a tone of wonder in his voice. Whether it was the reason for his departure or a result of his Herculean labour, he seemed to be suffering from a form of delusion, like someone striving for a goal that is sufficiently implausible to be taken for a profound truth. I wondered whether, after reaching Santiago, he would continue to Fisterra and whether there would be anything left of his battered shoes to burn at the *ara solis*.

He saw the bicycles resting on the parapet, and, since cycling is reputed to be an exacting mode of transport, and the Church allows pilgrims to undertake the journey on a bicycle or a horse, he assumed that we, too, were bound for Spain. '*Vous êtes pèlerins,*' he said, as though stating a fact. I agreed that we were, after a fashion. He nodded as though satisfied that the information was congruent with some complex calculation. We shook hands and wished each other luck. The sun was about to disappear behind the *oppidum*. There are no hotels in what was once an international hub of the Gaulish wine trade, and there was still a long hour of cycling ahead.

The future route now lay to the east, along the equinoctial line, to the borders of the Aedui and the Arverni. Eventually, the same line of latitude would lead to the vast Helvetian sanctuary above Lausanne and, beyond that, to the place in the Alps where the Rhone has its source and which was known to the ancient Celts as 'the Pillar of the Sun'. But these would be the stations of a later expedition whose distant terminus had yet to be discovered. More sounds of merriment came from the café across the street: the inhabitants of Mediolanum Biturigum were warming to their evening entertainment. It was time to return to the glowing screen and the lower world of the library, to find out how the paths of the gods had been brought to Middle Earth, and whether any of this was ever real or even possible.

PART TWO

6

The Size of the World

The barnacle-encrusted lump had been sitting under the portico of
the Athens archaeological museum for several months before anyone
noticed anything unusual. A year and a half before, in October
1900, some sponge-divers from Rhodes had been blown off course
by a storm and dropped anchor off the almost uninhabited island of
Antikythera. Sixty metres below was a shelf that had not been recorded
on any chart. When the winds had died down, they decided to look
for sponges before sailing for home. The first diver had been in the
water for no more than a few minutes when he tugged violently on
his rope and was pulled to the surface. Evidently suffering from
hallucinations caused by nitrogen narcosis, he claimed to have seen
a mass of human remains. A second diver went to investigate. He,
too, saw a dark mound of wreckage and then, protruding from the
mound, a beautiful bronze arm.

Two thousand years earlier, in about 80 BC, a large and elderly
ship carrying bronze and marble statues had sunk with all its crew
and cargo. It had probably been sailing to Syracuse or Rome when
the wind gods capsized it and locked up its treasures in the sea. After
its rediscovery, the arm eventually found its way to Athens. An
expedition was mounted and, with the help of the sponge-divers, the
contents of the wreck were salvaged.

The Antikythera wreck produced so many spectacular finds – a
bronze lyre, a marble bull, a philosopher's head, a Hercules, a bowl
of blue glass similar to one found at Alesia in Gaul – that no one paid
much attention to the formless bits of debris that were dumped under
the portico or deposited in cardboard boxes. It was not until one of
the lumps fell apart that the museum director spotted something that
was not only strange but, according to everything that was known

about the ancient world, impossible: embedded in the calcified wood was what appeared to be a gear wheel with tiny bronze teeth less than two millimetres long. The first inspections showed a series of bronze plates enclosed in a wooden case. Since then, increasingly sophisticated techniques have been brought to bear on the object known as the Antikythera Mechanism. Recently, a few more bits and pieces were discovered in a storeroom packed into boxes labelled 'Antikythera', and with the help of computer-gaming software and an eight-ton X-ray machine, most of the miraculous mechanism has now been brought back to life.

It took the form of a rectangular case about the size of a small shoebox. Some of the names of months engraved on its bronze plates suggest that it was manufactured in Corinth, presumably before that city was destroyed by the Romans in 146 BC. The device was practically an antique when it was taken on board the ill-fated vessel in c. 80 BC. There were two dials on the front and one on the back. A side-crank moved pointers on the dials and allowed the user to calculate the dates of solar and lunar eclipses, the phases of the Moon, the dates of the four Panhellenic Games, and probably also the positions of the sun and the five planets, and the rising and setting of certain stars. There was a choice of two calendars – Egyptian and Metonic.* The calculations were based on astronomical observations made by the Babylonians over the course of several centuries. It had epicyclic gearing (gears whose bearings are attached to other gears), which is otherwise unknown until the Middle Ages. This would have made it possible to multiply fractions and to replicate the apparently erratic motion of the moon across the sky. Despite the infinitesimal complexity of its workings, it would have been no more difficult to operate than an iPhone, though it must have taken some careful studying of the manual – thousands of Greek characters minutely engraved on the dials – to comprehend phrases such as 'spiral subdivisions 235'.

The exact purpose of the Antikythera Mechanism is still unknown. It may have been a scientific toy and an elegant illustration of micro-engineering (it was designed to be easily dismantled and reassembled).

---

* A Metonic calendar covered a cycle of lunar phases, which lasts about nineteen years. It has been suggested that a Druid education lasted twenty years so that a complete set of astronomical observations of the Metonic cycle could be collected.

As a calendar or an almanac, it was unnecessarily but delightfully precise. It would have been the perfect gift for an astronomer who wanted to hold the workings of the heavens in his hands or a geographer who wanted to find out exactly where he was on the earth. Whatever its purpose, it seems an almost alien presence in that world of brute force and basic machinery, and this was the most startling revelation of all: no one could possibly have known from the written record that such a thing had ever existed. And yet, unless the sponge-divers had been unbelievably lucky, there was more than one hand-held computer travelling about the Mediterranean in the second and first centuries BC.

That shapeless lump of wood and the glittering microcosm it contained are a rude reminder that only fragments of ancient wisdom have survived. A scholar who enters a Classics reading room with its beautifully published texts prepared by priestly editors is witnessing an illusion: behind the orderly accumulation of knowledge is a cavernous museum of many floors, devastated by war or natural catastrophe, most of its shelves and cabinets either empty or strewn with illegible clumps of charred parchment.

Inventions and discoveries were not instantly transmitted to the rest of the world. They could lie dormant in libraries for hundreds of years and then disappear for ever when the library was burned to the ground or when a librarian replaced an old text in the belief that it was out of date. Even the existence of a scientific instrument was no guarantee that the principles of its construction would be deduced and understood. In 263 BC, in the early stages of the war on the Carthaginians, Roman legions captured the Sicilian town of Catania. Among the trophies that were carried back to Rome was a curious invention called the *horologium solarium*. The sun cast the shadow of an upright stick onto a flat surface marked with lines and, in this way, indicated the hours of the day. The device was set up on a column facing the Senate House in Rome. For ninety-nine years, it gave the citizens of Rome the wrong time of day until finally someone realized what people on the Mediterranean coast of Gaul had known two centuries before: that the height of the sun and the angle of its shadow vary with latitude. Unless the earth shifted on its axis, a sundial made for Catania would never be accurate four degrees further north in Rome.

Since the Middle Ages, scientific wisdom has accumulated like interest in a savings account, but in the days of the ancient Celts, whole tribes and empires vanished within a few decades or were reduced to relict populations with no means of reproduction. The Celts believed that, one day, the sky would fall in and destroy the earth. This belief reflected their experience. Their own scientists and intellectuals, the Druids, were hunted almost to extinction: their last significant appearance in Roman history is as a band of screeching, foul-mouthed fanatics on a coast in North Wales. In some periods and domains, regression was the norm, and it would not be surprising if a future historian, confused by the backward counting of years BC, reversed the chronological data in order to produce a more logical sequence.

✿

It was almost three centuries before the Roman conquest of Gaul that one of the greatest expeditions in the ancient world took place, and over a thousand years would pass before anything similar was attempted. One day in the mid-320s, an ocean-going vessel rounded the rocky headland, passed under the beacon-tower and the temple of Artemis, and came to rest among the other ships in what is now the Vieux Port of Marseille. Massalia, founded three hundred years before, had become one of the most powerful cities in the Mediterranean. Aristotle had recently praised its enlightened oligarchy and its council of six hundred senators. Its houses stretched over the hills behind the port, where vines and olive trees had been planted. Ramparts kept out the Ligurian tribes who lurked in the forested ravines of the hinterland, but there were safe and well-travelled routes up the Rhone Valley leading to the lands of the wealthy, wine-addicted Celtic tribes. In the crowds that walked along the quays, there were Greek-speaking Celts and Gaulish-speaking Greeks. The warehouses and taverns were thronged with merchants and pirates who had seen a world many times bigger than the world of Homer's *Odyssey*. But even the most imaginative and cosmopolitan Massaliot would have found it hard to match the tales of the traveller who returned that day to his native city.

The traveller's name was Pytheas. He may have been commissioned by the senate or by a guild of merchants to prospect new trading routes, or perhaps, as a boy growing up in Massalia, he had contracted the incurable disease of curiosity. He would have read the sixth-century *Periplus* that described the coasts from Massalia to the Sacred Promontory, 'where the starry light declines', and the sea routes that led to the wintry lands under the Great Bear from where the tin and the amber came. Mediterranean city-states treated their explorers as secret agents and kept their logbooks under lock and key, but leaks were unavoidable, especially in a large port, and mariners are notoriously loquacious. Pytheas would certainly have heard of his fellow Massaliot, Euthymenes, who, in the early 500s, had sailed through the Pillars of Hercules, turned south and followed the coast for many weeks until he saw crocodiles and hippopotami swimming in the fresh water of a great river that flowed far out to sea. Down at the harbour, he would have talked to sailors who knew how to steer a steady course over long distances and whose knowledge of winds, constellations, tides and currents was only then being translated into mathematical equations.

Pytheas was conversant with the very latest developments in scientific theory. He may even have corresponded with Aristotle. He knew that the celestial pole around which all the stars revolved was an empty patch of sky that could be located from three stars in the constellations of the Little Bear and the Dragon. (There was no star at the pole in the third century BC.) Before leaving home, he set up a gnomon marked off into one hundred and twenty sections – a system which, in contradiction of the accepted chronology, suggests knowledge of the Babylonian division of the circle into 360. On the longest day of the year, the shadow cast by the noonday sun was $41^4/_5$ sections long. This indicates a latitude of 43.2° – one-tenth of a degree south of the harbour of Marseille, where the reading is supposed to have been taken. It was a remarkably precise figure and perhaps completely accurate: 43.2° is the latitude of Cap Croisette, where only the raggedy gnomons of telegraph poles spoil the view, and where there were fewer obstructions and disturbances than in Massalia. For the first time in recorded history, a man defined his position on the earth with an exact coordinate. When Pytheas stood on that windy headland on a sunny day in June measuring the length of the sun's shadow, he had already embarked on his voyage of discovery.

He sailed through the Pillars of Hercules – or, if the Carthaginian

blockade was in force, took the overland route along the rivers of
Aquitanian Gaul – to the Atlantic coast. He passed through Corbilo at
the mouth of the Loire. The mud of the estuary was already swallowing
the port. Long before the Romans arrived, it disappeared, and nothing
now remains of it, except perhaps a sandbank called the Banc de Bilho.
From Corbilo, he sailed along the granite coast of a peninsula called
Ouexisame in the Celtic tongue; its inhabitants were the Osismi – 'the
People at the End of the World'. The name has survived in 'Ouessant'
(Ushant), the island off Finistère which marks the western extremity
of Gaul. In February 1959, a few miles along the coast at Lampaul-
Ploudalmézeau, a man who had been collecting seaweed for his vegetable patch noticed a gold coin glinting among his lettuces. It had been
minted in the Mediterranean city of Cyrene in about 320 BC – a sign
of how far the Greek trading empire extended, unless it came from the
treasure chest of Pytheas himself. (Cyrenean gold coins would have
made better bartering tokens than the drab, bronze coins of Massalia.)

North of Ouexisame, there was no sight of land for a day or two,
until the stormy promontories of Belerion (Land's End and the Lizard).
This was the southernmost tip of the semi-mythical island or islands
called Prettanike. Pytheas sailed along the busy coast among the
coracles and canoes and larger vessels from the Atlantic lanes, to the
headland at the other end of southern Britain: Kantion (Kent).
According to one source, he then walked all the way through Britain.
The natives lived in houses made of reed or logs, and threshed their
wheat indoors because of the rainy climate. They made a beverage
from honey and grain, which they drank with a dismal potage of
millet, roots and herbs, having very little meat or fruit.

As he went, Pytheas calculated his latitude from the elevation of
the mid-winter sun. In one place, it rose four *peches* (about eight
degrees) above the horizon, which implies a latitude between the Peak
District and the Yorkshire Dales. The next reading showed a solar
elevation of only three *peches* (somewhere near the Moray Firth in
Sutherland). Here, in the middle of a fourth-century BC winter, the
history of Britain begins – not with Caesar's summer raiding parties
three hundred years later, but with the first identifiable visitor, a
scientific traveller with a name, a place of birth and geographical
coordinates, muddying his Mediterranean shoes on the soil of an
island whose very existence was in doubt.

He reached the northernmost part of Prettanike at a place called Orka – possibly Duncansby Head, which looks over to the Orkneys. He had now gone far beyond even the imaginings of Homer. He set sail again, perhaps in a native boat. Six days out from Orka was an island called Thoule (the Faroes or Iceland), and a place where the sun kept watch all night in summer, barely rising from its bed. Further still, he came to a region that was neither land nor sea but a mixture of all the elements 'on which one can neither walk nor sail'. In the fog banks and pack ice of the Arctic, he saw the earth in its troubled infancy or its confused old age.

He returned through the amber-rich Baltic and probably followed the river Dnieper to the Black Sea. In effect, Pytheas circumnavigated Europe. In the warmth and bustle of Massalia, or perhaps in a villa on Cap Croisette, he wrote up his journal. It was known by the title *Peri tou okeanou* ('On the Ocean'), and it became one of the most famous books of the ancient world. No copy has ever been found – though some palimpsestic remnant may yet be hiding in a monastery – and one of the greatest voyages of discovery ever made is known only from brief, generally hostile references in a handful of Greek and Latin texts. The main source is the *Geography* of Strabo (7 BC), the geographer whose name means 'one who can't see straight'. The fantastic tales of that impudent Greek from southern Gaul made him burn with envy. How could Pytheas have talked to people who lived six days north of Britannia and thus beyond the limits of the habitable world? It was well known in 7 BC that nothing north of Ierne (Ireland) supported human life; Ierne itself was the home of 'complete savages [who] lead a miserable existence because of the cold'. The exotic place names – Orka, Thoule, the Bed of the Sun – were obviously invented by Pytheas to give his incredible account an air of truth . . .

But even Strabo grudgingly admitted that there might be something to Pytheas's scientific observations: 'If judged by the science of the celestial phenomena and by mathematical theory, he might possibly seem to have made adequate use of the facts.' This was, after all, the great contribution of Pytheas: whatever the official reason for his expedition, he had been collecting the priceless gems of evidence that would make it possible to construct a map of the world.

✲

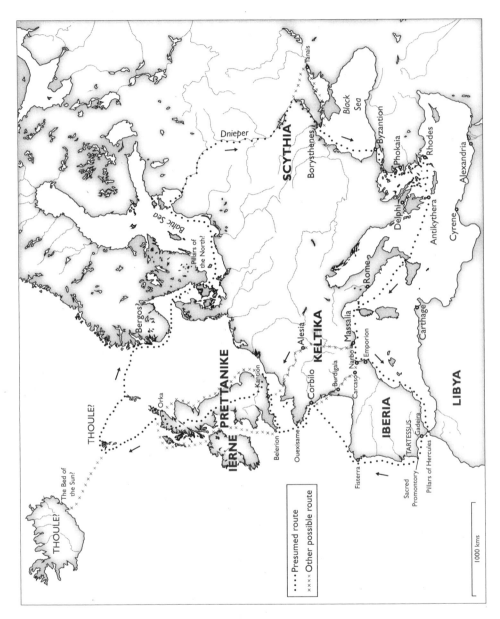

18. The Voyage of Pytheas

A scientifically produced map of the world in the fourth century BC seems as unlikely as the Antikythera Mechanism. If the warped, amoebic continents of medieval maps represent the sum of geographical wisdom, what formless fictions must have lived in the minds of the ancients? And yet, though precise measurements were the rarest of rare commodities, the principles were well established. Eighty years after the voyage of Pytheas, the chief librarian of the Library of Alexandria, Eratosthenes of Cyrene, made a momentous calculation. He had been told that at noon on the longest day of the year the sun at Syene (Aswan) shone directly down a well as though pouring its light carefully into the shaft without spilling a drop. A stick planted upright in the earth at Syene cast no shadow, whereas at Alexandria, eight hundred and fifty kilometres to the north, at exactly the same time, there was a very noticeable shadow. Given the distance between Syene and Alexandria (five thousand *stadia*) and the angle of the shadow to the sun's rays (about one-fiftieth of a circle or just over seven degrees), Eratosthenes concluded that the circumference of the earth must be 250,000 *stadia* (5000 x 50).

This is the earliest record of a rational mind embracing the whole earth. Inevitably, Eratosthenes' calculations were the approximate caresses of a lover who was unable to express the precision of his desire. He assumed that the earth was a perfect sphere, that Alexandria lay due north of Syene, and that Syene lay directly on the tropic (where the summer solstice sun is directly overhead at noon). It is impossible to say how close he came to the mathematical truth: the exact value of the *stadion* he used is unknown; the error was somewhere

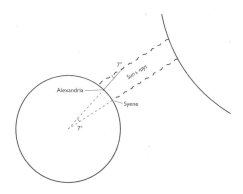

19. Eratosthenes' experiment

between two and thirty per cent of the actual figure. But the essential point was the application of theory to the cosmos: equipped with nothing but a stick, a distance measurement and simple geometry, Eratosthenes had established the basis of a world map.

Ancient accounts usually attributed discoveries to heroic individuals when in fact they probably dawned in different places and at different times. When Eratosthenes scratched the cosmic truth into the wax of a writing tablet, several vast realities of terrestrial existence were already widely known or suspected: the world was not flat, and since the sun was very large and very distant, it was mechanically absurd to assume that it orbited the earth. In the 320s BC, Pytheas knew that latitude could be calculated from the shadow of a gnomon, from the length of the longest day, or from the rising and setting of a star. When he walked through Britain, he felt the curve of the earth beneath his feet, and when he sailed on the ocean, he knew that the swelling tides were in some manner caused by the moon.

The information was available, and so were the means of fashioning it into imaginable forms. By modern standards, it was a motley collection of data. In the Library of Alexandria, Eratosthenes would have found a few precise readings from gnomons and water-clocks, astronomical observations made by Babylonian astrologers, measurements of distance provided by armies, camel-trains, the *mensores* (land-surveyors) of Alexander the Great, and the betamists (professional walkers) and 'rope-stretchers' who re-surveyed Egypt to re-establish land boundaries after each major flooding of the Nile. Ships putting in at Alexandria were searched and any scrolls found on board were confiscated; copies were made and the originals placed in the library, marked 'from the ships'. This wily acquisitions policy must have produced a fine collection of sailors' *periploi*, which listed river mouths and headlands, and gave distances in days of sailing.

Most of this geographical knowledge survives only as a muddle of rumour and misreporting in later Roman texts, but the early descriptions of the *oikoumene* (the inhabited earth) show that certain key coordinates had been identified – Rhodes, the Pillars of Hercules, Byzantion, Borysthenes, etc. When Pytheas sailed from Massalia, these points of reference were already being used to organize a conception of the earth that had once seemed a prerogative of the gods. Accurate depictions of the coastlines and continents were still many centuries

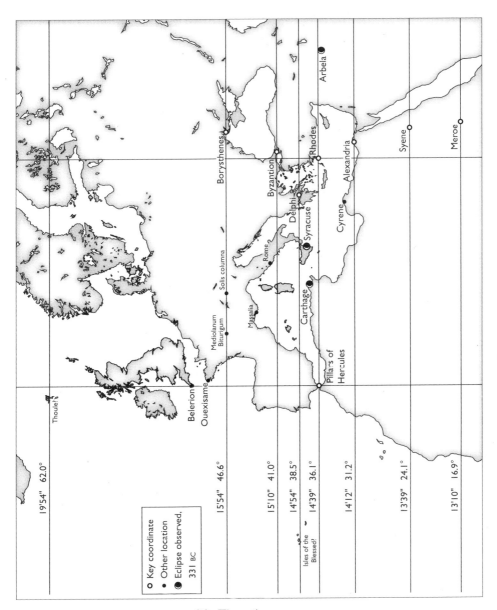

20. The *oikoumene*

The numbers on the left (hours and minutes) give the length of the longest day in 300 BC at that latitude. (The decimal degrees are those of the modern co-ordinate system.) The commonest intervals between *klimata* were half an hour; smaller divisions were also made. The latitude lines are derived primarily from Dicaearchus, Eratosthenes and Timosthenes. See also p. 143n.

away, but a semblance of the *oikoumene* could now be held within a human mind, thanks to one of the great inventions of the ancient world: the division of the terrestrial sphere into zones of latitude called *klimata*.

Determining latitude is fairly simple. Schoolchildren supplied with sticks and protractors regularly perform the exercise on sunny days. Determining longitude is far trickier and sometimes thought to have been beyond the capability of the ancient Greeks.

The erratic path of an ancient meridian or line of longitude can be seen towards the right of the map. The six places from Borysthenes (the mouth of the Dnieper) to Meroe (in the Sudan) were considered by Eratosthenes, for the sake of argument, to lie on the same north–south line. In reality, they occupy a time zone that covers almost six degrees of longitude: noon occurs at Rhodes twenty-two minutes later than at Meroe. For a sailor, the error would be catastrophic. The usual solution was 'latitude sailing': head north or south until the latitude of the destination is reached, then sail west or east until land is sighted. The same form of navigation was used by Columbus and Vasco da Gama almost two thousand years later. Once it became possible to calculate longitude as well as latitude, a ship could steer a direct, diagonal course along a rhumb line,* holding to the same bearing throughout the voyage, instead of laboriously following two sides of the triangle. But with no landmarks, a surface that never stood still and no chance of repeating the experiment, it was impossible to determine longitude at sea with any degree of accuracy until the invention of a reliable marine chronometer in the late eighteenth century.

The inconveniences of ocean sailing greatly magnify the problem of longitude, which is not quite as intractable as it seems. On land, various forms of triangulation can be used to create a network of coordinates. The gridlines of Greek colonies on the Gaulish coast and parts of the Celtic system of Mediolana were, in a sense, accurate maps of miniature worlds. On a national or global scale, something more manageable was required, but according to the written record, not even a theoretical solution existed until about 150 BC. It was then that the Greek astronomer Hipparchos suggested that meridians east

---

* On rhumb lines or lines of constant bearing, see pp. 132–3 and 295.

and west of a zero longitude (Rhodes) could be established by recording the local times at which a lunar eclipse was observed.

Here again, the sand in the hour-glass seems to flow in the wrong direction. If no means of determining longitude was devised before Hipparchos, how did Hannibal, for instance, manage to navigate his way along the Heraklean diagonal, and how was he able to rejoin the solar path after being forced to deviate from it? How could the pathways of the Celts have been anything but a wonderful mirage? A clue can be found, surprisingly, in Pliny the Elder's credulous encyclopedia of wonders, *Historia Naturalis* (c. AD 78). In a chapter which is bizarre even by Pliny's standards, he describes two ancient 'experiments', the purpose and result of which escaped him almost entirely. He knew only that they had something to do with the curvature of the earth, which 'discovers and hides some things to some, and others to others'.

Someone had evidently tried to explain to Pliny the problem of longitude. The first example describes a fictitious phenomenon reminiscent of the puzzle with which brains befuddled by jetlag often have to wrestle: one of Alexander's high-speed couriers could run 1200 *stadia* (about 200 kilometres) in nine hours, but only when he was heading west with the sun; the return journey took him six hours longer, despite the fact that it was downhill all the way. The other 'experiment' was just as confusing and equally impossible as described by Pliny. 'High beacon-towers' were erected by Hannibal in Africa and Spain. The beacons were lit at the sixth hour of day (noon). At the same moment, their light was seen in Asia at the third hour of night (9 pm).

This may be the only surviving indication of the kind of rapid, long-distance triangulations that enabled the Carthaginian general to follow the path of the sun. Hannibal and his astrologers performed this geodetic feat in 218 BC, perhaps with the aid of an early form of theodolite called the dioptra – a surveyor's rod with sights at both ends through which the relative positions of the beacons could be calculated (see p. 147). By then, the process may have been well established. A semi-instinctive form of rhumb-line sailing may have been adapted for use on land so that armies could navigate the continents like armadas.

There is even some unnoticed evidence of a longitude experiment further back in time, using astronomical rather than terrestrial measurements. In 331 BC, a lunar eclipse was observed at Arbela (Arbil, in Iraq), eleven days before the battle of Arbela at which Alexander defeated Darius III. The eclipse was recorded in at least three different places three thousand kilometres apart. All these places – Arbela, Syracuse and Carthage – lie in the same *klima* or latitude zone, as do two of the scientific capitals of the ancient world – Rhodes and Athens (fig. 20). Rhodes had recently become part of Alexander's empire. Like Hannibal, Alexander had an urgent need for accurate maps and global positioning techniques, and perhaps it was at Rhodes that his geometers and surveyors coordinated the world's first international scientific experiment.

Ultimately, the precision of these measurements depended on time-keeping. Most ancient records of eclipses give the times to the nearest hour or half hour. Since sunlight passes over the Mediterranean at about twenty-two kilometres a minute, the margin of error is enormous. Timing to the nearest minute was practically impossible, which is why ancient Greek and Latin have no word for 'minute'. The material evidence is barely enough to fill a small cardboard box. Fragments of four water-clocks have survived from Egypt and Greece. They appear to have been capable of measuring time to within ten minutes in a twelve-hour period, though more refined readings were apparently attainable: some of the day lengths reported by Pliny include thirds, fifths and ninths of an hour, and even, in one case, a thirtieth (two minutes). This would still have produced a very erratic meridian. The great advance in time-keeping came much later, in eleventh-century Spain, when an Arab engineer invented a water-clock with epicyclic gearing (p. 88). But historical chronologies are changing all the time. As we now know, the same technology was already performing its clockwork miracles in the second century BC. Someone on board a ship sailing west in the Aegean may have known exactly where he was before Poseidon reached up and confiscated the magical mechanism near the island of Antikythera.

✿

The measuring and mapping of the world coincided with the first great age of European exploration. Discoverers of distant places were usually said to have been blown off course and to have been led by the gods to lands ruled by monsters or by women of unimaginable beauty and sexual appetite. But some of those supposedly accidental voyages were so long and successful that the adventurers must have been prepared, both materially and scientifically. When Eudoxus of Kyzikos set off to reach India by circumnavigating Africa in the late second century BC, he had a well-fed, motivated crew which included doctors, craftsmen and 'flute girls'.

Not all those navigators arrived on uncultivated shores inhabited by Stone Age tribes. In the traditional European view of exploration, the bold adventurer is always more intelligent than the natives. While this was certainly true in the case of Hanno the Carthaginian, who reached equatorial West Africa in the early fifth century BC and captured three wild and hairy 'women' of the 'Gorillai' tribe, there is no reason to suppose that it was always the case. The people of Belerion on the south coast of England had been civilized by their contact with foreigners, and Pytheas was able to take his latitude readings throughout Britain without suffering the fate of some eighteenth-century French cartographers who were savagely attacked by suspicious natives. Pytheas's measurements of the elevation of the mid-winter sun are revealing in more than one respect. In order to take his readings at locations several degrees of latitude apart, he would have had to remain in Britain for over a year, and quite possibly several years, if the modest British sun failed to show itself in late December. Perhaps he really did endure two British winters, or perhaps the land of astronomically aligned stone temples was able to provide him with the information.

When the Gaulish tribes began to bisect their domains with parallels and meridians, the world was already shedding its mythical aura. The fabled Isles of the Blessed, the Elysium of demi-gods and heroes, were increasingly associated with real islands thought to lie somewhere in the Atlantic, a long way west of the inhabited world. There were sailors who claimed to have seen them: perhaps they had sighted or made landfall on the Canaries, Madeira or Cape Verde.

. With the Greek *klimata* as a guide, it is not hard to mount a virtual expedition, and the directions are easy to follow. Logically, to reach the Elysian Fields, one would sail due west on the latitude of Delphi, the *omphalos* of the earth, and hold to this bearing, riding the rays of the setting sun, to the place where Zeus released one of the two eagles or crows that met at Delphi. After ten thousand *stadia* (the distance given to the Roman general Sertorius by some Iberian mariners), the ship would come to a group of islands in the mid-Atlantic three and a half hours of daylight west of Delphi. In 1749, on the island of Corvo in the Azores, a rainstorm washed a black pot out of the foundations of a house. It contained a hoard of ancient coins. The coins have disappeared, and the finding will never be authenticated. But some of them were sent to Lisbon, and drawings were published in a scholarly journal in 1778. Most of the coins were clearly Carthaginian; two others came from the Greek city of Cyrene. They were dated to the late third century BC. The fact that the coins were discovered on the island furthest from Europe was thought to be particularly incredible, but an expedition to the edge of the world would hardly have sailed for home when there was still land to the west.

✿

As migrants, traders and mercenaries, the Celts, too, belonged to this age of exploration. It was only later that a shadow fell over the shrinking world: when the Romans landed in Britain in 55 BC, in the region called Cantium, there was no trace of Pytheas's expedition six generations before. 'Persistent enquiries' by Caesar produced little useful information and a good deal of misinformation. Tin, he was assured by a local informant, 'is found in the midland regions' ('*in mediterraneis regionibus*'), whereas Pytheas, along with countless Carthaginian, Greek and Celtic traders, had known that it came from Belerion in the south-west. Caesar asked about the islands where night was said to last for thirty days at the time of the winter solstice, but no one was able to confirm their existence. 'Accurate measurements' with water-clocks established the fact that the days were longer than in Gaul, which was hardly an original finding, and a spell of unusually good weather – or a misreading of Pytheas's account of the effects of the Gulf Stream – produced the surprising observation that 'the climate is more temperate than in Gaul'.

In Gaul and in Britain, Caesar was entirely dependent on local information, which is why it took him so long to discover the most convenient crossing of the Channel. At any given moment, his mental horizons were those of the visible world. His descriptions of particular sites are accurate enough for his battles to be re-enacted and his tactics

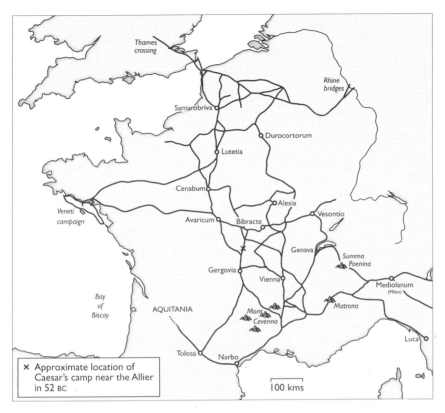

21. Caesar's movements in Gaul and Britain, 58–51 BC

analysed, but otherwise, his vision was as foggy as the Oceanus Britannicus. To reach Gaul from the Alps at the start of each campaigning season, he usually travelled in a north-westerly direction, which would have enabled him to believe that his skewed conception (shown in fig. 22) was more or less correct. Luck shielded him from the effects of ignorance. In the seventh year of the war, he decided not to return to the Roman part of Gaul, in part because of 'the difficult roads leading over the obstacle of the Cévennes'. Any trader could have told him that, from his camp near the river Allier, there was no need to cross the Cévennes. Instead, believing himself to be cut off from Italy, he marched towards the Rhine and set the scene for the final defeat of the Gauls.

One hundred and fifty years after Caesar, in AD 98, the Roman historian Tacitus decided to describe the geography of Britain using

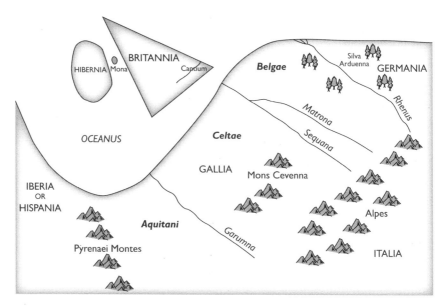

22. Caesar's conception of the Celtic lands
Based on *De Bello Gallico* (58–51 BC).

'ascertained fact' instead of guesswork. The fleet commanded by his father-in-law, Agricola, had circumnavigated the island, and he was able to describe it as a double-headed axe topped with a huge and shapeless tract of land (Caledonia) tapering to a wedge. To the east, the coast ran parallel to Germania. To the west, if one crossed the island of Hibernia (Ireland), one came to Hispania (Spain), which explained why the Silures of South Wales had 'swarthy complexions and curly hair'. Tacitus had often heard Agricola say that he could have conquered Ireland with a single legion and trapped the rebellious Britons between Spain and Gaul. But Ireland was never invaded, and the history of exploration was deprived of one of its finest *tableaux* – a Roman general standing on the Dingle Peninsula, peering at the Atlantic horizon in the hope of catching sight of the Iberian coast.

In the Highlands of Scotland, 'where earth and nature end', Agricola is supposed to have said to his troops, 'We do not have our enemy's knowledge of the country.' This would have been something of an understatement. A more accurate assessment of the Roman position is provided, in Tacitus's account, by the British leader, Calgacus, pointing at the Romans: 'a scanty band, dismayed by their

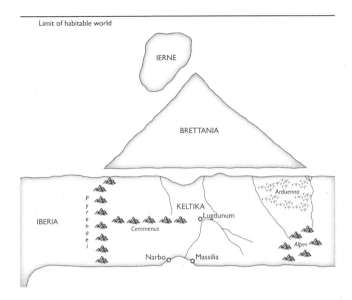

Limit of habitable world

IERNE

BRETTANIA

IBERIA

Pyrenadei

KELTIKA
Lugdunum

Cemmenus

Arduenna

Alpes

Narbo

Massilia

23. Strabo's conception of the Celtic lands

Based on Strabo's *Geography* (c. 7 BC). Massilia was the Roman name of Massalia (Marseille).

ignorance, staring blankly at the unfamiliar sky, sea and forests around them.'

Long before Agricola imagined himself reaching Spain by way of Ireland, traders, fishermen and adventurers had been sailing the unmapped seas, following the coasts of Spain and Gaul or, by observing the stars, the flight of birds and clouds rising over warm land, steering a diagonal course from northern Spain across the Bay of Biscay. They rounded the Armorican Peninsula (Brittany) and put in at international ports on the south coast of Britain – Mount Batten in Plymouth Sound, Poole Harbour and Hengistbury Head in Dorset. Before any Roman had set foot in Britain, the great navy of the Celtic Veneti tribe, 'whose knowledge and experience of all things nautical are second to none', according to Caesar, patrolled the Atlantic seaboard in their high-prowed ships with stretched-skin sails. They levied a tax on all who sailed in their territorial waters, which implies not only registration procedures and written records but also accurate knowledge of tides, currents and sea lanes.

The information was still there, but it was locked away in separate disciplines and professions, where it might as well have existed in different dimensions. A Roman surveyor in Agricola's army would scarcely have recognized the mental geography of his commander. No trader who had followed the rivers of Gaul would have believed, as Strabo did, that the Seine had its source in the Alps. Maps did exist: Tacitus, Pliny and Strabo were obviously thinking of particular maps when they described Britain as 'a double-headed axe', Italy as 'an oak-leaf' and Spain as 'an ox-hide', but they were describing the maps themselves rather than the reality they depicted, as though expecting the painting of a pudding to serve as a recipe.

The essential problem was practical rather than theoretical. In order to obtain accurate working measurements using the technology of his time, Eratosthenes would have had to assemble a team of intelligent, well-educated observers and station them at more or less regular intervals over a large part of the world. The observers would have been thoroughly trained in the sciences of measuring, surveying and astronomy. They would have had at their disposal a reliable communications system for transmitting the data. So that their results could be cross-checked and coordinated, they would have remained in position like parish priests for many years. The map-making expeditions of the Cassini family in the eighteenth century used ninety-five geometers to cover most of the area of modern France, but they had telescopes, magnetic compasses and sextants: at the very least, an expedition which lacked such technological refinements would have had one fixed observer for each triangulation point.

Ideally, the scientific body that collated the results would have had access to older, precisely dated records of eclipses. The organization would have been centralized or able to meet at regular intervals in a central location. It would have adhered to a strict code of scientific conduct that prevented it from allowing the temporary prestige of a tribe or a city from influencing the eternal truth of the survey. It would have operated in a period of relative political stability, or been able to call upon military protection. Above all, unlike the Cassini expeditions, it would have enjoyed an uninterrupted source of funding. With all this, a wonderfully accurate map of vast regions might have been created. For someone in Eratosthenes' position, such magnificent efficiency would have been the dream of a madman.

7

The Druidic Syllabus, I: Elementary

They had all heard about Druids but never seen one before. Diviciacus the Aeduan stood before the Roman Senate, leaning on his shield, and uttered the outlandish words with such eloquence that the interpreter was probably a distraction. Five years later, in 58 BC, in the midst of a savage war, Diviciacus would embrace his friend Julius Caesar with tears in his eyes, pleading for the life of his rebellious brother. Caesar would take the Druid's right hand and, comforting him, accede to his request. This was a man who possessed the art of inspiring an audience. The senators listened to what they already knew: somewhere beyond the Alps, great movements of tribes were disturbing the delicate peace. Wild Germans – 'whose way of life', said the speaker, 'cannot be compared to that of the Gauls' – had been hired by the Aedui's rivals, the Sequani and the Arverni. Now, the German mercenaries had turned on their employers and were threatening to bring hordes of 'untamed, barbaric men' across the Rhine. The Aedui feared a massacre.

As 'friends and kinsmen of the Roman people', the Aedui were important allies. Their name was familiar to most educated Romans. They were the 'Fiery Folk' or the 'People of the Hearth', who lived in a river port on the Arar (the Saône) and in a mountain fastness girt with a wall twice the height of a Celtic man – or three times the height of a Roman – and six kilometres long. Like the Romans, the Aedui claimed Trojan descent, and there was something of the purity of the age of heroes in the orator's braided hair, the lavish gold ornaments pinned to his woollen cloak, and his archaic pronunciation of place names. The quaint designs on his oblong shield might have been the faces of small animals tempted by an enchanter out of the wood and metal and fixed to the surface. The Senate would seriously consider granting the Aedui military assistance. Diviciacus was a barbarian and a Druid, but he, too, had a wife and children. He did not appear to be the kind of man who (as rumour suggested) would thrust his sword into a prisoner's bowels and then studiously observe the pattern of his writhings to discern the will of the gods, and it was hard to imagine that tall and stately figure shinning up a tree under a six-day-old moon, the crescent of a gold sickle glinting, to cut the sacred mistletoe from the oak.

Quintus Cicero had met Diviciacus at his older brother's house on the Palatine Hill. 'If there really are Druids in Gaul . . .' Quintus had said. 'Well, there are – because I know one!' His brother Marcus was interested in divination – one day, he would write a book on the subject, from a sceptical, modern point of view – and what better house-guest could he have? The Druid claimed to know the art of looking into the future (he was after all a diplomat), but he used a combination of augury and '*conjectura*', which suggested some rational inspection of the dubious evidence. Disappointingly, he had no tales to tell of human sacrifice. The practice must have died out in the olden days. The Druid, *mirabile dictu*, was a civilized, erudite man who could happily eat exotic food in a villa above the Roman Forum and write a eulogy of his host. He could discuss politics and law. He was an astronomer and a student of what the Greeks called '*physiologia*' – the scientific study of nature. Few Romans could boast such a panoply of accomplishments. His only obvious fault, apart from his ignorance of Latin, was his younger brother, Dumnorix, who had married their widowed mother to a rich and powerful Biturigan, taken a Helvetian bride for himself, and was flirting with any tribe that might help him to the supreme command of the Gauls.

Diviciacus, 'the Avenger'; Dumnorix, 'King of the Lower World' . . . These Gauls had names that seemed to speak of the distant dawn of the Roman empire, when an army of Celtic warriors entered Rome and walked in silent parade through the streets beneath the Palatine Hill. On that day in 387 BC, the Eternal City had been abandoned by all but the old noblemen who sat motionless in their doorways. To the barbarian Celts, they seemed the living statues of gods, until one warrior, more foolhardy than the rest, reached out and stroked one of the long white beards. The old man retaliated with his ivory stick; the spell was broken, and the massacre continued until every

Roman nobleman was dead. Even in the modern metropolis, more than three hundred years later, the old fears glowed like embers; there was something reassuringly farcical about those tales of Druidic practices. Later, the Romans would learn to fear the Druids – not the riddling, white-robed priests of a ridiculous cult, but the philosopher-politicians who could conjure vast armies out of the mist.

✿

Diviciacus, one of the few Druids known to us by name until the Hibernian magicians and Gaulish university professors of the fifth century AD, had endured a long journey to Rome. The shortest routes from Aeduan territory lay through the lands now controlled by German warriors. But Diviciacus knew the geography of Keltika like the plan of a temple. In 58 BC, he would devise for his friend Caesar 'a circuitous itinerary of more than fifty miles' through the difficult country between Vesontio (Besançon) and Mons Vosegus (the Vosges). To reach Rome in 63 BC, he would have travelled south along the valley of the Rhodanus, entering the Roman province in southern Gaul somewhere near Arausio (Orange). Turning to the north-east, he had climbed towards the snowy horizon on roads that ran alongside the rivers fleeing from the Alps, to Brigantium, and from there, in the footsteps of Herakles, to the Matrona Pass. As he descended into the land of vineyards, Diviciacus contemplated an uncertain future, but perhaps, as he thought of the wife he had left behind, the paths of his conjecturing also led him back in time, to the days when he had embarked on the first great journey of his life.

Boys and girls who left for Druid school had already reached the age of reason. Some young people, said Caesar, go to the Druids of their own accord ('*sua sponte*'). Others were sent by parents and relatives ('*parentibus propinquisque*'): the phrase implies that several members of the clan, not just the immediate family, clubbed together to provide a scholarship. Some went to the Druids for a general education; others remained under Druidic tuition for twenty years before becoming Druids themselves. Roman writers assumed that the education was reserved for children of the aristocracy, but a protégé of Diviciacus called Viridomarus had 'humble origins', according to Caesar, as did the three generations of Druids mentioned by the poet Ausonius in the fourth century AD. No doubt it was an advantage to come from a good family, but the essential qualification was intelligence. With such a comprehensive syllabus, the Druidic education system was necessarily meritocratic.

Those diligent, ambitious children of the Iron Age who '[flocked] to the Druids in great numbers', said Caesar, subjected themselves to the longest education in the ancient world. A Greek education began when the boy was seven, and usually lasted no more than eleven years. A pupil of the Druids remained in full-time education for as long as it takes a modern student to progress from nursery school to a doctoral degree. The family would lose a useful, intelligent child, but the advantages were enormous: not only were Druids exempt from tax and military service, they also settled disputes concerning inheritances and property boundaries, and they had the power to excommunicate offenders by banning them from sacrifices, which was the worst of all punishments.

No Druid school has ever been identified, perhaps because no one has looked for one. In AD 43, the Roman geographer Pomponius Mela claimed that 'the noblest of the Gauls' received their twenty years of Druidic education 'in caves and secret woods'. This was the civilized person's fantasy of hermits' glades and wizards' glens accessible only by some Celtic equivalent of Platform 9¾. Apprentice Druids who required writing tablets, measuring equipment and medical instruments, not to mention board and lodging, would not have spent twenty years in a dank cavern or a sylvan hut, though some part of the syllabus may have involved a contemplative retreat or a spell of enforced intimacy with nature. The Druids were said by several ancient writers to follow the precepts of Pythagoras. One of those writers, Hippolytus of Rome, observed that 'Pythagoras himself taught his disciples to be silent, and obliged the student to remain quietly in rooms underneath the earth'.

Some remarkably early evidence of a school has survived. It was in the Aeduan town of Augustodunum (Autun), between the *oppida* of Cabillonum (Châlon-sur-Saône) and Bibracte (Mont Beuvray). An analysis of the roads around Autun has shown that the *dunum* was already an important hub before the Romans named it after Augustus. It was there, in AD 21, that 'the noblest progeny of the Gauls devoted themselves to a liberal education'. Tacitus mentions this in passing in his account of the Gaulish revolt of that year. Since the Druids were considered a subversive political force and were subsequently outlawed by imperial decrees, it can hardly be a coincidence that the revolt began in a town where the 'noblest progeny of the Gauls' were receiving a liberal education.

The university at Augustodunum, founded more than twelve centuries before the Sorbonne, was still a famous seat of learning in the fourth century AD, when the porticoes of its schools were adorned with one of the lost treasures of ancient Gaul – a scale map of the world showing seas, rivers and towns and the distances between them. By then, the university was already a venerable institution. Professors who proudly called themselves sons of Druids (presumably in private) were teaching at Bayeux and Bordeaux. They represented a scholastic tradition older than Augustodunum itself. When Diviciacus qualified as a Druid in the early first century BC, he would have received his robes, not at Augustodunum, but at the *oppidum* of Bibracte, which was the capital of the Aedui before the Gallic War.

✤

Two slow cycling hours to the west of Autun, Mont Beuvray rises out of the forests of the Morvan plateau. The summit remains in sight throughout a day's travel on either side: its 'visibility footprint' covers several thousand square kilometres between Burgundy and the Massif Central. The nearest village, Saint-Léger-sous-Beuvray, lies eight kilometres to the east. From there, the road saunters off into beech woods before suddenly adopting the kind of gradients that signify a return to an earlier age: medieval mules were more patient than modern drivers, but even they would have baulked at the final ascent, which conjures up thoughts of penance and siege. In these parts of Gaul, the scale on an inclinometer could be marked off in centuries instead of degrees. Tracks like the one that climbs towards the *oppidum* from the Col du Rebout belong to a period when urban settlement took very different forms.

Roman visitors to Bibracte may well have felt that they were entering some other-worldly realm. On the undulating plateau at the summit of the mountain, monumental walls loomed out of the forest. All around were funeral pyres and orderly cemeteries that had been carefully maintained for many decades. After passing through the towering gateway, a visitor was greeted by the stench of tanneries and the forges' smoke. The pre-Roman capital of the Aedui was a teeming town of shops and small factories, covering an area about two-thirds the size of medieval Paris. The streets were made of compacted stone and gravel, with a layer of sand to prevent them from becoming slippery in the winter. After the industrial quarter came the residential suburb and, beyond that, the shops and the temple, with a wide-open view of wheat fields and coppiced woods. In the east, smoke could be seen rising from the lands of the Sequani where the iron was mined. If the weather was fine, the jagged white hem of the Alps marked the horizon.

Near the centre of the *oppidum*, an unusual object seemed to block the street. One of the most intriguing archaeological discoveries of the last hundred years, it was so well preserved that when it was excavated in 1987 it looked like a modern reconstruction – a basin in the form of a slender oval, beautifully formed from blocks of pink granite. For some reason, the stone had been dressed using techniques normally applied to limestone: the stone was local but the masons were Mediterranean. Several teams of archaeologists have been unable to determine its purpose. It was too shallow to have served as a cistern, and there was no nearby source of running water. Some have suggested a 'water cult' or a foundation monument. Only two things are certain: the lateral axis of the basin is the line of the summer solstice sunset and the winter solstice sunrise at Bibracte, and the oval itself is the result of complex geometrical calculations. It would have been a familiar object to the apprentice Druids, and we shall return to the pink-granite basin at the appropriate point in the curriculum.

Most of the inhabitants of Bibracte lived in warm, well-insulated houses of wattle and daub; some of them may have had slaves. The school would have been comfortable and well equipped. Standards of hygiene were very high. According the Greek historian Timagenes, the Gauls were extremely punctilious about cleanliness and elegance: 'You will never see in all these countries a man or a woman, however poor, either dirty or in rags'. The population of the Aeduan capital would have been particularly elegant. Though it stood on the summit of a mountain, it was one of the largest and best-supplied towns in eastern Gaul – '*maximum et copiosissimum*', according to Caesar, who chose to spend the winter of 52–51 BC there, six hundred miles from home. In a town of teachers and students, he would not have lacked

scribes, writing materials and reference works. The short passage on
the Druids in *De Bello Gallico*, once thought to have been copied from
an earlier source, is now recognized as an up-to-date description of
the Druid order and the most reliable of all texts on the subject. The
fact is rendered almost invisible by murky views of the Celtic past:
one of the classics of world literature was written in an Iron Age
oppidum.

✧

A young Aeduan arriving at Druid school, knowing something of the
superstitions that common people expressed on curse-tablets and at
shrines in the form of crude oaken images, might have hoped to be
provided with potions and magic spells. If so, they would have been
disappointed. Druidic science was an arduous discipline. The young
people, said Caesar, must 'learn by heart a great number of verses'
– he supposed that this was why the education could last twenty years;
'it is considered sacrilegious to commit the verses to writing'. For this
reason, the Druids are often said to have been illiterate, yet Caesar
went on to note that 'in almost all other matters, public and private,
they use the Greek alphabet'.* His own opinion was that rote learning
was a pedagogical device designed to keep the minds of young Gauls
healthy and alert. When, ten years later, during his siege of Alexandria,
he accidentally set fire to the Great Library, he might have pondered
the benefits of storing knowledge in thousands of trained minds.

Even the teachings that generations of Druids kept in their memories would one day disappear. Now, almost nothing seems to be left
of them. Yet patterns of thought sometimes remain visible like crop
marks in a field. The annals of the Celts, their religious and moral
precepts, the names of places and heroes were preserved in the tri-
partite forms familiar from Celtic art and theology, just as they were
later recorded in the triads of medieval Wales.

Triads were simple mnemonics that served as keys to greater
stores of wisdom. Some were verbal maps of a kingdom, like the
complex routes that were memorized by sailors, or like the Irish

---

* The same presumption of illiteracy is often extended to Celtic society as a whole,
though Diodorus Siculus reported that the Celts 'cast letters to their relatives onto
funeral pyres in the belief that the dead will be able to read them'. See also p. xv.

Dindsenchas ('the lore of places'), which inculcated a sense of real and sacred geography by recounting the route taken by a god or a hero. Others were signposts at the meeting of three roads that led to different shires of tribal lore: 'The Three Wives of Arthur', 'The Three Mistresses of Arthur', 'The Three Chief Rivers of the Island of Britain', 'The Three Unrestrained Ravagings of the Island of Britain', etc. Mnemonic rhymes are still a common form of personal data storage (the number of days in each month, the notes on the lines of the treble clef, the burning properties of wood), and many Druids who were sent to take charge of remote temples must have blessed their teachers for imprinting the useful formulae on their brains.

It is astonishing how the lightest breath on the dust of an ancient text can reveal a lost Druidic lesson. Statements about the Celts' beliefs often fall into threes and take a loosely strophic form. Caesar's famous statement that 'Gaul is divided into three parts' may have a Celtic origin, and Pomponius Mela's listing of the three peoples of Gaul may once have been a pair of triads:

> From the Pyrenees to the Garonne are the Aquitanians, from the Garonne to the Seine the Celts, and from the Seine to the Rhine the Belgians.
> The leading lights among the Aquitanians are the Ausci, among the Celts the Aedui, and among the Belgians the Treveri.

The flattering reference to the Aedui and to their allies, the Treveri, suggests that something very similar to this litany of origins once formed part of a history lesson at Bibracte.

When Timagenes was collecting information for his *History of the Gauls*, of which only a few excerpts survive, he heard the Celts' own story of their origins. Although the triadic verses were never written down, they were so well rooted in the minds of educated Celts that they came quite naturally to the lips of his informants:

> The Druids relate ['*memorant*': literally, 'bring to memory'] as a true thing that part of the population [of Gaul] was indigenous, but that others flooded in from the outermost islands and regions across the Rhine, driven from their homes by frequent wars and inundations of the fiery seas ['*fervidi maris*'].

Some say that after the destruction of Troy, a handful of Trojans fleeing from the Greeks, and scattering far and wide, took possession of these empty places.

The natives of these regions assert above all . . . that Herakles, son of Amphitryon, hastening to destroy the cruel tyrants, Geryon and Tauriscus, who were molesting Gaul and Spain, having overcome both, married a noble woman and begat many children who gave their names to the regions they ruled.

The names of those many Herculean children – and, in the matrilineal Celtic tradition, their mothers – would then have formed a geographical roll call of the Celtic tribes: Celtus, progenitor of the Celts; Galates, progenitor of the Gauls; Sardus, who gave his name to the Pyrenean Sardones; Bretannos, whose daughter gave birth to the Pretani.

The diversity of origins suggests a lively historical tradition. What Timagenes took to be competing views were probably the components of a broader picture that covered the entire Celtic world. It matches the historical evidence quite well, and it proves that, unlike some of their modern admirers, the ancient Celts never claimed a single ethnic origin (fig. 24).

Like all well-hidden secrets, the most important mnemonic riddle was there for all to see. The word 'Druid' was a cleverly tangled knot of meanings, and unravelling it would have required a long lecture on historical semantics. The *'uid'* belongs to the same family as the Sanskrit *'veda'* ('knowledge') and the Latin *'videre'* ('to see'). The *'dru'* could mean either 'very great' or 'oak'. Welsh and Breton forms derived from *'do-are-wid'* contain the word *'are'*, meaning 'eastward', 'in front of' or 'into the future'. Other words that were etymologically unrelated may have woven their connotations into the puzzle: *'druta'* ('swift'), *'drutos'* ('strong' or 'solid'), *'uidua'* ('tree' or 'wood').

The Greek historian Diodorus Siculus found this riddling habit of the Celts exasperating ('they use one word when they mean another'), and so do some modern etymologists who disagree about the exact meaning of 'Druid'. The argument is endless because the word is deliberately ambiguous. A Druid was a great sage or scholar who knew the secrets of the oak, or whose wisdom was as strong and

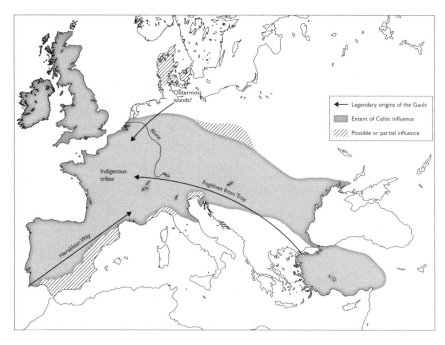

24. Legendary origins of the Gauls and the greatest extent of Celtic influence
From Timagenes' *History of the Gauls*.

solid as wood, who looked to the east and who saw into the future. Some nuances have probably faded away for ever, but enough remain to show what games a Druid master could play with the philosophical pun. '*Dysgogan derwydon meint a deruyd*', said a tenth-century Welsh poem: 'Druids predict all that will come to pass'.

Before the apprentice Druids could begin to predict the future, there was a vast amount to be learned. Apart from history and geography, they studied moral philosophy, religion and theology. The keystone of the Druidic creed was the Pythagorean belief in the immortality of the soul and a life after death. Caesar naturally considered the military advantages of a belief in the transmigration of souls: 'They wish above all to convince their pupils that souls do not perish ['*interire*'] but pass ['*transire*'] after death from one body into another, and this they see as an inducement to valour, for the dread of death is thereby negated.' Caesar's interpreter – perhaps Diviciacus himself – seems to have captured an echo of the rhyming pun that fixed the precept in the mind: '*non interire, sed transire*'.

According to the geographer Pomponius Mela, this was the only Druid teaching that ever 'escaped' into the wider world, yet the secret verses were so potent that fragments can still be picked up among Greek and Latin prose. 'The Druids express their philosophy in riddles, urging men to honour the gods, to do no evil, and to exercise courage.' This triadic litany, quoted by Diogenes Laertius from a work of the fourth century BC, is remarkably similar to a Welsh triad that was first written down in the thirteenth century AD: 'These are the three main principles of wisdom: obedience to the laws of the Almighty, concern for the common good, and courage in the face of the accidents of life.'

Perhaps the Druids were not so secretive after all. Some of their lessons were reserved for initiates, but much of the education was public. A teaching order that had managed to syncretise thousands of local gods and legends into a European pantheon, and which had more influence over the actions of individual states than the United Nations does today, was obviously not given to incomprehensible mutterings in secluded forests. The Gaulish gentleman who noticed Lucian of Samosata gaping in horror at the image of Ogmios-Herakles (p. 10) was either a Druid himself or a graduate of Druid school. 'Stranger,' he said, 'I shall explain the enigma of this portrait that seems to trouble you so.' The man spoke impeccable Greek and chattered away in the pleasantly teasing tones of a man of the world on the subjects of comparative religion, mythology, art and literature. He littered his conversation with quotations from Homer, Euripides and a Greek comic poet whose works are otherwise unknown. He had a seductively soothing pedagogical manner which charmed his troubled listener and enlightened him far beyond his expectations. As Cicero had discovered in Rome, a Druid's conversation could be delightful:

> You should not be surprised to see the tongue of Herakles, that embodiment of eloquence, leading men by chains attached to their ears. Consider the relation between ear and tongue: this tongue-piercing is not intended as an insult. Was it not one of your comic poets who said, 'The tongue of the chatterbox is always pierced at its tip'?

✿

At this point, after the history, the geography, the moral philosophy and religion, the Greek language and literature, the boys and girls who had gone to the Druids for a general education would return to their families. The exoteric curriculum gave way to the esoteric, and the students who remained would now be inducted into the higher mysteries of Druidism.

8

The Druidic Syllabus, II: Advanced

Behind all the other mysteries stood the tree that gave the Druids their name. According to Pliny, the Druids planted groves of oak, 'and they perform none of their religious rites without using its leaves'. This is one of several hints of Hellenic influence. The oak-wreathed head of the Greek sun god appears on many Celtic coins, and the oak groves of the Druids may have been designed for the kind of divination familiar to Odysseus, who journeyed to the remote shrine of Dodona 'to hear the lofty oak express the will of Zeus' in the rustling of its leaves. But an institution of such geographical and philosophical scope would have had many origins. In the never-ending realms of folklore, the branches of the oak point in all directions like the knotted fingers of a witch. The Celtic oak may have been a cosmic tree that spanned the three worlds, like the ash tree, Yggdrasil, of Norse mythology, or a relic of local, prehistoric beliefs that had been codified by the Druids. Caesar believed that Druidism had been 'discovered' ('*reperta*') in Britain (p. 10), and the preponderance of oak in English woodland may indeed have given rise to local cults that have left their trace in the hundreds of 'oak' place names that share an etymological origin with 'Druid': Darroch, Darwen, Derby, Derwent, etc.

The keys to Celtic mysteries usually lie in an observable reality rather than in a vague superstition. Oak is one of the best firewoods ('Oaken logs, if dry and old / Keep away the winter's cold'), and one of the best ways in which to get to know a tree is to prepare it for burning. Divine utterances are no longer perceptible in the rustling of oak leaves, but faces can still be seen in that most anthropomorphic of trees. Many of those faces have Celtic features. A few hours of attacking fallen oak branches with a bow saw and a splitting maul will produce a representative selection of ancient Celtic art works. The snags and antlered ends of dead branches are the beaked monsters of Celtic fibulae and flagon handles. The oval knots are the eyes of a Celtic god or the war-trumpet called a carnyx, and the pendant clusters of male flowers and the knobbly burrs that turn into beautiful whorls in the planed wood are the nodules and incrustations on gold armbands and torcs. Where a branch has cracked and pulled away from the trunk, the sinewy labyrinth of circles looks like the pattern book of a Celtic artist.

'The Celtic Druids investigated to the very highest point the Pythagorean philosophy', said Hippolytus of Rome; they practise divination 'from calculations and numbers by the Pythagorean art'.* The oak was an object of particular scrutiny. This was not the pagan 'tree worship' that Christian missionaries would try to eradicate, nor was it simply an artistic imitation of natural phenomena. Celtic art was a scientific attempt to decipher the secrets of creation, 'for offerings should be rendered to the gods by philosophers who are experienced in the nature of the divine and who speak, as it were, the same language as the gods' (Diodorus Siculus). In order to learn that language, they 'conducted investigations and attempted to explain the system of interrelations [or, in a variant text, 'the inner laws'] and the highest secrets of nature' (Timagenes).

The Pythagoreans believed that the universe could be explained by numbers. Two and a half thousand years before particle physics and the bio-inspired algorithms of computer science, a belief in the power of numbers was considered by most educated people to be a form of mystical obfuscation, but in the tangle of the oak grove there were shapes that seemed to obey the geometrical laws that had been described by Pythagoras. The contortions of the oak and the leaves and berries of the mistletoe appear in almost every imaginable Celtic object: a shield cover, the *phalera* of a harness, a cooking pot, a coin. Even when the design seems to be complete, the whole picture is never revealed. The principle of construction is always hidden, as it

---

* Pythagoras taught in the sixth century BC. 'Pythagorean' is the interpretation of classical, non-Celtic writers, who saw similarities between Druidism and Hellenic philosophies, just as later writers perceived analogies with Brahmanism. These filiations are neither implausible nor provable.

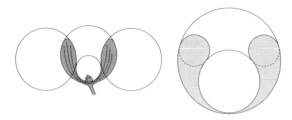

25. The geometry of the mistletoe

The face appears on a bronze *phalera* (harness ornament) of the fifth century BC from Horovicky (Czech Republic).

is in nature, and these swirls and mazy lines are easily mistaken for the meanderings of an individual artist's fantasy.

These cunning designs, which could evoke the elegant dance of a plant's leaves, the orbiting of spheres or the harmonious muscles of a horse, were one of the first great flowerings of the scientific spirit and one of the most disciplined and classical of ancient arts. The forms that remained in use over a large part of the Western world for almost a thousand years were probably created by artists under instruction from the Druids: in the forges of Bibracte, the apprentices would have learned to recognize the fibrous qualities of wrought iron and the alarming volatility of gold. The mythological connotations of these shapes are unknown, but the language they spoke is not so deeply encrypted that it can never be recovered.

The geometrical basis of early Celtic art was recognized only recently, and much of the work remains to be done. For the time being, a hypothetical Druidic design manual could begin almost anywhere – with a face in the British Museum, for instance, on the handle mounts of a 'bucket' or funerary urn that was placed in the grave of a Kentish Briton at about the time of Caesar's invasion (fig. 28). The secret of this emaciated, alien face has remained intact. But a Druid would have known that just as the stars and planets were regulated by an invisible system of circles and ellipses, the face was the visible witness of a complex pattern. Once the pattern has been deduced, its deeper meaning emerges: the mouth, the source of eloquence and prophetic utterance, forming the lowest extremity of the figure, turns out to be the true centre of the design. It also occupies the centre of four Pythagorean triangles, which, for reasons that will shortly be mentioned, means that this face that watched over the cremated

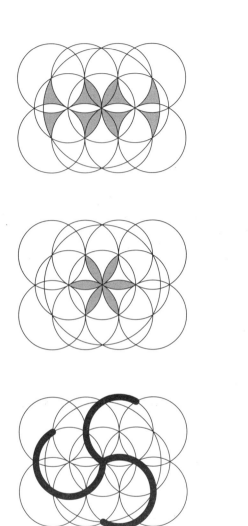

26. The geometry of Celtic art

Once the geometrical pattern has been deduced from the *phalera* (top), it proves to be applicable to many other objects. *Phalera* from the Somme-Bionne chariot burial (France), 450–400 BC. Flower from an inner panel of the Gundestrup Cauldron (Denmark), 175–150 BC. Bronze appliqué from a flagon, Dürrnberg bei Hallein (Austria), 400–350 BC.

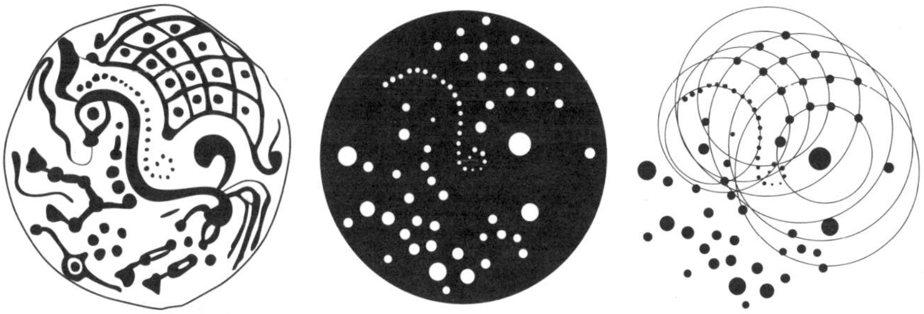

27. Gold coin of the Parisii

A gold coin of the Parisii tribe, first century BC. These coins can be analysed in various ways. Two implicit patterns are shown on the right. The symbols are astronomical. The horse itself may represent the constellation of Ursa Major.

remains of a man or a woman of Cantium contained the fragments of a compass by which mortals could find their way on Middle Earth and in the world beyond.

It used to be said – and sometimes still is – that the 'symbols' of Celtic art were 'copied' from other civilizations by Iron Age artists who laboured under the same cerebral limitations that Victorian scholars attributed to savages: 'The Celt was a clever adaptor, but weak as an innovator' (this was written in 1980). To the Celts themselves, knowing from their observations of nature and the heavens that eternal truths are not presented in an instantly comprehensible form, the humanized gods of Greece and Rome were childishly literal idols. When Brennos, the leader of the Celtic expedition to Delphi, entered a shrine and saw gods of wood and stone standing about like real people, he burst out laughing.

☼

Some phrases of the gods' language can be deciphered in the pink-granite basin of Bibracte (first century BC). So much information is stored in its subtle curves that it might have served as a teaching aid. The basin is the geometrical result of two circles, overlapping at one-fifth of their diameters. Lines drawn from the centre of the oval to the centre of one of the circles and to a point of intersection form a Pythagorean triangle – a right-angled triangle with lengths that are a Pythagorean triad: 3, 4 and 5. Pythagoras himself may have invented the figure, but there is no trace of this geometrical experiment in the

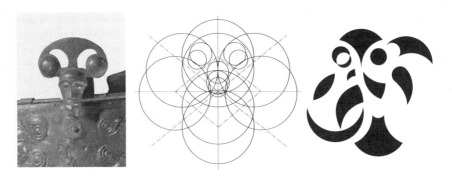

28. The face on the Aylesford Bucket
The face on the Aylesford Bucket (c. 50 BC), and the compass-drawn design that produced it. Other characteristically Celtic shapes that can be derived from the same design are shown on the right.

Pythagorean books of Euclid's *Elements* (c. 300 BC), and the basin may be the witness to an independent tradition of Druid mathematics.

The oval formed by two intersecting circles was not primarily a symbol but the materialization of mathematical truths. Later, when the intrinsic logic of the figure had been forgotten, it became an esoteric emblem: the 'mandorla' (almond) or '*vesica piscis*' (fish bladder) was the secret insignia of early Christians. In Christian iconography, it was associated with the vulva and used to frame the baby Jesus or the Madonna. It may have had a similar sexual connotation for the Druids, which would account for the use of red clay and pink granite. (The granite closest to Bibracte was grey; the pink granite came from the Mont de Fer, eight kilometres further east.) Perhaps, like its Christian equivalent, the sky-reflecting pool was the portal that linked the upper, middle and lower worlds, and the portal through which every human being passed.

The apprentice Druids and Druidesses would have explored this smooth, mysterious object in all its surprising detail. The female shape that later contained the Christ child emerging from his mother's womb was an Iron Age scientific calculator. Though it hardly bears comparison with the Acropolis or St Peter's Basilica, the pink-granite basin of Bibracte is one of the most remarkable religious monuments of Europe. (It also happens to be the best-preserved Celtic stone structure.) The Pythagorean triangle has two angles of 53.13°. This was,

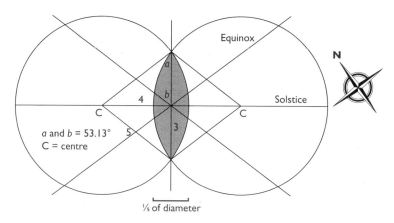

Equinox

N

Solstice

a

b

4

C

C

3

5

a and b = 53.13°
C = centre

⅕ of diameter

29. The pink-granite basin at Bibracte

to within four-fifths of a degree, the angle of the solstice sun at Bibracte. Accuracy of this order in the measurement of angles is often thought to have been unattainable without theodolites, but here, in one of the clearest numerical utterances of the gods – two intersecting circles and a Pythagorean triangle – is proof that solar pathways could be measured quite simply. The fact that this solstice angle happens to be the angle produced by the sacred Pythagorean triad of 3, 4 and 5 must have struck the Druid mathematicians of Bibracte as a particularly auspicious coincidence.

☼

Having acquired a working knowledge of the language of the gods, the apprentices would have been ready to perform duties at the temple. They would have learned how to celebrate the four great festivals and to calculate their dates,* and the correct manner in which to hold a sacrificial victim (one hand around the knee, the other clutching the waist). (Fig. 30.)

Until the early 1980s, it was assumed that most Celtic temples were clearings in a wood. Then the eight-year-long excavation of a third-century BC Bellovacian shrine at Gournay-sur-Aronde changed

---

* The four Celtic festivals occur on the 'cross-quarter days', halfway between solstice and equinox: Samhain – winter solstice – Imbolc – vernal equinox – Beltane – summer solstice – Lughnasadh – autumn equinox.

30. The Gundestrup Cauldron (detail), c. 175–150 BC

the imagined scene completely. Celtic temples are now known to have been solid wooden structures with ambulatories and well-defined areas marked off for particular forms of sacrifice. A Greek traveller would have recognized the arrangement and perhaps some of the ceremonies. In the centre of the temple, aligned on the solstice or the equinox, was a hollow altar lined with wood. Inside, the putrefying remains of sacrificial victims – pigs, sheep, dogs or humans – filtered down into the lower world. Other victims hung like tapestries on the outer palisade: their flesh would be taken up to heaven by scavengers and the elements, which is why the Celtic and Iberian soldiers on Hannibal's expedition insisted on leaving their comrades' bodies unburned on the battlefield.

The Greek terms for the two forms of sacrifice were 'chthonic' ('under the earth') and 'Olympian' or 'ouranian' ('heavenly'). Each temple was a double portal: some spirits passed from the world of the living to Albos, the 'white' world of the heavens; others descended to Dumnos, the world of 'darkness' or 'the deep'. The temples were, in effect, an early form of church, with more pungent and literal reminders of death than stale incense and a musty crypt.

The vestments of the 'oak sages' themselves are depicted on the silver Gundestrup Cauldron, which was discovered in a Danish peat bog in 1891. It shows scenes of Druidic rites and unidentified Celtic myths. The tall figure who plunges a sacrificial victim into a vat wears what an expert on Celtic dress has described as 'tight trousers akin to cycling shorts'. The close-knit ribbing of the costume is also reminiscent of the thin, vertical striations of oak wood. The tasselled skull-cap looks like the cup and stalk of the acorn of the pedunculate oak, and the pattern on the laced slippers recalls the stylized oak-leaves of Celtic designs. This is, to all appearances, a man dressed to look like an oak. In a costume made of brown sheep's wool, a Druid, or a pupil in Druid school uniform, could have passed through the oak wood less noticeably than a deer. Modern Druids who wish to resemble their predecessors should consider exchanging their white robes for oak-patterned Lycra, oak-leaf slippers, acorn caps for winter and oak-leaf headdresses for summer.

As Druidism spread to the remotest parts of Europe, new temples had to be built. A Druid would be expected to direct the architectural operation according to the will of the gods. Since the gods spoke in riddles, it is not surprising that there is something odd about the shape of Celtic temples. The four corner posts and ditches typically describe a clumsily drawn square or rectangle. These 'subrectangular enclosures' seem to have been laid out by a sloppy surveyor who always managed to put at least one of the corners in the wrong place. A British structural archaeologist, analysing Celtic enclosures in the south of England, noted in 2009 that 'nothing was quite square', and asked, 'So were [the Celts] just rubbish at surveying?' 'Either prehistoric southern England was a land of botchers and bodgers, or they were doing it deliberately and systematically. I chose the latter option and called the phenomenon "systematic irregularity".'

Five years earlier, in an article on Celtic temples in the Vexin region to the north-west of Paris, a French archaeologist had pondered the same problem. He noticed that, in every case, a line drawn through the major axis of the skewed rectangle produced two triangles that were mirror images of each other. These peculiar shapes appeared to have been produced by attaching a loose length of rope to two poles, then stretching it out on either side to define the other two points. The pattern did after all have a geometrical rationale, but, in

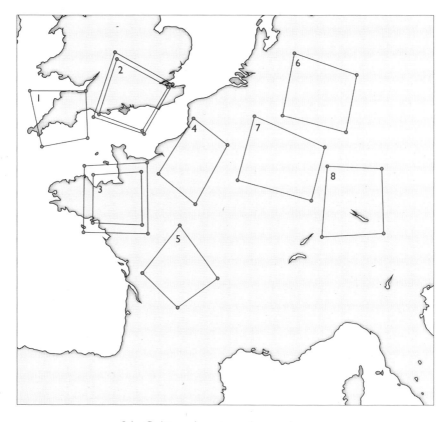

31. Celtic subrectangular enclosures

Examples of Celtic subrectangular enclosures in England, France and Germany. Key: 1. South Cadbury. 2. Casterley Camp. 3. Oisseau-le-Petit. 4. Bruyères-sur-Oise. 5. Arnac-la-Poste. 6. Hardheim. 7. Oberesslingen. 8. Holzhausen.

characteristically Druidic fashion, the underlying principle was concealed. Like the labyrinthine oak, the apparently lopsided ground plan contained a logic that was visible only to initiates.

The question remains: why such an awkward design? Was it simply a geometrical puzzle or a hasty way of drawing an approximate rectangle? But there are many easier ways in which to draw a four-sided figure, and why would carpenters and roofers whose wooden houses were greater feats of engineering than any Greek or Roman temple have tolerated such a poorly drawn and inconvenient plan?

Something spectacular lies behind the configuration of these enigmatic structures, but it was only after a self-taught course in Druidic

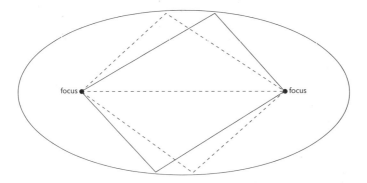

32. The ground plan of a Celtic temple

To draw the ground plan of a Celtic temple, attach a thread to two pins placed at the foci; drag the thread with a pencil and, keeping it taut, trace out the ellipse. NB: the pink-granite basin at Bibracte is an oval, which is distinct from an ellipse.

science that I realized what it was. As philosophers 'bound together in fellowships according to the rules and example of Pythagoras' (Timagenes), the Druids would have been aware of the heavenly shape that Pythagoras was said to have been the first to recognize. The sun's apparent motion against the background of stars over the course of a year describes a slanted circle called the ecliptic. This is the elliptical loop along which the planets and the twelve constellations of the zodiac appear. For a culture that attached such importance to the motion of the sun, this would have been a crucial discovery.

The surveying operation involving two poles and a length of rope is the simplest method of drawing an ellipse. Though there was nothing on the ground to show it, these apparently defective rectangles are the geometrical figures that define the yearly course of the sun. The temples and other sacred enclosures that were once a prominent feature of the landscape were constructed as though the heavenly ellipse surrounded them. And just as the line of the solstice sun had been materialized in the Via Heraklea, this other solar pathway was mapped out on the earth in thousands of places from Bavaria to the Atlantic Ocean.

This was the shape of worship in Europe for hundreds of years. The path of the sun was implicit in the precinct of the temple, and the points of the four Celtic festivals might have been marked at the correct points of the zodiacal ellipse like Stations of the Cross. In this virtual ellipse, the shadow of a Druidic rite can be seen. The Celts, like most cultures, performed ceremonies of circumambulation. According to Posidonius, they turned to the right (that is, to the south) when honouring their gods, which was also the direction in which St Patrick and other Celtic saints turned when they consecrated a church or a well, processing around the site '*deisiol*' ('to the right' or 'sunwise'). The invisible ellipse of the Celtic temple suggests that the saints were following not just the direction of the sun but its path through the heavens.

The Druids' arcane observance of 'the inner laws of nature' has functioned extremely well as a cloaking device. It has defeated the archaeological computer programs that were designed to identify significant patterns of post-holes, and this entire chapter in the history of religion and architecture has remained hidden for two thousand years. Until now, the string construction of the ellipse was thought to have been unknown in the West before the late sixteenth century AD. The unostentatious cleverness of the Druids has made it possible to go on believing that the Romans, with their tidy squares and rectangles, were a technically superior civilization. It is no wonder that these masters of invisibility would make such a fearsome resistance force when they reassembled in Britain after the conquest of Gaul.

✢

Twenty years was probably barely enough time for a complete Druidic education. No doubt there were many sub-disciplines and areas of specialization. Some Druids studied the medicinal properties of plants – 'selago' (fir club moss), whose smoke could heal a sick eye, 'samolus' (brookweed), which preserved swine and cattle from disease, and mistletoe, which was an antidote to any poison. Apart from the elephantine blasts produced by a reconstituted carnyx, ancient Celtic music is entirely lost, but Pythagoras's investigations of harmonic intervals would certainly have formed part of the curriculum. The Celtic bards played an instrument similar to the lyre, and Druid musicians may have composed the acoustic equivalents of geometrical designs.

Druids who contemplated a career in politics would have studied civil and criminal jurisprudence, including the legal corollaries of a belief in the transmigration of souls (the settlement of debts was sometimes delayed until the next world, and money was lent in the expectation that it would be repaid by the deceased). They studied the internal administration of the order and the protocol for electing a new chief Druid. Like Diviciacus, some Druids became experts in intertribal affairs, and, although they never bore arms, they had to be familiar with political and military strategy: 'Often, when two armies approach each other in battle with swords drawn and spears thrust forward, these philosophers step forth between them and cause them to cease, as though casting a spell over wild beasts.' (Diodorus Siculus)*

One day, many years after arriving at the school, an apprentice, already on the verge of middle age, would stand under the night sky, perhaps where a viewing platform had been set up on the eastern edge of Bibracte. This was the most scientifically advanced part of the course. It would enable the Druid to predict the future and to prepare Middle Earth for the advent of the gods:

> The Druids discuss and impart to the youth many things regarding the stars and their motion, the size of the universe and the earth, the nature of things, and the power and majesty of the immortal gods. (Caesar, *De Bello Gallico*, VI, 14)

Pomponius Mela says something very similar, but in a form that seems to echo the original triad: '*Hi terrae mundique magnitudinem et formam, motus caeli ac siderum et quid dii velint, scire profitentur.*' ('They profess to know the size and shape of the earth and the universe, the motion of the sky and the stars, and what the gods want.')

This is the triadic equation of mathematical divination: take the geodetic data (the spherical shape of the earth, its size and its zones of latitude), factor in the necessary astronomical observations (eclipses, shadow lengths, solstice angles), and the result of the calculation will reveal the will of the gods – '*quid dii velint*' (specifically, how to orient the altar, the direction in which to attack an enemy, the most auspicious trajectory for a tribal migration).

Unlike those of the Babylonians, the Druids' astronomical observations have not survived, except, by implication, in the five-year

---

* This may have been a function of female Druids: Plutarch and Polyaenus attributed the power to stop battles to 'Celtic women'.

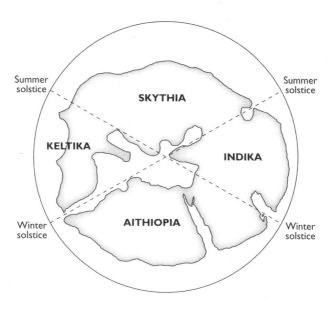

33. Division of the world by Ephorus, c. 350 BC

solar-lunar calendar engraved on a sheet of bronze that was dug out of a field in the foothills of the Jura. But their observations can be inferred from the system of Mediolana and the long-distance roads of Gaul. Studying the theorems of Pythagoras, the Druids would have been as familiar with Greek science as the Celts of the Mediterranean, and since theirs was the only intellocracy in Europe, and the only fellowship of scientists organized on such a scale, they may have added to what the Greeks had taught them. Caesar's verb '*disputant*' ('they discuss') shows that this was not a fossilized body of knowledge. Like university professors, the Druids taught, but they also conducted research and modified their teachings to take account of the latest stage of scholarly debate.

They would have been acquainted with *klimata* and the division of the inhabited world by Ephorus (c. 350 BC) into four zones based on the solstice angles of the sun.

Aristotle would have been known to them as a leading authority on the teachings of Pythagoras but also as the philosopher who had refined the system of *klimata*.

The diagonals or solstice lines are the lines known to sailors as rhumb lines: the navigator chooses a bearing and holds to that

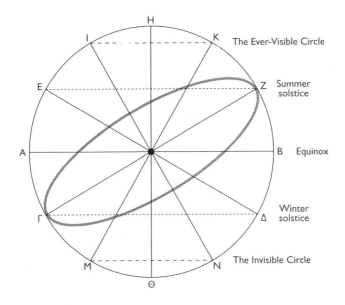

34. Division of the world by Aristotle

Aristotle, *Meteorology* (350 BC), II, 6, and the zodiacal path identified by Pythagoras. The twelve directions were conventionally named after the winds that blew from those quarters. The 'Ever-Visible' and 'Invisible' Circles (referring to the setting of stars) are the Arctic and Antarctic Circles.

bearing until the destination is reached. The centre of the Aristotelian earth was Rhodes, where the angle of the solstice sun in the fourth century BC happened to be exactly sixty degrees or one-sixth of a circle. (This is the angle of the solstice lines shown in the two diagrams above.) To an observer in more northerly latitudes, the angle was noticeably different, but on the geometrical evidence of the pink-granite basin and countless everyday objects of Celtic art, the Druids had the means of adapting the Aristotelian system to Celtic climes. They also had a huge, uninterrupted land mass on which to practise their navigation and to match their movements to the calculated will of the gods.

The newly qualified Druid who descended from the mountain after twenty years would know that the gods were present in every corner of the natural world, that nature itself was a temple and Middle Earth a mirror of the upper world. The temple presided over by the Druid was a material expression of those truths, a form of obedience to the immortal gods. Like the botanizing, star-gazing parish priests of later centuries, the Druid would continue to observe and record 'the inner laws of nature'. And, as branches of the sacred oak, possessing the secrets of the earth and the sky, and knowing their motions and dimensions, thousands of Druids all over Europe would contribute to the building of another temple so vast that it would turn Middle Earth into a world in which the gods would be at home. This was the miraculous efficiency of which Eratosthenes and other lone scientists could only dream.

PART THREE

9

Paths of the Gods

With the benefit of a Druidic education, something wonderful appears on the face of Europe, something that has not been seen since the late Iron Age – a map more than two thousand years old and in an almost perfect state of repair. In its fullest form, it shows a comprehension of the earth without precedent in the ancient world. This was the heavenly vision that would help to determine the patterns of settlement and movements of population that created modern Europe.

Mediolanum Biturigum – the unlikely hub of the Gaulish wine trade, now called Châteaumeillant – was the sacred centre of Gaul in the time of the Bituriges. It stood on the longest possible meridian and on an equinoctial line running from the Atlantic to the Alps (p. 62). A Druid versed in Greek science would have known that it had been chosen for other reasons too. Mediolanum Biturigum lies two hours due west of one of the key intersections of latitude and longitude in the Greek *oikoumene*: the mouth of the Borysthenes. It also lies thirty longitudinal minutes east of another key intersection – the Pillars of Hercules, where the Mediterranean meets the Atlantic. And on the line of latitude that runs one hour to the south of Mediolanum stands Delphi, the centre of the ancient world.

The system of Mediolana had been a patchy organization of local territories. Now, perhaps as early as the fourth century BC, the system was developed with such scientific rectitude that a magnificent pattern began to spread across the Continent like the roots and vessels of a great living tree. The Druids could hardly have chosen a better *omphalos*. Taking their bearings from the Greeks, they created a new, Celtic centre far to the west of Delphi. This siting of a prime Mediolanum is one of the earliest perceptible events in the gradual shift of power from the Aegean and the Mediterranean to the North

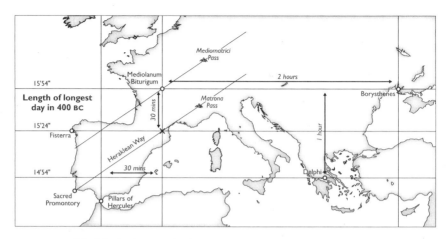

35. Mediolanum Biturigum and the Greek *oikoumene*

Sea that would continue for the next two thousand years. It affirmed the place of Gaul in the wider world, and, for the first time, joined the lands of the barbarian Celts to the civilized homeland of Herakles.

✻

The exploration of this tree begins with a simple calculation. The commonest division of *klimata* or lines of latitude based on the length of the longest day was thirty minutes. The line of latitude that runs exactly thirty minutes to the south of Mediolanum reaches the Atlantic near one of the 'ends of the earth' called Fisterra or Finisterre. But the point of intersection that lies due south of Mediolanum (marked 'X' on the map) seems utterly devoid of historical significance. In the foothills of the Pyrenees, in a convoluted region of limestone gullies where the medieval Cathars hid from their persecutors, the river Aude crashes through the Gorges de la Pierre-Lys. The jagged escarpment that seems to block the northern entrance is called 'la Muraille du Diable' ('the Devil's Wall'). Until the eighteenth century, when a local priest persuaded his parishioners to cut a road through the canyon, the hamlet of Belvianes was a cul-de-sac. Yet Celtiberian coins have been found there: Balbianas, as it was known in the eleventh century, was probably the estate of a Romanized Celt called Balbius. The inhabitant of this Pyrenean 'bag-end' lived just four kilometres from the small town of Axat beyond the southern entrance to the canyon. Axat owes its name to the Atacini tribe and was probably their tribal capital.

The former territory of the Atacini now knows little of its proto-historic past, but it could plausibly trace its history back to a certain day in 218 BC when a Carthaginian army crossed the Pyrenees, because the point marked 'X', half an hour of daylight south of Mediolanum, stands precisely on the Heraklean Way.

The idea presents itself like a gold coin glinting on the ridge of a freshly ploughed field. The location of the prime Mediolanum matches not only the Greek lines of latitude and longitude, but also, with even greater precision, the solstice line of the Heraklean Way. This impeccable geographical coincidence suggests a radiant invention that would otherwise appear to have existed only in the abstract form of philosophers' diagrams – a system of *klimata* based not only on equinoctial lines running west to east, but also on the diagonal lines of the solstice. Logically, if the latitudinal position of Mediolanum Biturigum was determined by the Heraklean Way half an hour to the south, the route created by the mythical founder of the Celts should be mirrored by another solstice line half an hour to the north.

As though by divine decree, a line projected from Mediolanum Biturigum on the same standardized solstice bearing as the Via Heraklea (p. 14) leads directly to the foot of the *oppidum* on an oval hill in Burgundy where a Celtic princess, the sister-in-love of Pyrenea, took Herakles to her bed. This was Alesia, 'the hearth and metropolis [literally, 'mother-city'] of all Keltika' (fig. 37): 'It has always been held in honour by the Celts . . . and for the entire period from the days of Herakles, this city remained free and was never sacked.' This cosmopolitan place, whose citizens came 'from every tribe', is the likeliest site of the '*locus consecratus*' where, according to Caesar, the Druids assembled 'at a fixed time of the year' to settle legal disputes.* The territory was administered by a small tribe called the Mandubii ('The People of the Horse'). As the tribe that occupied the region of the watershed and guarded the routes that joined the Mediterranean to the British Ocean, the Horse Folk enjoyed the protection of their powerful neighbours. The fabled impregnability of their *oppidum* was presumably a result of the tribe's internationally recognized neutrality, and it was partly for this reason that Alesia would be chosen by

---

* On the location of this 'consecrated place' mentioned by Caesar, see pp. 316–17.

Vercingetorix, leader of the Gauls, as the site of their final battle with the Romans.

From his elliptical path above Middle Earth, the sun god who had loved the princess of Alesia enjoyed a glorious view. Mirroring its southerly counterpart, the northerly line running parallel to the Heraklean Way passes through the tribal capitals of the Agesinates, the Mandubii (Alesia) and the Lingones, through the 'oak' sanctuary of Derventio (Drevant), and the towns that are now Nevers and Semur-en-Auxois (another place said to have been founded by Herakles). Finally, twenty longitudinal minutes to the east of Mediolanum, the solstice line arrives with the accuracy of a Gaulish spear at the main gate of one of the most important Celtic sites in Europe.*

The Fossé des Pandours in the Vosges massif, where the *route nationale* snakes down towards Strasbourg, was once a vast *oppidum* covering a hundred and seventy hectares. It was the capital of the Mediomatrici tribe – the 'Mothers of Middle Earth' – and it guarded the pass now called the Col de Saverne. This is the main gateway from France to Germany and from the Lorraine plateau to the valley of the Rhine. Its Gaulish name is unknown, but, as the pass of the Mediomatrici, it may have had the same maternal connotations as the Matrona. Both passes were portals through which the sun was reborn and poured its light over the lands of the western Celts.

This northerly counterpart of the Matrona Pass, providentially positioned on the northern equivalent of the Heraklean Way, was the physical confirmation of a cherished legend: after completing his journey from the Sacred Promontory to the Alps, Herakles had wandered all over Keltika, bestowing his protection and prestige on the tribes that lived along the great rivers of northern Gaul. And this geo-political symmetry was just one feature of a celestial design that was drawn on the lands that stretched from the Alps to the Atlantic and from the 'outermost islands' to the Pillars of Hercules.

✳

This mapping of a great land mass by solstice lines has a peculiarly Celtic appearance. It adopts the Aristotelian or Pythagorean system of twelve wind directions, but instead of dividing the circle of the

---

* These and other lines are illustrated on the large map on p. 154.

earth into twelve equal segments, the solstice lines follow the bearing of the Via Heraklea. The original path of Herakles hugs the curve of the Mediterranean coast and heads for the rising sun of the summer solstice, following the longest possible line through Keltika from the end of the world at the Sacred Promontory. This was the baseline of the Druidic system, just as a section of its successor, the Via Domitia, was used as a baseline by the makers of the eighteenth-century Cassini map. The tangent of the real and legendary route creates a more subtle harmony than the equal divisions of the Pythagorean compass rose (p. 133), a geometric petalling of the circle which contains a beautiful truth. Just as the arcs and tangents of Celtic art obey the coded laws of nature, the pattern of meridians, parallels and solstice lines expresses one of the fundamental secrets of the sun god.

The standardized tangent of the original Via Heraklea is identical to the tangent of its northerly sister. In modern terms, the angle is 57.53° east of north. Even in short-distance ancient measurements, accuracy to within any fraction of a degree is considered significant, and a survey tolerance of at least one degree is usually applied. The extreme precision of the Celtic lines seems at first impossible in the absence of theodolites and compasses, but to Druids versed in Pythagorean geometry, the solution would have been obvious, and it must often have been applied when they were settling boundary disputes.

Eleven steps to the east and seven steps to the north – or the same number of knots in an Egyptian rope-stretcher's rope – make two sides of a right-angled triangle whose tangent angle is 57.53°. This whole-number ratio – 11:7 – is the simple formula that produces a Heraklean line.

Though it appeared to be a figment of legend, geography and the motion of the sun, there is something almost miraculously convenient about the path of Herakles. For a Druid mathematician, seeking correlations between the ideal world of numbers and the random arrangements of material reality, this ratio of two prime numbers, 7 and 11, would have had a particular significance.

The value of pi (π) – the ratio of a circle's circumference to its diameter – was a Holy Grail of ancient mathematics. The elusive, irrational number required for a precise calculation of the circumference and area of a circle was one of the most mysterious and powerful

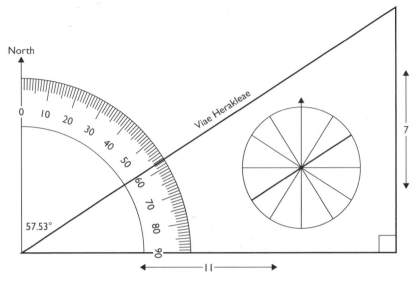

36. The Heraklean ratio

utterances of the gods. The actual value of pi, to four decimal places, is 3.1416. The Egyptian Rhind Papyrus (c. sixteenth century BC) records a calculation that gives a value of 3.1605. The Babylonians and, later, the Roman army used a ratio of 25/8 (3.125) but were often content with a rough-and-ready 3. Some time before 212 BC, using regular 96-sided polygons inscribed inside and outside a circle, Archimedes proved that the value of pi lay between 223/71 and 22/7 (or 3.1408 and 3.1428). This was an impressively close approximation and a notable event in the history of mathematics.

Yet it now appears that the latter figure had been inscribed on the face of the earth more than a century before Archimedes. One of the treasures left behind by Herakles was a pathway based on pi divided by 2, the ratio of half a circle's circumference to its diameter (11/7 equals 1.5714, which is half of 3.1428). As though by the purest chance, the Druidic system contained the closest approximation to pi in the ancient world. Herakles had supplied his Celtic sons and daughters with the geometrical secret of his solar wheel, and once that wheel had been reinvented and set in motion on the earth, there was no end to the wonders it might create.

✿

With the formula in hand, the first obvious question is this: was a third Heraklean diagonal created half an hour of daylight to the north, in Belgic Gaul?* Once again, when the formula is applied, a sequence of significant places appears. A solstice line projected from the point that lies half an hour due north of Châteaumeillant passes through or close by several major *oppida*. Most of these were probably tribal capitals before the Romans: Vannes, which owes its name to the Veneti tribe and which commanded Quiberon Bay; the city of Rennes, which became the Roman capital of the Rediones and was probably the pre-Roman capital, too, since it was there that they minted their coins; le Haut du Château near Argentan, the largest *oppidum* of the Arvii; Pîtres, the likely capital of the Veliocasses, surrounded by a complex of necropolises; and a 'Camp de César' on the banks of the river Samara, in the lands of the Viromandui or whichever tribe inhabited that part of Gaul in the fourth century BC.

Within Gaul, the coincidences are far more striking than any pattern produced by lines drawn at random. At the north-eastern end of the line, near the modern Belgian border, the coherence is less marked: the line passes within one and two thousand metres respectively of Cambrai and Famars, which were towns of the Nervii, before arriving exactly in the centre of the town of Mons, currently thought to have started life as a Roman *castrum*. (See the large map on p. 154.)

At this stage of the reconstruction, there are three Heraklean lines traversing Gaul, with a centre at Mediolanum Biturigum (Châteaumeillant) and another possible focal point at Alesia.

In the Aristotelian or Pythagorean system, the summer solstice lines are mirrored by winter solstice lines (see the diagrams on pp. 132–3). Taking Alesia – the 'hearth and mother-city of all Keltika' – as the point of intersection, the corresponding winter solstice line runs

---

* If so, the line would be slightly closer to Châteaumeillant than Châteaumeillant is to Belvianes: since *klimata* or lines of latitude are based on length of day rather than distance on the ground, the lines become increasingly crowded as they approach the poles, which is one reason why the theory of equidistant Mediolana would never have revealed a pattern.

Except where stated, the assumed tolerance is less than ten seconds of day length (even measuring the length of day to the nearest minute would have been a remarkable achievement). The bearings are precisely accurate. Far less rigorous criteria are normally applied to the tangents of Roman roads and to the orientation of towns and temples.

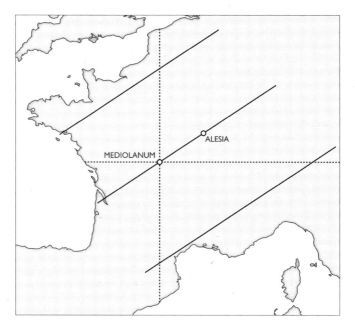

37. Summer solstice lines

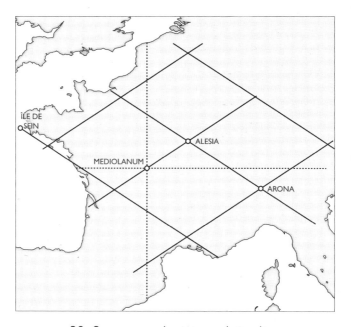

38. Summer and winter solstice lines

north-west to the chief *oppidum* of the Senones (the Camp du Château near Villeneuve-sur-Yonne), to the Mediolanum that became the capital of the Aulerci Eburovices (Évreux) and to the cape beyond the port of Le Havre that was known as Caput Caleti (the headland of the Caleti tribe). In the other direction, it runs by the foot of the greatest of the Helvetii's sanctuaries, on the Mormont hill, and meets the original Heraklean Way at Arona on the banks of Lake Maggiore.

There is a thrilling sense of hidden mechanisms in seeing an abstract design function so efficiently as a guide to early Celtic history. Arona, where two solstice lines intersect, is known to archaeologists as one of the great cultural crossroads of protohistoric Europe. Beyond Arona and the fortress above the lake, the line passes through the village of Golasecca, which has given its name to the Golaseccan culture of the early Iron Age. It served as a bridge between the Etruscans of Italy, the Hallstatt civilization beyond the Alps and the rich tribes of the Marne and the Moselle famed for their chariot-burials. This was the cultural equivalent of Alesia to the north-west, and so it appears on the Heraklean grid. Continuing to the south-east, the line arrives in the centre of the Mediolanum which is now Milan.

To complete the pattern, two further winter solstice lines should run to the north and south of the Alesia line. But even allowing greater margins of error (up to one degree and one minute of daylight), there are few signs of the same coherence. The contrast is revealing: both lines lie outside Celtic and Belgic Gaul. The northerly line, beyond the Rhine, passes close to some of the biggest *oppida* in Europe – Magdalensberg, Biberg and Donnersberg – but with nothing like the same precision. Although the Romans exaggerated the cultural differences of 'Germanic' tribes, many of whom were clearly Celtic, their history is different from that of the Gaulish tribes, and they may never have accepted the jurisdiction of the Druids. (Caesar was told that there were no Druids in Germany.)

The southerly winter solstice line leads to the lands of pre-Celtic, Ligurian tribes and, in the opposite direction, through Aquitanian Gaul to the Armorican Peninsula. It would have crossed at least sixty kilometres of open sea, to the consternation of a long-distance surveyor. In those Atlantic waters sprinkled with islands and charted mentally by generations of sailors, an accurate survey line would not have been impossible. Even without precise measurements, it would have been obvious that the sun of the winter solstice set over the headlands of Brittany and the lands of the Osismi, 'the People at the End of the World'. And perhaps, after all, the measurements were precise: a line projected from the point due south of Alesia on the Via Heraklea reaches the tiny Île de Sein, which, in Breton folk-lore, was the island to which the souls of the dead processed at low tide. In the days of the ancient Celts, it was the home of nine female Druids. The geographer Pomponius Mela described their peculiar convent in the mid-first century AD. Since they lived at the end of a solstice line, it was only fitting that they demanded of those who sought their wisdom a degree of navigational skill:

> Sena, in the British sea, facing the coast of the Osismi, is famous for a Gaulish oracle, tended by nine priestesses who take a vow of perpetual virginity. They are called Gallizenas [probably '*Galli genas*', 'Gaulish maidens'] and are said to possess the singular power of unleashing the fury of the winds and the seas by incantations, of turning themselves into any animal they choose, of curing what is elsewhere considered incurable, and of knowing and predicting the future. But they reveal the future only to navigators, and only if they deliberately set out to consult them.*

✵

The probability that the solstice lines of Gaul would pass through so many important Celtic places by chance is exceedingly remote. (Just for the record: within Gaul, even allowing one thousand metres on either side of each line, the likelihood of only five tribal centres occurring on the lines by chance is 1 in 87 million; the probability for the sites that are bisected by the lines is approximately 0.43^{24}, which is effectively zero.) But probabilities are often false prophets. The reality of historical research is that, if a coincidence is amazing, it probably

---

* Two further coincidences on this Aquitanian and Armorican line, apart from those mentioned later (p. 156): 1. The point south of Alesia from which the line is projected lies just outside the village of Bezouce (Gard), which is thought to have been the capital of a tribe, the Budenicenses, whose existence is attested only by two inscriptions. 2. The point of intersection with the Alesia line lies a few hundred metres from the castle of La Rochefoucauld – a possible *oppidum* site and the home, in the tenth century AD, of a man said to be a son of the Fairy Mélusine, who was also present at Châteaumeillant. (But Mélusine was an exceptionally well-travelled fairy.)

is a coincidence, and when two thousand years have elapsed, material proof is thin on the ground.

The feasibility of the system is not in doubt. Most of the problems confronting long-distance land surveyors who wanted to draw a straight line between two mutually invisible points could be solved by trigonometry. Devices for measuring angles, such as the dioptra-and-protractor, developed in the third century BC, were used primarily by astronomers. Terrestrial surveyors rarely bothered with such refinements. The protohistoric positioning unit was the groma – a vertical stick with horizontal cross-bars and plumb lines which made it possible to draw straight lines and right angles. Little else was needed – just a right-angled triangle with two sides whose lengths were measured in whole numbers. One of the two sides was aligned on the local meridian. Due north could be found by marking the point at which the shadow of the gnomon was shortest, or, more accurately, because of the fuzziness of the shadow, by finding the middle of a line drawn between the shadow points at two symmetrical hours of the day (for example, 10 am and 2 pm). The operation could be repeated *ad libitum* as the survey progressed. Over long distances, errors would be averaged out and cancelled.

Inaccuracies resulting from the application of flat, Euclidean geometry to the spherical earth are inconsequential over a few degrees of latitude. Within the zones occupied by Gaul, Iberia or Britain, the curvature of the earth can be ignored. From Mediolanum Biturigum to the pass of the Mediomatrici – a distance of over four hundred and fifty kilometres – the deviation would be approximately 2.5 metres or the length of three Celtic swords. This is partly why some of the medieval sailors' maps known as portolan charts were so remarkably accurate within areas similar in size to those covered by the Druidic survey.*

There are some spectacular examples of the effectiveness of these ancient measuring tools. In the second and third centuries AD, Roman surveyors laid out the fortified frontier called the Limes Germanicus. For eighty kilometres, it follows a perfectly straight line through the hills of the Swabian-Franconian forest; on a twenty-nine-kilometre stretch south of Walldürn, the directional error is less than two metres.

---

* See the note on portolan charts, p. 303.

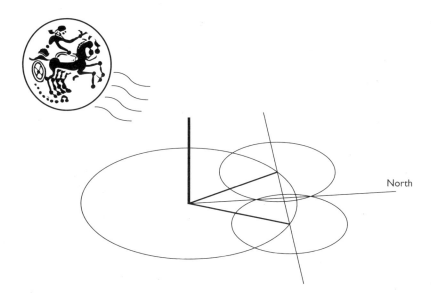

39. Determining true north

In the early eighth century AD, using practically the same technology, but with the help of an astronomer, a Buddhist monk, I-Hsing, surveyed a meridian of two thousand five hundred kilometres from the southern border of Mongolia to the South China Sea, which is the distance that separates the northern tip of the British mainland from the Pillars of Hercules. Some qanats (ancient underground aqueducts) in China and on the Iranian plateau stretched for tens of kilometres and were accurate to within a few centimetres, despite requiring a three-dimensional survey. The Celtic pathways had the advantage of existing only as imaginary lines in two dimensions. Astronomical observations would have made them even more accurate, and perhaps, like medieval determinations of the qibla (the direction in which Muslims face when praying), they inspired further trigono-metrical refinements.

Of course, the fact that the Celts were theoretically capable of plotting long-distance lines does not prove that the lines existed. The forms that proof might take can easily be imagined but not obtained. A Druid of the late Roman empire, seeing his store of knowledge depleted by age, might have inscribed the pattern on a piece of parch-ment, disguising it as a decorative illumination. The design might have been effaced as the work of a pagan or left to moulder in a monastery, its meaning lost for ever – unless some details of the system had been preserved in a verbal map, like the triads that record the origins of the Gauls, the legends that allow the course of the Via Heraklea to be plotted, or the Irish poem in which Cú Chulainn, son of Lugh, recounts his route to the maiden Emer: '[I came] from the Cover of the Sea, over the Great Secret of the Peoples of the Goddess Danu, and the Foam of the Two Steeds of Emain Macha; over the Garden of the Great Queen and the Back of the Great Sow; over the Glen of the Great Dam, between the God and his Druid' . . . But to place most of those sites on a map is a practical impossibility.

✤

Expeditions into the bleary realms of speculation sometimes return empty-handed only to find the answer waiting at home. I had seen the 'map' several times without realizing what it was. It takes the form of written texts that describe one of the great migrations of the Celtic tribes, condensing the events of two centuries into brief but detailed narratives. The basic elements of the tale are known to be true. Between the fourth and second centuries BC, Celtic tribes settled in northern Italy, the Danube Basin, the Balkans and Turkey. It was a long, complex process, and yet, as historians have often observed, it seems to show a common purpose and the hand of a coordinating power.

The historical reality of mass Celtic migrations is well established. In 58 BC, a confederation of Swiss tribes headed by the Helvetii gathered at Genava (Geneva). Their intention was to walk across Gaul and to settle in the lands of the Santones, whose western border was the Atlantic Ocean.* Preparations began two years before the departure. Every acre of arable land was sown with corn, and when the harvests had been gathered in, the migrants' resolve was strengthened by the simple expedient of setting fire to every town, village and private dwelling (twelve towns and four hundred villages, according to Caesar's information).

---

* The date set by the Helvetii for their migration was around the time of the spring equinox, when the sun sets due west – the direction in which they intended to travel. Heading west from their assembly point, Geneva, they would indeed have reached the lands of the Santones, just to the north of La Rochelle.

Even Caesar was impressed by the Helvetii's logistical competence: 'Writing tablets were found in the Helvetian camp on which lists had been drawn up in Greek characters. They contained the names of all the migrants, divided into separate categories: those able to bear arms, boys, old men and women.' He quoted the tablets in the first book of his *Commentaries on the Gallic War*:

Tribe	Heads
Helvetii	263,000
Tulingi	36,000
Latobrigi	14,000
Rauraci	23,000
Boii	32,000
Total	368,000

of whom 92,000 *are able to bear arms*

Whatever the reason for the transplantation of 368,000 people from the Swiss plateau to the Atlantic coast – depleted farmland, a sense of stagnation in the military elite or a reversion to the old nomadic ways – these mass-migrations are a cultural trait of Celtic societies. Belgic tribes, who had come from the east, settled in southern Britain at a time when they were prospering in Gaul. Some of the Parisii left the Seine for the Humber and founded a colony in Yorkshire. Many centuries later, most of the Scots who left their homeland for the New World were not victims of the Highland Clearances; they were Lowlanders who had made enough money in the booming industrial economy to become mobile and ambitious.

The greatest of these migrations was the Gaulish diaspora instigated by the Bituriges. Six ancient authors mention it – Livy, Polybius, Diodorus, Pliny, Plutarch and Justinus. Livy's is the most detailed account. His source was certainly Celtic, and he must have recognized the legend as a verbal map, but without perceiving its underlying logic.

We have received the following account concerning the Gauls' passage into Italy. It was in the days when Tarquinius Priscus was king of Rome. The Bituriges were the supreme power among the Celts, who form one third of Gaul, and it was always they who gave the Celts their king.

At the time in question (the early fourth century BC),* the king of the Celts was a 'brave and wealthy' man called Ambigatus. The name appears to mean 'he who fights on both sides' or 'the two-handed warrior'. Under his rule, Gaul had prospered. The harvests had been copious, the tribes had multiplied, and, now that his hair was turning white, King Ambigatus had to face the consequences of his success: Gaul was bursting at the seams. 'It seemed scarcely possible to govern such a multitude of people.'

Following Celtic tradition, in which property passed through the female line, Ambigatus sent for his sister's two sons, both energetic and enterprising young men. One was Bellovesus ('worthy of power'), the other Segovesus ('worthy of victory'). To each prince, the Druids were to indicate a direction, and the tribes, accompanied by an army large enough to ensure their safety, would follow the paths assigned to them by the gods. Where the augural ceremony took place, Livy does not say. The most likely site of a Biturigan palace is Avaricum (Bourges), but in the solemn circumstances, Mediolanum Biturigum (Châteaumeillant) would have been the most appropriate location: just as the Greeks mapped the home country onto the colonized territory, the first city founded by Bellovesus in the new land would be called 'Mediolanum'.

The Druids obtained the judgement of the gods. Segovesus was pointed in the direction of the Hercynian Forest, beyond which lay the windy plains of central Europe. His brother Bellovesus was given 'a considerably more pleasant route': he was to lead his people into Italy. If Plutarch's version can be believed, the followers of Bellovesus could hardly wait to expatriate themselves: they had tasted Italian wine, 'and were so enchanted with this new pleasure that they snatched up their arms, and, taking their families along with them, marched to the Alps'.

At this point, Segovesus disappears from the tale. His contingent of men, women and children set off for the boundless forest of oak in which we shall try to find them later on. Meanwhile, the more

---

* Tarquinius Priscus was on the throne at the time when Massalia was founded (c. 600 BC), but the legend conflates different periods. The Etruscan city of Melpum, on the site of the future Mediolanum (Milan), was destroyed in 396 BC, and the Celts entered Rome in 387 BC. The Biturigan hegemony probably dates from the fourth century BC.

fortunate Bellovesus gathered together the surplus population of seven tribes in what was evidently an expedition on the scale of the Helvetian migration witnessed by Caesar.

The first group was made up of migrants from the following tribes: the Bituriges, the Arverni, the Senones, the Aedui, the Ambarri, the Carnutes and the Aulerci. They headed off in the auspicious direction and came to the lands of the Tricastini. The Tricastini lived in the Rhone Valley to the north of Arausio (Orange), in a region where, a few centuries later, the migrants would have been able to satisfy their wine-lust to their hearts' content. The letters 'TRIC RED',* etched in the stone of the Roman cadastral map of Orange, show that the Tricastini's territory once extended from the Rhone to the limestone bluffs of the Dentelles de Montmirail.

There, the followers of Bellovesus looked to the east and beheld a daunting obstacle: 'Beyond stretched the barrier of the Alps.' In those days, according to the tale, only Herakles had found a way through the Alps, and so they stood, 'fenced in, as it were, by high mountains, looking everywhere for a path by which to transcend those peaks that were joined to the sky and so to enter a different sphere of the earth' ('*in alium orbem terrarum*').

Described in these cosmic terms, the migration was a pilgrimage with no return, a mass enactment of the human journey from this world to the next. The Alps were to the Celts what the Red Sea was to the tribes of Israel. The answer came in the form of what the legend calls a sacred duty. Word reached the migrants that Greeks from Phocaea had landed at Massalia and were being attacked by local tribes called the Salyi. Seeing this as a sign of their own destiny, they went to the aid of the colonists and 'enabled them to fortify the site where they had first landed'.

Having fulfilled their religious obligation, and reaffirmed their affinity with the Hellenic world, the Bituriges and their allies crossed the Alps by the pass of the Taurini (the Matrona) and the valley of the river Duria. Near the river Ticinus, they defeated the Tuscans and then settled in a country that belonged to a people called the Insubres. According to Livy, 'Insubria' was the name of a territory in

---

* '*Tricastinis redditi*': (lands) restored to the Tricastini.

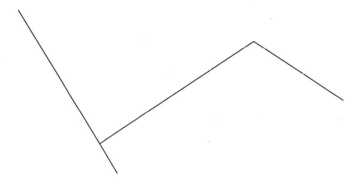

40. The pattern of migration

the lands of the Aedui, which seemed a good omen, 'and so the city they founded there was called Mediolanum' (Milan).*

Livy goes on to describe the colonization of northern Italy by all the other Gaulish tribes that followed in the wheel-tracks of the Bituriges and their compatriots. First, by the same Alpine pass, came the Cenomani, then the Libui and the Saluvii. The next group, composed of Boii and Lingones, took a slightly different route, crossing the Alps by the Poenina (the Great St Bernard). Last of all came the Senones – presumably another contingent of the tribe that had joined the initial migration. Polybius gives a similar list, but he describes the Insubres as settlers rather than as the original inhabitants of Milan.

Most of this is historically true. North-eastern Italy was Celtic from the early fourth century until the Roman victory of 191 BC. Many settlements that became Roman towns were founded by Celts. Senigallia, on the Adriatic coast, preserves the name of the Senones, who also gave their name to Sens. Mezzomerico was once Medio-madrigo (from the Mothers of Middle Earth). Bologna, Brescia, Ivrea, Milan and Turin are all Celtic names. The Massalian episode prob-ably dates from the same period. A century or so after the foundation of Massalia, when new trade routes were opening up along the Rhone, Massalian merchants would have sought the protection of tribes to the north. The most powerful trading port on the Gaulish Mediterranean would certainly have had to reckon with 'the supreme power in Gaul'.

---

* For these and the following sites, see the large map on p. 154.

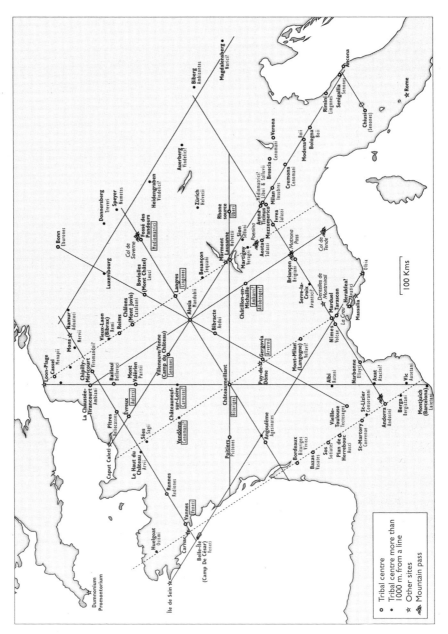

Legend (map):
- ○ Tribal centre
- ● Tribal centre more than 1000 m. from a line
- ★ Other sites
- Mountain pass

100 Kms

Map labels (tribal centres and sites):

Ancona *Nericii?*
Rome ★
Magdalensberg *Norici?*
Biberg *Ambisontes*
Senigallia *Senones*
Rimini *Lingones*
Chiusi *(Senones)*
Boii
Verona
Modena *Boii*
Bologna *Cenomani*
Cremona *Cenomani*
Brescia *Cenomani*
Libui & Sallumi
Milan *Insubres*
Mediomatrici?
Arona
Ticinus
Mezzomerico?
Ivrea *Salassi*
Aosta *Salassi*
Sion *Seduni*
Poenino
Martigny *Veragri*
Matrona Pass
Col de Tende
Olbia
Briançon *Brigiani*
Dentelles de Montmirail
Serre-la-Croix *Avantici?*
Marduel
Tarascon *Avatici*
Heraklea?
La Croix
Massalia
Nîmes *Volcae*
Auerberg *Vindelici?*
Speyer *Nemetes*
Donnersberg *Treveri*
Heidengraben *Vindelici?*
Zürich *Helvetii*
Rhone source *Uberi*
Heidenmauer
Fossé des Pandours *Mediomatrici*
Bonn *Eburones*
Luxembourg
Col de Saverne
Bovielles (Mont Châtel) *Leuci*
Langres *Lingones*
Besançon *Sequani*
Normont
Lausanne *Helvetii*
Alesia *Mandubii*
Bibracte *Aedui*
Châtillon-en-Michaille *Ambarri?*
Chalons (Mont Lewis) *Catalauni*
Reims
Vieux-Laon (Bibrax?) *Remi*
Namur *Aduatuci*
Mons *Nervii*
Cassel *Menapii*
Loon-Plage *Menapii*
Chipilly-Méricourt *Viromandui?*
Bailleul *Bellovaci*
Châlons *Ambiani*
La Chaussée-Tirancourt
Mont Valérien *Parisii*
Villeneuve/Yonne (Camp du Château) *Senones*
Gergovia *Arverni*
Puy-de-Dôme
Mont-Milan (Langogne?) *Vellavi?*
Albi *Rutteni*
Narbonne *Elisyces*
Axat *Atacini?*
Vic *Ausetani*
Bourges *Bituriges*
Châteaumeillant
Evreux *Aulerci*
Sées *Sagii*
Châteauneuf-sur-Loire *Carnutes*
Vendôme *Cenomani*
Pîtres *Veliocasses*
Angoulême *Agesinates*
Poitiers *Pictones*
Bordeaux *Bituriges Vivisci*
Sos *Soziates*
Bazas *Vasates*
Plan de Herrebouc *Ausci*
Vielle-Toulouse *Tectosages*
St-Martory *Convenae*
St-Lizier *Consoranni*
Berga *Bergistani*
Andorra *Andosini*
Montjuïch (Barcelona) *Laietani*
Le Haut du Château *Arvii*
Rennes *Redones*
Vannes *Veneti*
Carnac
Belle-Île (Camp de César) *Veneti*
Huelgoat *Osismi*
Caput Caleti
Île de Sein
Dumnonium Promontorium

41. Tribal centres and the migration to Italy

The names in boxes are those of tribes who migrated to Italy. A solar line – sometimes more than one – passes directly through a Gaulish tribal centre in twenty-five cases and within 1000 metres of the site's perimeter in twelve further cases (on average, 750 metres). In Italy, beyond Milan, the system suggests a general direction of migration rather than an exact trajectory.

The legend is entirely plausible, except in one respect: the god-given itinerary looks very odd indeed. Unless Bellovesus and his followers mistook the lacy ridge of the Dentelles de Montmirail for a range of mountains, the territory of the Tricastini is a strange place from which to contemplate the distant Alps. Either they ignored the direction assigned to them by the Druids, or the gods' instructions were exceedingly complicated: south-south-east, a deviation towards Massalia, then north-east, and finally south-east to New Mediolanum (fig. 40).

This all sounds like a *post facto* justification of military conquest, a boastful bardic tale designed to make the events fit a spurious divine plan. Yet Livy, like most ancient historians, accepted the divinatory basis of the expedition. Justinus, too, in describing the Celtic colonization of Italy and later migrations to the east, said – presuming that

---

Several minor *oppida* on the lines have been omitted (e.g. Les Baux-de-Provence, Mondeville by Caen, Malaucène, Vézénobres, etc.), as have tribes whose names or capitals are unknown (e.g. the Budenicenses and the inhabitants of Marduel and Tarusco). Some tribes or tribal names may differ from those of the fourth century BC.

Speculative journeys along the lines will reveal many other likely sites for which there is, at the time of writing, insufficient archaeological evidence (e.g. Dôle, Jouarre, Luxembourg, Montpellier, Najac, Treviso).

Bearings – taken where possible from the nodal points of Mediolanum Biturigum and Alesia – are those provided by the tangent ratio of 11:7 (57.53°, 122.47°, etc.), with the exception of the Alesia–Bibracte–Gergovia line, which, for geographical reasons, is 28.2° from north rather than 28.8° (see pp. 197–8).

The creation of a settlement obviously depended in part on topography, and so some leeway was presumably allowed. With a slightly broader margin, several more tribes could join the total of thirty-seven. Major *oppida* occurring more than 1000 metres from a line are indicated on the map: Arvii (1.5 km), Cenomani (1.5), Remi (at Bibrax) (1.7), Bergistani (2.4), Laietani (2.4), Atacini (3.1), Seduni (3.5), Ruteni (3.6), Consoranni (4.0), Atrebates (4.1), Morini (4.1), Nervii (4.1), Sagii (4.4), Ausetani (4.8), Osismi (4.8), Sequani (5.0), Veragri (5.0), Aduatuci (5.3). In retracing ancient surveys, especially over such long distances, common sense calls for certain adjustments. Future explorers of the system should feel free to experiment.

Druids used the same method as Roman augurs – that the Celts 'penetrated into the remotest parts of Illyricum under the direction of a flight of birds, for the Gauls are skilled in augury beyond other nations'.

To a Druid, this hieroglyphic would have had the luminous logic of a work of art. What Livy and the other historians were unwittingly describing was a solar expedition reminiscent of Hannibal's march through Iberia and Gaul. With the Druidic map as a guide, we can now retrace the exact route of the Celtic migration led by Bellovesus. The bisecting solstice line from Mediolanum Biturigum (the dotted line on fig. 41) leads past the great temple of Lugh on the Puy de Dôme (pp. 208–9) and across the stony plain of the Crau, where the enemies of Herakles were pelted with boulders from the sky. It ends at the bay of Massalia and the *oppida* by the inland sea of Mastromela which is now the Étang de Berre. (One of those *oppida*, Saint-Blaise, is considered the likeliest location of the lost city of Heraklea near the mouth of the Rhone, which had disappeared by the time Pliny heard of it in the first century AD.) (See the map on p. 154.)

The Mediolanum line meets the Aquitanian–Armorican line (p. 146) at a point marked on ancient itineraries as 'Trajectus Rhodani'. Here, at the meeting of roads from Mastromela and the Matrona, was one of the major crossings of the Rhone, where Tarusco (Tarascon) looks over to the *oppidum* of Ugernum (Beaucaire). In the Middle Ages, Beaucaire was the site of the biggest international fair in Europe, and it was already a trading hub in the fifth century BC, when wine amphorae were arriving from Massalia and Greece. Herakles himself had been there: 'Tarusco' recalls the name of the monster Tauriscus who, according to the Druids' account of Gaulish origins, was defeated by Herakles on his march through Keltika. The line then continues to the bay of Olbia (Hyères), a trading port founded by Massaliots in the fourth century BC.

Here again, we pick up the trail of the migrants. Olbia is mentioned in a different context by Strabo as one of four Massaliot cities that were 'fortified against the tribe of the Sallyes and the Ligures who live in the Alps'. The Sallyes are the same as the Salyi, the troublesome tribe that was defeated by the followers of Bellovesus when they came to the aid of the Greek colonists. Olbia was closely linked with a native *oppidum* on the neighbouring hill, and the excavator of Olbia suggests that in defending themselves against the attacks of Ligurians, the Massaliots cooperated with Celtic tribes who had settled on the coast.

It now appears that when the Bituriges and their compatriots contemplated the distant Alps from the territory of the Tricastini, they were looking through the eyes of the sun god. On their solar path to the lands of the Salyi and the Massaliots, they would have crossed the river Gard just downstream of the ford where the Roman aqueduct, the Pont-du-Gard, still stands. At that exact spot, they found themselves for the first time on the Via Heraklea. The point of intersection is marked by the *oppidum* of an unknown tribe. Its crumbling masonry, on the Marduel hill opposite Remoulins, is the oldest known urban enclosure in eastern Languedoc (c. 525 BC). This was one of the three most important towns of the region. It stood at the meeting of two major roads and guarded the ford.

Fording the river, the travellers turned onto the Via Heraklea and climbed towards the limestone hills. The Heraklean line passes three small *oppida** and then the Dentelles de Montmirail as it heads for the Alps. Since the only way through the mountains was the col forged by Herakles, the migrants would naturally have taken his solstice route across 'the pass of the Taurini'. This is the pass more commonly known as the Matrona or Montgenèvre. After entering Italy through this Heraklean gateway, they would have followed the river Duria (the Dora), which flows from the Matrona and alongside the Heraklean line to Arona, the cultural crossroads of Iron Age Gaul, Switzerland and Italy (p. 145).

Picking up the winter solstice line from Alesia, they then travelled south-east to the point at which the river Ticinus (the Ticino) leaves Lake Maggiore. Somewhere near that river (the site is unspecified), the migrants defeated the Tuscans. The battle is thought to have taken place in the river basin between Castelletto sopra Ticino and Golasecca. Both places stand on the solstice line.

The journey of the first contingent of pioneers is almost over: the Alesia line – a long cord attached to the mother-city of the Celts –

---

* Les Courens (Beaumes-de-Venise), Saint-Christophe (Lafare), le Clairier (Malaucène).

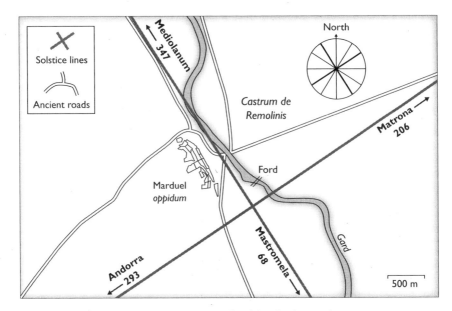

42. Solstice lines at the Marduel *oppidum*
Distances from the intersection are given in kilometres.

at last leads directly to the Mediolanum which is now the city of Milan.

A few weeks or several years later, the reliability of the system having been tested and proved, other tribes follow the same Druidic route-map, pushing further into north-eastern Italy and founding Celtic towns along the route of what became the Via Aemilia. 'South of the Padus, in the Apennine district, beginning from the west, the Ananes [an unknown tribe] and then the Boii settled. Next to them, on the coast of the Adriatic, the Lingones, and south of them, still on the sea-coast, the Senones' (Polybius). The Libui and the Saluvii settle in the vicinity of the Ticinus near the site of the battle (Livy).

The Lingones, whose Gaulish capital stands on the line from Alesia, seem to have been offered a shortcut by the Druid augurs. The account recorded by Livy says that the Lingones crossed the Alps by the Poenina, which is now the Great St Bernard. Since the Poenina was impassable for wheeled vehicles (according to Strabo), one of Livy's editors suggests that this was a mistake for the Matrona, but the map of Middle Earth shows that a crossing by the Great St Bernard, though arduous for humans, would have been perfectly acceptable to the gods: for the Lingones, as for the Remi and the Catalauni, the most direct solar route to the Heraklean Way passes over the Great St Bernard.

The final episode of the great migration, reported by Diodorus, involved the Senones, who came from the area of Sens, a hundred kilometres south of Paris. For some reason, the Senones had been assigned the territory furthest from the Alps. Coming as they did from the chillier part of Burgundy, they found the Adriatic intolerable: 'Because the region was scorching hot, they were distressed and eager to move, and so they armed their younger men and sent them out to seek a land where they might settle.' Several thousand young Senonians then marched off to Clusium (Chiusi).

Meteorologically, it was a bizarre choice by the sweltering Senones: Clusium lies more than half a degree of latitude to the south, but it also lies on a solstice line that reaches the coast directly between the two Senonian settlements of Ancona and Senigallia. From Clusium, the young Senones set off for Rome.

This took place in 387 BC, about ten years after the likely date of departure from Mediolanum Biturigum. Perhaps the silent procession of Celtic warriors into Rome, along the streets lined with old bearded noblemen, had been part of the original plan, just as Delphi was the target of one of the later groups (pp. 171–3). For the Romans, the invasion was a punitive raid provoked by the killing of a Gaulish chieftain at Clusium by a Roman ambassador. But from the vantage-point of the Druids and the sun god, Rome was a logical terminus of the labyrinthine route. Diviciacus may have known this when he stayed there with Cicero in 63 BC: the winter solstice line from Mediolanum Biturigum, with an imperceptible variation of eight-hundredths of a degree or $1/4500$ of a circle, leads to the Palatine Hill. To be absolutely precise, it leads to the site of the future Vatican City.

✻

The precision of the Druidic system is quite amazing. The capitals of the tribes that took part in the great migration appear as though by magic on the grid of solstice lines: the Aedui, the Arverni, the Aulerci, the Bituriges (represented by Mediolanum Biturigum), the Lingones and the Senones. Not all the pre-Roman capitals are known, but the *oppidum* of Vindocinum (Vendôme) on the Mediolanum

Biturigum line and the *oppidum*-like site of Châteauneuf-sur-Loire on the meridian might now be considered possible early tribal centres of the Cenomani and the Carnutes.*

The weirdly accurate projection of the upper world onto Middle Earth confirms what several historians have suspected: that many tribes other than those mentioned by Livy and Polybius took part in the migration. No fewer than thirty-seven tribal centres occur on the lines, which implies a coordination of the population on a huge scale. Some of those tribes may have joined their neighbours or assisted the migrants who passed through their territories. The Ambiani or their fourth-century predecessors, for instance – whom Livy may have confused with the Ambarri – clearly belong to the same network: the bisecting solstice line from Alesia passes within a few metres of the thatched Gaulish house at Parc Samara and leads exactly to the western entrance of the *oppidum*.

This beautifully choreographed diaspora is a stunning example of the Druids' belief in 'the power and majesty of the immortal gods' (p. 131). First came the myth, and then, by a deliberate process of religious and scientific observance, the reality. It proves that the migration legend was not a retrospective fantasy, a heroic tale told after the event. The legend was a faithful record of the original plan. This is not such an unusual pattern of collective behaviour: wars and migrations are often inspired by myths and national legends. But the sheer scope and accuracy of the Celtic enterprise are unparalleled.

Until now, it has been impossible to show exactly how divinatory calculations determined historical events. The Druids who directed the tribes were not fraudulent conjurers who made a nation's destiny depend on the twitch of an entrail or the parabola of a bird's flight. They were the coordinators of an immense work of art that was one of the most ingenious and effective federal systems ever devised. It

---

* Five other tribes can be added to the partial lists supplied by Livy. The Salassi from Aosta settled at Eporedia (Ivrea). The Insubres or Insubri are named as settlers by Polybius: the first part of 'Insubri' means 'path' or 'direction'; the second suggests an offshoot of the Uberi who lived at the source of the Rhone and the Pillar of the Sun on the equinoctial line from Mediolanum Biturigum. The Mediomatrici gave their name to Mezzomerico. The Allobroges are mentioned in this connection by Geoffrey of Monmouth. The Veneti were said by Claudius to have invaded Rome with the Insubres.

gave the tribes a view of Middle Earth that had once been the prerogative of the gods and that would not be seen again by earth-bound
mortals until the cartographic marvels of the Renaissance.

The standing stones of 'Celtic' Brittany, which belong to a much
earlier civilization, represent a more localized form of organization.
At Carnac, prehistoric menhirs march towards the solstice sun in
approximately aligned avenues hundreds of metres long. But the
Druidic alignments were something quite different from those lumber-
ing, labour-intensive sun-paths. Though some sections of the lines,
like parts of the Via Heraklea, would eventually be materialized as
roads (p. 205), they existed primarily as intellectual abstractions,
created by mind instead of muscle. They were the avenues and henges
of a new age in which science and technology were the means of
discovering the designs of the living gods.

'*Hi terrae mundique magnitudinem et formam, motus caeli ac siderum
et quid dii velint, scire profitentur.*'* Under the scientific direction of
the Druids, history became the visible expression of the gods' will.
But the will of the gods is not identical with the desires of human
beings. The coordinated colonization of northern Italy and the capture of Rome – the city that lay at the end of the winter solstice line
from Mediolanum Biturigum – were the catalysts that stimulated the
expansion of a Roman empire. Perhaps the Druid augurs knew that,
some time in the distant future, Alesia the mother-city would be the
site of a great battle. They believed that one day, the sky would fall
and the earth be destroyed by fire and water. When they brought the
heavens down to earth, they made the Celts the servants of the gods
and the agents of their own destruction.

---

* 'They profess to know the size and shape of the earth and the universe, the motion
of the sky and the stars, and what the gods want' (p. 131).

10

The Forest and Beyond

We left Segovesus and his band of migrants marching glumly towards the enormous Hercynian Forest. While the tribes led by his brother Bellovesus were basking in the vineyards of northern Italy, a more obscure but even grander odyssey was under way. It covered such a vast area that the Druidic calculations were inevitably less precise. Yet the trajectories of this other mass migration show the same adherence to the sun's course, even two hours of daylight east of Mediolanum Biturigum, to the centre of the classical world and the shores of another continent.

The name of the Hercynian Forest, first recorded by Aristotle in 350 BC, is Celtic – 'Ercunia', or, in the very old days, before the language had changed, 'Perkwunia', meaning 'oak'. The other word for 'oak' was '*dru-*', as in 'Druid'. Ancient Celtic seems not to have distinguished different species of *quercus*, and so the two words must have referred to the tree in different guises. The Ercunian was the wild, uncultivated oak, the centenarian giant that had never spread its lattice shade in a Druid's grove and whose acorns fed animals that had never seen a human being. Its domain was larger than an empire. The breadth of the forest, Caesar learned, was nine days for someone travelling without baggage, but its length was a matter of conjecture – sixty days, according to Pomponius Mela, more if Caesar's information was correct. The forest began in the lands of the Nemetes, the Helvetii and the Rauraci who lived along the Rhine. Some people from that part of Germania had trekked through the tangled gloom for sixty days but had never reached the other side, nor even found a creature who could tell them where it ended.

'Impervious to the passage of time', the Hercynian Forest was thought to be as old as the world itself. Remnants of what was once the largest natural feature in Europe survive in patches of woodland and forest. The town of Pforzheim, which is now the northern gateway to the Black Forest, was once Porta Hercyniae. Some of the migrants led by Segovesus would have passed through the Bavarian or Bohemian Forest which marks the borders of Germany, Austria and the Czech Republic. The names, 'Bavaria' and 'Bohemia', are mementos of the restless Boii tribe, who took part in so many Celtic migrations that no one knew for sure – perhaps not even the Boii themselves – where their homeland had been.

The forest followed the north bank of the Danube, and then, in the lands of the Dacians, near the western edge of the Carpathian mountains, it 'turned left', according to Caesar's information, away from the river. It stretched so far that it '[touched] the *fines* ['territories' or 'borders'] of a great many nations'. (The word '*fines*' suggests that, like other forests, it served as a buffer between tribal groups.) There is only one other shred of evidence: a tribe that settled near the bend of the Danube in the Roman province of Pannonia (western Hungary) was called the Hercuniates. The 'Folk of the Hercynian Forest' are described by Pliny and Ptolemy as a '*civitas peregrina*', a wandering tribe that had come from foreign parts. Three sites have been identified as *oppida* of the Hercuniates in the region of Lake Balaton, but it would be as hard to retrace their footsteps through the forest as it is for an archaeologist to distinguish an Iron Age settlement from mounds raised by fallen trees and rocks assembled by their clawing roots.

Into this sunless expanse the Druids sent Segovesus and his followers, condemning them and their descendants to a diet of berries and beer. Sailors adrift on the ocean are surrounded by clues to their whereabouts; a traveller in a forest the size of half a world is confined to small dark spaces that endlessly recur like the scene of a nightmare. The guiding stars are eclipsed by branches and blurred by the breath of the forest. A stranger in Hercynia could navigate only by the soft cloak of mosses on the north face of oak trunks and by the diffuse glow of the dawn. Sometimes, there was a hill from which to take a sighting, or a moonlit clearing where sawn trunks showed where hunters had tried to catch the jointless elk. According to Caesar, there were 'vague and secret paths' through the forest, but Pomponius Mela described it as '*invia*' ('trackless'). Beyond the Rhine, the solar route-map seems to be of little help, though it is hard to believe that the

Biturigan Druids sent a royal prince and thousands of migrants blundering off into totally uncharted territory.

From Mediolanum Biturigum, the solar direction assigned to Segovesus would have taken him to the east-north-east. Recounting the same legend, Plutarch says that a group consisting of 'many myriads of warriors and a still greater number of women and children' 'crossed the Rhipaean mountains, streamed off towards the Northern Ocean, and occupied the remotest parts of Europe'. The mythical Rhipaean range lay somewhere to the north in whichever inhospitable clime ancient writers chose to place it. The crucial detail is that Segovesus, like his brother, crossed a range of mountains. The east-north-easterly solstice line from Mediolanum would have taken him to Alesia and across the Vosges by the pass of the Mediomatrici, mirroring Bellovesus's crossing of the Matrona. From there, it was a short distance to the land of the Nemetes ('The People of the Sky Sanctuary'), who, in Caesar's day, lived on the western edge of the forest. (These routes are shown in fig. 43.)

The Mediolanum–Alesia solstice line passes within five kilometres of Speyer (the Roman Noviomagus Nemetum). Crossing the Rhine, the migrants would then have entered the Odenwald south of Heidelberg. Unless they journeyed on to the north and vanished into parts of Europe that were never Celtic, they would have turned to face the rising sun of the winter solstice: the line that runs exactly one hour of daylight to the north of the Alesia line passes through the Bohemian Forest. After an age that was only a short time in legend and the life of the forest, a group of migrants led by a descendant of Segovesus arrived at the place which is now the capital of Slovakia. In the second century BC, on the hill where Bratislava Castle looks down on the Danube, an *oppidum* was built by the wandering tribe of Boii who had already colonized part of northern Italy.

This far to the east, where the Danube begins to leave the trackless forest for the Great Hungarian Plain, there is only the faintest hope of finding any solar evidence of tribal movements. The earlier system of Mediolana, from which the Druidic system evolved, was almost exclusively Gaulish. Before the period of expansion, 'Middle Earth' may have been conceived of as the part of the European isthmus bounded by the Alps, the Pyrenees, the Mediterranean and the Atlantic. This was the Gaulish homeland of well-ordered rivers and mountains which Strabo described in a passage that seems to echo a lost Celtic legend: 'The harmonious arrangement of the country appears to offer evidence of the workings of Providence, since the regions are laid out, not haphazardly, but as though in accordance with some calculated plan.' Beyond Gaul, there are just a few outlying Mediolana, some separated from the others by hundreds of kilometres. The northernmost of these latter-day Mediolana is Metelen near the Dutch-German border. In all of Europe east of Switzerland, only two Mediolana are known: the town of Wolkersdorf north of Vienna, and a staging post near Ruse in Bulgaria on the Romanian border. To find traces of the Celtic network of 'sacred centres' in the Hercynian Forest and beyond is surprising. To find three of those rare sites on the same Hercynian trajectory is entirely unexpected.*

The forest tribes, Caesar learned, 'know nothing of road measurements'. But measurement on the ground would have been useless in a trackless forest, and even if someone had spent sixty days walking through Hercynia, journey times over natural terrain were a crude gauge of distance. The only practical way for Celtic tribes who lived on either side of the forest to obtain some measure of its expanse was geodetic. Bratislava lies sixty longitudinal minutes east of Mediolanum Biturigum; nine latitudinal minutes is about one hundred kilometres, which might have been the breadth of the forest at its narrowest point. (It seems astonishingly appropriate that the reported dimensions of the forest – nine days wide and sixty days long – correspond so closely to the geodetic measurements: Roman writers may have understood these numbers to refer to days of human travel rather than to the timetable of a sun-chariot.) By whichever paths they reached their destination, the Celts who settled on the hill which is now a part of Budapest had the means of knowing that the length of their longest day was practically the same as at Alesia, and that their *oppidum* lay on a solstice line from Bratislava and the Bohemian Forest.

✿

* The bearing from Metelen to Wolkersdorf is within 0.15° of the Gaulish standard (122.32°). The bearing from Wolkersdorf to Ruse, despite the great distance, is accurate to within one point of a 128-point compass (124.74°). Medieval portolan charts used a 32-point compass.

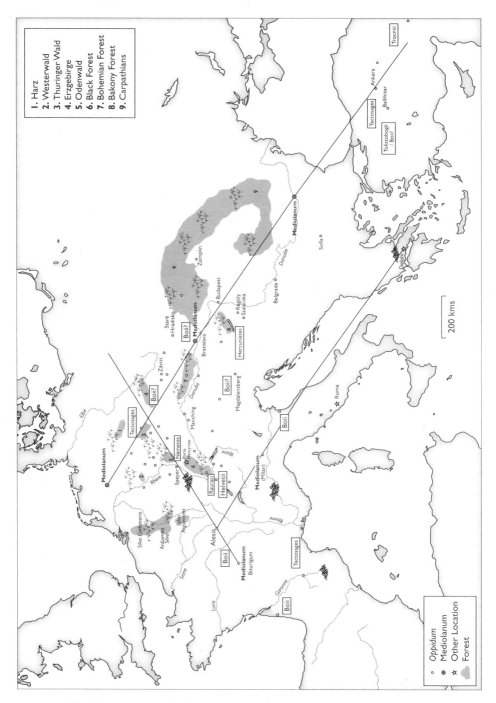

43. *Oppida* east of Gaul and remnants of the Hercynian Forest
The Hercuniates might have reached their new home (the *oppida* around Lake
Balaton) by travelling due east along the equinoctial line from Mediolanum Biturigum,
via the capital of the Helvetii and the sources of the Rhone and the Rhine.

The leaves and branches that fall in a broadleaf wood quickly form a thick blanket under which forest creatures sleep through the winter and which gradually turns into the heavy earth of a sepulture from which nothing will awake. A few isolated coordinates are of little more value than coins that have worn smooth. Almost everything to do with the Hercynian Forest is either impenetrable or implausible – the giant oaks engaged in wrestling contests that lasted centuries; the bovine *urus*, slightly smaller than an elephant, that raced through the trees at tremendous speed; the Hercynian bird whose feathers glowed in the night like fires. The Mediolana that seem to mark a migration route through the forest may each have been part of a local system, or they may simply have been named after places in tales that were told about the homeland in the west. The names of the trans-sylvanian Celtic tribes were eventually recorded when the lands they had colonized became the Roman provinces of Noricum, Pannonia, Dacia, Moesia and Galatia, but the tribes had moved so frequently and so far, intermarrying, dying out and re-emigrating, that sometimes even the direction of the original migration is in doubt.

The history of the Celtic diaspora of the fourth to second centuries BC is a long and twisted tale of invasions and expulsions, settlements and extinctions. It should make even the most ardent Celtic supremacist despair of ever identifying any fundamental ethnic trait of *Homo celticus*. Some tribes adopted local customs so completely that by the time they became known to the Romans, their only clearly Celtic feature was their name. Mercenaries went to work in distant lands accompanied by their wives and children. The Galatians of Asia Minor – the 'foolish' recreants of St Paul's epistle – owed their name to Celtic immigrants from Gaul. Several hundred of their finest warriors served as Cleopatra's bodyguard. Later, the same elite troops were employed by Herod the Great. The infant who was to become King of the Jews might have been beheaded in Bethlehem by a Celtic sword.

Woven in amongst these grand and ragged tales of tribes ranging over a continent are all the microscopic mysteries of trade, the interminable journeys of trinkets and treasures carried by merchants or passed from hand to hand, stolen, sold or copied. Every museum that has a Celtic collection is a trove of insoluble enigmas. How the silver Gundestrup Cauldron ended up in a Danish peat bog somewhere

44. Horses depicted on Celtic coins and their approximate
geographical origins
Most of these coins date from the first century BC.

near the northern Pillars of Hercules, no one knows. (The metalwork suggests that it was manufactured in the region of Bulgaria, but was it commissioned by natives of the 'outermost islands' or brought back from the east by the 'Germanic' tribes, the Cimbri and Teutones, whose kings had Celtic names?) Whole chapters of a civilization's history lie undeciphered in cabinets and coin drawers. As they moved across the Continent like a herd of sacred transhumant animals, the sun-horses of Celtic coins morphed and evolved. If a historian of ancient art could devise an equation of shapes and curves and zoo-morphic astronomy, it might be possible to retrace the movements and filiations of the tribes, and to recover some of the myths that are encoded in those quaint and lovely creatures.

Just as the flocks of birds passing over the ocean of trees followed their own unvarying solar routes, a general trend is perceptible in the wanderings of Celtic migrants. Young men went east in search of treasure and adventure – some to the north-east, many more to the south-east. With the late exception of the Helvetii's foiled migration (pp. 149–50), westward movements were either a return to the home-land or the result of disaster: the Celts who had come to Gaul from beyond the Rhine, according to the Druids, had been 'driven from their homes by frequent wars and inundations of the fiery seas'. Only the defeated and the exiled walked towards the dying sun with their shadows tarrying behind. There is no good evidence that the west-ernmost regions by the Atlantic were invaded and settled by Gaulish tribes in this period, and the question to be asked about the Celtic inhabitants of Ireland and the Iberian Peninsula is not, 'Where did they come from?', but 'When did they become Celtic?'

The 'vague and secret paths' along which even Caesar refused to send his legions when 'the woods closed over the fleeing enemy' will never be known, but sometimes, in the chronicles of classical writers, there are signposts and even pieces of map. One journey in particular is sufficiently well documented to show where the migrants entered the forest and where they left it. Along with the capture of Rome in 387 BC, it was the most daring of all the Gaulish odysseys. The tribes would talk about it for centuries to come, and when the bards sang their long tales of the great adventure, the descendants of Bellovesus and Segovesus would have seen, as though from one of the great hill forts of Bohemia towering over the forest,

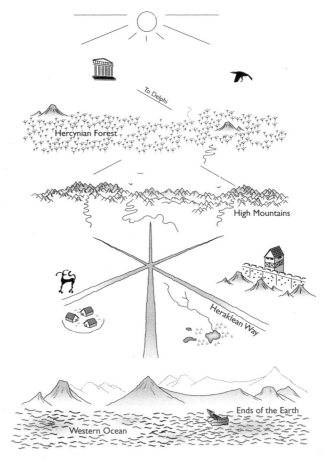

45. The expedition to Delphi. (East is at the top.)

a comprehensive vision of the wide world beyond the tidy shires of Gaulish Middle Earth.

☼

'In days gone by', said Caesar, a sub-tribe of the Volcae called the Tectosages ('Wealth-Seekers'), 'because of the great number of their population and the insufficiency of their farmland, had sent colonies across the Rhine. They took possession of the most fertile parts of Germany around the Hercynian Forest and there they settled.' This is almost certainly a fragment of the Biturigan migration legend: the Tectosages had come from the region of Toulouse in south-western Gaul. It had been a long trek from Aquitania to the Rhine, but soon the tribe was stirred again by the old restlessness. In the early third century BC, another contingent of 'Wealth-Seekers' left for the east with two other tribes: the Trocmii, whose origins are unknown, and the Tolistobo(g)ii, who were probably a branch of the ubiquitous Boii.

Following the winter solstice trajectory through the Hercynian Forest, they would have reached its eastern edge near the shores of the Black Sea. Here, they entered a world in which historical events were recorded in writing, and so they can be seen, as it were, in the open, no longer hidden by the trees, crossing the Hellespont in 278 BC and colonizing the land that came to be known as Galatia. The Tectosages eventually settled at Ancyra (Ankara). Each of the three tribes was divided into four sub-tribes, and the twelve tetrarchs held their annual council at a place called Drunemeton ('Sanctuary of the Oak'). Coins of the Tectosages from the region of Toulouse, almost three thousand kilometres to the west, seem to represent the same political system – a cross, with a symbol of wealth or authority in each of its quadrants: a crescent moon, a nest of stars, an ellipse, sometimes a sheaf of wheat and almost always an axe.

To the people whose lands they ravaged, the itinerant Celts were an appalling horde of semi-human drunkards. Some of the Tectosages butchered their way down the eastern Adriatic. According to the Greek geographer Pausanias, they raped the dead and the dying, and selected the plumpest babies for their feasts. Pushing on through Macedonia, they crossed the river Spercheios. Some used their shields as rafts; others simply waded across – because, said Pausanias, the Celts are 'far taller than any other people'. As the Greek cities assembled their armies, it was becoming apparent that this chaotic rampage had a goal. The horde reached Heraclea, but instead of attacking the town, it battled on towards the pass of Thermopylae.

Beyond Thermopylae lay the fabled land of wine and wisdom where the sun god returned to the earth. The horde knew exactly where it was and why it had come there. The leader of the expedition to Rome in 387 BC had been a warrior called Brennos; the leader of the Greek expedition in 279 BC was another Brennos – from '*branos*', the Celtic word for 'crow'. The two expeditions, a century apart, were astronomically symmetrical. Rome lay on the solstice line from Mediolanum Biturigum; the goal of the later expedition – Delphi – lay on the solstice line from Alesia.* A day's march from Thermopylae, white temples stood on the slopes of Mount Parnassus. There, the Massaliots, along with many other Greek cities, had their treasury, filled with statues and other offerings to the gods, because it was in the place called Delphi ('womb') that the two eagles or crows released by Zeus had met and defined the centre of the world.

The battle tactics of the Celts seemed so ridiculously suicidal to Pausanias that he assumed that they had no seers or priests to advise them. At Thermopylae, the sun rose and the barbarians rushed into the pass. A heavy fog was rolling down the mountains, and the Greeks were waiting. Thousands of Celts were massacred in the gullies or trampled into the marshes of the floodplain, yet the survivors struggled on 'without even begging leave to recover their comrades' bodies, caring not whether they were buried in the earth or devoured by wild animals and birds of prey'. The original source used by Pausanias evidently had some knowledge of Celtic religion: at Thermopylae, the souls of the Celtic dead would travel to the upper world or to the lower. Perhaps they knew that the hot springs of Thermopylae had been created by Herakles when he had tried to quench the fire of the Hydra's poison, and that its sulphurous caverns led directly to the underworld.

For the Greeks, what happened at Delphi in 279 BC was an inconceivable calamity: the hinged wings of an iron crow flapping on his helmet, a Celtic chieftain rummaged through Apollo's sanctuary. The Cyrenean poet Callimachus wrote of the invasion only a few years after the event in his *Hymn to Delos*:

> Latter-day Titans shall raise up against the Hellenes
> A barbarian sword and the Celtic god of war,
> Rushing from the extreme west like snowflakes,
> Or as numerous as stars when their flocks are thickest in the air.

In Greek accounts, the disaster at Delphi has two different endings. Some say that the Celts looted the sanctuary and stole its treasures. Others softened the blow to Greek pride by imagining a miraculous intervention: the gods overwhelmed the barbarians with thunder and lightning, an earthquake, a snowstorm that caused a landslide, and a

---

* Within one point of a 128-point compass (124.62°). See p. 165n.

mass hallucination that made them think that their comrades were speaking Greek. They stabbed one another to death and their leader Brennos committed suicide by drinking undiluted wine.

No material evidence has been found of any destruction at Delphi in 279 BC, either by Celts or by earthquake. A raid of some sort took place, but it is unlikely that Delphi had been chosen for its treasures: there were far more lucrative and accessible places to plunder. This cruel and costly expedition to the centre of the world had a symbolic, religious aspect: it was a heroic episode in a national epic acted out by an army of belligerent, wine-drinking pilgrims. Both Callimachus and Pausanias significantly describe 'the mindless tribe of Galatians', not as eastern neighbours of the Greeks, but as people from the other end of the earth – 'the barbarians who came from the Ocean' or 'from the extreme west'. The logic of Celtic geography is unmistakable: the Tectosages had journeyed from the sunset to the sunrise on the paths of the sun god. Their leader, Brennos, personified the crow, which in Irish mythology is associated with the god Lugh. When he stood at the *omphalos* of the world, taking into his body the concentrated nectar of the sun, this was not the mortification of a drunken soldier, but a ceremony of sacrifice and communion.

✿

For the Celts, Delphi was not the end of the story, but the rest of the world found out what had happened to the Delphic treasure only many years after the expedition, when the Tectosages of Gaul had become vassals of Rome. The crow had sailed back over the forest to its home near the Ocean, as though the odyssey would reach its conclusion only when the circle or ellipse was complete. A sanctuary that became the chief *oppidum* of the Tectosages stood above the river Garonne to the south of Tolosa (Toulouse). There, the survivors of the expedition told tales of the endless forest and the sunny lands beyond. Some may have proudly displayed a Greek helmet, a Carpathian bride or the severed head of a German preserved in cedar oil.

As for the treasure, it was considered the property of the gods, and disposed of accordingly. Posidonius, who travelled in southern Gaul in the early first century BC, learned that it was worth about fifteen thousand talents and consisted of unwrought gold and silver bullion. Bars of solid silver had been melted and hammered into the size and shape of mill-stones, and placed where the 'frugal, god-fearing' Celts traditionally stowed their riches:

> It was the lakes, above all, that gave the treasures their inviolability, and into them, the people let down heavy masses of silver or even gold. . . . In Tolosa, the temple, too, was hallowed, since it was much revered by the inhabitants of the region, and for this reason, the treasures there were excessive, for many people had dedicated them to the gods and no one dared lay hands on them.

Posidonius was describing the practice known as ritual deposition. Such enormous quantities of precious metals were consecrated to gods of the underworld and deposited in wells, pits, rivers and lakes that the archaeological record shows a scarcity of Gaulish gold towards the end of the Iron Age. Though the Tectosages all knew where the treasure was hidden, it remained untouched until the Roman conquest of southern Gaul: in 106 BC, a Roman proconsul, Quintus Servilius Caepio, drained the lakes and made off with the bullion. Terrible punishments had traditionally been meted out to anyone who tampered with public treasure. Since Caepio was a powerful Roman, his punishment had to be left to the gods. According to a legend reported by Timagenes, Caepio was sent into exile and all his daughters became prostitutes.

It is unlikely that the cursed Caepio discovered the true Delphic treasure: the shrines of Delphi were not repositories of gold and silver bullion; most precious metal in the region of the Tectosages came from their mines in the foothills of the Pyrenees. Whatever its form and origin, the true value of the treasure was symbolic. The Tectosages had travelled to the centre of the world, taken the gold of the sun from its place of birth, and buried it in their homeland in the extreme west. The ritual of deposition may have resembled Egyptian burials of the mummified sun god. The details escape us completely. But we do know that the expedition forged a geographical and sacred link between the centre of the Greek world and the Western Ocean.

✧

'Many large rivers flow through Gaul, and their streams cut this way and that through the level plain, some of them flowing from bottomless lakes and others having their sources and affluents in the mountains, and some of them empty into the ocean and others into our sea.' Diodorus, like Strabo, seems to have acquired some accidental knowledge of the complicated three-dimensional geometry of the Celtic universe. Perhaps there was a mythical underground river that encircled the earth and allowed the sun god to travel back to his place of birth; perhaps the river was the Ocean itself, which, as Pytheas the Massaliot had discovered, eventually merged with the sky. But beyond the landscaped symmetries of Middle Earth, the universe of the ancient Celts is as mysterious as the Hercynian Forest.

The physical treasure itself may be easier to recover than the lost Celtic myths. The word used by Posidonius in describing its hiding places is *limnai*, the plural of *limne*, meaning a marsh, a pond or a shallow lake, 'a pool of standing water left by the sea or a river'. Some elderly Toulousains, interviewed in the 1950s, remembered swimming in shallow ponds which appeared along the ancient course of the river in the Pont des Demoiselles quartier in the south-east of Toulouse. Nothing of value was ever found there, and although gold, jewels, torcs and armbands from the Lower Danube have been discovered in the former lands of the Tectosages, none of them can be traced as far as Greece.

No doubt these were the ponds that were drained by the greedy proconsul. Posidonius says that the *limnai* were 'in Tolosa', but there were other marshy places, outside the Roman city, closer to the pre-Roman home of the Tectosages. The *oppidum* above the river at Vieille-Toulouse has wide views to the south-west, over the ponds of what is now the Parc du Confluent. Here, the Garonne, which flows to the Atlantic, is joined by the Ariège, which rushes down from the mountain pass where the Heraklean Way crosses the Pyrenees. River confluences are classic sites of ritual deposition. The quiet little patch of woodland by the confluence, criss-crossed by signposted paths, may once have been a holy place. A treasure might have been unknowingly extracted from the gravel pits and dumped on a driveway or a path, but since even a heavy object, rolling on a bed of pebbles, urged by the conjoined force of two rivers, will travel many metres in a year, a sacred relic from the centre of the earth may at last have completed its long journey to the Ocean at the end of the world.

11

Cities of Middle Earth

The expedition to Delphi in 279 BC marked the high-water point of the Celtic tide. Less than a century later, the Celts of northern Italy were defeated by the Romans, who then advanced along the Mediterranean into southern Gaul. In 125 and 124 BC, Roman armies crossed the Matrona in the footsteps of Herakles. The ostensible aim was to defend their old allies, the Massaliots, against the troublesome tribes of the hinterland. In exchange, the Romans were granted a narrow strip of land running all the way from Italy to Hispania. In 123 BC, a Roman garrison was established below the *oppidum* of the Salyi at a place where hot springs bubbled up from the limestone. The place was named Aquae Sextiae after the Roman consul, Gaius Sextius Calvinus. Its modern name is Aix-en-Provence.

A glance at a modern road map shows what a crucial position it occupies: a day's march north of Massalia, the Salyi's *oppidum* in the hills above Aix-en-Provence is one of the noisiest Iron Age sites in France. The nearby autoroutes lead to Italy by the coast, to the Alps by the valley of the Durance, and to the Pyrenees by the plain of the Crau and the Via Domitia. Two years after the creation of Aquae Sextiae, in 121 BC, all these arterial routes were controlled by Rome. A coalition of Allobroges and Arverni, led by the Arvernian king Bituitos, fought a Roman army near the town of Biturrita (Bédarrides): the name is Celtic and means 'ford of Bituitos'.

The site of the battle was probably chosen by the Gauls, since this is where the Heraklean Way crosses the Rhone. (This policy of fighting battles on solar paths was to have spectacular consequences in the Gallic War: p. 192.) According to a legend recounted by Orosius in his *History Against the Pagans* (c. AD 420), Bituitos was confident of victory: 'Seeing such small numbers of Roman soldiers, he boasted

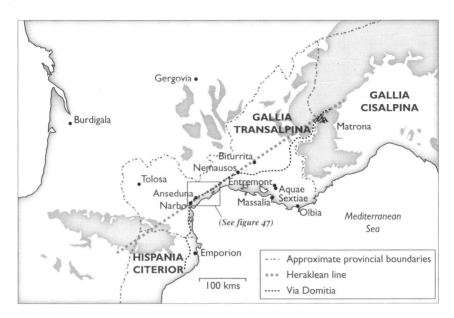

46. Southern Gaul in 106 BC

that they would scarce feed the dogs that he had with his army'. But the sun god failed to shine on the Celts, and the war dogs were rewarded with an unexpected feast of one hundred and fifty thousand Celtic corpses.

That year, the new Roman province of Gallia Transalpina was founded. The ancient path of Herakles was converted into a high-speed road – the Via Domitia – along which slaves and other vital necessities were rushed from Spain to Italy. Independent Gaul was now cut off from the Mediterranean and forced to deal directly with the Romans. No one, apart from the Druids, could have suspected that, even as the shadow of Rome fell over Western Europe, Celtic science and the sun god were creating their own heavenly masterpiece of social engineering.

✿

A generation or two after the founding of Gallia Transalpina, most of the territory that had belonged to Gaulish aristocrats was owned by Roman businessmen and veterans. Their names are dotted all over the map of southern France as though an enormous auction had taken place – which, in some parts, is what actually happened. The lands

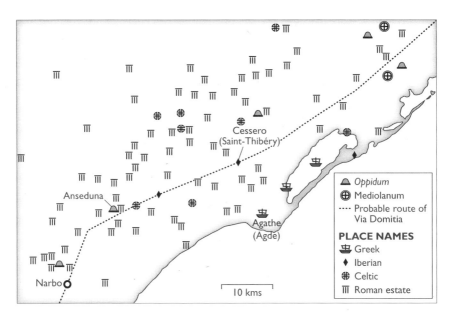

Map legend:
- ▲ Oppidum
- ⊕ Mediolanum
- ···· Probable route of Via Domitia

PLACE NAMES
- ⚱ Greek
- ◆ Iberian
- ⊕ Celtic
- Ⅲ Roman estate

Place labels on map: Cessero (Saint-Thibéry), Anseduna, Agathe (Agde), Narbo

10 kms

47. The Romanization of southern Gaul

that Herakles had made safe for his sons and daughters were confiscated and privatized. A few Celtic place names survive. Most of them refer to gods and geographical features – Lodève, from *luto* ('marsh'), Cers, from Circius the wind god – but they are greatly outnumbered by the names of Roman individuals: Loupian from Lupianus, Thézan from Titianus, Valras from Valerianus.

With what remained of their estates, the natives were obliged to supply the conquerors with corn, cavalry and money. In some respects, little had changed: tolls and taxes had been collected long before the Romans, and there is no evidence that the Celts of Gallia Transalpina sank into the despondency of the vanquished. Some of them learned to speak Latin and to add water to their wine. Quite a few of those 'Roman' estates belonged to Gauls who acquired a new name when they became Roman citizens. Those who lived along the former Heraklean Way enjoyed the benefits of Roman enterprise as never before. In Narbonne, near a beautifully paved, slave-built section of the Via Domitia, the vaulted cellars of the *horreum* stored the grain, the wine and the olive oil that the new economy produced.

As swiftly as meltwater from the Cévennes rushes over the dry riverbeds and covers the *garrigue* with flowers, some of this new wealth found its way into the Gaulish hinterland. Fifteen kilometres north-east of Narbonne, the pine-scented terraces of the *oppidum* of Anseduna* look down on the coastal plain where a meticulous surveyor seems to have scored the Heraklean diagonal across the compliant fields. The place had been destroyed in the late third century BC, probably at the time of Hannibal's invasion. When the Romans arrived, it was a ruin, but with the creation of the province, the old town was plumbed into the system of Mediterranean trade, and it sprang to life again. Oil lamps, glass bottles and imported tableware were suddenly everyday items. The finds displayed in the small museum at Ensérune paint a sunny picture of life in Roman Gaul – a hand-held sundial etched on a piece of Samian ware; round counters used in a game; clay legs, with holes for the threads, on which a child's puppet danced to places that can only be imagined. One inhabitant of Anseduna had the daily pleasure, when she scooped up the last ladleful of food, of finding a three-dimensional ceramic frog grinning up from the base of the dish.

The proconsul who stole the Delphic treasure in 106 BC did not find a cowed, colonial population: he had been sent to Tolosa to quell a revolt, and there were many other signs of lively resentment in Gallia Transalpina. The natives had to endure the thievery of corrupt officials, but some of them were educated and self-confident enough to take their complaints to Rome. One of the officials who had been lining his own pockets was Marcus Fonteius, governor of the province from 74 to 72 BC. He was tried in Rome and defended by no less an orator than Cicero. The Celts had evidently made a good case. Cicero felt it necessary to frighten the jury with the old clichés:

> Do you think that, in their military cloaks and trousers, they come to us in a humble and submissive spirit? . . . Far from it! They go strolling about all over the forum in high spirits and with their heads held high, using threatening expressions and terrorising people with their barbaric and inhuman language. . . .
>
> These are the nations that once marched so far from their homes, all the way to Delphi, to attack and plunder the Pythian Apollo, the oracle of the earth . . . These are the people who pollute their altars and temples with human victims. . . .

---

* The name is recorded in AD 899 and probably means 'boundary hill fort'. Its modern name is Ensérune.

Other nations, when they wage war, beg the immortal gods for their favour and indulgence; these nations waged war against the immortal gods themselves.

The Roman colonization of southern Gaul was not a sign of inherent weakness in Celtic society. Until recently, French historians saw the dawn of Gallic civilization in the gleam of Roman armour coming over the Alpine passes; now, they stress the continuity of Celtic culture by referring to the imperial age of Gaul as 'the Roman interlude'. The economic and social changes wrought by the Romans – or, indirectly, by the expansion of their empire – were incalculable. In Gallia Transalpina, there was a revolution in livestock breeding, irrigation and mining. This was partly the result of Roman expertise, but it was also a native response to new conditions. The best farmland had been taken by the Romans. The poorer soils had to be improved and turned to profit: there were taxes to be paid and wine to be bought.

Some changes were already taking place when the Romans arrived. In the old days, material wealth had served primarily to enhance the prestige of kings: the Arvernian Bituitos had invested heavily in military equipment made of precious metals, while his father Louernios ('the Fox') had earned the gratitude of his subjects by marking out a banqueting zone larger than a city and laying on a public feast that lasted several days. Now, the coins that were minted by Gaulish tribes were tokens rather than treasures. Half a century before the rest of Gaul was conquered by the Romans, the most powerful tribes established a monetary union. This ancestor of the Eurozone should count as one of the most impressive achievements of what looked increasingly like a Celtic nation: the barbarian Celts had generated the political will, coordinated the tribal mints, and set exchange rates within Gaul and with the trading empires of Massalia and Rome.

Conquest and enslavement were not the inevitable prelude to civilization. The biggest change of all, which transformed the lives of millions of people from the Danube to the British Ocean, owed far more to the Celtic sun god and Druidic science than to Roman sophistication.

✿

The system of solar paths may have expressed the Druids' love of mysterious patterns, but it survived and grew because it served several practical purposes. Its usefulness as a navigational *aide-mémoire* is obvious: by memorizing a few key locations and their place in the system, a Druid geographer (or any reader of this book) could function quite effectively as a talking *table d'orientation*. As a political and administrative tool, it could be used to organize territorial divisions and large-scale migrations, and because it was based on simple equations and celestial geometry, it gave the Druids' judgements the irrefutable authority of cosmic truth. It had the solidity of a religious conviction: by imposing a graceful harmony on the physical geography of western Europe, it made it easy to believe that Middle Earth was not a chaotic arrangement of elements but a deliberate, divine creation.

The paths of the sun joined the source of the Rhone to its delta, the Alps to the Pyrenees, and the Mediterranean to the Ocean. They coordinated the four principal gateways to the east (the Matrona, the Poenina, the pass of the Mediomatrici and the Col de Tende), the four headlands at the ends of the earth (the Sacred Promontory, Fisterra, the Île de Sein and Belerion), and the sources of fifteen major rivers.* The whole system might have been the plan that Herakles had carried with him on his travels when he was reorganizing the landscape of western Europe. (See fig. 41.)

But when Druid theologians contemplated this vast concurrence of terrestrial geography and celestial mathematics, they must have wondered: was this a proof of divine providence or an intellectual dream that could never quite come true? As artists and scientists, they knew that every product of the human mind is an approximation, that for every radiant coincidence there are a thousand dull discrepancies, and that, in the world of mortal beings, physical reality would always have the last word.

Some of the points of intersection are geographically significant – the tidal island of Loon Plage, the ford at the Marduel hill, the crossings of the Rhone at Tarusco and Biturrita. More often, the lines

---

* Ariège,* Aube, Creuse, Drôme, Durance, Duria (Dora), Garonne,* Indre, Marne, Meuse,* Orne, Rhine, Rhone, Somme, Yonne. (The asterisk indicates the traditional rather than hydrographic source.)

meet at a point where geography shows no particular inclination to commemorate the path of a sun god. The line from Châteaumeillant to the Rhone delta passes by the sacred mountain of the Arverni, the Puy de Dôme, but without bisecting the summit; instead, it crosses a spring called 'Source de l'Enfer', which, despite its name ('Hell's Spring'), is just a trickle of water. Châteaumeillant itself is hardly the most spectacular *omphalos*, and although Alesia stands on a hill, there are, as Caesar observed, several 'other hills of a similar height' all around it. Even from the window of the slow train from Dijon to Paris, it is easy to miss the mother-city of the Celts. The system of solar paths could never be a flawless reflection of the upper world, because, after all, one might suppose, even the Druids couldn't move mountains . . .

✧

Despite their unobstructed view of one of the most important historical sites in France, the inhabitants of the middle section of the Rue des Remparts in Châteaumeillant keep their west-facing shutters closed, even in the daytime. On the other side of the narrow street, a steep bank of turf scalped by a mowing machine rises to the height of a second storey. On top of the bank, a motionless tidal wave of vegetation looms over the rooftops. The whole monstrosity, including the hedge, is almost fourteen metres high.

This gargantuan earthwork is the surviving eastern edge of one of the first towns or *oppida* to appear in Europe north of the Alps. About two hundred *oppida* have so far been identified, from Britain to the Danube Basin. Some were the size of a small field, a few were larger than Hyde Park or Central Park, but most are so distinctive that they can occasionally be detected on a relief map or spotted in a landscape without prior knowledge of the archaeological record. A typical Celtic *oppidum* occupies a flattish area of high ground which seems to have been designed by nature as a world apart. A river, a ravine or the sea almost surrounds the plateau; the remaining side is barricaded by a geometrically regular ditch and a bank of earth. Sometimes, there are heaps of tumbled stones that once formed a decorative rather than defensive wall.

Only a few *oppida* have been excavated. They were divided roughly into residential, industrial and religious districts. Unlike the smaller,

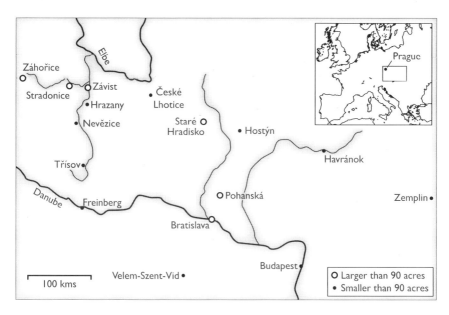

48. *Oppida* of Bohemia

sporadically occupied hill forts which served as places of refuge, the *oppida* were densely populated throughout the year. For some reason, towards the end of the second century BC, people whose ancestors had always lived in open settlements and isolated farms began to come together and live like town-dwellers. The process of proto-urbanization may have started in the east, after the expulsion of the Celts from northern Italy (c. 180 BC): it was then that the Boii developed a system of *oppida* to the north of the Danube (fig. 48). The historical evidence tells a slightly different tale. In Italy, the Romans were able to defeat an entire tribe by capturing a single, central place, which suggests that previously un-nucleated populations were already coalescing and, in the literal sense, becoming civilized. In areas such as northern France, Wales and northern Britain, where older, rural ways of life persisted, military conquest was slower and more costly, requiring the destruction of farmland and the felling of entire forests.

The first *oppida* in Gaul emerged about half a century after the Bohemian *oppida*. The earliest, which include Bibracte and Château-meillant, were practically unoccupied until the end of the second century BC (c. 110). Some were founded just a few years before the Roman invasion of 58 BC, which is why they were once thought to have been built as fortresses. But most of the *oppida* were far too large to be defended, and their walls were designed for visual impact rather than solidity. They were not thrown up in a panic but developed in a leisurely fashion over a generation or more. It was only after seven years of fighting Roman armies that the Gauls, 'for the first time', says Caesar, defended a position by building fortifications.

The *oppidum*-planners seem to have designed their new towns with religious rather than military criteria in mind. They built them around ancient, pre-Celtic shrines that dated back to the Bronze Age or even to the Neolithic. Perched on their promontories and plateaux, the loftiest *oppida* have the impressively impractical appearance of alien settlements drawn by science-fiction illustrators. They are, in fact, as mysterious as they look. Anyone who has clambered up an artificially steepened hill to see the site of an Iron Age town will have asked the question that archaeologists have been trying to answer for several decades: why did Celtic people of the late Iron Age make their towns so absurdly inconvenient when they were supposed to function as markets rather than citadels? The impetus for their creation was apparently economic: the first Gaulish *oppida* coincided with the creation of a Gaulish currency, and from the very beginning they were used as centres of trade and mass-production (fig. 49). Why, then, did they abandon the earlier settlements at river confluences and road junctions, and force themselves to negotiate enormous physical obstacles in order to import their raw materials and export their products?

Another puzzle can now be added to the mystery of the inconvenient *oppida*. The Druidic network, which incorporates the chief *oppida* of about forty tribes, dates back to the fourth century BC: the solar paths match the migrations to Italy and reflect the power structure in Gaul at that time. Yet the *oppida* barely existed before 110 BC. Paradoxically, the solar paths are at least three hundred years older than the *oppida* they bisect.

In 2004, a French archaeologist proposed a theory to explain the impracticality of the Gaulish *oppida*. This theory also happens to provide a solution to the second puzzle, and it should now be considered the likeliest explanation. When the *oppidum*-dwellers moved to their new homes, they were moving to sites that already had a history. The shrines that lie at the heart of the *oppida* were many centuries old. The history-loving Celts would have told stories about these

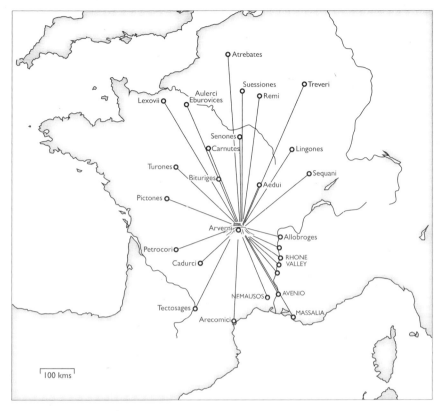

49. Coins found on the plateau of Gergovia

The provenance of coins found on the plateau of Gergovia suggests the commercial sphere of a major *oppidum*.

hallowed sites, just as the evocative ruins of their own *oppida* later became the subjects of medieval legends which attributed their construction to Caesar, Attila or the Devil.

The island-worlds that looked down on the surrounding land had been sacred to the ancestors of the *oppidum*-dwellers. There were thousands of such places, marked by standing stones, burials or derelict wells. Some of those charismatic sites may still have served their ancient purpose in the darkest days of the Gallic War, when the *oppida* lay in ruins or were occupied by Roman troops. As the tribes were plotting the great uprising of 52 BC, Caesar learned that 'the leaders of the Gauls were convening councils in woods and remote places'.

With the founding of the Roman province of Gallia Transalpina and the sudden surge in trade, it became essential to bring together the artisans and skilled labourers who were scattered about the countryside like weavers and blacksmiths before the Industrial Revolution. Some of the ancient holy places were chosen – no doubt by divination and astronomical measurement – to be the sites of the new towns. In this way, instead of being forced to congregate in the Iron Age equivalent of a soulless 'new town', the workers would be induced to follow the same steep paths as their pious ancestors. At first, the new workshops and foundries were devoted to the building of the *oppidum* – the temple and houses, the looming, lavish wall of carved beams and iron spikes – but when the *oppidum* was completed, the factories would be turned over to the manufacture of tools, weapons, textiles and jewellery that would be traded and sold all over Gaul. By then, the rural population would have discovered the delights of civilization. Within a few years, the streets of the *oppidum* would be paved with the sherds of wine amphorae that visitors still trample underfoot today.

It was a brilliant solution to the problem of disorganized labour and a population reluctant to change its ways. For a modern equivalent, one would have to imagine the development of urban settlements around Stonehenge or Glastonbury Tor – which is, in effect, what happens every year at the time of the summer solstice and the Glastonbury Festival. Religious fervour is entirely compatible with commerce. A similar phenomenon could be seen in France until quite recently. Once a year, remote places where angels or the Virgin Mary had performed miracles were transformed overnight into lively fairs to which pilgrims flocked from miles around.

The Druidic network was vital to this reorganization of Celtic society. There was already a geomantic system onto which the new, economic system could be grafted. Just as the great migrations to the east had been ordered by the paths of the sun, the chief *oppidum* of each tribe was selected for its auspicious solar coordinates. The movement of the rural population to the *oppidum* was itself a form of internal migration controlled by the ultimate authority in the sky.

The fact that the first towns in barbarian Europe, like the temple-cities of Egypt and the solstice-oriented towns of the Etruscans, were placed under the aegis of the sun god is not the sign of a backward, theocratic society. Having already fashioned a religion out of a thousand local cults, the Druids of the late Iron Age now combined tribal tradition with economic development. Yet material prosperity was not an end in itself. In coordinating the new tribal centres of Gaul, the Druids were creating something that no other European civilization ever attempted on such a scale. As Eratosthenes and other ancient geographers knew, the world of humans showed a distressing disregard for the eternal truths of astronomy and mathematics. The meridian drawn through Alexandria, Rhodes, Byzantium and other prestigious places was wildly erratic (p. 98). The obvious though apparently insane solution to this incongruence of terrestrial reality and the upper world was to modify the reality, and this is what the Druids did when they laid the foundations of modern Europe. It was as though the creator of a medieval *mappa mundi* had set out to reorganize the physical world so that when he returned to the scriptorium, everything from Paradise to the Pillars of Hercules could be drawn in exactly the right place.

✻

This was the state of Independent Gaul when the province of Gallia Transalpina acquired a new governor in 61 BC. He was a man of thirty-nine years whose family claimed descent from the goddess Venus. He had sailed on the Western Ocean with a Roman army, massacred the Celtic tribes of the Iberian coast, and reached Brigantium (A Coruña) in the north, from where it was said that one could sail to Hibernia and the tin-rich Cassiterides islands. His ambitions were vast and required correspondingly enormous sums of money. When this Herakles of the modern world crossed the Matrona and journeyed to the province along the old Heraklean Way, he knew that a land far bigger than Italy lay to the north. Like all Romans, he had heard of the treasure of Tolosa, the gold torcs that had been stripped from the bodies of the defeated Arverni, and the slabs of gold as large as a hand that lay just beneath the surface in the lands of the Tarbelli of Aquitania. At Aquae Sextiae, in 102 BC, his uncle Marius had won a famous victory against the Germanic tribes who had rampaged through Gaul for seven years. It was a connection of more immediate use to him than his divine ancestry and one of the reasons why Gaius Julius Caesar would enjoy the unwavering loyalty of the legions when he began to enshroud the land of the Druids in darkness.

12

The Gods Victorious

In the autumn of 57 BC, fifty-three thousand men, women and children, comprising the entire surviving population of the Aduatuci tribe, were crammed into a small *oppidum* in what is now southern Belgium. The exact site is unknown – it might have been the citadel of Namur – but the number is certainly accurate since it was given to Caesar by the traders who bought the Aduatuci as slaves. The Gallic War was nearing the end of its second year, and it was already proving astonishingly lucrative. In only a few months of campaigning, the Romans had driven the Helvetii and their allies back to their homelands – reducing their population by about two-thirds – and conquered practically every northern tribe between the Rhine and the Atlantic. That autumn, Caesar reported to the Senate that 'all of Gaul has been pacified'. When he came to write up his annual reports for his *Commentaries on the Gallic War*, he would be able to add a triumphant postscript to Book Two: 'Upon receipt of Caesar's letters, fifteen days of thanksgiving were decreed, which had never happened before.'

Roman businessmen might have feared that Gaul would be a logistical nightmare, but they had every reason to be delighted with the Gaulish infrastructure. The land of the Druids had been turned into an enormous emporium and distribution centre. Huge quantities of booty and endless caravans of human merchandise headed for Rome, while horses, provisions, naval armaments and other military equipment flooded into northern Gaul from Italy, Spain and the province of Gallia Transalpina. Compared to the intense activity of the private companies with contracts to supply the Roman army, fighting took up only a small part of the war: between 58 and 51 BC, there were fewer than four battles a year. On a map, the itineraries of the legions look like a tangle, but through the eyes of an import-export manager, the commercial rationale of the Roman campaigns is obvious. In the more prosaic passages of his *Commentaries*, Caesar himself sometimes makes the business plan explicit. While the fifty-three thousand Aduatuci were being marched off towards Italy, the Twelfth Legion was sent to guard the Upper Rhone in order to liberate Roman traders from 'the very great dangers and very great customs duties' that had hampered them in the past.

By the end of 57 BC, the Gallic War was practically over. Most of the remaining six years were devoted to mopping-up operations, the quelling of revolts and the installation of puppet kings and tribal governments friendly to the Romans. In 55 and 54 BC, Gaul was still sufficiently 'pacified' to allow Caesar to burnish his reputation with an abbreviated 'conquest' of the land at the end of the earth. Eight hundred ships made the trip from Portus Itius (near or at Boulogne) to somewhere north of Portus Dubris (Dover). The flotilla included several private vessels chartered by merchants who were eager to prospect the new market.

The expeditionary force to Britannia travelled eighty miles inland and crossed a river called the Tamesis, 'which can be forded – with some difficulty – in only one place'. Roman *dignitas* usually demanded a bridge, but with British shock troops suddenly appearing along the roads on their high-speed chariots, the soldiers, according to Caesar, waded across the river with only their heads above water. A poet called Varro Atacinus, who was a native of Gallia Transalpina, had already written an epic poem about the first year of the war.* The amphibious crossing of the Thames was exactly the kind of material that would enable poets to celebrate Caesar's exploits. (A popular historian was unlikely to wonder why the roads of the Britons ended when they came to a river.) Cicero himself had written to request some colourful details that he could use to describe the conquest of Britannia, and Caesar had obliged with 'a copious letter': 'the approaches to the island are known to be guarded with wondrous walls of massive rock'. Unfortunately, the pickings were poor, Cicero reported to a friend:

---

* Only one line survives of Varro's *Bellum Sequanicum*: '*Deinde ubi pellicuit dulcis levis unda saporis . . .* ' ('Then, when the smooth swell of a sweet taste enticed . . . '). This may be an allusion to the wine-inspired migrations of the Celts.

It is also now ascertained that there isn't a speck of silver on the island, nor any prospect of booty apart from captives, and I fancy you won't expect any of *them* to be highly qualified in literature or music!

Shortly after the defeat of Cassivellaunus, the warlord who had been chosen to lead the British resistance, Caesar was sitting in a room paved with mosaics and marble somewhere in southern Britain near Verlamion (St Albans). A soldier with a drawn sword stood behind him while he dictated letters to a slave. Caesar was said to be capable of composing several letters at the same time, even on horseback. The previous spring (55 BC), while crossing the Alps to rejoin the army in Gaul, he had written a grammatical treatise on the subject of analogy. The room in which he sat had not been furnished for his personal comfort. His baggage train always included a supply of mosaic squares and marble veneer so that important guests such as Roman merchants and foreign kings could be properly entertained. He wrote to Cicero: Britain had been 'dealt with' (which was to say, the four kings of Cantium and the warlord Cassivellaunus had surrendered): 'Hostages taken, but no booty. Tribute, however, exacted.'

The letter was dated 'Shores of Nearer Britain, 26 September'. The wooden tablets were tied with string and sealed with wax. They would reach Cicero in Rome on 24 October, two days after a letter from Cicero's brother Quintus, who had joined Caesar as *legatus*. The adventure had been largely fruitless though not on the whole unpleasant. Quintus had written five plays in his spare time. The fact seems to have slipped between the floorboards of history: the first literary works known to have been composed in the British Isles were four Greek tragedies and a play called *Erigone* (lost in the post between Britain and Rome). In the fabled land beyond the edge of the known world, Roman soldiers had staged a theatrical performance – probably of *Erigone*: the mythical subject would have provided light relief and a chance to laugh at the barbarians. Erigone's father introduces his compatriots to wine. Mistaking their intoxication for a fatal illness, they stone him to death. It was a joke among the Romans that the Celts had started adding water to their wine because they thought it might be poisoned.

That September, just before the equinox, the army and all the travelling *negotiatores* set sail after dark with a cargo of British prisoners and reached Gaul at daybreak. From Portus Itius, Caesar returned to Samarobriva. After the summer droughts, there was a shortage of grain, exacerbated by the Roman policy of destroying the enemy's wheat fields. A population already weakened by war would have to suffer the horrors of famine. The minimum daily requirement of the Roman army in Gaul – without counting fodder – has been estimated at one hundred tons of wheat. In assigning their winter quarters to the legions, Caesar spread them over a wider area than before 'in order to remedy the lack of corn'. In the autumn, tribes from Armorica (Brittany) and the Rhineland rose up against the Romans, and 'throughout that winter, there was barely a moment when Caesar was not receiving intelligence of the councils and commotions of the Gauls'. But the disciplined legions prevailed, and 'not long after those events, Caesar had a more peaceful time of it in Gaul'.

✿

The sun god of the Celts is practically invisible until the end of the Gallic War, which is hardly surprising since the only accounts of the war are the seven books of Caesar's *Commentaries*, the eighth book, written by his lieutenant Aulus Hirtius, and various historical fragments and anecdotes, none of which is Celtic. Apart from conventional references to 'Fortuna', Caesar says nothing of the actions of gods and never mentions the divinatory powers of his friend, Diviciacus the Druid. Yet the Druid augurs, who 'settle nearly all disputes, whether public or private', and who frequently used their influence to stop battles, certainly played a major role in coordinating Gaulish military strategy.

Hirtius mentions a certain 'Gutuater' or 'Gutuatrus' who was accused of masterminding the great uprising of 52 BC. The word '*gutuater*' has been found on several inscriptions: it was not, as Hirtius supposed, a man's name, but a title – 'master of invocations'. Later, when the Druids had been outlawed, the word was used as a generic term for 'priest'. The *gutuater* who instigated the rebellion in 52 BC was a predecessor of Sacrovir ('holy man'), who led the revolt of AD 21 in the university town of Augustodunum (Autun), and of the Druids of Anglesey, who were 'the power that fed the rebellion'.

These powerful, priestly figures – Gutuater, Sacrovir and the Anglesey Druids – remained undetected until their final defeat. Many more must have fled after the Gallic War and vanished into Britannia. They are little more than ghosts in the historical record. Yet evidence can be found of their conduct of the war. A consistent strategy bears the marks of Druidic computation. Whenever the site of a battle was chosen by the Celts, it lay somewhere on the solar network. Bituitos of the Arverni, like Hannibal before him, had fought the Romans where the Via Heraklea crosses the Rhone. Sixty years later, the Gauls placed themselves whenever possible in auspicious solar locations. Caesar himself diplomatically followed 'the custom of the Gauls' when convening general councils of the pro-Roman tribes, though he certainly had no idea how those places of assembly had been chosen, and just as he had been unable to discover even the most basic facts about Britain, he had only the faintest inkling of Druidic warcraft. The closest he came to a perception of Celtic strategy was in his dealings with the Suebi.

> The Suebi, according to their custom, had called a council and given orders . . . that all who could bear arms should assemble in one place. The place thus selected was near the centre ['*medium fere*'] of their territories, and they resolved to await there the arrival of the Romans and to do battle on that spot.*

From a modern military point of view, the stubbornness of the Celtic armies seems tragically self-defeating. In eight years, their tactics barely changed. When the Gaulish leader Vercingetorix urged the adoption of Roman practices (scorched earth and fortifications), he was treated as a young upstart by the Gaulish nobles. But he, too, would follow the directions of the Druids. To expect the Celts to have learned practical lessons from the Romans would be to misunderstand the nature of religious thought. In fighting their battles where the gods decreed, they were fulfilling a divine purpose. The earth that the Romans were devastating was not the only world.

---

* The unnamed place may have been somewhere in the Thuringian Forest (no. 3 in fig. 43) between the Elbe and the Rhine.

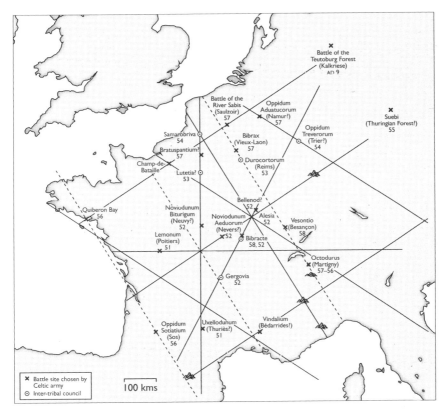

50. The Gallic War and Gaulish strategy

The thousands who died on the paths of the sun god would be reincarnated. At a certain moment in his battle with the Nervii, Caesar came very close to seeing this mysterious process with his own eyes:*

> But the enemy, even in the last hope of salvation, showed such great courage that, when those in the front rank fell, the men behind stepped onto their prostrate forms and fought on from their corpses.

✿

---

* This was the so-called battle of the Sambre. Pierre Turquin showed conclusively in 1955 that the river 'Sabis' of Caesar's text is not the Sambre but the Selle, and that the battle took place on the site of the village of Saulzoir (Nord). This is now corroborated by the Druidic system: Saulzoir lies precisely on the northern solstice line (fig. 50).

Almost every one of those battles was won by the Romans. Not all were military triumphs. Some were not even battles, unless fleeing children can be counted as enemy combatants:

> The rest of the multitude, consisting of boys and women (for they had left their homes and crossed the Rhine with all their families), began to flee in all directions, and Caesar sent the cavalry in pursuit. Hearing the noise in their rear, the Germans saw their families being slain; they threw away their arms and abandoned their standards.

Caesar's report to the Senate on the German massacre appalled Cato, who thought that it brought shame on the Roman people. Pliny later described Caesar's career total of 'one million one hundred and ninety-two thousand men' killed as a 'crime against the human race' (*'humani generis iniuria'*), but he acknowledged that circumstances had forced Caesar's hand: to the imperial mind, Caesar was avenging 'insults' to Rome and consolidating the frontiers of the empire, and if the buffer zone eventually stretched to the ends of the earth, that was all to the good.

Within eight years, a large percentage of the population of Gaul was wiped out. The pre-war population can be roughly estimated at eight million. Caesar's figures suggest a total military force of two million: the Helvetian census (p. 150) implies that combatants, who included women, made up a quarter of the total population. Eight million people could easily have been supported by Gaulish agriculture in its pre-Roman state. The death count is obviously hard to establish. 'A great number' is Caesar's usual indication of the tally – he uses the phrase *'magnus numerus'* twelve times, coupled with verbs meaning 'to kill' – but there are enough statistical details to give a sense of scale:

> Helvetii and allies: reduced from 368,000 to 110,000.
> Nervii: reduced from 60,000 men to fewer than 500; of 600 senators, only 3 survived.
> Aduatuci: about 4000 killed; 53,000 sold into slavery.
> Seduni: over 10,000 killed.
> Veneti: most of the tribe killed in battle, the remainder sold into slavery, and the entire senate put to death.
> Aquitanian and Cantabrian tribes: 'barely a quarter' of 50,000 left alive.
> Bituriges (at Avaricum): reduced from 40,000 to 800.

These figures refer to civilian as well as military casualties. The 39,200 killed at Avaricum (Bourges) included 'women, children and those weakened by age'. People who died later on as a result of famine and disease are, of course, missing from the figures. Taking only the war years into account, an average death toll applied to all the tribes that were slaughtered 'in great numbers' suggests total figures in the region of one million dead and one million enslaved, which is the estimate given by Plutarch in his *Life of Caesar*. The number of Gauls and Germans sold into slavery probably exceeds the number of slaves shipped to the American colonies in the eighteenth century.

The wholesale massacre of Celts was not just a result of the fortunes of war and the circumstances of particular battles. On three occasions, Caesar applies the verb *'depopulari'* to Roman operations. This is usually translated as 'ravage' or 'plunder', but at least once, it has its literal sense: 'depopulate'. The comprehensive extermination of tribes was a deliberate strategy, made possible, in part, by the Gauls' mobilization of entire populations. (Celtic soldiers went to war with their families in tow.) After the battle with the Nervii in 57 BC, Caesar noted that 'the race and name of the Nervii were nearly annihilated'. Four years later, it was the turn of the Eburones to have 'their name and *stirps* [current generations and all future descendants] obliterated'.

Even ignoring the loss of income and labour, these quasi-military operations were often counter-productive. Tactical genocide had at least two serious drawbacks. First, as Caesar had observed when the Helvetian migrants left their homeland, large parts of the country were left defenceless against potentially less tractable enemies from across the Rhine, though the danger could be mitigated in the short term by the destruction of buildings and crops. Second, what remained of society in the zones of annihilation was catastrophically destabilized. As the war went on, far beyond the months when Caesar had first reported that 'all of Gaul was pacified', the Celtic armies took on a different appearance. For the remainder of the war, the legions would be harried by bands of 'desperadoes', 'robbers' and 'runaway slaves'. In the lands of the Unelli (the Cotentin Peninsula), 'a great multitude of wreckers and thieves came together from all parts of Gaul, called away from their farming and daily chores by the hope of plunder and a passion for war'.

It was something of a miracle that the greatest military coalition of Celtic tribes in history emerged from this disaster zone that stretched from the Ocean to the Rhine.

✣

One day at the end of the winter of 53–52 BC, the sun rose at Cenabum (Orléans), and the Roman merchants who had been living in the town since before the war were massacred. The Gaulish message system transmitted the news to the Massif Central and the plateau of Gergovia. There, in the chief *oppidum* of the Arverni, 'a young man of the highest ability and authority' called Vercingetorix ('Great Warrior King') put the next stage of the plan into action.

Ambassadors were sent throughout the western half of Gaul, from the Parisii to the Ruteni and along the Atlantic seaboard. Their mission was to assemble a pan-Gallic army. Cowards and appeasers were to be tortured and burned to death; less serious offenders would have both ears cut off or one eye gouged out. There seems to have been little need of such encouragements: almost all the tribes of Independent Gaul declared their support for Vercingetorix – even the Aedui, who until then had remained loyal to Rome. When Caesar learned of the rebellion, he returned from Italy, placed the province in a state of emergency, and marched his soldiers over the snowy Cévennes. This time, when he reached the Loire and the heart of Gaul, he would be confronting a nation determined to recover its freedom.

As far as one can tell from Caesar's account, Vercingetorix was a ruthless and effective general. His father, Celtillus, had been elected supreme leader of the Gauls. But Celtillus had tried to turn the republic into an absolute monarchy and had been executed by the state. Vercingetorix was suspected of harbouring the same design, but the political institutions of the Gauls were remarkably flexible. (Caesar twice refers to their propensity for taking a vote as 'fickle-ness' and 'eagerness for political change'.) In Britain, Cassivellaunus, who had tyrannized his neighbours the Trinovantes, had been asked to organize resistance to the Romans. Now, the son of an executed dictator was entrusted with the salvation of Gaul. Even after several defeats and his destruction of twenty Biturigan *oppida* in a vain attempt to starve the Roman army, Vercingetorix was hailed as 'the finest of leaders'.

At Gergovia, the young Arvernian general seems to have won a great victory against the Romans. A century later, Plutarch reported that the Arverni 'still show visitors a small sword hanging in a temple, which they say was taken from Caesar'. According to Caesar himself, Roman discipline broke down at Gergovia: 'The soldiers thought that they knew more about victory and its means than their commander-in-chief.' (In the *Commentaries*, successes are attributed to a singular 'Caesar', whereas setbacks are usually described with a generalized plural.) With the province of Gallia Transalpina already trembling at the thought of a barbarian horde less than three days' march to the north, Caesar would not have wanted to inform the Senate that disaster had stared him in the face at Gergovia, but so many soldiers, merchants and slaves were arriving in Italy with tales of the war in Gaul that he was forced to make concessions to the truth. 'Having achieved what he intended [at Gergovia], Caesar ordered the retreat to be sounded . . .' He admitted to the loss of forty-six centurions and 'somewhat fewer than seven hundred soldiers'.

If the war had ended at Gergovia, Vercingetorix might have become the leader of a unified Gaul. A nation would have existed on the north-western frontiers of the Roman empire in which the benefits of Roman civilization were enjoyed without the humiliation of military defeat. At Alesia, a gigantic bronze statue commissioned by Napoleon III shows Vercingetorix as a moustachioed Viking. This is not the barbarian general who spent the last five years of his life in prison on the Capitoline Hill before being paraded in Caesar's triumph and then strangled in his cell. This is the military genius who told his army that 'not even the whole earth could withstand the union of Gaul'. Since almost fifty tribes with proud traditions of belligerence elected him as leader and followed him to the end, he deserves his place in history as the first French national hero. The problem is that having defeated Caesar at Gergovia, this Napoleon of the Iron Age now did something so 'unusual and extraordinary' that, as Montaigne and countless other disappointed patriots have pointed out, 'it appears to defy military custom and logic'.

Gergovia lies on the solar path that joins the burial place of the Delphic treasure to the mother-city of the Celts (Alesia). One hundred Roman miles from Gergovia, on the same solar trajectory, stands the Aeduan capital of Bibracte. This is where Vercingetorix next appeared, at a general council of all the tribes. He was again proclaimed commander-in-chief 'by popular vote'. From Bibracte, following the same line, he marched to the north-north-east. At the same time, Caesar was skirting the edge of the Lingones' territory and heading for the lands of the Sequani in the hope of finding a safe route south to the province.

Caesar's itinerary was the ancient 'tin route' along the upper Seine: it would have taken him past the hilltop ruins of a yellow palace where the Lady of Vix had lived over four centuries before. A few hours' march from Alesia, he met the Gaulish army. Following the line from Gergovia and Bibracte, Vercingetorix would have intercepted Caesar near the Celtic settlement of Bellenod. The river mentioned by Caesar in his account of the battle would be the infant Seine, and the hill that the Gauls defended the place once called 'les Châtelots', which indicates a fortified enclosure.

The German cavalry recruited by Caesar charged up the hill and routed the Gauls. Several important prisoners were taken, including the man whom the Druids had elected chief magistrate of the Aedui. It was then that Vercingetorix seemed to relinquish command to a higher authority. He retreated to Alesia and immured himself and all his army inside the *oppidum*. On that elliptical hill at the heart of Heraklean Gaul, an army of eighty thousand settled in and waited for the attack. 'Why', asked Montaigne, 'did the leader of all the Gauls decide to shut himself up in Alesia? A man who commands a whole nation must never back himself into a corner unless he has no other fortress to defend.'

The Gaulish army, according to Caesar, occupied 'the part of the hill that looks towards the rising sun'. A sanctuary has been found there, near a healing spring, dedicated to a Celtic equivalent of Apollo. The Romans immediately began to surround the hill with turreted ramparts, fields of pits and sharpened stakes, trenches twenty feet deep and a moat filled with water diverted from the river Ozerain. Caesar was as busy as a spider when it feels the first twitch of the fly. His lovingly detailed description of the siege works translates his glee at Vercingetorix's blunder. Before the *oppidum* was completely encircled, Vercingetorix ordered a levy of all the tribes: '12,000 each from the Sequani, Senones, Bituriges, Santones, Ruteni and Carnutes; 8000 each from the Pictones, Turoni, Parisii and Helvetii', etc. The total number of soldiers requisitioned was 282,000.*

About three weeks later, the pan-Gallic relief force assembled in the lands of the Aedui. Since Celtic armies marched and fought in tribal regiments, the horde would have been an ethnographic map of Gaul. Some were dressed in chainmail (a Celtic invention), others in leather cuirasses. All of them carried brightly painted shields and cloaks fastened at the shoulder with a brooch. Their cloaks and trousers were striped, with checks of many different colours. Some of the warriors wore iron helmets crested with wings or a solar wheel. Those from the poorer regions wore sheepskin skull-caps and stuffed woollen bonnets. Their hair was blanched and stiffened with lime-water so that it looked like the mane of a horse. Others were clean-shaven and had feathered, wreath-like hairstyles. They might almost have passed as Romans.

A census was taken (this was the source that Caesar would use when he wrote up his account): 258,000 soldiers had answered the call. Accordingly, the Roman fortifications formed two lines of defence – one facing the *oppidum*, the other facing the plain from where the relief army would arrive.

By entombing his warriors in the sacred town of Herakles and Celtine, and by summoning a quarter of a million soldiers to the same place, Vercingetorix or the Druid augurs had presented Caesar with a general's dream – the chance to inflict total defeat on the combined forces of the enemy. The siege began in late August or early September and lasted long enough for the jaws of famine to tighten on the eighty thousand. The population density of the beleaguered *oppidum* would have been four times that of modern Paris. After about thirty days, the civilian population was evacuated, but their exit was blocked by the Romans and they died of starvation under the eyes of the besieged. When the relief army arrived, it was massacred by the legions within sight of the ramparts.

Inside the mother-city, another council was convened: it was decided that Vercingetorix should surrender. He donned his finest armour and trotted out of Alesia – according to Plutarch – on a beautifully caparisoned horse. He rode in a circle around Caesar,

---

* See the map of the Gaulish confederation on p. 34.

dismounted, dropped his armour on the ground, and sat at the conqueror's feet. The survivors were divided up among the Roman soldiers. In place of booty, each man received a slave, and since, by that stage of the war, the legions were labouring under the weight of plundered treasure, even a half-starved porter was a boon.

✿

The Alesia that can be seen today on the hill above the village of Alise-Sainte-Reine is the Roman town that replaced the *oppidum*. The oldest part is the temple to Ucuetis, a god of metalworkers. Its stone footings, next to the *table d'orientation*, trace the ground-plan of an earlier temple. The museum of Alesia is unaware of the fact, but unlike the other buildings, the Celtic temple is oriented by its major axis on the solstice line from Châteaumeillant. There are few other signs of Druidic calculations – the army that faced the rising sun, two sorties launched by the Gauls when the sun was highest in the sky, and Vercingetorix's final circumambulation of Caesar. These are the only hints that Alesia had once been the focal point of a solar sanctuary as large as Gaul itself.

At Alesia, the Gaulish cause was lost. But there was to be one other 'last stand'. Throughout that winter and the following spring (51 BC), the legions were busy stamping out the fires of rebellion that still burned in other parts of Gaul. In early summer, a Gaulish army was defeated at the siege of Lemonum (Poitiers), which lies on the same latitude as Châteaumeillant. Vercingetorix's most trusted general – a leader of the Cadurci tribe named Lucterius – escaped from Lemonum and joined forces with a leader of the Senones called Drappes. They assembled a ragged army of two thousand warriors. Lucterius was already known to Caesar as 'a man of the utmost audacity', but the Cadurcan's plan was more than audacious, it was suicidal. Abandoning the ruins of central Gaul to the Romans, Lucterius and Drappes would march south to attack the Roman province.

The direct route from Lemonum to Narbo, the capital of the province, led through the lands of the Cadurci, where Lucterius had his power-base. He and his army passed the Duranius (the Dordogne) and struck out across the region of limestone plateaux where the rivers run through deep gorges. Here, where the warmth of the south begins to prevail over the moist winds of the Atlantic, Lucterius was in his home territory. Word reached him that two Roman legions had set off in pursuit. He realized, says Hirtius, that 'to enter the province with an army in the rear would mean certain destruction'. But the region later called the Quercy (from 'Cadurci') was the natural habitat of fugitives. Long before the Celts, a primitive race had lurked in the tortuous caverns that led to the lower world. In the valleys of the Lot, the Aveyron and the Viaur, the crags that jut out of the woodland at river-bends look like citadels, and the citadels look like crags.

Lucterius chose what appeared to be an impregnable *oppidum*. Its name was Uxellodunum, from *uxellos* ('high') and *dunum* ('hill fort'). Before the war, Uxellodunum had been a protectorate of his tribe. It was a natural fortress: a river almost surrounded it, 'very steep and rugged cliffs defended it on all sides', and on the narrow strip of land that connected the *oppidum* to the outside world, 'the waters of a copious well burst forth'. Its only obvious weakness was a large area of high ground facing the *oppidum* from which anyone trying to enter or leave could be seen.

Despite the meticulous topographic description by Hirtius, no one knows where the last major battle of the Gallic War was fought. 'Uxellodunum' was a common Celtic place name, and several *oppida* in the same region may have shared it,* but since the final resting-place of Independent Gaul is a matter of national historical importance, the French Ministry of Culture, in 2001, following the lead of Napoleon III, declared the plateau of the Puy d'Issolud in the Lot *département* to be 'the official site' of Uxellodunum. Six hundred and thirty-four arrow-heads, sixty-nine catapult darts and other Roman weaponry prove that a battle took place there in the mid-first century BC. Unfortunately, not a single detail of Hirtius's description corresponds to anything at Puy d'Issolud, and a war of words still rages between the three towns that claim to have been Uxellodunum.

Three kilometres to the east of the Gaulish meridian, on the borders of the Cadurci and the Ruteni, there is a place that no one has ever suspected of being Uxellodunum. It matches Hirtius's description

---

* 'Uxellodunum' survives in Exoudun, Issudel, Issoudun and a few other place names. Most have probably vanished. The Uxelodunum (*sic*) on Hadrian's Wall above Carlisle is now Stanwix ('Stone Way').

exactly. The village is now called Pampelonne. The steep-sided promontory on its eastern edge, in a tight bend of the river Viaur, bears
the old name of the town, Thuriès. A hamlet, first recorded in 1275,
once clung to the cliffs; its last remnants disappeared when the hydro-
electric dam was built in the 1920s, but the impressive ruins of a
medieval castle still bear witness to its strategic importance.

Thuriès castle stood on the Iron Age route that connected
Aquitania to the lands of the Arverni. It was the stoutest fortress in
the region; its lords grew rich on tolls exacted at the river crossing
– which is why, one day in the 1360s, a small band of Gascon mercenaries led by the Bastard of Mauléon, wearing handkerchiefs on their
heads and talking in high-pitched voices, gathered at 'the magnificent
spring' on the edge of Thuriès. After filling their pitchers at the
fountain, the six 'women' strolled into town, then summoned their
companions with a horn-blast from the ramparts – 'and that', as the
Bastard explained to the chronicler Jean Froissart, 'is how I captured
the town and castle of Thurie [sic], which have brought me more
profit and revenue every year . . . than I could ever make from selling
the castle and all its dependencies.'

Some places are predestined to be battle-sites. Many centuries
before Thuriès fell to the Bastard of Mauléon and his band of
bogus women, the last Gaulish army, following the direct route
from Lemonum to Narbo, would have come to what is now the
Puy d'Issolud, the 'official' Uxellodunum. Near the bridge over the
Dordogne, a battle was fought with arrows and catapults. Continuing along the same direct line to Narbo, the survivors would then
have reached the Thuriès *oppidum* above the river Viaur. Knowing, as
Hirtius says, that it would have been madness 'to enter the province
with an army in the rear', the fugitives decided to make a stand.

Thuriès, which Hirtius may have conflated with the other *uxellodunum* or 'high hill fort' on the route, does in fact lie on or close to
the borders of Gallia Transalpina. It also lies on the borders of the
Cadurci and the Ruteni, which is what Hirtius's description implies.
Thuriès was a frontier town with a major river crossing on the long-
distance route to Aquitania. This might explain why Caesar decided
to leave central Gaul to help out at the siege of Uxellodunum: 'He
reflected that, though he had conquered part of Aquitania through
[his lieutenant] Publius Crassus, he had never been there in person.'

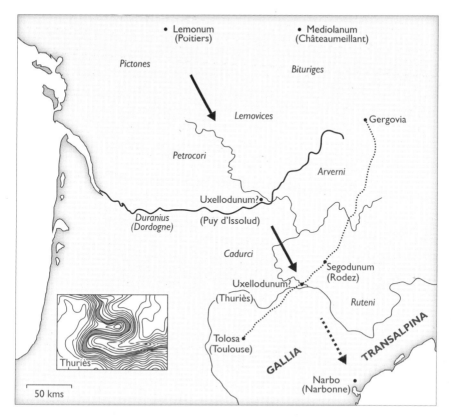

51. The route to Uxellodunum

The dotted line represents the ancient route from the Auvergne to Aquitania.

The *oppidum* lay conveniently on the route to Aquitania, which is where Caesar, after supervising the siege, would decide 'to spend the latter part of the summer'.

The key to Uxellodunum was the 'copious well' below the *oppidum* walls. The Romans eventually succeeded in drawing off its water by 'cutting the veins of the spring' with mineshafts. The inhabitants of Uxellodunum surrendered, but not because they were dying of thirst. A prisoner explained the logic of their decision to Caesar: 'They attributed the drying-up of the well, not to the devices of men, but to the will of the gods.' To the Romans, this was a mark of primitive superstition, but the Celts were at least as advanced as the Romans in mining techniques, and the digging of mineshafts can hardly have passed unnoticed. From the Celtic point of view, the Romans were acting as agents of a higher authority. The course of the siege – and of the entire war – had been governed all along by the upper world.

At Uxellodunum, within an arrow's range of the Gaulish meridian, Independent Gaul came to an end. Before he left for Aquitania, Caesar wanted to ensure that this would be the last sputtering of rebellion. The solution was made possible by what he saw as his reputation for 'lenitas' ('mildness' or 'softness'). No one would accuse him of acting out of 'natural cruelty' if he inflicted an 'exemplary punishment' on the people who had borne arms against the Romans. He would allow them to stay alive so that they could serve as advertisements of Roman justice: 'Itaque omnibus qui arma tulerant manus praecidit'. 'Praecidit' means 'cut off'; the noun, 'manus', is sometimes translated as 'the right hand', perhaps because the fourth-declension accusative plural looks like a singular. The correct translation is 'the hands'. The legions once again gave proof of their tireless efficiency, perhaps, too, of their frustration at 'the oppidum-dwellers' stubborn resistance'. The deliberate spoiling of human merchandise would show that Caesar was in earnest . . . The operation was performed, and, that autumn, the men and women of Uxellodunum saw the sun of southern Gaul ripen what remained of their crops but were unable to reap the harvest, having no hands with which to hold their tools.

✿

A winter in Gaul, described by Diodorus Siculus in the first century BC:

> And the land, lying as it does for the most part under the Bears, has a frigid climate and is exceedingly cold. For during the winter, on cloudy days, snow falls on the earth instead of rain, and in clear weather, ice and heavy frost are so abundant that the rivers freeze over and are bridged by their own waters. For not only can small bands of travellers who happen to pass that way continue their journey on the ice, but even huge armies with all their beasts of burden and heavily-laden vehicles are able to reach the other side quite safely. . . . And since the natural smoothness of the ice makes the crossing slippery, the Celts scatter chaff on it to make the going more secure.

In the historical record, the years following the conquest of Gaul are covered with a blanket of snow. We know only that, between 46 and 27 BC, local rebellions broke out among the Bellovaci, the Treveri and the

Morini, but a generation of warriors had died, and the legions who camped in the *oppida* watched over hungry populations of grandparents and children. The archaeological record shows that, with a few exceptions, the old *oppida* were gradually abandoned for more practical settlements on lower ground. These became the Roman towns whose imperious remains still dominate the muddy scrapings of Iron Age excavations.

The siting of the new towns was determined, not by the paths of the sun, but by the motions of men. By the mid-first century AD, many of the *oppida* had fallen into disrepair. Some shrines were still tended; columns of smoke could be seen rising from charcoal-burners' fires and metalworkers' forges; but beyond the building-sites and streets of Augustonemeton (Clermont-Ferrand) and Augustodunum (Autun), Gergovia and Bibracte stood on the horizon like memorials to a lost world.

The short journeys of the *oppidum*-dwellers from hilltop to plain were the last migrations in the heroic age of the Continental Celts. The tide had been going out since the expedition to Delphi, and it would continue to ebb until Celtic societies lingered only on the shores of the Ocean in countries that the legions would have been happy to leave to the savages. From the siege and destruction of the Celtiberian *oppidum* of Numantia in 133 BC to the massacre of the Caledonian tribes at the battle of Mons Graupius in AD 83 (p. 265), the history of the Celts in their westward retreat seems to call for the plangent, piped tones of national self-pity that never fail to accompany their filmed adventures.

The Druidic network seemed to fade like a shadow when a cloud covers the sun. Their teachings had never been inscribed on paper or stone, and the system of solar paths left few material traces on the landscape. Some sections of road followed the paths – the tin route from the north of Paris to the *oppidum* at Fécamp, or the route from the Alps to the British Ocean through the lands of the Lingones and the Remi. Just as parts of the old Heraklean Way had become sections of the Via Domitia, these routes were incorporated into the Roman road network. They still exist – their solstice alignments unrecognized – like the foundations of pagan temples buried under churches. But apart from these sparse strands of tartan weave, the surveys that produced the Roman network show no evidence of solar orientation.

The roads of the Romans were centred on the town of Colonia Copia Felix Munatia, later renamed Lugdunum (Lyon). Like the

52. Principal Roman roads of Gaul
The thicker lines indicate sections of road on Celtic orientations.

three Gaulish Mediolana that became important junctions in the network (Châteaumeillant, Évreux and Saintes), 'Lugh's hill fort' might have been chosen as a place of religious significance to the natives: it lay ten minutes to the east of the Gaulish meridian and one quarter of a *klima* to the south of Châteaumeillant. But its location at the confluence of the Rhone and the Saône was above all a matter of commercial and administrative expediency.

With Lugdunum as its capital, Gaul was divided into provinces in 27 BC. The gods played no part in this reorganization. A single province encompassed the foothills of the Alps and the ports that faced Britannia, while the chilly coasts of Armorica came under the same jurisdiction as the sunny vineyards of Lugdunum. The shape of early Roman Gaul has become so familiar that its bizarre configuration is

53. The provinces of Gaul

The provinces of Gaul after the Augustan Settlement of 27 BC, and the Roman logic of their borders. The dotted line represents the earlier western border of Gallia Narbonensis.

never questioned or explained. To the Romans, no explanation would have been necessary. The new boundaries accurately reflected Gaul as seen by a Roman geographer. This was the shapeless earth of mortals, charted without the guidance of a sun god.

✿

In the Roman capital that is now Lyon, the magnificent though slightly outdated Musée de la Civilisation Gallo-Romaine appears to have been taken over by Celtophile exponents of counterfactual history. If Vercingetorix had defeated Caesar at Alesia, and if Lucterius had crossed the borders of the province and reclaimed the Heraklean Way, this is what one might expect to see: the monumental plinths of marble statues carved in the first century AD with the names of important Gauls, publicly declaring their pride in their Celtic heritage:

> To Lucius Lentulius Censorinus of the PICTAVI,* amongst whom he has held every post of honour, commissioner of the BITURIGES VIVISCI . . .

> To Quintus Julius Severinus of the SEQUANI . . . patron of the most splendid corporation of boatmen of the Rhone and the Saône, twice honoured by the Council of decurions of his city with statues bearing witness to his integrity.

> To Caius Servilius Martianus, ARVERNIAN, son of Caius Servilius Domitus, priest of the temple of Roma and Augustus, the three provinces of Gaul.

The names of warlike tribes whose homelands had been ravaged by Caesar are displayed with all the pomp of a victorious nation. Elsewhere in the museum, a bronze tablet discovered in Lyon reproduces Emperor Claudius's speech to the Senate in AD 48. Claudius proposed that loyal and wealthy citizens of Gallia Comata be allowed to sit in the Senate. 'Hairy Gaul' was no longer beyond the pale. Soon, the tribes of Gaul would rename their principal towns, replacing the Roman name with that of the tribe, which is why metropolitan France is one of the most visibly Celtic countries in Europe. The Remi live in Reims, the Bellovaci in Beauvais, and the Turones in Tours; Auvergne is the province of the Arverni; the Bituriges, who were nearly exterminated by Caesar, still inhabit Bourges, and the Parisii still have a capital on the Seine.

Gaul recovered from the war, psychologically and materially, within two or three generations. Unlike other vanquished civilizations, the Gaulish Celts did not punish or deny their gods. They continued to worship them under the Romans. A year or so after Claudius's speech, the Arverni commissioned a colossal statue of Mercury (the avatar of Lugh) from a famous sculptor for their temple on the Puy de Dôme. It cost forty million sesterces and was the largest statue in the world until the same sculptor was ordered to produce an even larger statue of Nero.

---

* The Pictavi or Pictones of Lemonum (Poitiers).

Though it was built of stone instead of wood, the temple of Mercury on the summit of the Puy de Dôme has the traditional, deceptive shape of Celtic shrines. Its corners look like right angles, but one axis is oriented on the local summer solstice, the other on the solar path from Châteaumeillant. Like so much else in Celtic Gaul, these details have slipped into oblivion, but they show that Lugh was still a living presence in the Roman empire. His power was acknowledged by the Romans when it was decided that the birthday of Emperor Claudius, who was born in Lugdunum, should fall on the feast day of Lugh (1 August).

At Alesia and Uxellodunum, the gods' will had been done. According to Caesar, the Druids sacrificed large numbers of people 'for state purposes'. They preferred to use convicted criminals, but 'when there [was] a shortage of such people', they sacrificed the innocent. The eight-year-long war in which so many warriors and civilians had passed into the other world had been a heavy harvest. Usually, the sacrificial victims were packed into gigantic dolls in the image of gods with wicker limbs, which were then set on fire. The besieged *oppida*, crammed with thousands of people, had performed the same religious function. This holocaust can hardly have been the original objective of the Gauls, but it was not the final disaster that it would have been for other nations. The gods had been propitiated, and the Druids were vindicated by the subsequent prosperity of Gaul.

✿

Defeat and subjugation are supposed to be defining characteristics of the Celts. Archaeology has muddled that simple, romantic tale. The exodus from the *oppida* was not necessarily a trail of tears. The process had begun before the war and it continued long after the conquest. Little is known about the early stages of Roman urbanization in Gaul. In the *oppida* that became Roman towns, the thatched huts of the natives were swept away and replaced with stone buildings. Architects and engineers imposed a simple street-plan based on two axes – the *cardo maximus*, which ran approximately north–south, and a bisecting *decumanus maximus*. These axes frequently followed the alignment of the main roads that led to the town, but the overriding criterion was convenience. Solar orientation in Roman towns and forts is extremely rare. The road that enters Amiens from the south-east on a Celtic solstice bearing was ignored by the Roman town-planners, who matched their street-grid to the course of the river Somme.

There is, however, some compelling evidence that the Druidic system was not immediately abandoned. It may even have been adapted to the new world. The streets of Reims are aligned on the solstice line that joins the Great St Bernard Pass to the British Ocean. The same phenomenon can be seen in the Roman towns of Autun, Metz and Limoges. These alignments, which have kept their secret until now, may reflect the special favour that was shown to certain tribes: the Remi had always been allies of the Romans; the Mediomatrici of Metz and the Lemovices of Limoges sent soldiers to Alesia but were involved in no other battles; the Aedui had rebelled only at the very end of the war, and soon regained their status as 'Friends of the Roman People'.

Unbeknownst to their modern inhabitants, the streets of these Gallo-Roman towns are the aisles of a temple dedicated to an ancient sun god. Perhaps this materialization of solar paths was to have been the next stage in the development of the system. If Gaul had remained independent, the upper world might have been more comprehensively mapped onto Middle Earth, but many of the priestly planners who would have masterminded the operation had left the country after the Gallic War.

'*Non interire, sed transire . . .*': 'Souls do not perish but pass after death from one body into another, and this they see as an inducement to valour, for the dread of death is thereby negated' (p. 116). At the end of the war, many living souls had passed over from Gaul to Britannia, where, as Caesar was told, Druidism had been 'discovered'. In earlier days, Belgic tribes had migrated to the island that Pytheas had known as Prettanike. Perhaps older traditions of Druidism had been preserved there: 'Those who wish to make a more assiduous study of the matter generally go to Britain in order to learn', said Caesar. Some of the Druids who crossed the Channel in the autumn of 51 BC would have been revisiting places and people they had known as students.

Merchants and fishermen putting out from Portus Itius or one of the smaller Channel ports might have carried fare-paying passengers fleeing from the Romans. Even after the battle of Uxellodunum, there had been cavalry skirmishes in the north of Gaul. A leader of the

Atrebates called Commios, whom Caesar had used as an ambassador to Britain in 55 BC, having turned against the Romans, had been 'infesting the roads and intercepting convoys'. But even if the Channel ports were placed under surveillance, no one would have paid much attention, for instance, to an elderly Druid boarding a slave ship or a fishing vessel. It was only much later that the Romans learned to fear the political power of the Druids and outlawed their order.

The Romans would hear of Commios again. Twenty years on, he was installed as king of the British Atrebates: coins bearing his name were issued from a town called Calleva (Silchester). Precisely when and where he escaped from the Romans, no one knows. In the late 70s AD, the Roman governor of Britain, Frontinus, heard a cheerful tale of a Gaulish refugee outwitting his Roman pursuers:

> Defeated by the deified Caesar, Commius the Atrebatan was fleeing from Gaul to Britannia. He happened to reach the Ocean when the wind was fair but the tide was out. Though his ships were stranded on the shore, he nonetheless ordered the sails to be unfurled. Caesar, who was pursuing, saw the billowing of the sails in a full breeze. Imagining Commius to be making good his escape, he abandoned the pursuit.

The port of Leuconaus (Saint-Valéry-sur-Somme) lies at the end of the solstice-oriented route from Samarobriva (fig. 16). At low tide, the ocean recedes by as much as fourteen kilometres. On the open horizon of the Bay of the Somme, a sail can be seen at a great distance, out as far as the point where the sand-flats merge with the sea. It might have been from there that Commios sailed for Britain. The legend credits him with the glorious deception, but there is something unmistakably Druidic in that beautiful and magical illusion serving a vital purpose.

When the tide came in, a fair wind would have carried the refugees across the Channel in a single night. At dawn, along the coast that was 'guarded with wondrous walls of massive rock', as Caesar had told Cicero, there were many safe harbours; some of them were busy international ports. The hinterland of Britannia was beginning to prosper, and it would be left in peace by the Romans for the next ninety-four years.

The home of Druidism was not quite as uncivilized as Cicero had supposed. The British king who was defeated by Caesar spoke Latin, and despite what Roman historians believed, Herakles himself had set foot on the island. One version of the legend of Celtic origins identifies the father of Celtine as a certain Bretannos. The name is otherwise unrecorded and resembles no word other than Prettanike or Britannia. Somewhere in that cold and foggy land, perhaps along its southern coast, there had once lived a princess sufficiently well endowed, in person and in larder, to seduce a sun god from the Mediterranean.

PART FOUR

13

The Poetic Isles

This book was to have ended here, with the defeat of the Gauls and the exodus of Druids to Britain. 'Their science crossed the ocean', said Pliny, 'and reached the void of Nature' (by which he meant Britannia). It was in this cul-de-sac of the north that Druidism or some of its religious traditions had been 'discovered', according to Caesar. He, or his Druid informant, called it a '*disciplina*', which suggests an institution capable of organizing a body of knowledge into a curriculum. But where were the schools of Iron Age Britain? And where, for that matter, were the towns? 'The Britanni', said Caesar, 'fortify their tangled woods with a ditch and a rampart and call it a town'. The British king, Cassivellaunus, spoke Latin, but he must have learnt it on the Continent, just as the sons of Highland chiefs in seventeenth-century Scotland left their glens to go and study at the Sorbonne in Paris.

The sorcery of received ideas covers the British Isles with a coarse and heavy cloak. It is hard to picture a system of solar paths stretching so far from its Mediterranean origin and easy to believe that, after the conquest of Gaul, Britannia waited in its primeval squalor for the Roman landlords to come and install the plumbing and the central heating. Not until AD 43 would a beacon fire be lit on top of a watch-tower on the Kentish coast to announce to the Continent that Britannia belonged to the Roman empire.

But if Britannia truly was a homeland of Druidism, and if, as Caesar was informed, 'those who wish to make a more assiduous study of it generally go there to learn', it can hardly have been such a backwater. There is, in fact, a trace of Druidry in the Celtic name of the islands, though its meaning has been lost for almost two thousand years. 'Prettanike' was the name heard by Pytheas in the fourth century BC; 'Britannia' was the form familiar to Caesar. The inhabitants would originally have been the 'Pritani' or 'Pret(t)anoi'. The name belongs to a group of words whose Indo-European root means 'to cut', 'to form', 'to shape'. In early medieval Ireland, the 'figured folk' of Britain were assimilated to the 'painted' or 'tattooed' Picts of Scotland. Convention has sealed the interpretation, and the accepted history of Britain now begins with a population of barbarians who smeared themselves with the blue dye of woad.

Some Celtic tribes, like the 'painted' Pictones or Pictavi of Gaul, were named for their visible attributes. Many others had names that referred to religious ritual: the People of the Dance (Lingones), of the Sanctuary (Nemetes), of the Cauldron (Parisii); the Shining Ones (Leuci), the Bright Ones (Glanici). The Pritani of Britannia probably belonged to the latter group. The name is often found, as Prito, Pritto, Pritillius or Pritmanus, on fragments of Iron Age and Gallo-Roman pottery from Gaul and northern Germania. Like 'Mason' or 'Smith', the name was the mark of a profession. In ancient Celtic, '*pritios*' had the same dual meaning as the Greek '*poietes*': a creator, a craftsman, an enchanter and a poet.

The protohistoric inhabitants of Britain were not, by name, the face-painted belligerents beloved of British nationalists. They were makers, not destroyers. They excelled in the arts of verse and incantation. The name 'Prettanike' belongs to the distant age when an early form of Druidism existed in the British Isles. The scientific traditions of the Druids may have been Hellenistic, but their bardic and religious heritage belonged to the ancient land that should now be reimagined as the Poetic Isles.

✧

The legend of a Mediterranean sun god impregnating the daughter of a mythical King Bretannos reflects the realities of trade and cultural transmission in the first century BC. Even for mortals, the Oceanus Britannicus was not a barrier. Branches of the Atrebates and the Parisii had migrated to Britain; the Catuvellauni of the Thames Basin were probably relatives of the Catalauni of Champagne. In the regions closest to the Continent, pottery, coins and burials show a similar culture developing on both sides of the Channel in the aftermath of the Gallic War. And far beyond the civilized south-east, there are

Legend:
- ○ Tribal centre
- ■ *Nemeton* (sanctuary)
- * Lugh place name

Cornavii
Lugi
Smertae
Caereni
Decantae
Carnonacae
Taexali
Vacomagi
Creones Caledones
Venicones
Epidii
Damnonii
Votadini
Selgovae
Anavionenses
Novantae Carvetii
Brigantes
Parisii
Deceangli Corieltauvi
Cornovii
Ordovices Iceni
Dobunni
Silures Trinovantes
Catuvellauni
Atrebates
Belgae Cantiaci
Durotriges Regni
Dumnonii

100 kms

54. British tribes

The tribal names are known from ancient historians and geographers, the *civitas* capitals of the Romans and inscriptions. In northern Scotland especially, the limits of tribal territories are a matter of speculation.

places that bear the name of the god Lugh, and many others that were *nemetons* or 'sky sanctuaries' of the Druids (fig. 54).

If the Gaulish system of solar paths was extended across the Channel, the evidence should be easy to discover. Though the ethnographic information is scantier than it is in Gaul, enough British tribal centres have been identified to make corroboration possible. But at first, the patterns that are so vivid in Gaul are nowhere to be seen. Nothing in Iron Age Britain suggests that the Heraklean ratio of 11:7 was ever applied to any system of paths or hill forts. There is just the faintest whirring of a Druidic mechanism, but it comes from a place that lies a long way from the south coast, in a corner of the county of Shropshire, in the lands of the Cornovii.

The market town of Whitchurch, which claims to be 'old but not old fashioned', prides itself on being the birthplace of the man who wrote the light opera *Merrie England*. It lies just three kilometres from the Welsh border. The town is recorded by Ptolemy and by two other ancient sources as 'Mediolanum'. Disregarding its neighbouring hills, Whitchurch, like Milan, interprets its ancient name as 'middle of the plain'. This is the only known Mediolanum in England, though there was a 'Medio*m*anum' (probably a scribe's misspelling) somewhere in mid-Wales,* and the Medionemeton on the Antonine Wall. Otherwise, the map of British Middle Earth is almost blank.

Unlike the Scottish Medionemeton, which was the mid-point of a survey line joining sea to sea (p. 52), Whitchurch is not an obviously significant 'middle sanctuary'. It stands at a junction of Roman roads, but then so does almost every other place whose ancient name has survived. It does, however, possess some curious properties, which make it a British twin of the prime Gaulish Mediolanum, Château-meillant.

Like Châteaumeillant, Whitchurch-Mediolanum occupies a border-

---

* The likeliest location of 'Mediomanum', which the Ravenna Cosmography (c. AD 700) places between Levobrinta (Forden Gaer) and Seguntio (Caernarfon), is Tomen y Mur, a Roman fort complex and legendary palace of Lleu (Lugh). The Cosmography also lists a 'Mediobogdum', once thought to have been the Roman fort at Hardknott Pass, but now identified with the fort near Kendal in the 'middle of a bend' in the river Kent, four kilometres west of the meridian. The '*medio*' in this case may be purely geographical.

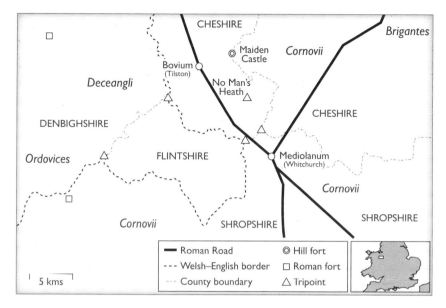

55. The area of Whitchurch (Mediolanum)

These are the historic county boundaries, before the reforms of 1965 and 1974.
One of the 'tripoints' (where three boundaries intersect) is a 'quadripoint': four
parishes meet at the place called No Man's Heath.

land that was probably a buffer zone between Celtic tribes. Parish,
county and national boundaries, some of which date back to pre-
Roman times, form such a tight knot in the vicinity of Whitchurch
that a walker who finds a fascination in such things can set off from
the town centre at dawn and stand on five triple intersections or
'tripoints' before noon.

Whitchurch also shares with Châteaumeillant one of those happy
accidents of geography that the Druids of Gaul exploited so skilfully.
Châteaumeillant – the Mediolanum of the Bituriges – stands on the
longest line that can be drawn through Gaul from north to south.
Whitchurch – the Mediolanum of the Cornovii – stands on a meridian
that runs almost the entire length of Britain. Anyone who has tried
to trace a north–south route through the non-consecutive sheets of
a road atlas will know that Britain is awkwardly skewed to the west.
Leaving the part of southern England known as the West Country,
and heading due north, one ends up in eastern Scotland; the Atlantic
waters of the Severn Estuary are on the same line of longitude as the

Firth of Forth, which is an inlet of the North Sea. The Whitchurch meridian is the longest line that can be drawn through the tilted island of Britain. It crosses three estuaries, but not the open sea, before reaching the northern coast of Aberdeenshire.

As a line of mid-longitude (p. 62), the Whitchurch meridian could hardly be bettered. It begins at a hill called Beacon Knap above the Dorset coast and ends at Portsoy or Port Saoidh, whose name means 'Harbour of the Warrior' or 'the Scholar'. By contrast, the line of mid-longitude that was chosen by the British Ordnance Survey – and perhaps, too, by the first Roman surveyors – crosses one hundred and seventy kilometres of the North Sea.

A legend preserved by medieval scholars suggests a native British tradition of long-distance surveying predating the Roman conquest. One of the first to have recorded it was Geoffrey of Monmouth, whose *Historia Regum Britanniae* ('History of the Kings of Britain') was written in about 1136. According to the *Historia*, in the old days before the Romans, a mythical King Belinus ordered a causeway to be built 'which should run the whole length of the island, from the sea of Cornwall to the shores of Caithness, and lead directly to the cities that lay along that extent'. Like Herakles on the Via Heraklea, Belinus conferred on all who travelled on his roads 'every honour and privilege, and prescribed a law for the punishment of any injury committed upon them'. Whatever the source of the legend – a tale told by a Welsh bard or a manuscript found by Geoffrey in Oxford – it has the mark of the Druids: the name of the mythical road-building monarch is that of a Celtic god of light, Belenos or Belenus.

The Druids' geometric plotting exactly matches the mythical truth. The Gaulish meridian, projected from Châteaumeillant to Loon Plage and across the Channel, would have missed the British mainland by about thirty kilometres. In order to extend the system into Britain, retaining the points of reference that defined the place of Celtic lands in the wider world, the Druids would have chosen the meridians or lines of longitude that run ten-minute increments to the west of the prime Gaulish Mediolanum. And this is what the map reveals: the more westerly of the two lines, directly connecting Heraklean Gaul to the homeland of the Druids, is the Whitchurch meridian.

Given what we now know about the Druids, the coincidence can hardly be called astonishing, though it is, all the same, astonishing.

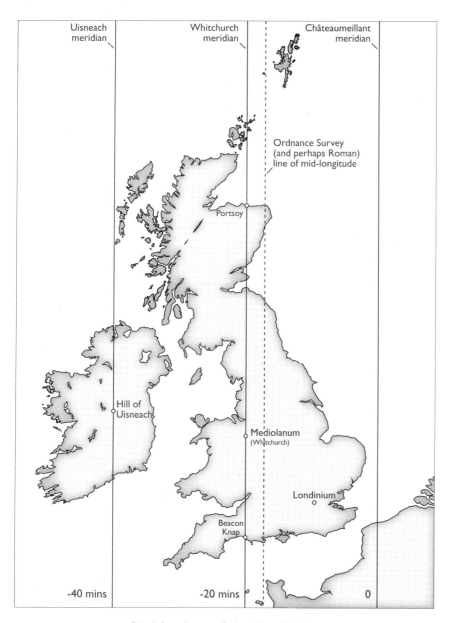

Ordnance Survey
(and perhaps Roman)
line of mid-longitude

Portsoy

Hill of
Uisneach

Mediolanum
(Whitchurch)

Londinium

Beacon
Knap

-40 mins

-20 mins

0

56. Meridians of the British Isles

As is the tidy fact that if the same operation is extended to the west, into the remotest of Celtic lands, the next meridian passes through the Hill of Uisneach (within twenty-nine seconds of daylight). In Celtic mythology, the Hill of Uisneach, with its royal burials and ring forts, was the sacred centre or *omphalos* of Ireland (see p. 274).

✿

Without the corresponding solstice lines to reveal a network of solar paths, the Whitchurch meridian is a slender thread on which to hang even a virtual expedition. Yet that slender thread traces out a comprehensive mystery tour of ancient Britain and the geometric basis of a wonderfully coherent system.

Shortly after leaving Beacon Knap in Dorset, the meridian passes by the foot of Glastonbury Tor, near the site of a *nemeton*, and then through the village of Nempnett Thrubwell, whose name has the same origin. Comparatively few British tribal capitals are known, but the meridian bisects several of them, as though in obedience to the commands of Belinus: the road 'should run the whole length of the island . . . and lead directly to the cities that lay along that extent'. These tribal capitals include more than half the likely centres of Scottish tribes.* The meridian also encompasses twenty hill forts, some of which may have marked an ancient Welsh frontier.

On several sections of its unerring course, the Whitchurch meridian shows a remarkable attraction to boundaries and their intersections. After reaching the tripoint where Wales meets the Anglo-Saxon kingdoms of Mercia and Wessex, it follows the Welsh border for twenty-two kilometres, then crosses back into England near the tripoint of Gloucestershire, Herefordshire and Monmouthshire. At Whitchurch, at approximately one-third of its total distance, it crosses the boundary region shown on the map (fig. 55). Further north, before the Mid Hill that marks two-thirds of its length, it crosses the lonely clearing in the Kielder Forest where Cumberland and Northumberland meet Scotland.

One of the meridian's most intriguing characteristics is its close relationship with long-distance routes. In Dorset, it bisects an important town of the Durotriges called Lindinis (Ilchester). In the early

---

* Rubers Law, Trimontium, Traprain Law and the Caterthuns, on which, see p. 266.

days of the Roman conquest, this was the southern terminus of the
Fosse Way, which runs diagonally across the country to Lincoln and
forms what many historians believe to have been the first Roman
frontier in Britain. After crossing the Severn Estuary at a hill-fort
complex of the Silures tribe, it meets the southern terminus of another
ancient route, marked by the eighth-century earthwork known as
Offa's Dyke. Over its entire length, the meridian passes over eight
and perhaps nine Roman road junctions, as though the Romans had
somehow keyed their network into the ancient road of Belinus.

Of course, one straight line is not a network, and there are so
many hill forts, especially in south-west England and the Welsh
Marches, that if an ant walked across the printed map, its trail would
probably take in about the same number of significant places.
Appropriately, the meridian passes through the hills and dales that
were the stamping-ground of Alfred Watkins, the discoverer or
inventor of ley lines (p. xiv). In the dense scatter of pre- and protohistoric sites in Herefordshire and Shropshire, the possibilities for
single-minded expeditions along an 'Old Straight Track' are practically
endless.

As Watkins found, different eras merge in these forts and refuges
that were inhabited for thousands of years. Out of this confusion of
eras, oral tradition conjures simple figures to speak for all the centuries. One of those figures is the Devil, whose 'Mouthpiece' – on the
meridian by the deserted village of Witchcot – is nothing more
mysterious than an old sandstone quarry. Another is the real or
legendary King of the Britons, Arthur. He first appears at Glastonbury
Tor, one of the fabled locations of the Holy Grail and a portal to the
Underworld. Arthur's second appearance on the meridian is at the
cliff-top fort of Little Doward on the Welsh–English border, above
a great bend in the river Wye. It looks down on a village coincidentally named Whitchurch (one of eight Whitchurches in England).*
According to a legend transmitted by Geoffrey of Monmouth, it was
here that the fifth-century warlord Vortigern was besieged and burned

* The mid-point of the Antonine Wall survey line is Medionemeton. The site most
likely to have performed the same function on Hadrian's Wall is the halfway house
of Vindolanda. The name is also recorded as Vindolana, which might be translated
as 'white church' or Whitchurch.

to death by the Romano-British hero Ambrosius or, as he appears in this telling of the tale, Merlin. In the bowels of the fort, a round 'room' in 'King Arthur's Cave' is said to have contained a table of the same shape . . .

The Whitchurch meridian is astronomically compatible with the Gaulish system, but it presents only a few pieces of the puzzle, and Whitchurch itself differs from Châteaumeillant in one important respect. Châteaumeillant visibly sits at the centre of Gaul, whereas Whitchurch could never be described as the centre of Britain. If the system had been translated directly from Gaul to Britain, another line of longitude should have run ten minutes to the east, between the Whitchurch and the Châteaumeillant meridians. It would have passed through central London, with a likely point of origin at Thorney Island, where the Thames could be forded at low tide. Perhaps it was there, on the future site of Westminster Abbey, that Caesar's army waded across the river in 54 BC. But in contrast to the Whitchurch meridian, the London line has little of ancient interest, apart from a tripoint on Flag Fen near Peterborough. Its treasures and tribal centres belong to a much later age: Tate Britain, Number 10 Downing Street, the British Library and the Great Court of the British Museum.

Beyond these longitudinal paths, the clouds descend and thicken, until the British sun unexpectedly appears.

✻

In the meadows and cricket fields of the University Parks, where much of this book was ruminated, even people who consider Oxford to be the centre of the civilized world can recapture some of its early insignificance. Most tourists never venture this far north of the college lanes. The spires are eclipsed by trees, and there are few signs of academic life apart from white-coated technicians moving among their apparatus behind the glass front of a science building. Ironically, the University Parks are the only important protohistoric site in a city whose every stone is a memorial. During the long, dry summer of 1976, linear marks appeared in the fields and were identified by archaeologists as 'a substantial ritual focus' dating from the Bronze Age or earlier. Practically nothing of that 'ritual focus' is visible today. It was still in use after the arrival of the Romans, but the town itself hardly seems to have existed before AD 911, when it was recorded as Oxenaforda.

Oxford's principal connection with the world of the Celts is J. R. R. Tolkien of Exeter College, and so it is not surprising that the following peculiar and unexplained detail has received almost no attention.

The Mabinogion is the collective title of Welsh tales that were probably first written down in the eleventh century. Despite the medieval interpretations and embellishments, these tales, like the Irish myths, preserve fragments of legends dating back to the days of the ancient Celts. Since many of the locations can be identified, they often seem to speak of people and things that are very close at hand.

One such tale is 'The Meeting [or 'Adventure'] of Lludd and Llevelys'. Beli the Great, King of Britain, has died. His eldest son, Lludd, has inherited the kingdom. He rules it prosperously and makes London his capital. But the island is troubled by three 'plagues', one of which takes the form of two squabbling dragons. Lludd seeks the advice of his youngest brother, who has become King of France. After secretly equipping a fleet, Lludd sails for France; his brother sails out to meet him, and this is the advice Llevelys gives him:

> When you arrive home, have the length and breadth of the island measured, and where you find the exact centre, have a pit dug. In the pit, place a vat full of the best mead that can be made, and cover the vat with a silk sheet.

Lludd returns to Britain, has the length and breadth of the island measured, and finds its exact centre to be Rhydychen, which is the Welsh name of Oxford. Somewhere in Oxford, he digs the pit; the dragons fall in and drink up all the mead. Lludd wraps the unconscious monsters in the silk sheet and locks them 'in a stone chest in the most secure place he could find in Eryri'. (Eryri is Snowdonia, the mountain massif of North Wales.) 'And thereafter, the place was called Dinas Emreis [or Ambrosius], though before, it had been Dinas Ffaraon Dandde' ('Hill Fort of the Fiery Pharaoh').

The place where Lludd buried the dragons is well known. It was recently acquired by the National Trust. Below Mount Snowdon, the disintegrating hill fort of Dinas Emrys guards a road that joins the Llanberis Pass to the Aberglaslyn Pass. These are the two main routes through Snowdonia to the Menai Strait and the Isle of Anglesey (fig. 69). In the Welsh tale, little else is said about the dragons, but in the *Historia Brittonum* ('History of the Britons'), written in about

828, they are identified by the boy-prophet Myrddin Emrys (Merlin Ambrosius) as symbols of the native Welsh and the Saxon invaders. The hill fort itself, which may already have been a mound of rubble when the *Historia Brittonum* was written, is said to be the dilapidated royal palace of Vortigern, whose towers collapsed as soon as they were built.

These anachronistic interpretations, devised several centuries after the original myth and woven into the much older narrative, form the basis of most modern retellings of the tale. Though the nation of Wales did not exist, the nub of the tale is supposed to be the red dragon, which now appears on the Welsh national flag. Oxford, having no obvious connection with the birth of a Welsh nation, is omitted as an irrelevant detail. Yet the dragons transported by Lludd from the centre of the kingdom in Oxford to 'the Hill Fort of the Fiery Pharaoh' are not simple emblems of nationalism: they strongly suggest a Celtic solar myth, while Llevelys, King of Gaul, is related, by name and by deeds, to the Irish Lugh. The scribe notes that 'Hill Fort of the Fiery Pharaoh' was the earlier name of the fort, implying that one of his sources was even older than the ninth-century *Historia Brittonum*. The tale had taken shape when there were neither Saxon nor Roman soldiers in Britain.

The Druidic experiment is easily performed: measure the rhumb-line trajectory of the dragons from Oxford to Dinas Emrys. At the conclusion of the experiment, two facts appear. First, the path of the dragons is a solstice line – not the standard Gaulish trajectory with a ratio of 11:7, but something closer to the actual solstice as seen from Britain. Second, the halfway point of the line falls near 'The Devil's Mouthpiece' and a village north of Ludlow called Middleton. Llevelys had evidently given his brother some excellent and accurate advice: the village of Middleton lies precisely on the Whitchurch meridian.

These two facts present themselves with the sound of an iron key turning in a lock.

✳

This is what the treasure chest contains: the mathematical formula of the British Druidic system, and a map of the Poetic Isles before the Roman conquest. The temptation (not to be resisted) is to go rushing about the map of Celtic Britain like a historian with a day pass on a time machine. But first – to save time on the road – the theory and the formula.

The meeting in mid-Channel of the two royal brothers, Lludd and Llevelys, may be the remnant of a legend which recounted the translation of the Druidic system from Gaul to Britannia. Lludd of Britain is the elder brother. He inherits his father's kingdom, the homeland of Druidism. But his younger brother, Llevelys of Gaul, is 'a wise man and a good counsellor'. It is Llevelys, avatar of Lugh and ruler of a land in which Pythagorean science is taught to the young, who provides the necessary data, and the means of converting the Mediterranean solar network into a British equivalent. Having discovered by precise measurement the *omphalos* of his kingdom, and having calculated the trajectory of the sun dragons, Lludd will be able to bring the protection and prestige of the sun god to Britannia.

The formula supplied by the wise Llevelys is as secretly simple as a Celtic design. To return for a moment to an earlier part of this book, the exact points at which the solstice sun rises and sets were practically impossible to determine. The sun's light is refracted by the atmosphere, and a terrestrial horizon is never completely flat. In Gaul, therefore, a standard solstice angle had been chosen. It matched the trajectory of the Via Heraklea and the convenient ratio, 11:7, which contains the formula for producing a circle (p. 142).

This Mediterranean standard was perfectly usable even in northern Gaul, but by the time the solar paths reached British climes, the angle would have been visibly out of kilter with the locally observed solstice. The sun would no longer appear to rise and set in 'the right place'. A new, British standard had to be devised.

This was perhaps the first time in history that Britain deliberately distinguished itself from a Continental system. In modern terms, the solstice angle chosen as the British standard was 53.13° east of north, while the Gaulish angle was 57.53°. (Remarkably, the difference between these two standard angles – 4.4° – is almost exactly the actual difference between strictly calculated solstice angles at the latitudes of Châteaumeillant and Oxford – 4.63°.) The cross-Channel adjustment produced a trajectory which matched what the inhabitants of Britain saw when they observed the rising and setting of the solstice sun, but, like the Gaulish angle, the British angle had to be brought in line with a mathematically convenient and Druidically significant ratio. Suddenly, that vat of mead in which Lludd traps the dragons at the centre of his kingdom looks very familiar . . .

In the Aeduan capital of Bibracte in Gaul, a pink-granite basin was filled with a liquid that served a ritual purpose (pp. 123–5). The basin was astronomically aligned, reflecting the upper world both visually and mathematically, while its elliptical concavity suggested a birth passage and a connection with the lower world. Mead is a product of both worlds: it comes from the bees of the air and the wheat that taps the nutrients of the earth. Cauldrons and tankards filled with mead were buried with tribal chiefs in some of the German *oppida*. Perhaps, then, this was the sacred beverage that filled the basin at Bibracte. In the absence of the tell-tale waxy deposits it is impossible to be sure, but it is quite certain that the Bibracte basin shared something real and magical with the vat of mead at the Oxford *omphalos*. The geometrical formula for the basin's ellipse was 4:3. This is the elementary ratio that produces a perfect Pythagorean triangle, and – as Llevelys would have known when he handed the formula to his brother – this is also the ratio of the solstice line that connects the Oxford *omphalos* to the fort of Dinas Emrys.*

Here, locked in legend for two thousand years, is the formula – 4:3 – that would be used by British Druids to pattern a land mass one-third the size of Gaul. It was concise enough to be written on a tiny piece of parchment, and it contains so much information that it pushes the date at which the recorded history of Britain can be said to begin back before the Romans. Interpreted Druidically, those Celtic legends are the dream of a lost volume of the encyclopedia devoted to a forgotten letter of the alphabet. In the waking world, it sits there on the shelf, waiting to be read.

✴

Before the expedition can set off with a Druidic GPS calibrated on the British ratio of four and three, one question remains to be answered. When Lludd had the length and breadth of his kingdom

---

* Measured to the nearest hundredth of a degree, the line crosses the lake, Llyn Dinas, at the foot of Dinas Emrys. Both the lake and the hill fort were fabled burial places of the dragons, of Merlin's gold and of the Throne of Britain.

measured, why did his surveyors find the centre to be in Oxford? Iron Age and even Roman Oxford was such a peripheral place that its appearance in the tale seems to be one of those stray, eccentric details that litter the Celtic legends.

A lateral-thinking Druid would have known that Oxford was important precisely because it was peripheral. The distribution of coins minted by southern British tribes shows that Oxford stood at the intersection of three major tribal territories: the Catuvellauni of Verlamion (St Albans), the Atrebates of Calleva (Silchester) and the Dobunni of Corinium (Cirencester). Oxford itself may have been a neutral enclave like Alesia, its protected status guaranteed by its strategic importance. The small Mandubii tribe of Alesia is known only from a solitary reference in Caesar's *Gallic War*. Perhaps an equally small tribe of Oxubii has disappeared entirely.*

The exact centre of the Oxford *omphalos* (deduced from the calculations that follow) was on the site of one of the city's earliest Christian institutions. Beyond the Westgate and the railway station, a traveller heading for the Cumnor Hills crosses what was once an international frontier, where the Anglo-Saxon kingdoms of Wessex and Mercia met, and where the Thames still sometimes rises from its bed of gravel to flood the western approaches to the city. This is one of the busiest and least photogenic crossings of the Thames. As the river reaches Oxford, it suffers from indecision and splits into several streams. Only after Folly Bridge and the University boat houses does it regain its composure and set off purposefully for London.

Among those dithering, sloppy streams along the Botley Road, there once stood a magnificent abbey. All that remains of the abbey is a small section of rubble wall near Osney cemetery. Before the monks drove out its demons, Osney ('Osa's Island') was probably a pagan site. An archaeologist has suggested that the circle formed by the river channels around the castle and the former abbey marks the outline of a defensive enclosure or *oppidum*. (The circle is clearly visible on aerial photographs.) It is more than likely that the river crossing was defended: it was a vital link in a wider network. Even today, Oxford is a hub of the road system, and an accident on its

---

* 'Oxubii' ('People of the Ox') was the name of a Mediterranean Gaulish tribe in the region of Fréjus.

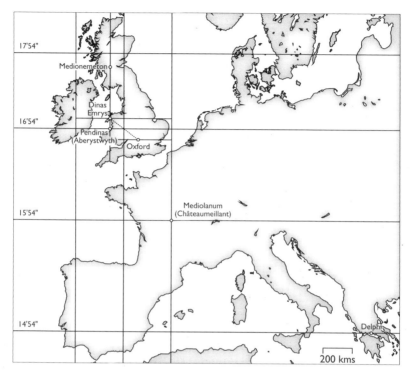

57. The place of Britain in the *oikoumene*

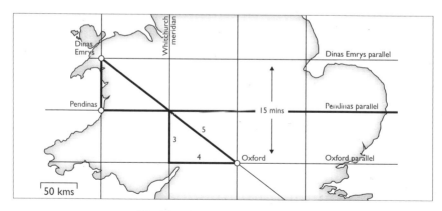

58. The dragons' solstice line

ring road can affect traffic throughout a large part of southern England.

Oxford (or, as it may once have been called, Mediolanum) was a turntable of the two systems. It was one of the prime coordinates of the new, British system based on the 4:3 ratio, and, like Whitchurch, it was also integrated with the Gaulish system and thus with the Greek *oikoumene*.

The line of latitude that runs one hour of daylight to the south of Châteaumeillant passes through Delphi. The line that runs one hour to the north of Châteaumeillant passes through the great hill fort of Pendinas, which looks down on Aberystwyth and Cardigan Bay in mid-Wales. This Welsh line of latitude, which belongs to the ancient mapping of the world, is also an essential part of the British system. At the approximate mid-point of its course, the dragons' solstice line from Oxford meets the Pendinas line of latitude, forming a Pythagorean triangle. Due north of Pendinas itself lies the hill fort of Dinas Emrys, and so, when the solstice line arrives at Dinas Emrys, it completes another Pythagorean triangle. The two systems – the British and the Continental – are exquisitely consistent. Despite the local adjustment to the British solstice angle, Dinas Emrys and Oxford each lie one quarter of a Greek *klima* (± 15 seconds) north and south of the Pendinas line.

The Druids' genius for marrying mathematics and geography was just as effective in Britain as it had been in Gaul. In the tale of Lludd and Llevelys, the latitudinal line drawn through Oxford across the breadth of the kingdom helps to determine the geometrical centre, but this was not just an abstract projection: the line also traces a natural route from sea to sea. Though there are no earthworks to show it, the Oxford parallel is a southern equivalent of Hadrian's Wall and the Antonine Wall. South of the Humber, this is the narrowest crossing of the island of Britain, from the Severn Estuary to the *dunum* that is now Maldon on the Blackwater Estuary.

In Gaul, some of the solar paths had been materialized as roads (p. 206). The Oxford line, too, may have existed as a physical artery. A north–south route is thought to have crossed the Thames at Oxford, and a west–east route is just as likely: some of the traffic that crawls along the Botley Road past the remnant of Osney Abbey is bound for the Severn Estuary and Wales. Here, too, legend confirms the

Antonine Wall

Hadrian's Wall

Oxford parallel

59. 'The breadth of the island'

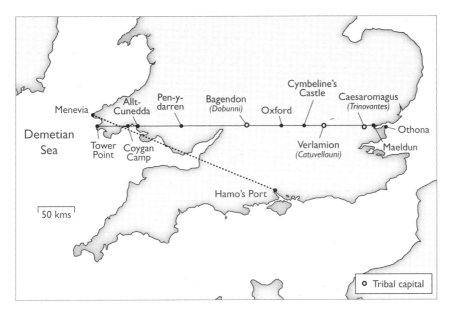

60. The causeway of Belinus

The causeway running the breadth of the kingdom, and Geoffrey of Monmouth's attempted reconstruction (dotted line). Verlamion is St Albans, and Caesaromagus is Chelmsford. Three forts on the line have legendary associations: Allt-Cunedda, named after a King of the Britons; Pen-y-darren Roman fort in Merthyr Tydfil (Tydfil was a daughter of the King of Brycheioniog, an early British kingdom); Cymbeline's Castle (perhaps echoing a local legend) refers to the tribal leader Cunobelinus ('hound of Belenos'). Tower Point is at St Brides, named for the Celtic goddess and Christian saint Brigit. Coygan Camp was a prehistoric, Iron Age and Dark Age fort. Othona was a Roman port. Maeldun (a Celtic name) is Maldon in Essex.

calculation. In his *Historia Regum Britanniae*, Geoffrey of Monmouth describes a route running latitudinally across Britain from sea to sea. After creating the causeway that ran 'the whole length of the island from the south coast to the north',

> Belinus commanded another causeway to be made over the breadth of the kingdom, which is to say, from the town of Menevia on the Demetian Sea, to Hamo's Port, running east to west, and leading directly to all the towns that lie between.

This latitudinal line that was supposed to bisect all the interjacent towns sounds remarkably like one of the Gaulish solstice lines along which major towns or *oppida* occur. But as Geoffrey of Monmouth puzzled over his ancient source, plotting its mysterious coordinates on a blurry mental map, he made a hopeless muddle of the Celtic geography. Menevia was the Roman name of St Davids in Pembrokeshire; Hamo was a legendary Roman commander who gave his name to Southampton. This was largely guesswork on Geoffrey's part: his line makes no sense as a latitudinal route. It runs roughly north-west to south-east, not 'east to west', it fails to pass through any significant town, and one-third of its course is over water.

The solution lies in the most obviously Celtic detail that survived from the original legend: the 'Demetian Sea', the part of the Irish Sea that washes the Pembrokeshire coast. It owed its name to the Iron Age Demetae tribe of south-west Wales, and it was there, on the Demetian coast, that the line crossing the breadth of the kingdom would have ended. Though no Roman roads have been found running west or east from Oxford, the earlier instructions of Belinus must have been carried out to the letter. The Oxford line of latitude passes through enough important towns, forts and tribal capitals to have satisfied the king's requirements.

Lludd must have been delighted with his brother's advice. Despite its awkward elongations, Britain, like Gaul, appeared to have been divinely arranged, 'as though in accordance with some calculated plan' (p. 165). The ancient kingdom was now attached to the Continent and the wider world by the paths of the sun, and yet, with its own prime meridian and its own standard solstice ratio, retained its peculiar independence, which makes Lludd, son of Beli the Great, a very British king.

14

The Four Royal Roads

Between the conquest of Gaul (58–51 BC) and the Claudian invasion of Britain (AD 43), the Druidic system was not just extended across the Channel, it also reached a new level of sophistication. Its evolution in Gaul had been brutally arrested; in Britain, the influx of Druids and stronger trade links with the Continent allowed it to flourish. The Whitchurch meridian, two ten-minute increments west of the Châteaumeillant meridian, was a Continental import. The intermediate line through London – a town that Lludd was said to have rebuilt – may have remained significant as a meridian, but the new, British solstice angle produced new lines of longitude at roughly five-minute intervals: through Pendinas (Aberystwyth), Whitchurch, Oxford, and a fourth line to the east whose importance will shortly become apparent.

The solstice ratios (11:7 in Gaul, 4:3 in Britain) were equations that could be applied in different circumstances and adapted to political and commercial necessity, but they were also used to fashion lasting features of the inhabited land. The lines that radiated from the Oxford *omphalos* to Dinas Emrys and other points of the Druidic compass produced a graceful coordination of Iron Age sites. Three or more tribal centres lie on the Oxford parallel, and at least a further five on the Whitchurch meridian. The Pendinas / Aberystwyth parallel, after passing through two county tripoints and the place that became the Roman town of Tripontium near Rugby, reaches its intersection with the easternmost line of longitude at a fortified settlement of the Iceni tribe called Wardy Hill. (See the large map on p. 240.)

At first, some of these places seem devoid of significance, but as the older landscape comes into view, they turn out to have been busy and important. The fenland fortress of the Iceni at Wardy Hill lies at a latitude–longitude intersection and on a solstice line from Oxford. In the other direction, the same line appears to go astray: it misses the capital of the Dumnonii (Exeter) by three kilometres. But this is a line that exists in the Iron Age, not in Roman Britain, and so, logically, it ends at the Exeter suburb of Topsham. This former river port, where the river Exe becomes navigable, is now known to have been the original tribal centre.

The Dumnonian settlement at Topsham was excavated only recently. Many other places on the solstice lines may one day prove to have pre-Roman roots. Some are already seen as probable tribal centres. The Dinas Emrys line continues north-west across the sands of Abermenai Point to the Druid stronghold of Anglesey and Holy Island. It passes through Aberffraw, which became the capital of Gwynedd – one of the Welsh kingdoms that were formed from the old tribal territories after the departure of the Romans. In the other direction, it passes within five hundred metres of a suspected Iron Age settlement near Worcester Cathedral – perhaps the home of an obscure tribe called the Weogora – and, after the tripoint of Kent, Surrey and Sussex, it arrives on the south coast at Fairlight Cove, near the scene of a more recent invasion – Hastings (p. 262).

The size of the canvas on which the sun-paths sketch a lost land-scape is hard to estimate. The towns of the Iceni and the Dumnonii are separated by more than three hundred kilometres. On the Whitchurch meridian, the Durotrigan town of Lindinis (Ilchester) lies almost five hundred kilometres south of the Votadini's capital at Traprain Law (also known by its older name, Dunpelder). Due west of Traprain Law and the *oppidum* site of Edinburgh, the Pendinas–Dinas Emrys meridian arrives with the precision of a god-transported dragon at the place on the Antonine Wall called Medionemeton. If the Druid surveyors operated at this level of accuracy, there is no reason why the entire island should not have been charted by Belinus and Lludd.

＊

At this distance in time, it seems incredible that two partial maps of the British Druidic system should still exist. The first can be seen in the British Library, which happens to stand on the London meridian. The second is embedded in another map which is familiar, in one

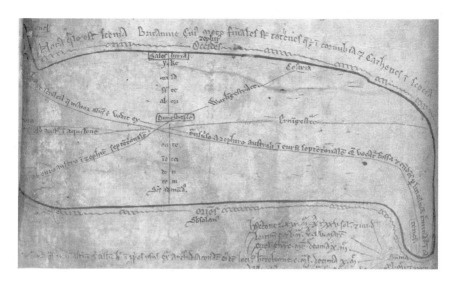

61. The Four Royal Roads, drawn by Matthew Paris

form or another, to most British schoolchildren because it depicts the Roman road system.

Some time between 1217 and 1259, a Benedictine monk called Matthew Paris was working in the scriptorium of the abbey of St Albans. St Albans had once been Verlamion, the capital of the pagan Catuvellauni; the Romans called it Verulamium and turned it into one of the most important towns of southern Britain. The first British Christian martyr had died there. Now, in the thirteenth century, it was a centre of learning, a rival of Oxford, which – though knowledge of the fact had long since been lost – lay on the same Druidic line of latitude.

The monk drew what appears to be a crude map consisting of a black oval and four red lines. He described it as a 'schema Britanniae' – an outline of Britain. Compared to his other, more flowery maps of the British Isles and the Holy Land, Matthew Paris's *Schema Britanniae* is a dull, geometrical doodle. This obviously inaccurate document was once considered to be 'of extremely slight interest to most scholars of this period'.

The monk had no atlas, no encyclopedia, and no gazetteer other than the old Roman itineraries. He had read Geoffrey of Monmouth's *Historia Regum Britanniae*: his own copy, containing his marginal notes, has survived. He also knew Henry of Huntingdon's *Historia Anglorum* ('History of the English', c. 1129). There were probably other, older manuscripts, brown and blotched with damp, their half-legible words like the whispers of a dying saint. There may even have been a map, copied from an ancient design or a *mappa mundi* like the one that had been displayed at the school of Autun in Gaul (p. 111). The monastery library of St Albans contained treasures that could be found nowhere else.

The subject of the drawing was the marvellous pattern of highways known as the Four Royal Roads. These roads were not some fantastic fable: they existed and were still in use. Three of them were Roman, though the legend claimed that they had been built before the Romans; they were called by the names they had acquired in Saxon times: the Fosse Way, Watling Street and Ermine Street. The fourth road, the Icknield Way, was prehistoric. Historians warn that these Four Royal Roads were primarily a rhetorical trope or figure of speech, not to be taken too seriously.

Eager to discover the literal reality of these fabulous ways, Matthew Paris had read that the southern and northern ends of Britain were 'Totnes in Cornwall and Caithness in Scotland', and so he drew a wobbly oval to encompass both places, joining them with an S-shaped line, unaware that Caithness does indeed lie due north of Totnes. Then he drew a neat red line joining Salisbury in the west (at the top of the map) to Bury St Edmunds in the east, and a bisecting line along the major axis of the oval. To these he added two diagonal lines to represent the roads mentioned by Geoffrey of Monmouth as part of the network ordered by Belinus: 'Two others he also made obliquely through the island for passage to the rest of the towns.'

Like any scholar who wanted to preserve and elucidate an ancient text, the monk now contributed his own interpretation. He knew that half a day's journey to the north of St Albans, the Icknield Way crossed Watling Street at the priory of Dunstable. This, he assumed, must be the crux of all four roads, and so he wrote the name 'Dunestaple' in the centre and drew a box around it. The devil who peered over the shoulder of medieval monks as they copied out their sacred texts must have grinned horribly when he saw the mistake. If the monk of St Albans had possessed the knowledge of a Druid, the truth would have struck him like a revelation. But no shaft of light fell across the scriptorium floor to trace the pagan path of the solstice sun and to show that the line he had drawn between Salisbury and Bury St Edmunds passed, not through Dunstable, but through the very centre of St Albans where he sat, unwittingly drawing a map of Druidic Britain (fig. 62).

This line, like some magically created pilgrim route to the pre-Roman past, is exactly oriented on the British solstice. It has no correspondence in the Roman road system. No Roman road or prehistoric pathway links the places on the line, and yet they all appear along it as precisely as though the original cartographer in the days of legend had acquired a map of Britain on the Mercator projection. Unbeknownst to Matthew Paris, the solstice line which he labelled 'Ykenild Strete' connects the ancient abbeys of Saffron Walden, Ixworth, Bury St Edmunds, St Albans, Reading and Salisbury,* as well as several other places whose Iron Age significance is suggested by a name or by archaeological finds: Ashdon, Welwyn, Abbots Langley, Abbotts Ann, Winterbourne Abbas and Abbotsbury Castle. It passes through a suburb of Andover called East Anton, which was once a major road junction: its Celtic name was Leucomagus, the 'shining' or 'bright' 'market'. Beyond Salisbury, as if to appose a Druidic seal to the itinerary, the line reaches the Dorset coast near the southern end of the Whitchurch meridian.

If anyone ever doubted that Christian sites replaced earlier pagan sanctuaries, here is the astronomical proof. The name 'Ykenild' or 'Icknield' was applied in the Middle Ages to various segments of prehistoric pathway and drove road running roughly west to east. The origin of the word is unknown. Two places that preserve the name – Ickworth and Ixworth – are exactly bisected by the St Albans line. Two others that were associated with an 'Icenhilde weg' in the tenth century (Wanborough and Hardwell in Uffington) are on the Oxford line from Wardy Hill to Topsham which precisely parallels the St Albans line. They lie just below White Horse Hill and the chalk escarpment on which the prehistoric Ridgeway crosses the Chilterns. Perhaps the mysterious word at the root of 'Icknield' was once the collective name of these solar paths.

---

* On the transferral of Salisbury Cathedral from Sorviodunum (Old Sarum) to its current site in 1220, see p. 286.

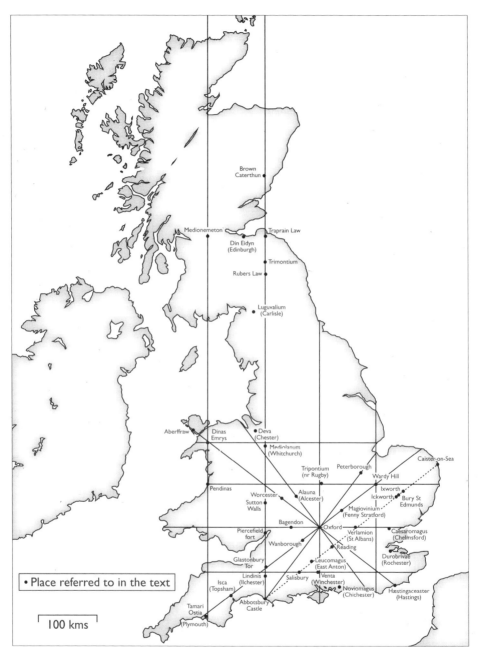

Brown
Caterthun

Medionemeton
Din Eidyn
(Edinburgh)
Traprain Law

Trimontium

Rubers Law

Luguvalium
(Carlisle)

Aberffraw
Dinas
Emrys
Deva
(Chester)

Mediolanum
(Whitchurch)

Tripontium
(nr Rugby)
Peterborough
Caister-on-Sea

Wardy Hill

Pendinas
Worcester
Alauna
(Alcester)
Ixworth
Ickworth
Bury St
Edmunds

Sutton
Walls

Bagendon
Magiovinium
(Fenny Stratford)

Piercefield
fort
Oxford
Verlamion
(St Albans)
Caesaromagus
(Chelmsford)

Wanborough
Reading
Durobrivae
(Rochester)

Glastonbury
Tor
Leucomagus
(East Anton)

Isca
(Topsham)
Lindinis
(Ilchester)
Salisbury
Venta
(Winchester)
Hæstingaceaster
(Hastings)

Noviomagus
(Chichester)

Tamari
Ostia
(Plymouth)
Abbotsbury
Castle

• Place referred to in the text

100 kms

62. The British network
The network so far. All bearings are exact (tan ratio 4:3).

Matthew Paris's *Schema Britanniae* can now be seen for what it is – a remnant of the oldest map in British history. For all its errors and approximations, it preserves the accurate coordinates of an oral tradition that predates the Roman conquest. Beyond this solstice line, in all directions, stretches the great network of Belinus and Lludd, which no single map, legend or book could encompass.

✿

The three other Royal Roads of British legend – the Fosse Way, Watling Street and Ermine Street – were, understandably, conflated by the medieval scholars with the roads of the Roman conquerors. They were among the earliest to be built after the invasion of AD 43, and they seem at first to have no connection with pre-Roman Britain. Considering the apparently undeveloped state of the British hinterland, these great arteries are so impressively precocious, probably completed for the most part within a generation of the Roman invasion, that archaeologists sometimes wonder whether the Romans based their roads on a native network. But since the Britanni are assumed to have been content with meandering tracks and muddy causeways, this is considered unlikely.

The truly peculiar feature of the first long-distance Roman roads in Britain is their extreme accuracy. The angular alignments are so precise that when the road-builders set out from their starting point, they must have known to within a few paces where they were heading, even when the terminus lay far to the north or west. No Roman text describes the building of these roads, and their Latin names are unknown, but the roads themselves are long sentences whose structure and grammar remain quite comprehensible.

Modern surveyors who have studied the Roman network insist that before these roads could be made, an extensive survey must have been carried out. The explanation only makes the achievement more remarkable. Roads of conquest, as today in Afghanistan, are often constructed in advance of a front line, but without air support and satellite positioning, it would have been practically impossible to survey a target area that had yet to be conquered – unless, that is, the foundations of a road system had already been laid . . .

The London to Chichester road, or Stane Street, as it came to be known, seems to be a typical example of Roman expertise. It can be followed from London Bridge along Clapham Road and Tooting High Street, and, if the historical pedestrian manages to keep to the same straight line for sixty Roman miles, the inevitable end-point will be the Eastgate in Chichester. Stane Street is not one of the legendary Four Royal Roads, but it shares with them a curious, Celtic property. The ruler-straight road sets off from the Eastgate in Chichester in what appears to be the wrong direction: instead of heading north-north-east to London, it runs east-north-east to the village of Pulborough. Only there, after twenty-two kilometres, does it correct itself and turn towards the metropolis (fig. 63). Perhaps the surveyors' intention was to avoid a hillier route across the Sussex Downs – not that Roman road-builders shied away from ferociously steep gradients – but the trajectory of Stane Street is hardly an improvement on the direct line. An easier and faster route would have been the course of the present A285 through Duncton, which keeps to lower ground and follows the projected London line more closely.

The inescapable conclusion is that the road from Noviomagus (Chichester) was originally aimed, not at Londinium, but at the Celtic port of Durobrivae (Rochester) on the river Medway. Noviomagus was the capital of the Regni tribe; Durobrivae was one of the two chief *oppida* of the Cantiaci tribe. Both tribes had strong trading ties with Gaul, both had reasons to build roads before the advent of the Romans, and since the god Lugh was 'the guide of their paths and journeys' (p. 72), the original surveyors angled their road in accordance with his eternal laws. This 'Roman' road, which seems to change its mind at Pulborough, runs exactly parallel to Matthew Paris's Icknield Way, towards the sun that rises over the North Sea at the time of the summer solstice, on a Pythagorean ratio of four and three.

Here, in the network that is supposed to be the great and lasting contribution of Rome to the future prosperity of Britain, the Pythagorean harmonies of the Celts are clearer than ever. During the last century of Britain's independence, something vast and magnificent was evolving, of which the Chichester road is just one example. Although the Druids' wisdom was later contaminated by misinterpretations and coloured by the theology of the medieval scholars who recorded its remnants, the truth survived in a recoverable form. None of the medieval scribes could possibly have known this, but the four

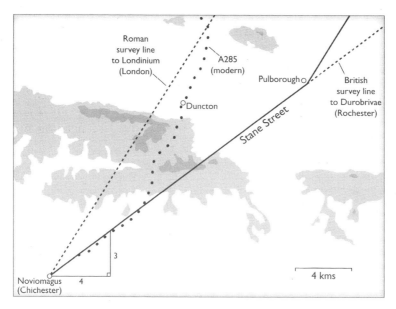

63. Stane Street

Stane Street: from Chichester to London or to Rochester? The Roman survey line on the left represents the direct route between Chichester and London Bridge. It can be followed on the ground along certain stretches of former Roman road such as Clapham Road and Tooting High Street. The puzzle is this: why does the actual Roman road (the continuous line on the map) deviate so far from the survey line, instead of, for example, following the shorter route of the current A285? A possible answer is that a convenient stretch of British road or path already existed, oriented on the summer solstice and connecting the British towns of Noviomagus and Durobrivae.

roads identified in legend as the work of a king or god called Belinus have something quite precise and distinctive in common: these are longest surviving roads in the 'Roman' network to be aligned on the British solstice angle.

It now appears that these Royal Roads were indeed, as the legend claimed, older than the Romans. They were singled out in the legend from other lines in the network as prime examples of the Celtic system. Each road represents one of the four British solstice bearings (36.87° and 53.13°, and the bisecting lines, 126.87° and 143.13°). The fabled configuration of roads thus produces a complete Druidic blueprint: the Icknield Way is the summer solstice line, bisected by

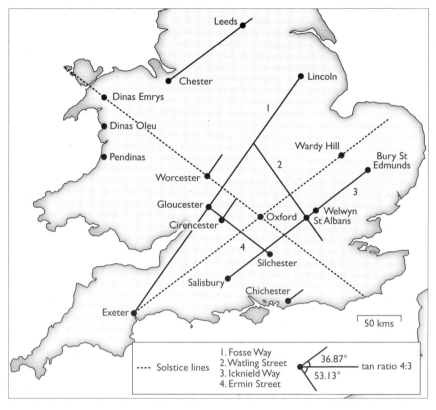

64. The Four Royal Roads and the Roman road system

All these survey lines have a tan ratio of 4:3. The Exeter–Lincoln line (the Fosse Way) implies a survey tolerance (acceptable deviation from the survey line) of 0.59°. The southern terminus of the Roman Fosse Way was probably Ilchester, which lies on the Whitchurch meridian: this Roman road has a tan ratio of 3:5 (bearing 30.96°, with a survey tolerance of 0.44°.)

Watling Street; Ermin Street is the winter solstice line, bisected by the Fosse Way.*

---

* Ermine Street, which ran approximately north from London, shows no obviously significant bearing, whereas Ermin Street (north-west from Silchester) follows the British solstice bearing. Medieval scholars chose what they believed to be the more important 'Ermyngestrete', though in some versions of the legend (e.g. Robert of Gloucester's thirteenth-century *Chronicle*), 'Eningestret' is paired with 'Ikenildestrete', as it is on the map above: 'Lyne me clepeth eke thulke wey, he goth thorgh Gloucer, / And thorgh Circetre [Cirencester] euene also'.

As for the towns that lie along these lines, some, as one might expect, are Roman, but others date back to the pre-Roman Iron Age. In several cases, the 'Roman' survey lines are actually a closer match for Iron Age than for Roman Britain. The solstice line from Silchester runs, not to Roman Cirencester and Gloucester, but – via the foot of White Horse Hill – to their nearby Iron Age predecessors, Bagendon and Churchdown Hill. If the same line is extended to the Welsh coast, it arrives at the hill fort of Dinas Oleu ('the hill fort of Lleu' or 'Lugh') at Barmouth – halfway between Dinas Emrys and Pendinas on the Medionemeton meridian.

The Roman towns themselves may turn out to have existed before the conquest. The evidence is scarcer than it is in Gaul, and at this point in the book there was to have been a speculative passage on the possible solar alignment of late Iron Age towns in Britain. Then, in August 2011, archaeologists from the University of Reading announced that they had uncovered definite evidence of the grid pattern of a native settlement beneath the Roman town of Calleva Atrebatum (Silchester). The Romans could no longer take the credit for the first planned towns in Britain. There was one further detail, about which the official report was understandably discreet, since such things are associated with neo-Druids, ley-line hunters and other muddiers of material evidence: the original British grid of Calleva, unlike the Roman north–south, east–west grid, was aligned on the summer solstice.

✿

The Romans were always surprised by the interregional alliances formed by British tribes. It is just as surprising to see a coordinated British nation emerging before the Romans first landed on the south coast. The British ratio of four and three can be detected on a microcosmic level in certain objects of British Celtic art such as the Aylesford Bucket or the Battersea Shield (figs. 66 and 67); it is also visible on a larger scale, in the temple at Camulodunum (Colchester), whose alignments can now be connected to the history of Iron Age Britain (p. 259). An intriguing passage in Ranulf Higden's version of the Four Royal Roads legend (c. 1342) suggests that the geometrical formula permeated British Iron Age society on every level and at every scale:

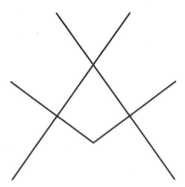

65. The pattern of the Four Royal Roads
Each road is aligned on one of the four British solstice bearings.

> Molmutius, King of the Britons [father of Belinus], the twenty-third,
> but the first to give them laws, ordained that the immunity of fugi-
> tives should be enjoyed by the ploughs of the tillers of the soil, by
> the temples of gods and by the ways that lead to the cities.

The 'ploughs' ('*aratra*') were ploughland considered as a unit of
land measurement. The exciting implication is that the solar equation
was applied, not just to roads and temples, but also to the organization of the countryside. Just as the streets of British Calleva were
oriented on the summer solstice, the field systems of Iron Age Britain
may have been patterned by the solstice sun. There is a similar echo
of a grand Druidic plan in Geoffrey of Monmouth's *Historia Regum
Britanniae*. According to his unknown source, the Royal Roads were
created when the *civitates* (states or cities) of Britain were unable to
agree on their boundaries. This was certainly a reference to the days
when national policy was decided by the Druids, one of whose functions was to settle boundary disputes. The new alignments were devised
to settle the matter once and for all, and to 'leave no loophole for
quibbles in the law'. In Britain, as in Gaul, the sun supplied the
formula with which no tribe or individual could disagree.

From this formula, fragments of a tribal map of ancient Britain
might be pieced together, and the countryside that still exists will
begin to shimmer with an unanticipated harvest. Many of the solar
paths bisect the points where three or more shires and parishes meet.
Some of those places still bear names that consecrate their ancient

66. British solstice bearings applied to a roundel of the Battersea Shield

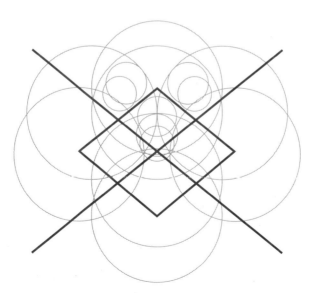

67. British solstice bearings applied to the face on the Aylesford Bucket

significance – Three Shire Oak, Four Shire Stone, No Man's Heath, etc. (p. 297). Unlike diocesan boundaries, which tend to follow natural features, the historic county boundaries often pass through almost featureless landscapes, as though some earlier world has vanished along with the visible logic of its configuration. These territorial divisions are thought to date from the Saxon kingdoms which emerged from the ruins of Roman Britain. The theory that the Saxon kingdoms in turn were based on Iron Age tribal territories now looks entirely plausible.

These protohistoric alignments would be overwritten and obscured by all the later Roman roads that covered the province of Britannia. The Celtic alignments were like cryptic designs on an old parchment that an artist incorporated into new, less geometrical patterns. The medieval scholars who recorded the legends nevertheless communicated the outline of the earlier Druidic network. With the information that remains, and the formula of the Druidic system, the feats of the first Roman road-builders no longer seem so incredible. Celtic Britain appears as on a cloudless day, when there can never be enough time for all the expeditions the sun will allow.

The virtual atlas of these solar paths is so voluminous that if the whole system were described in detail, the preceding two hundred pages would be a brief introduction by comparison. A few possible journeys are described in the epilogue, but since one of the aims of this book has been to show how an apparently abstract, mystical system is corroborated by archaeological evidence and historical events, the more urgent task is to use the map of Celtic Britain to follow the warriors and scholars of the Poetic Isles as they enter the lists of recorded history in AD 43.

15

The End of Middle Earth

Of all the books that were never written or that disappeared in the ruins of a library, one of the greatest losses to history must be the autobiography of Caratacus. When the Roman invasion force landed on the coast of Cantium (Kent) in AD 43, Caratacus, son of Cunobelinus, was the ruler of a large part of southern Britain. He became the leader of the British resistance, and held out against the Romans for eight years. By the time he was captured in AD 51, his fame had spread as far as Italy. He was taken to Rome, along with his brothers, wife and daughter, to be displayed in a triumphal ceremony. Normally, the ceremony would have ended with his execution, but when Caratacus was brought before Emperor Claudius, he delivered such an impressive speech in Latin, and then another speech to Claudius's wife Agrippina, that he was spared the punishment that had been meted out to Vercingetorix a century before. 'I had horses, men, arms and wealth,' he is supposed to have said. 'Is it any wonder that I was reluctant to part with them? Just because you Romans want to lord it over everyone, does it follow that everyone should willingly become a slave?'

The wife and brothers of Caratacus then delivered speeches of their own, expressing 'praise and gratitude'. Claudius granted them their freedom, and the Caratacus family settled down to live in Rome. 'After his release', according to the Roman historian, Cassius Dio, 'Caratacus toured the city, and, having seen how big and shiny everything was, he said, "When you have these and other such things, why do you covet our little tents?"'

With the Roman legions still laying waste to his native land, Caratacus had to be careful. 'Little tents' was a flattering understatement. Wealthy Britons of the first century AD lived in large and comfortable houses stocked with expensive imports. Their diets were more interesting than those of many British people until the mid-twentieth century. They drank wine from wine glasses and flavoured their food with coriander, dill and poppy seeds. A small charred stone excavated from a pre-Roman well in Calleva (Silchester) in 2012 suggests that when she dined out in Rome, the daughter of Caratacus would not have been amazed to taste an olive. If Britain had nothing to compare with the marbled magnificence of Rome, it was probably because, like their Gaulish counterparts, the kings of Britain felt no need of monumental architecture. The Roman invasion was unlikely to change their minds: the imperious Temple to the Divine Claudius that the Romans built in Camulodunum (Colchester) would be seen by the Britons as a blot on the landscape and 'a citadel of perpetual tyranny'.

Nothing else is known about the life of Caratacus in Rome. The story that he and his daughter became Christians and brought the new religion back to Britain is entirely spurious. If he had any dealings with devotees of a proscribed religion, they would not have been Christians, whom Claudius had just expelled from Rome, but Druids, whose 'cruel and horrible rites' the same emperor had banned. The Druids were popularly imagined to be soothsayers and healers with a propensity for human sacrifice and political agitation, but an earlier decree, which forbade Roman citizens from becoming Druids, shows that a Druid could also be an educated speaker of Latin. Since Claudius had recently persuaded the Senate to admit citizens of 'Hairy Gaul' to the senatorial class, it would not have been extraordinary if there were Druids living in Rome. Somewhere in that city of shiny monuments, a meeting might have taken place. With the solar map of Britannia unfolded in his listeners' minds, this is the tale Caratacus might have told.

＊

The invasion of AD 43 caught Caratacus unprepared. He lost a battle somewhere in the south-east, and then another on the river Medway – probably near Durobrivae (Rochester) at the end of the solstice line from Noviomagus (Chichester). In one of those battles, his brother Togodumnus was killed. When the Romans crossed the Thames and marched on Camulodunum (Colchester), Caratacus shifted his campaign to the west. He retreated through the Cotswolds and across the Severn Estuary. Eventually, in about AD 49, he reached the lands of the Silures of South Wales.

Even at this early stage in the conquest of Britain, the conventional view of disciplined Romans and chaotic Celts is untenable. Caratacus had ruled a small empire in the Thames Valley. Now, a child of the civilized south-east, he became the undisputed leader of the 'swarthy, curly-haired' Silures – 'a particularly ferocious' people, said Tacitus, whose cunning was matched by the 'deceptiveness' of their terrain. For a supposedly anarchic group of clans, the Silures were an effective political entity, able to form alliances over wide areas, 'luring' other tribes 'into defection', as Tacitus snidely puts it, 'by bribing them with booty and prisoners'.

Along the ridges and valleys of South Wales, a guerrilla war was fought that has left no visible trace. From there, Caratacus moved the theatre of war again, to the north, into the lands of the Ordovices, a week's march from Roman-occupied Britain. His forces were now augmented, says Tacitus, by 'those who dreaded the thought of a Roman peace'. His aim was presumably, in part, to open supply routes to the large tribal federations in the east – the Cornovii and the Brigantes – but there was another reason for his gradual retreat to the north-west. Behind the windy bulwarks of Snowdonia lay the holy island of Mona (Anglesey), where the Druids had their stronghold.

Like Finistère, Fisterra and the Sacred Promontory, Mona was one of the ends of the earth. As an island, it belonged to this world and the next. Its connection with the lower world is well attested: between the second century BC and the period when Mona finally fell to the Romans (AD 78), hundreds of bronze and iron artefacts were cast into a lake in the north-west of the island. (The lake, Llyn Cerrig Bach, is now a marshy lagoon on the edge of a military airfield.) The artefacts included swords, slave chains, blacksmiths' tools and cauldrons. Some of them came from Hibernia, others from Belgic Gaul. They might have been brought as votive offerings by the students who travelled to Britannia to study Druidism.

Now, perhaps, for the first time in their long war against the Celts, the Romans had an inkling of the sacred geography that determined the movements of the enemy. The strategic value of Mona was obvious: the sea was its moat but also its highway. From the harbours

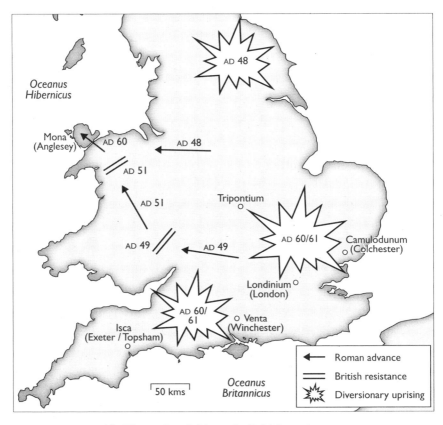

68. The role of Mona in British resistance

of Mona, a troop ship could sail to northern Britain, to Hibernia or to the lands of the Dumnonii in the south-west. While the Romans consolidated their conquest of the south and east, the island fortress of the Druids became 'the haven of fugitives' and 'the power that fed the rebellion' (Tacitus).

Charted chronologically, the movements of the British forces form a pattern of which Mona is the oblique focus. In AD 48, governor Ostorius Scapula marched against the Deceangli of North Wales but was prevented from attacking Mona and its 'powerful population' by a sudden uprising among the Brigantes to the east. Soon after that, Caratacus took command of the Silures of South Wales. His strategy, too, seems to have been governed by the need to defend the sacred island: as Caratacus moved north, his lines of resistance always protected Mona. Later, the revolt of the Iceni and their allies would coincide with Suetonius Paulinus's attack on the island and force him to call off his destruction of the Druids' shrines (p. 257).

Some historians argue that Druid priests and their island base played a negligible role in the British resistance. This was not the view of the Roman commanders. Agricola considered the invasion of Mona an 'arduous and dangerous' undertaking. When Suetonius Paulinus launched his attack, he was hoping to outdo a rival general, Corbulo. In his mind, the conquest of that small island in the Oceanus Hibernicus would be an achievement equal to Corbulo's recent subjugation of Armenia.

The common soldiers, who included large numbers of Germans and Celts, agreed with their commanders. As they advanced through the hallucinatory landscapes of highland central Wales, they were conscious of approaching a place from which an occult power radiated. They had been reluctant even to cross the Oceanus Britannicus. 'Indignant at the thought of campaigning beyond the known world', according to Cassius Dio, they had cheered up only when a flash of light had shot across the sky from east to west – sunwards – in the direction of Britannia. Now, as they chased Caratacus to the north, they saw the clouds gather into a dark thunderhead. It loomed over the mountains of Snowdonia, beyond which the world came to an end. When Roman troops stood at last on the shores of Mona in AD 60, they would be 'paralysed by fear' at the sight of 'women dressed like Furies in funereal attire, their hair dishevelled, rushing about amongst the warriors, waving torches, and a circle of Druids raising their arms to the sky and pouring forth dreadful curses'.

Only the Druids and the British commanders could see the whole panorama. The dragons' solstice line from Oxford to Dinas Emrys crosses the Menai Strait at Abermenai Point, where the earliest recorded ferry connected Mona with the Dinlle Peninsula, whose name means 'fort of Lleu' or 'Lugh'. It was there, no doubt, at the narrowest crossing, that the Roman legions would push their flat-bottomed boats through the sandbanks and the shallows to find themselves confronting the weird army of Druids. Beyond the strait, the line reaches Holy Island off the north-west coast of Mona and the white mountain of Holyhead which guided sailors on the Hibernian Ocean (fig. 69).

In AD 51, the sun god who had mustered the Gaulish tribes at

Alesia a century before induced Caratacus to make what a recent historian has called 'a crucial error': like Vercingetorix, 'Caratacus consolidated his forces for a last stand, giving the Romans exactly what they wanted: a set-piece battle'. The site of this final battle has never been discovered,* but on the map of Middle Earth, the solar signposts point to a place which corresponds in every detail to Tacitus's description.

The road connecting the two mountain passes that lead to Mona is guarded by the fort of Dinas Emrys, known in older days as Dinas Ffaraon Dandde ('Hill Fort of the Fiery Pharaoh'). Here, as we saw (p. 230), three solar paths converge: the dragons' solstice line from the *omphalos* of Oxford is intersected by lines of latitude and longitude. The hill was once an Iron Age settlement. Now, the only noticeable remains are those of a thirteenth-century tower. Nearby, a *'lapis fatalis'* ('Stone of Destiny') called the Carreg yr Eryr ('Eagle Stone') marked the meeting-point of three *cantrefi* – the medieval districts that are thought to have been based on Celtic tribal kingdoms.

For Caratacus, the fabled hill fort at the intersection of three solar paths was a British equivalent of Alesia. It also happened to satisfy his strategic requirements. The battle was fought, according to Tacitus, 'in the lands of the Ordovices' and in a place where 'advance and retreat would be difficult for the enemy but easy for the defenders'. In front of the fortress ran 'a river of uncertain ford' or 'of varying depth' (*'amnis vado incerto'*): this would be the lake-fed river Glaslyn, which swells rapidly with the rain but which is fordable at other times. Downstream of the lake called Llyn Dinas, the valley is almost blocked by the hill of Dinas Emrys. All around, an 'impending' or 'menacing' 'ridge' or 'range of mountains' (*'imminentia iuga'*) daunted the Roman commander. This can hardly refer to the modest hills of Shropshire where the battle is often assumed to have taken place.

---

* Few of the other traditional candidates fit Tacitus's description: Caer Caradoc near Church Stretton (a negligible river, and in Cornovian rather than Ordovican terri- tory; the name 'Caradoc' is a corruption of 'Cordokes'); Caer Caradoc near Clun (a negligible river); Llanymynech (where advance and retreat would have been relatively easy); the Herefordshire Beacon or British Camp (no river). The most likely sites, apart from Dinas Emrys, are Breidden Hill and Cefn Carnedd, both above the river Severn.

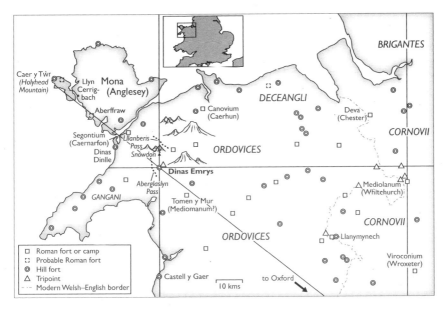

69. North Wales and Dinas Emrys

North Wales and the strategic significance of Dinas Emrys. Most of the Roman forts were probably constructed in the 70s or 80s AD, after the defeat of Caratacus.

The stories that cling to Dinas Emrys like the river-mists are as confused as the archaeological remains. After Caratacus' death, a memory of his great battle with the Romans may have survived in bardic records or local legends, which then became entangled with the original myth. Centuries later, when the Romans had abandoned Britain to the Celts and the Saxon invaders, the tales of other warriors were woven into the text. By then, the faces of the old Celtic gods and heroes were little more than abstract patterns in the weave. And yet, in certain lights, they can still be recognized.

In early medieval legends, the beleaguered king who chooses Dinas Emrys as his fortress is not Caratacus but the British warlord Vortigern, forced by the Saxons to flee to the remote west. This would have happened four hundred years after the time of Caratacus. Vortigern's 'magi' – a common medieval Latin translation of 'Druids' – instruct him to build a citadel. The masons start work, but, every night, the towers mysteriously collapse. The magi then advise Vortigern to 'find a fatherless boy, kill him, and sprinkle the citadel with his blood'. The sacrificial boy turns out to be the orphaned son of a Roman nobleman.

His name is Ambrosius (in its native form, Emrys) or Ambrosius Aurelianus.* The boy escapes death by revealing the true cause of the towers' collapse: underneath the fort, inside the hill, there is a pool in which two dragons lie buried.

The legend of the Roman boy whose blood was to protect the citadel is reminiscent of one of the 'cruel and horrible rites' of the Druids (p. 250). During their nine-year campaign, the forces of Caratacus would have acquired prisoners and hostages, and the son of an important Roman may well have served as a blood offering before the battle. His name preserves the religious significance of the sacrifice: 'Ambrosius' means 'immortal', and 'Aurelianus' comes from '*aureus*' (the adjective means 'golden' and was commonly applied to the sun).

On the eve of the battle at the sacred hill fort where Lludd had buried the dragons and where three solar paths converge, the 'Immortal Sun' was symbolically interred. A treasure, later said to be the Throne of Britain or the gold of Merlin, was entombed beneath the hill or in the nearby lake, just as the gold of Delphi had been deposited in the pools of Tolosa (p. 174). The belief in reincarnation was one of the principal tenets of the Druids; it was subsequently expressed in the legend of King Arthur and his sleeping knights, and in the stories of a saviour crucified by the Romans who descended into hell and ascended into heaven. One day, the warriors of Caratacus who died in battle would rise again like the sun in the eastern sky.

On the gentler slopes of the hill, Caratacus 'piled up stones to serve as a rampart', but, says Tacitus, 'the rude and shapeless stone construction' was swiftly demolished by the Romans. Perhaps this is the historical origin of Vortigern's crumbling citadel. The Britons, caught between the legionaries and the auxiliaries, were overwhelmed. The wife and daughter of Caratacus were captured; his brothers surrendered. Caratacus himself escaped to the north-east, where the queen of the Brigantes, Cartimandua, hoping to tighten her delicate hold on power, handed him over to the Romans. From northern Britain, Caratacus crossed the conquered land in chains. It would

---

* This was the name of a Romano-British chieftain. The later version, by Geoffrey of Monmouth, identifies the boy as the mathematician, astronomer, bard and prophet, Myrddin or Merlin.

have taken over a month to reach Rome, and on that long journey through Britain, Gaul and Italy, there would have been plenty of time to compose the speeches that would save him and his family from execution.

The tribes of South Wales fought on, inflamed by a report that governor Ostorius Scapula had called for the very name of the Silures to be 'utterly extinguished'. The island of Mona was left to its own devices for another nine years. It was not until AD 60 that the soldiers of Suetonius Paulinus crossed the Menai Strait, massacred the Druids, and set about the unsoldierly task of extirpating groves of oak. But even then, their victory was incomplete. While they desecrated the Druids' groves in the far west of Britain, where the dying sun turned the ocean red, news reached them from the mainland that a great fire was rising in the east. The whole province of Britannia was in revolt. This time, the military application of Druidic science would have devastating consequences for the Romans.

✿

While Suetonius Paulinus was rushing from Mona towards Londinium 'amidst a hostile population', a messenger arrived with an order for the camp prefect of the Second Augustan Legion, based at the fortress of Isca Dumnoniorum (Exeter). The prefect would normally have been third in command, but the Mona campaign had left the fortresses undermanned, and Poenius Postumus found himself in sole charge of the legion. He was ordered to proceed immediately to the province and to join forces with Suetonius Paulinus.

For some reason, the camp prefect disobeyed the order. Between Isca Dumnoniorum in the far south-west and the Roman province in the east lay the hill forts of the Durotriges, the most impressive of which was Maiden Castle near Dorchester. Seen from the air, its mazy earthworks resemble the knotted oak-wood swirls of Celtic art, which suggests that they served an apotropaic as well as a practical, strategic purpose. Traces have been found at Maiden Castle and other forts in the region of hand-to-hand fighting and ballistic assault. While the evidence is often associated with the invasion of AD 43, many of the signs of destruction are more consistent with a date of AD 60–61. If Poenius Postumus failed to join his commander, it was probably because he, too, had a rebellion on his hands.

The attack on Mona had sparked off two simultaneous revolts – one in the south-west, extending perhaps as far as Noviomagus (Chichester) and Venta Belgarum (Winchester), the other in the south-east, affecting an area of about ten thousand square kilometres. Seventeen years after the Roman invasion, the British tribes must have retained a message system as efficient as that of the Gauls. 'Secret conspiracies' had been hatched by the Iceni, the Trinovantes and their allies. Now, the gods themselves appeared to be taking a hand.

The Roman merchants and administrators who had settled in Camulodunum (Colchester) were unnerved by strange occurrences. A statue of Victory was found flat on its face, as though it had been fleeing from the enemy. 'Frenzied women' screamed prophecies of destruction in the streets. As though in confirmation, a ruined city was seen in the waters of the Thames Estuary. In the English Channel, the flood tide ran blood-red, and the ebb tide revealed 'effigies of human corpses'. The witches of Camulodunum, like the torch-waving Druidesses of Mona, could strike fear into a Roman heart, and the most disturbing news of all was that the rebel leader was a woman.

Boudica, queen of the Iceni, whose name means 'Victorious', is the first heroine of British history. Every modern retelling of her tale mentions the rape of her daughters and the whipping she received at the hands of the Roman administrators who were bleeding the province dry. The only evidence for these outrages is Boudica's rabble-rousing speech to her troops, reported (or invented) by Tacitus. The sexual humiliation of the Icenian royal family was supposed to explain how a woman – albeit one 'possessed of greater intelligence than often belongs to women' (Cassius Dio) – came close to reconquering a Roman province. Boudica's bloody rampage through southern Britain showed what could happen when a Celtic woman's righteous passion was unleashed. It hardly needs saying that to wreak comprehensive destruction on several major settlements within a short period is impossible without a well-coordinated and well-supplied military campaign. Boudica was a soldier and a politician. The rape of the princesses and the scourging of the queen may well have taken place, but they also belong to the rhetoric of rebellion, and they provided the Celtic troops with a *casus belli* more inspiring than the financial malpractice of Roman officials.

The most obviously Druidic detail is missing from many popular accounts of Boudica's meteoric career, either because it seems too weird to be true, or because it sits awkwardly with the image of Boudica as a mother and a victim of Roman male aggression. Boudica addressed her troops, according to Cassius Dio, in a 'harsh voice', from 'a tribunal made out of marshy [or 'fenny'] earth'. She wore a tartan tunic and a thick cloak. A mass of auburn hair fell to her hips. In her lap, a throbbing creature waited to be released from its prison. The queen opened her arms, and a hare bounded off in a direction which the Druids proclaimed to be auspicious.

The brown hare (*Lepus europaeus*) will flee in a straight line for a kilometre or more, and usually in the same direction as the wind, which made it the ideal choice of animal for a Celtic commander who wanted to convince her troops that the gods agreed with her plan. The likeliest location for this ceremony of divination is the fortified settlement of Wardy Hill in the Isle of Ely, where the easterly line of longitude meets the Pendinas line of latitude and the solstice line from Oxford (fig. 62). The 'hill' rises no more than ten metres above sea level, but in the Cambridgeshire fens it occupies a commanding position. Excavations in the early 1990s showed that Wardy Hill was an important defensive site long before a pillbox was erected on its summit in World War Two. It was a major settlement of the Iceni tribe: 'a resident élite persisted here', even during the Roman occupation.

Traced on the map of Middle Earth, Boudica's 'rampage' is a perfectly coordinated dance of destruction. The solstice line from Wardy Hill runs as straight as a brown hare to Erbury (or Clare) Camp, which was one of the largest fortresses of the Iceni's allies, the Trinovantes. It then arrives at the ceremonial centre of Camulodunum. This was the capital of the Roman province and the first town to be destroyed by Boudica's army. The Romano-Celtic temple is thought to have pre-Roman origins. This now seems all the more likely since the temple is aligned on the British solstice angles: one axis coincides with the solstice line from Wardy Hill; the other points directly at the next place on Boudica's itinerary: Londinium.

A layer of burnt debris from the time of Boudica's revolt has been found at several sites in London. It extends south of the Thames to Southwark, where Boudica is assumed to have crossed the river. At

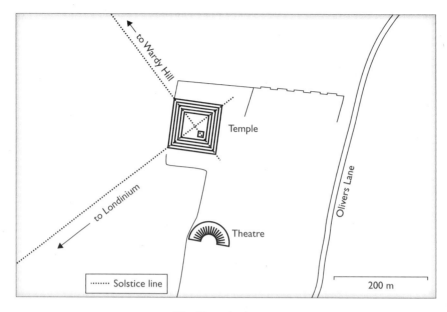

70. Camulodunum

The religious centre of Camulodunum, near Gosbeck's Farm, Colchester. (After Dunnett and Reece.) The alignments are accurate to within less than one degree.

this point, when this book was in rehearsal, the map of Middle Earth appeared to be in error: if Boudica followed the solstice line south-west from Camulodunum, she would in fact have crossed the Thames several kilometres downstream, at a site of no apparent interest, where the Woolwich Power Station once stood. Then a bulletin arrived from the archaeological front line. Because of 'the constant threat from treasure-hunters', the discovery had been kept secret since 1986. Now, in 2010, with the completion of the Waterfront Leisure Centre car park, the Kent Archaeological Rescue Unit could reveal that 'a major fortified Iron Age settlement' had been discovered on the Woolwich Power Station site:

> Constructed about 250 BC, centuries before the foundation of the City of Londinium by the Romans, this major site on the south bank of the River Thames controlled the river for over 200 years. [Its inhabitants] lived surrounded by massive earth ramparts and deep defensive ditches. . . . The complete defensive circuit would have enclosed an area of at least 15–17 acres. . . . This major

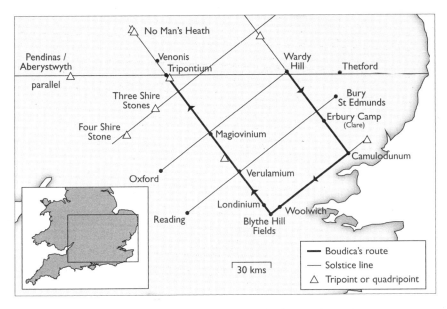

71. The pattern of Boudica's revolt

riverside fort . . . also dominated a wide area and was effectively the capital of the London Basin for part of the Iron Age.

The solstice line from Camulodunum exactly bisects this 'capital of the London Basin'. Passing to the south of Greenwich Park, the line continues to a solar intersection and a Roman road junction at the foot of Blythe Hill Fields in Lewisham. From the top of the hill, the scouts of Boudica's army would have looked down towards the merchant ships and barges, and the new Roman houses on the north bank of the Thames. They now turned to follow the trajectory of one of the Four Royal Roads of Britain – the road later known as Watling Street.

Along that ancient path protected by the gods, they slaughtered their way into Londinium, perhaps re-crossing the Thames at Southwark – or, if they followed the solstice line exactly, between Blackfriars Bridge and Waterloo Bridge, where a rare Celtic parade helmet with two bronze horns was dredged from the river in 1868. Their route would have taken them by Russell Square and Euston Station (not the neighbouring King's Cross, where a local legend places the grave of Boudica), then over Hampstead Heath and along

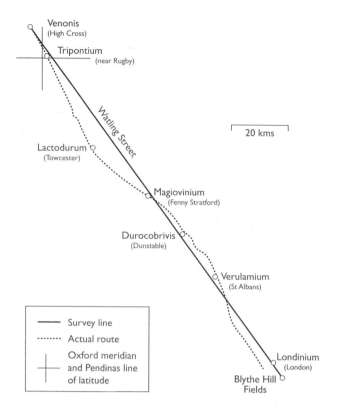

72. Watling Street

The presumed survey line and actual route of Watling Street. The course of the road through London is unknown. Beyond London, this line would have reached the south coast near Hastings. It matches the survey zone of the eighteenth-century London-to-Hastings road via Lewisham, Bromley, Farnborough, Sevenoaks, Tonbridge, Lamberhurst and Robertsbridge. This road is not currently identified as Roman.

the Great North Way to the next Roman town to be destroyed – the former capital of the Catuvellauni, Verulamium (St Albans).

With the smoking ruins of three centres of Roman power behind her, Boudica may have been intending to complete the pattern of destruction by returning to Icenian territory along the solstice line from Oxford (fig. 71). Meanwhile, after abandoning Londinium to its fate, the troops of Suetonius Paulinus had regrouped somewhere to the north of Verulamium. The camp prefect having failed to arrive from Isca Dumnoniorum with the Second Augustan Legion, the

Romans were outnumbered, but a battle had become inevitable. They faced the Britons from a narrow pass with woodland in the rear and a plain in front. (These are the only topographical details given by Tacitus.) The soldiers who had recently been scared witless by the Druids of Mona had to be encouraged by Suetonius to ignore the appalling din of war-trumpets and 'empty threats' (Druids' curses). 'You see before you more women than warriors,' he told them in an ill-advised attempt to steady their nerves.

Since Watling Street was the main artery between Wales and London, the battle is plausibly referred to as the battle of Watling Street. The exact site is unknown. The archaeologist who excavated the settlement of Tripontium on Watling Street near Rugby suggested in 1997 that the battle took place on the nearby Dunsmore Plain. This happens to be one of the battlefields recently identified by 'terrain analysis techniques', and the even more recent Druidic analysis agrees.

The Pendinas / Aberystwyth line of latitude bisects Watling Street at Tripontium and the meeting point of three counties, just to the east of the Oxford meridian (figs. 71 and 72). Until 2007, the site was occupied by the giant masts of radio transmitters, which made excavation impossible. A vast housing estate is about to bury whatever evidence remains. Perhaps, one day, a Celtic sword or a Roman lance will be forked out of a garden in Boudica Avenue or Suetonius Close. Any human remains may well be female. The Roman soldiers surged out of the pass in a wedge formation. Hampered by their wagons and baggage, the Britons were unable to retreat, and 'our soldiers', says Tacitus, 'did not refrain from slaying even the women'.

According to Tacitus, who liked to present his pampered Roman readers with the spectacle of barbarian stoicism, Boudica committed suicide by taking poison. In the mopping-up operation, the Romans 'laid waste to' the lands of 'tribes that were hostile or unreliable'.* In Cassius Dio's less heroic account, Boudica survived the battle but fell ill and died. Her soldiers had been ready to fight on, but the death of their queen struck them as the final defeat. They gave her 'a costly burial', and then 'scattered to their homes'.

No mention of this is made in the historical accounts, but a

---

* The participle, '*vastatum*' ('ravaged'), may indicate a deliberate depopulation of tribal territories.

painstaking excavation has shown that at about that time the great ceremonial enclosure of the Iceni at Thetford in Norfolk disappeared. It lay on the same line of latitude as Pendinas, Tripontium and Wardy Hill. The entire complex – its grand circular buildings and nine concentric palisades – was systematically dismantled by Roman soldiers. The oaks were extracted from their postholes by digging or by pushing and pulling. The Thetford complex was neither a military nor a residential site, but the Romans had learned to fear the Druids and their oaks, and it was safer to remove them altogether than to consign the sacred place to flames from which the trees might rise again.

✿

Ten years after the death of Boudica, most of what is now England was under Roman domination. Wales hung on to its independence until the mid-70s, and, despite the earlier massacre of Druids, the island of Mona held out even longer. In AD 78, a new governor, Gnaeus Julius Agricola, finally completed the cleansing operation from which Suetonius had been recalled by Boudica's revolt. The Britons 'sued for peace and surrendered the island'. With the Druids' threat annihilated, Agricola was free to move north, to encounter 'new peoples', and to 'lay waste to their lands as far as the Tay'. By AD 83, only the tribes of northern Caledonia were unsubdued.

One night, somewhere beyond the Firth of Forth, while the soldiers of the Ninth Legion slept in their camp, the sentries were butchered by 'Caledonian natives' and the camp was overrun. Agricola arrived during the night with the cavalry. By dawn, the Britons were fleeing through 'the marshes and the woods'. Nothing further is reported until the following summer, when Agricola learned of the death of his baby son in Rome, and decided to seek 'a remedy for his grief in war'. He sent the fleet ahead with orders 'to plunder several places and to spread terror and uncertainty'.

'Still buoyant despite their earlier defeat', the Caledonian tribes demonstrated the characteristic Celtic ability to swarm like honey bees when the hive is attacked: 'By embassies and treaties, they called forth the whole strength of all their states.' More than thirty thousand warriors began to mass at a place whose name, in its Latin form, was Mons Graupius.

This is the first occasion on which a proto-Scottish nation appears in history. Unfortunately, the first named event in the annals of Scotland has been condemned to wander homelessly about the map: the location of 'Mons Graupius' is a mystery. There are currently about thirty contenders, but since the human geography of Iron Age Scotland is largely conjectural, and since most ancient battles leave few physical traces, no single place has emerged as the favourite.*

The name 'Graupius' is always said to be obscure, despite the fact that the Celtic word '*graua*' is found in dozens of place names. It meant 'gravel', and the second part of the name is probably its frequent companion: 'hill' or 'summit', from the Celtic '*penno*', the Latin forms of which are '*pennius*' or '*pen(n)is*'. Gravelly hills are not exactly rare, but with Tacitus's description of the battle site, a map of contemporary Roman forts, and, crucially, the Druidic map of Britain, the last stand of the British Celts can at last find a home and perhaps a monument more fitting than the planned seventeen wind turbines on the nearby Nathro Hill.

Lines of latitude divided the ancient world into *klimata*. One line passed through Delphi, another through Châteaumeillant, and another through Pendinas above Aberystwyth. The next line in the sequence, one hour of daylight north of Pendinas, crosses Scotland from Ardnamurchan Point in the west, by Rannoch Moor and the north shore of Loch Tummel, to Montrose Basin in the east.† The harbour of Montrose lies a day's sail north of the probable site of the Roman naval headquarters, Horrea Classis ('granaries of the fleet') in the Firth of Tay. A few kilometres inland, the great meridian that runs almost the entire length of Britain intersects the Montrose parallel on the river plain below one of the most spectacular and least-known sites of Iron Age Scotland.

---

* The battle may have been fought somewhere in the Grampian Mountains, but the name 'Grampian' is a false clue: it was first applied to the mountains of the southern Highlands by a sixteenth-century Scottish historian whose Latin text misspelled 'Graupius' with an 'm'.

† By an inscrutable coincidence, this line of latitude passes close to a small white house on the outskirts of Pitlochry at the foot of the Pass of Killiecrankie called Tigh na Geat (formerly, Taigh nan Teud, or 'House of the Harpstring'). The house was once said to mark the southerly limit of the Lords of the Isles' influence and the exact centre of Scotland.

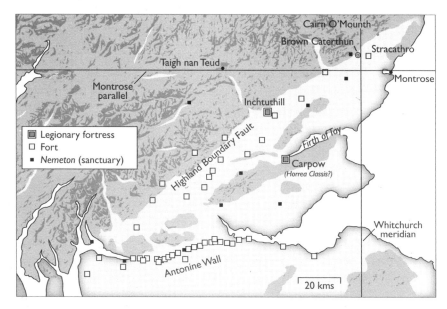

73. Central Caledonia
Central Caledonia at the time of the battle of Mons Graupius

The twin hills called White Caterthun and Brown Caterthun were major Iron Age forts. Both were 'multivallate' (with several concentric ditches and ramparts). Brown Caterthun is the closer of the two to the meridian and the meeting point of two counties and two parishes. The track to the summit leaves the rich farmland of Strathmore and rises gently through the springy heather, cutting through the mounds that were once the footings of ramparts. The water that gushes from a spring at the top of the hill has carved a thin gulley through the black loam, exposing the sandstone gravel that lies just beneath the surface.

Even on a hazy day, the luminous logic of the site appears as on a relief model in a museum. In the plain below, two battles were fought in the Middle Ages. In 1130, an invading army of five thousand was defeated by David I of Scotland. In 1452, the rebel Earl of Crawford was defeated by a royalist coalition of clans from the northeast. More than a thousand years before, the intimidating sails of Agricola's fleet might have been seen on the sparkling horizon. Between Brown Caterthun and the harbour, the buildings of Stracathro Hospital mark the site of the legionary fortress that was once the most northerly permanent outpost of the Roman empire.

It is easy to see why the Romans felt that they had come to what Tacitus calls the *'terminus Britanniae'*. The line of Roman forts runs diagonally along the Highland Boundary Fault until it reaches Stracathro. Looking north from the summit of Brown Caterthun, when the cloud-battalions part and the sun rushes over the moorland, there is a magnificent panorama of another country. This is where the Highlands and a military commander's nightmare begin. As Tacitus has the British leader Calgacus say in his pre-battle speech: 'There are no nations beyond us – nothing but waves and rocks.'

The Caledonians arranged themselves with their front line on the plain and the other ranks rising up the slope of the hill in tight formation. Eight thousand Roman foot soldiers and three thousand cavalry took up position in front of the camp. 'The flat country between was filled with the noise of the [British] charioteers racing about.' Until the very last minute, young men and old warriors had been arriving from regions unknown to the Romans. Since the valley sloping down towards the Firth of Clyde in the west was occupied by Roman forts, the warriors would have reached the battleground by the high roads from the north and by the Cairn O'Mounth pass, which had been a portal to the Highlands since prehistory.

The battle at the end of Middle Earth was a triumph for the tactical brilliance of Agricola. His grief found a powerful remedy: ten thousand Britons fell; 'equipment, bodies and mangled limbs bestrewed the bloody earth'. The remaining twenty thousand turned and ran 'in disarray, without regard for one another, scattering far into the trackless waste'. After the battle, a strange custom of the vanquished was observed: many of the fighters set fire to their homes and slaughtered their own wives and children. That night, beyond the camp where the Romans celebrated the victory and their plunder, the wind brought the sound of men and women wailing 'as they dragged away the wounded or called to the survivors'. At daybreak, victory showed its true face:

> An enormous silence reigned on every side. The hills were desolate, smoke rose from distant roofs, and the scouts who were sent out in all directions encountered not a soul.

The survivors had vanished as though the battle were already a legend. Agricola returned to winter quarters and received the report

of his naval commanders, who had sailed around the north of
Caledonia, thereby contributing valuable information to the Romans'
knowledge of the world. The tribes of remotest Britannia were left
in peace to fight among themselves, while, a long way to the south,
in their shiny new towns, the Romanized British enjoyed luxuries such
as couches and chairs, red Samian ware, colourful rings and trinkets
in the fashionable Celtic style, and oil-lamps made in Italy and Gaul.

The olive oil that was used as lamp fuel was expensive to import,
but for the few who could afford it, the oil was worth its weight in
gold. That gleaming nectar of the warm Mediterranean made it
possible to cheat the sun and to stay up far into the night, drinking
wine and telling tales of Caratacus and Boudica, and of the days when
the sun god had come to earth and made it safe for mortal beings.

16

Return of the Druids

The twenty thousand who fled from Mons Graupius vanished into a land of which very little is known. A century after Agricola, the Romans had pulled back behind Hadrian's Wall, and Caledonia was once again a land of myth. In the early third century, Cassius Dio described a hardy race of Caledonians living off roots and bark, and capable of surviving for days on end in swamps with only their heads above water. The only reliable sighting of the northern Caledonians is in Tacitus's account of a renegade cohort of German auxiliaries in Agricola's army. After killing a centurion and some soldiers, they hijacked three galleys and set off on 'a grand and memorable exploit'. They, rather than Agricola's admiral, are the first people known for certain to have sailed around the north of Britain. Provisions exhausted, they went inland in search of water and food, and 'encountered many Britons who fought to defend their property'. Some of the Germans eventually returned, as slaves, to the Rhineland, where 'their tales of the extraordinary adventure made them famous'.

The Caledonians themselves, having 'red hair and long limbs', were considered by Tacitus to be Germanic in origin. Since the German tribes had no Druids, this might explain why, in vivid contrast to southern Britain, there are few signs of a solar network in Caledonia. Even if the angles are adjusted to more northerly climes, any hypothetical solstice lines are as indistinct as shadows on a sunless day.

The map of Middle Earth reflects a cultural divide: it suggests a sphere of Druidic influence in the parts of Britain closest to the Continent which had been colonized by Belgic tribes. In the early Middle Ages, Britain was conventionally divided into north and south by an imaginary line running west from the Humber Estuary, following what would have been the old southern borders of the Brigantes.

North of the line, in the kingdom of North-Humbria, the pan-tribal authority of the Druids may never have been recognized. When Caratacus the Catuvellaunian had thrown himself on the mercy of the Brigantian queen, Cartimandua, no Druidic council had prevented her from handing him over to the Romans.

The territory that is now Scotland had no perceptible Heraklean Way or Royal Road, and yet the Caledonian tribes seem to have known where they were in relation to the rest of the world. Some of their capitals lie on the Whitchurch meridian (p. 240), others on the meridian that passes through Dinas Emrys and Medionemeton, and still others on a third line of longitude that runs through the western Highlands. Whatever their ethnic origins, the names of these tribes are clearly Celtic,* and so is this alignment of centres of power on the meridians.

There are no equivalents of the myth of Lludd and the dragons to provide a clue to a Caledonian *omphalos*, only untraceable local traditions which purport to identify the centre of Scotland. Each of these traditions identifies a different centre, but when the various sites are plotted on the map, they suddenly seem to be in harmony. One 'centre of Scotland' is the little white house on the Montrose parallel (p. 265n). Four others line up on the meridian which passes through Dinas Emrys. The first is the 'middle sanctuary' of Medionemeton. The second is Gartincaber Tower near Doune (a folly built in 1799 on a site believed to be the geographical centre of Scotland). The third is the village of Fortingall, where a two-thousand-year-old yew tree twists on its crutches in the middle of an ancient monastic site. (On the edge of the village, which is also the fabled birthplace of Pontius Pilate, a stone circle stands at a place, Duneaves, whose name comes from '*nemeton*'.) The fourth 'centre' on the same meridian rises behind Fortingall to the north: this is the great granite cone of the mountain called Schiehallion. Its Gaelic name – Sìdh Chailleann – means 'Fairy-hill of the Caledonians'. In the language of lowlanders, its name was Maiden Pap, which means 'Middle Mountain'.[†]

---

* Caereni, 'Shepherds'; Caledones, 'People of the Rugged Fortress'; Carnonacae, 'Hornèd Ones'; Cornavii, 'Sailors'; Damnonii, 'People of the Lower World' or 'Keepers' or 'Magistrates'; etc. The tribes are listed in Ptolemy's *Geography* (second century AD), probably from information supplied by Agricola's officers.

[†] 'Pap', meaning 'nipple' or 'breast', was a common name for a hill. 'Maiden' is incorrectly assumed to refer to the mountain's fancied resemblance to a virgin's breast.

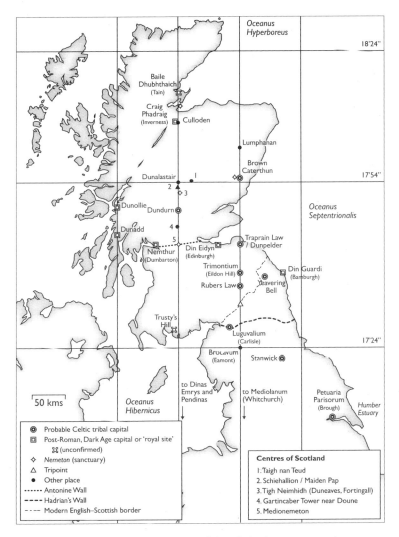

Map labels:

Oceanus
Hyperboreus

18'24"

Baile
Dhubhthaich
(Tain)
Craig
Phadraig
(Inverness)   Culloden

Lumphanan

Brown
Caterthun

Dunalastair   1   17'54"
2
3
Dunollie Dundurn
Dunadd   4
5   Traprain Law
Nemthur   / Dunpelder
(Dumbarton)   Din Eidyn
(Edinburgh)
Trimontium
(Eildon Hill)   Din Guardi
Rubers Law   (Bamburgh)
Yeavering
Bell

Oceanus
Septentrionalis

Trusty's
Hill
Luguvalium
(Carlisle)   17'24"
Brocavum
(Eamont)   Stanwick

to Dinas
Emrys and
Pendinas   to Mediolanum
(Whitchurch)   Petuaria
Parisorum
(Brough)   Humber
Estuary

50 kms   Oceanus
Hibernicus

Legend:
- ◉ Probable Celtic tribal capital
- ▣ Post-Roman, Dark Age capital or 'royal site'
  - ⊞ (unconfirmed)
- ◇ Nemeton (sanctuary)
- △ Tripoint
- ● Other place
- ······ Antonine Wall
- ▬▬▬ Hadrian's Wall
- ---- Modern English–Scottish border

Centres of Scotland
1. Taigh nan Teud
2. Schiehallion / Maiden Pap
3. Tigh Neimhidh (Duneaves, Fortingall)
4. Gartincaber Tower near Doune
5. Medionemeton

74. Centres of Scotland and the Caledonian meridians

Some capitals of Dark Age kingdoms founded after the departure of the Romans were probably the successors of Iron Age capitals. The only plausible solstice diagonal in Caledonia is the trajectory of the 'Royal Road' along which Boudica marched from Wardy Hill to Camulodunum. This is the longest diagonal that can be drawn through Britain. It passes to the west of the tribal capital of the Carvetii tribe, Luguvalium (Carlisle), through Brocavum (Eamont), Blatobulgium and several other Roman forts, and along the route of the A74 via Gretna Green to the site of the Glasgow Necropolis. It is shown as a dotted line in figure 79.

In the historical silence of the Highlands, it is hard to distinguish human messages from stray sounds carried by the wind. This striking alignment of 'centres' does all the same have a compellingly Celtic air. It suggests that Caledonia was connected to the rest of Britain and the Celtic world almost two millennia before Scotland and England were joined by the Acts of Union.

Did some memory of pagan meridians survive in bardic tales and witches' lore? When Macbeth of Scotland made his last stand at the village of Lumphanan in 1057, he or his geomancers might have known that the battleground lay directly on the Whitchurch meridian. Successive developments over many centuries of prehistoric sites such as Stonehenge show that when tribal memory was preserved in astronomical alignments and visible features of the landscape, it could have a very long life. In 1746, the Caledonian tribes suffered a defeat even more catastrophic than the battle of Mons Graupius. Despite the marshy terrain, the Jacobite rebels chose a moor to the east of Inverness for their decisive engagement with the government army. But only a Highlander for whom a thousand years were a short spell in the collective memory of his clan would have known that Culloden Moor is bisected by the line that runs through the middle of Scotland.

✿

From Caledonia, the sun of the winter solstice appeared to return to the Ocean beyond an island that was the last outpost of the inhabited world. The Massalian explorer Pytheas had been told that its name was 'Ierne'. The origin of the word is unknown, though it survives in the modern name of Ireland: Eire. The Romans, having heard that 'complete savages lead a miserable existence there because of the cold', called it 'Hibernia' ('the wintry land'). It was also said that despite the wretched climate, the grass of Hibernia was so lush and plentiful that 'the livestock eat their fill in a short space of time and, if no one prevents them from grazing, they explode'.

Because Ireland was never conquered by the Romans, its pastures are prolific in tales dating back to the days of the ancient Celts. They were first recorded in the early Middle Ages, but echoes of the founding myths had reached the outside world long before. In the early fifth century AD, in his *History Against the Pagans*, Orosius reported that 'a very tall lighthouse' had been erected in the city of Brigantia

(A Coruña) in north-western Spain 'for the purpose of looking out towards Britannia'.

The implicit notion that the British Isles might be visible from Spain probably reflects a tale passed on by a trader, a slave or a refugee like the deposed Irish chieftain who sought asylum with Agricola. The eleventh-century compilation of legends known as *The Book of Invasions* (*Lebor Gabála Érenn*) tells the story of Breogán, a Celtic king of Galicia, who built a gigantic tower in Brigantia. (Hearing this, a Roman would have recognized the lighthouse called the Tower of Hercules.) 'On a clear winter's evening', Breogán's son climbed to the top of the tower and saw a distant green shore. He promptly set sail with 'thrice thirty warriors'. 'They landed on the "Fetid Shore" of the Headland of Corcu Duibne' in the south-west of Ireland.

These pre-Christian legends embrace so many diverse and specific details that the saga of Irish origins defies summary but not belief. If Breogán's son sailed due north from Brigantia, he would have come to the hill of Ard Nemid in what is now Cork Harbour. This, according to Ptolemy's *Geography*, was the part of Hibernia inhabited by a tribe called the Brigantes.* Perhaps the Irish Brigantes had heard of the city of Brigantia in Spain and imagined their Iberian forefathers crossing the Ocean with the stiff breeze of destiny in their sails. It is impossible to know how much historical truth the legend conveys. Some promontory forts in south-western Ireland have Iberian-style defences, and the lives of the early Irish saints contain many allusions to Iberia and Lusitania (Portugal). Archaeology suggests that Hibernia's ties with the rest of Keltika were tenuous, but this may simply reflect the fact that so many Irish Iron Age sites have yet to be excavated. Many have been destroyed – and still are being destroyed – by road building and peat extraction. At the time of writing, the chief material proof of Ireland's Mediterranean connections is the skull of a Barbary macaque – the species of monkey that still scampers over the Rock of Gibraltar – which crossed the Ocean, dead or alive, some time between 390 and 20 BC.

The monkey's skull was discovered under the great burial mound

---

* Names derived from '*briga*' ('high place') are common in the Celtic world, especially in Iberia. There is no known connection between this tribe and the Brigantes of Britain.

at Navan Fort in Northern Ireland. Navan Fort is the Emain Macha of Irish legend, one of the 'royal sites' at which the early medieval kings of Ireland held assemblies and ceremonies of inauguration. The intricate earthworks and timber circles of these royal sites show that they were already the religious centres of Ireland in the Iron Age. They were chosen, like many of the *oppida* of Gaul, because they were known to be places that had been sacred to the pre-Celtic inhabitants of the island. One of the royal sites – the complex of barrows and enclosures on the Hill of Uisneach – is identified in legend as the *omphalos* of Ireland. Uisneach was the sacred centre, the burial place of Lugh, where a Druid lit the first fire in Ireland. It stood in a territory called 'Mide' (the Middle Land). The rest of the island was divided into four kingdoms, which became the medieval provinces of Ulster, Connacht, Leinster and Munster.

Celtic society survived for so long in Ireland that these places of legend can be seen emerging into recorded history with their identities intact. In gloating over the demise of the great pagan shrines, the ninth-century Christian author of *The Martyrology of Óengus* (*Félire Óengusso*) unintentionally produced a miniature gazetteer of Iron Age Ireland:

> The mighty burgh of Temra [Tara] perished at the death of her princes: with a multitude of venerable champions the Ard mór [great height] of Machae [Armagh] abides.

> Ráth Chrúachan [Rathcroghan, the ring-fort of Cruachan] has vanished . . . fair is the sovranty over princes in the monastery of Clonmacnoise.

> The proud burgh of Aillinne [Dún Ailinne] has perished with its warlike host: great is victorious Brigit; fair is her multitudinous cemetery [Kildare].

> Emain's burgh [Emain Macha] has vanished, save only its stones: the Rome of the western world is multitudinous Glendalough.

> The old cities of the pagans, wherein ownership was acquired by long use, they are waste without worship, like Lugaid's House-site.

These pagan centres can be plotted on a map, and any solar patterns hidden in Iron Age Hibernia should appear. The most obviously Druidic feature is this: the *omphalos* of Uisneach is connected by a solstice line to the royal sites of Cruachan and Dún Ailinne. The bearings are close but not identical to the British standard (within 1.4° and 1.6° respectively). Two other royal sites – Cnoc Áine and Emain Macha – are also roughly aligned on the Uisneach *omphalos*, within a range of 2.2°.

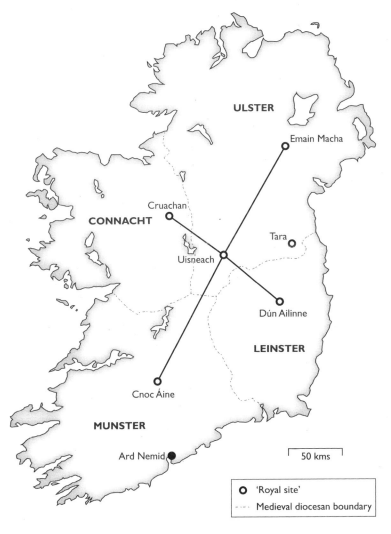

75. 'Royal sites' of Ireland

'Royal sites' of Iron Age Ireland. The Hill of Tara, the seat of the kings of early medieval Ireland, plays no part in this pattern. It may have been used only sporadically, or acquired its eminence only later.

1. Tullyhogue Fort
2. Belfast (hill forts)
3. Tynagh
4. Clonmacnoise
5. Kells (hill fort)
6. Croghan Hill
7. The Curragh
8. Dublin
9. Innisfallen (Killarney)
10. Ardmore
(St Declan's Stone)

50 kms

76. The Irish network

The range of bearings of the three west-east diagonals is 57.96°–59.94°. Assuming perfect alignments, the system would have been based on a tan ratio of 9:5. The line joining Uisneach to Dún Ailinne is a winter solstice line; the corresponding line to Cruachan points to sunset on 1 August (the feast of Lughnasadh).

Despite the slight inaccuracies, a pattern materializes like a piece of jewellery in an archaeologist's trench. The fortress and 'royal site' of the Grianan of Aileach was one of the key coordinates used in an early division of Ireland. It lies north of Uisneach on a bearing of

2.9°. This skewed meridian is mirrored by two similarly tilted north–south lines which link the other four royal sites (fig. 76).

This peculiarly Hibernian variation on the solar network is remarkably coherent. The Uisneach meridian bisects the two diagonal lines, forming two parallelograms. Logically, a corresponding site should exist to the south of Uisneach on the line from the Grianan of Aileach. This would be Ardmore, which predates St Patrick and is probably the oldest monastic settlement in Ireland. In the nineteenth century, thousands of pilgrims were still paying their pagan devotions to a miraculous stone and a holy well at Ardmore, enacting an 'annual scene of disgusting superstition' involving the not-entirely-ritual consumption of whiskey.

One other 'royal site' remains to be accounted for: Raffin Fort in County Meath is not mentioned in the medieval texts, but it, too, 'displays all the features typical of a royal site and is considered to belong to this group'. The solstice lines now begin to trace out a lost history of Ireland. On the same bearing as the other two diagonals – within less than one quarter of a degree – the line from Raffin Fort passes through the hill fort that became the monastery of Kells, then through the Uisneach *omphalos*, to the monastery of Clonmacnoise, which was one of the great centres of learning in early medieval Ireland. The westerly point of intersection lies just outside the village of Tynagh. The missionary who Christianized Tynagh was said to be a son of Lugh, which suggests that the site was once a cult centre of the Celtic god.

This elegant pattern may be further evidence of the spread of Celtic culture to Ireland by trade, migration or even deliberate inculcation. A possible sequence of events can be pieced together from legend and by analogy with other Celtic lands. The earliest partition of Ireland described in *The Book of Invasions* used a natural frontier, the Esker Riada. This 'road', formed of glacial ridges of sand and gravel, splits the island roughly into north and south. At this point in the history of Hibernia, there was no *omphalos* or sacred centre: the division was purely terrestrial.

Then a people called the Fir Bolg arrived after an odyssey of several generations which had taken them through Greece and Spain. It was the Fir Bolg who chose Uisneach as the centre, presumably using celestial rather than geographical measurements. *The Book of*

Invasions describes their partition of Ireland as a '*tóraind*' (a 'marking-out' or 'delimiting'). As in Gaul, certain prehistoric sites were chosen and then redeveloped – equipped with banks, ditches, towers and palisades. If the architects of these royal sites retained some of the crude solstitial alignments of the Neolithic monuments, this would account for the inaccuracies of the Hibernian system. When the first Christian missionaries landed in Ireland, they followed in the footsteps of the Druid 'missionaries', and their monastic houses were the direct descendants of Druid schools.

The solar map of Ireland is as rich in virtual expeditions as a railway timetable. It no longer seems a merely picturesque coincidence, for example, that the sun of the winter solstice, seen from Uisneach, rises over Croghan Hill (no. 6 in fig. 76), where St Brigit founded the first convent in Ireland. Other places on the lines may turn out to have been centres of pagan worship, and perhaps the idiosyncrasies of the system will prove to be consequential. The strangely tilted meridian which runs three degrees west of south from the Uisneach *omphalos* could be the result of careful calculation. If the line is projected as it would have been on a medieval portolan chart, it arrives with eerie precision at the exact point from which Breogán's son and his armada sailed for Ireland. When he climbed the tower in Brigantia later known as the Tower of Hercules and saw the distant green shore, his mind's eye did not deceive him.

Like the Britons and the Gauls, the Irish developed a system which reflected their fabled origins. Archaeologists have shown that the chronology of the Irish legends is astonishingly accurate. The same precision may be encoded in the solar network. Recently, scholars have begun to talk of Celtic culture spreading, not from central Europe, but from the far west. It would have travelled along the Atlantic sea lanes from one 'end of the earth' to the next – from the Sacred Promontory to Fisterra and Brigantia, and from there to Finistère, Belerion and the other 'Sacred Promontory', on the south-eastern tip of Ireland.

The earliest written records in Europe beyond the Aegean are inscriptions made in a language called Tartessian. The oldest inscriptions use the Phoenician alphabet and date from the eighth century BC. Tartessian was spoken in south-western Iberia. If the partial decipherments are correct, this language belongs to the same sub-group as the Celtic languages of Gaul and Britain. Like the Irish legends and the lives of Irish saints, these inscriptions may be the distant echoes of an ancient maritime trading empire based on slaves and luxury goods. The rhumb line that connects the Tower of Hercules to Uisneach would represent one of the oldest trade routes in Europe. If the line is projected further still, it arrives with the same uncanny accuracy at the Sacred Promontory on the extreme south-western tip of Iberia, where the sun of the winter solstice returned to the lower world (fig. 77), and where the road from the ends of the earth began its long journey to the Alps.

✵

Here, on the shores of the Western Ocean, another book begins. It is tempting to believe that the story of Celtic Middle Earth had a sequel, and that the Druids continued to practise and teach in the early Christian era. The fifth-century saint referred to in the *Martyrology of Óengus* as the 'victorious Brigit' (one of the patron saints of Ireland) was the daughter or foster-daughter of a star-gazing Druid who predicted that she would 'shine in the world like the sun in the vault of heaven'. According to one account, Brigit's father had come, like Breogán's son, from Lusitania. Her feast day is the day of Imbolc (the first of February), one of the four Celtic festivals, and her name – 'the Shining One' – is that of a Celtic goddess. The woman herself, who tended a fire surrounded by a circular hedge that no man could cross, might have been raised as a priestess of her divine namesake.

The word 'Druid' was applied to Christian saints and hermits, and even to the Son of God. But a word is not proof of continuity. The '*draoidhe*' who were defeated by St Patrick lived five hundred years after Julius Caesar described the Druids of Gaul as a scientific intelligentsia. The diplomat and scholar Diviciacus would have had little in common with the fifth-century Irish Druid Lucatmael, who, in a miracle-contest with St Patrick, induced 'demons' to cover the land in a waist-high blanket of snow.

In Continental Europe, the body of knowledge that had once demanded a twenty-year-long education was either lost or subsumed into the classical curriculum. The fourth-century Gaulish poet Ausonius claimed that '*professores*' teaching in Bordeaux were scions

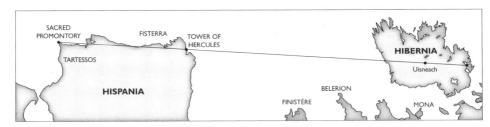

77. From Hispania to Hibernia

of ancient Druid families, but the implication was that Druidism belonged to the past. Some of the Druids' religious functions – consecrating temples, measuring boundaries, counselling kings – survived in pagan cults, which were absorbed rather than abolished by the Church. Their temples – according to the instructions of Pope Gregory I in c. 600 – were converted ('if they be well built') rather than destroyed, 'for surely it is impossible to efface all at once everything from their strong minds'.

While Druidism persisted in popular religion, the art that had been the geometrical form of its wisdom went beautifully to seed. The 'Ultimate La Tène' style of illuminated manuscripts such as the Book of Kells (c. 800) is decorative rather than mathematical; 'Celtic' Christian crosses may resemble pagan sun-wheels and evoke the pattern of solstice lines radiating from an *omphalos*, but their geometry is inconsistent and contains no secret messages from a Druid underworld.

The intellectual decline of Celtic art is especially evident in the enigmatic carved stones of the Picts of Dark Age Scotland. Most of the carvings were made in the eighth and ninth centuries, more than a thousand years after Celtic art first appeared in Europe. One of the commonest figures in the Pictish repertoire combines the crescent-shaped 'pelta' of Celtic art with two 'compass lines', which could be the solstice bearings of a solar grid, or the finger and thumb of a measuring hand. But these, too, are inconsistent. Even after decades of scholarly study, the Pictish symbols are still mysterious, and it now looks as though they were mysterious to the Picts themselves. The intriguing designs they saw on antique pieces of equipment and jewellery were a code they were never able to crack. They copied the

78. A Pictish carving

From a Pictish stone found in the Orkney Islands. (After Murray, p. 230)

curiously truncated shapes, unaware that each one had once been the visible part of an invisible whole.

※

When the first Christian chapels were built in Britain and Gaul, the creator of the Heraklean Way had long since ascended into the heavens. Meanwhile, stiff with cold and frost, and in a remote region of the earth, far from the visible sun, these islands received the light of the true Sun – which is to say the precepts of Christ – showing to the whole world his splendour, not only from the temporal firmament, but from the height of heaven, which surpasses all things temporal.

In Gaul, the 'true Sun' shone brightest where the Romans had founded their towns and where the great cathedrals would be built. But it also shone on obscure and half-abandoned places that had been sacred to the Celts. On the mountain where the *oppidum* of Bibracte had stood, a chapel replaced the temple. *Nemetons* turned into Christian shrines, and sites named after the god Lugh acquired chapels dedicated to a 'St Luc'. At least one Mediolanum changed its name to 'Madeleine'. In Alesia, the mother-city of the Gauls, a Christian girl was said to have been martyred in 252. St Regina (Sainte Reine) had been decapitated, and where her severed head had struck the ground, a miraculous healing spring gushed out.

The story of the saint of Alesia is typical of the early process of Christianization. The pagan gods of Alesia's healing spring were

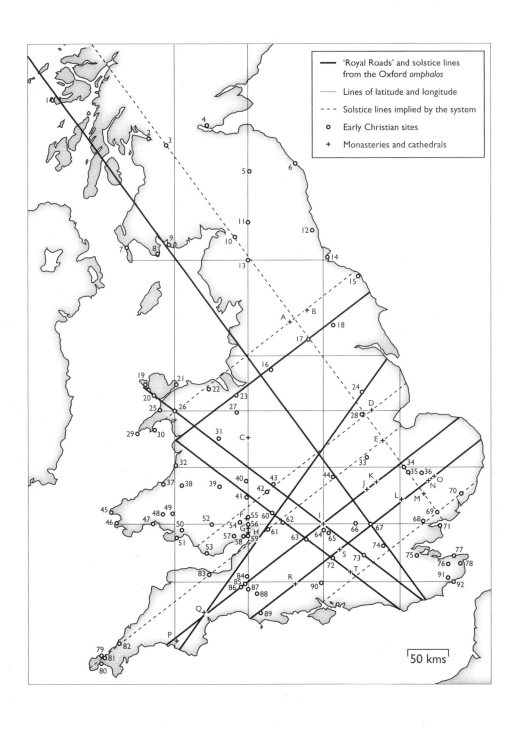

▬▬	'Royal Roads' and solstice lines from the Oxford *omphalos*
—	Lines of latitude and longitude
---	Solstice lines implied by the system
○	Early Christian sites
+	Monasteries and cathedrals

50 kms

79. Christianity and the solar network

The early Christian sites (first foundation, up to the mid-seventh century) are plotted without prior reference to solstice lines. For exact coordinates, see www.panmacmillan.com/theancientpaths. In Wales, pre-eighth century monasteries are shown. Hoards containing Christian artefacts are omitted because provenances are uncertain (Mildenhall, Traprain Law, Water Newton, etc.), as are Christian embellishments and private chapels in Roman villas. Later monasteries and cathedrals (c. 974–1248) are selected for their association with the system (e.g. those on the 'Royal Road' between Salisbury and Bury St Edmunds: p. 239).

Key:

Early Christian sites (list of coordinates at www.panmacmillan.com/theancientpaths): 1. Iona. 2. Dumbarton. 3. Glasgow (Govan). 4. Dunfermline. 5. Mailros (Melrose). 6. Lindisfarne. 7. Kirkmadrine. 8. Whithorn. 9. Ardwall Isle. 10. Carlisle. 11. Bewcastle. 12. Jarrow. 13. Eamont. 14. Hartlepool. 15. Whitby. 16. Manchester. 17. Leeds. 18. York. 19. Caergybi. 20. Aberffraw. 21. Penmon. 22. St Asaph. 23. Chester. 24. Lincoln (St Paul in the Bail). 25. Clynnog Fawr. 26. Dinas Emrys. 27. Bangor on Dee. 28. Ancaster. 29. Bardsey. 30. St Tudwal's Island East. 31. Meifod. 32. Llanbadarn Fawr. 33. Ashton. 34. Ely. 35. Soham. 36. Icklingham. 37. Llanarth. 38. Llanddewi Brefi. 39. Glascwm. 40. Leominster. 41. Hereford. 42. Malvern (St Ann's Well). 43. Worcester. 44. Bannaventa. 45. St Davids. 46. St Brides. 47. Coygan Camp. 48. Carmarthen. 49. Llanarthney. 50. Llangyfelach. 51. Bishopston. 52. Merthyr Tydfil. 53. Llantwit Major. 54. Raglan. 55. Dixton. 56. Llandogo. 57. Caerleon. 58. Caerwent. 59. Mathern (St Tewdric's Well). 60. Gloucester (Churchdown Hill). 61. Uley. 62. Bagendon (church in *oppidum*). 63. Dragon Hill, Uffington (chapel). 64. Abingdon. 65. Dorchester-on-Thames. 66. Cholesbury. 67. St Albans. 68. Witham. 69. Colchester. 70. Sutton Hoo (?). 71. Bradwell (Othona). 72. Silchester. 73. Chertsey. 74. Westminster. 75. Rochester. 76. Canterbury. 77. Reculver. 78. Richborough. 79. St Ives (St Ia's). 80. St Michael's Mount. 81. Phillack. 82. Perranporth (St Piran's Oratory). 83. Carhampton. 84. Glastonbury Tor (St Michael's). 85. Bradley Hill. 86. Muchelney. 87. Ilchester. 88. Sherborne. 89. Poundbury (Dorchester). 90. Winchester. 91. Lyminge. 92. Folkestone (St Eanswythe).

Monasteries and cathedrals (selected): A. Bolton Priory. B. Fountains Abbey. C. Haughmond Abbey. D. Haverholme Priory. E. Croyland Abbey. F. Monmouth Priory. G. Tintern Abbey. H. Chepstow Priory. I. Osney Abbey. J. Newnham Priory (Bedford). K. St Neots Priory. L. Walden Abbey (Saffron Walden). M. Clare Priory. N. Bury St Edmunds Abbey. O. Ixworth Priory. P. Reading Abbey. Q. Plympton Priory. R. Exeter Abbey. S. Salisbury Cathedral. T. Waverley Abbey.

officially obliterated in the ninth century, when a 'Life of St Regina' was concocted from the hagiography of another saint. Nothing was said of the battle that had been fought at Alesia in September 52 BC, though the day on which the saint is still remembered (7 September) may be the exact anniversary of Vercingetorix's defeat. Thousands of other sites were ideologically cleared to make way for the new religion. Monasteries and hermitages were founded in places said to be so wild and barren – *'in terra deserta, in loco horroris et vastae solitudinis'** – that only demons had been able to live there until the grace of God had made them fertile.

In the long dawn of western Christianity, older landscapes some-times deepen the view like anachronisms in a dream. When St Columba and St Patrick processed 'sunwise' around chapels and holy wells, they were performing a Druidic ritual in the name of a new god. (As the native of a *nemeton*,[†] Patrick may well have been familiar with Druidic rites.) In the curved ambulatories of their churches, monks paced out the invisible ellipses of Celtic temples. Pope Gregory had instructed that animal sacrifice should be allowed to continue, provided that the animal be eaten afterwards in a holy feast and 'no longer sacrificed as an offering to the devil'. Many other ceremonies must have been retained, even as their meanings were erased.

Traces of this merging of two religions are surprisingly evident in the British solar network. Several major Christian sites are strung along the Whitchurch meridian like beads on a rosary: Mailros Abbey, Lanercost Priory, Tintern Abbey, Chepstow Priory, the monasteries of Llandogo and Dixton near Monmouth, the church on Glastonbury Tor, and the ancient chapel at Eamont near Penrith, where the kings of Dark Age Britain accepted Christianity as the official religion of the Isles in 927.

Apart from the lonely church on the Bewcastle Waste in Cumbria, which the Romans knew as 'Fanum Cocidi', the shrine of a Celtic god, these holy places seem to have been created *ex nihilo*. Yet they and many others adhere to the British solstice lines as though, along

---

* Deuteronomy, 32:10 (the phrase was usually quoted from the Vulgate). King James version: 'In a desert land, and in the waste howling wilderness'.

† Nemthor or Nemthur, which is probably Dumbarton (one of several possible birthplaces).

with some of the Iron Age tribal boundaries, knowledge of the system had somehow been preserved.

Evidence of the first Christian sites in Britain is sparse and not always easy to interpret. It consists of saints' lives and chronicles, inscriptions, lead fonts and other ecclesiastical remains, and cemeteries in which the skeletons are oriented on the sunrise. Far more is known about the great abbeys and priories of the monastic revival of the tenth to twelfth centuries, but there are no documents to explain why they, too, often match the solar paths. Monastic histories were stitched together from fictional accounts of the abbey's patron saint, forged charters and snippets of folklore, suitably Christianized. No ambitious institution would have advertised its pagan roots. When Osney Abbey was founded as a priory in 1129 on sodden meadows beneath Oxford Castle, no reference was made to the site's legendary status as the *omphalos* of Celtic Britain. The unpromising location was selected because the founder's wife liked to walk along the riverbank and often stopped by a tree in which – miraculously, it seemed to her – magpies used to gather 'and ther to chattre, and as it wer to speke onto her'. The garrulous birds, her confessor explained, were souls in purgatory seeking rest. Accordingly, the priory was built on that very spot.

Abbeys, priories and even hermitages were founded where they would be fed by the flow of pilgrims' money. They stood where people had passed or congregated in pagan times. Travellers' tales and local legends were incorporated into the founding myth. Monks and abbots, too, believed in witches and demons; they knew and feared the names of the pagan gods. Their mental maps of the abbey's environs included magic wells and trees, and the mounds where fairies went to and from the lower world. Some of the medieval abbeys were joined to other holy sites by straight tracks called 'fairy paths', 'trods' or 'corpse roads'. These tracks were said to have been made by the feet of saints or angels. Some were remnants of longer routes such as the Icknield Way, and although the paths were prehistoric, Christian pilgrims walked along them towards a new life with the sun's light in their eyes or their shadows rushing ahead to the horizon.

This is the mystery glimpsed in the scriptorium at St Albans: the solstice line labelled 'Icknield Way' on the map of the Four Royal Roads passes through five abbeys and one cathedral (Salisbury), despite the fact that most of those institutions had existed for less than a century. How did a new cathedral come to find itself on an ancient solar path? The mystery would be impenetrable without a legend which explains how the site was chosen. From the top of the old cathedral inside the circular earthworks of the Iron Age *oppidum* three kilometres to the north, the Bishop of Old Sarum or his bowman shot an arrow. Where the arrow landed, the new cathedral would be built. Instead of falling to the ground, the arrow pierced a deer, which ran to the banks of the river Avon. It died, somewhat inconveniently, on a marshy floodplain, on the site of the future Salisbury Cathedral.

The deer's sense of direction in the throes of death was as keen as that of Boudica's hare. It died on a piece of land called Myrfield or 'boundary field' at which three ancient territories met. This zoomantic divination practised or sanctioned by a medieval bishop is one of the rare clues to an actual process of transmission. Druids, too, deciphered messages in the struggles of slain animals. Whether or not they grasped the whole picture, hermits, seers and pagan worshippers ensured that the sacred places of the new religion would be aligned, like its altars and graves, on the paths of the old sun. Hermits colonized Druidic sites, and on those sites, abbeys were founded – which is why, when St Patroclus of Bourges made his cell 'in the deep solitudes of the forest' in the early sixth century, his secluded retreat already had a Celtic name: Mediocantus or 'Middle of the Wheel'. In churches standing on the foundations of temples, and in basilicas built from the rubble of *oppida*, half-converted congregations heard words of wisdom very similar to those they had learned from the Druids:

'Honour the gods, do no evil, and exercise courage.'
'Death is but the middle of a long life.'
'Souls do not perish but pass after death from one body into another.'

More than a thousand years after the advent of the Celtic gods, their sun was still shining on the mortal earth. All over Europe, pilgrims followed the roads that could be concealed but not destroyed. The new religion was spreading its own map over the world, and although the sacred centre was now Jerusalem and many of the co-ordinates of the Celtic earth had been erased, certain places that had fallen into obscurity recovered some of their ancient glory. Every year, hordes of Christians passed through Châteaumeillant, the *omphalos* of Gaul, heading south-west to the Pyrenees and the shrine of the apostle James at Compostela. They imagined themselves to be guided by the blur of the Milky Way, which is still known in some parts as 'the Way of St James'. The white road in the heavens had once been associated with Herakles and his mother's milk, and with the glowing trail that was left by the dying sun as it descended towards the Ocean.

Half an hour of daylight south of Châteaumeillant, beyond the mountain forests that Herakles had turned into the world's biggest funeral pyre, the latitude line of the northern Mediterranean leads to Santiago de Compostela and, from there, to the End of the Earth called Fisterra. The 'Altar of the Sun' vanished long ago. It may have stood on the hill above the lighthouse or on the site of the twelfth-century church of Santa María das Areas, where pilgrims still pray to a miracle-working Christ of the Golden Beard.

Centuries before, Carthaginian vessels had passed the Altar of the Sun as they sailed north on the tin route to Finistère and Belerion. The rocky headland on the Costa da Morte was the scene of many shipwrecks, and treasures may still be awaiting rediscovery beneath the Atlantic storms. According to the legend of the Fisterran Christ, a statue with a golden beard was cast into the waves from a ship in distress, to lighten the load or to calm the raging winds by propitiation. For an unknown length of time, it was lost in the Ocean. Then, one day, it was caught in a fisherman's net. Like many other images of ancient gods, it was interpreted as a miraculous image of Christ. But a golden beard had been one of the attributes of the Carthaginian Herakles. He could still be seen in all his splendour in the fifth century, on the African shores of the Mediterranean, before Christians removed his beard and felled his mighty trunk. His ritual death, in an ancient storm at the end of the earth, was the god's salvation. He plunged, like the sun and the souls of the dead, into the roaring sea, and the ship that had carried him sailed on in the certain knowledge that light would soon be spreading from the east.

Epilogue

A Traveller's Guide to Middle Earth

When this book was on the verge of being written, I walked through central London on the Celtic meridian. This is the line of longitude that would have run between the meridians of Whitchurch and Châteaumeillant if the solar network had been translated directly from Gaul to Britain, as, indeed, it may have been at an early stage (p. 224). I wanted to confront the magical mathematics of Middle Earth with the randomness of present reality, and to counteract the excitement that turns every suspicion into a truth.

Coincidences had become everyday occurrences. A few days before, the Druid network had shown its astonishing power to illuminate the long-buried past by revealing the location of the legendary court of King Arthur. The line that crosses England half a *klima* north of the Aberystwyth parallel meets the Whitchurch meridian in Greater Manchester. The intersection lies in the Wigan suburb of Standish. Two thousand years ago, Standish was a Roman road junction called Coccium . . . Once again, the solar paths and the Roman road system were in mysterious harmony.

To be precise, the point of intersection is at the end of a cul-de-sac running off Old Pepper Lane, where a track leads into the council-owned woodland of Shevington Moor. The other edge of the wood, one hundred and fifty metres to the east, is skirted by the Royal Road from Tripontium. It was along a southern section of this trajectory that Boudica had marched to her last battle with the Romans.

When the solar paths were plotted on the virtual map, a fourth line became visible: this was the summer solstice path running northeast from the dragons' tomb of Dinas Emrys. Then a word appeared on the computer screen as though the solar network could generate digital hallucinations: '*CAMELOT*'. The pattern unfurled itself like

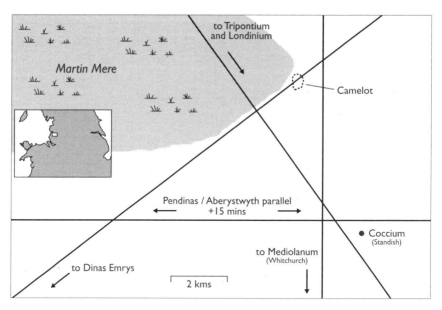

80. The solar location of 'Camelot'

a flag in a sudden breeze: Hannibal, Vercingetorix, Caratacus, Boudica and now, it seemed, Arthur, King of the Britons, had all been followers of the sun god. 'Arthur's Cave', on the Whitchurch meridian, marks the site of Merlin's victory over Vortigern (pp. 223–4). On the same meridian, the monks of Glastonbury had excavated an ancient royal burial containing what they claimed were the remains of King Arthur and Queen Guinevere. It was possible after all that in post-Roman Britain, when the old Celtic territories were re-emerging as Dark Age kingdoms, the court of Camelot had been sited at an auspicious nodal point of the network.

The approximate date of Camelot's foundation was revealed almost in the same instant by the two words which appeared beneath 'Camelot': 'Theme Park'. For some unfathomable reason, in this zone of solar intersections, the latest incarnation of Merlin, according to the Camelot website, 'can be found performing his illusions twice a day in his spellbinding magic show which takes places in the Castle'.

❁

As soon as a geometrical pattern is imposed on the inhabited earth, significance rushes in like water into a channel dug in a damp field.

The London meridian crosses the Thames at Vauxhall Bridge near the site of a Bronze Age causeway and heads north to Westminster. A short distance away, beyond the Houses of Parliament – as though the network had been common knowledge all along – stands the equestrian statue of Queen Boudica, her commanding bronze thighs conveying an unusually positive impression of an Iron Age aristocrat's diet.

At the time of Boudica's rebellion, Westminster was an island. A medieval charter described it as a *'locus valde terribilis'* – 'a truly terrible place'. Despite the mirthful interpretation of the word by Westminster schoolboys, *'terribilis'* means 'awe-inspiring' or 'venerable'. Thorney Island was a sacred place. One of the earliest Christian churches had been founded there, according to a sixth-century legend, by King Lucius of Britain. No king of that name ever existed, and so 'Lucius', like 'Luc', is probably a corruption of the name of the god 'Lugh' or 'Lugus'. An early British chronicle stated that the primitive church was replaced by a temple to Apollo, then restored in AD 488 by Ambrosius Aurelianus, the Romano-British chieftain whose name, like that of Apollo, evokes the immortal sun.

As the mouths of the Tyburn stream silted up, Thorney Island was joined to the north bank of the Thames. The area is now a temple to the governing spirits of the Poetic Isles. The meridian passes through Poets' Corner in Westminster Abbey, across Downing Street, through the Cabinet Office and Horse Guards Parade, and along the east side of Trafalgar Square. Druid architects would have been amazed by these vast stone alignments, though they might have wondered why the orientations were so approximate.

Every city swarms with coincidence. It was only now, several weeks after discussing this book with my editor, that I realized that the meridian bisects the restaurant where the discussion had taken place, and that it continues north to the left-luggage office of St Pancras Station, where the bicycles had completed their journey back from Mediolanum Biturigum. Geomantic expeditions are not for the neurotically disposed. At the Euston Road entrance to the British Library, and in the Great Court of the British Museum – both bisected by the meridian – a voice proclaimed the 'Druid network' to be nothing but a huge and complex system of personal reference, a testament, not to the Druids' genius, but to the ruthless ingenuity of the unconscious mind.

On the first floor of the museum, a few steps from the meridian, a trained volunteer was sitting at a table. She was inviting members of the public to handle a selection of Roman artefacts, as though to convince them of the reality of the past. In the same room, between Prehistory and the Romans, I looked again at the face on the Aylesford Bucket and the other-worldly features that contain the formula for the map of Celtic Britain. I peered at the microscopic gold coins and tried to remember the human or divine faces and the shapes of the celestial horses as they can be seen in magnified illustrations. How those objects were produced without a powerful lens is hard to say.

One of the glinting, mysterious discs in the British Museum's cabinets is the oldest Celtic gold coin found in Britain, and one of the most beautiful objects of the ancient world. It shows the flowing oak-leaf hair of a sun god or a Druid and a star-field of indecipherable symbols surrounding a horse. A terminal connected to the museum database makes it possible to inspect the tiny details. The catalogue entry explained that the coin had probably been minted in northern Gaul in the second century BC and brought across the Channel as a gift or as a trade item: 'Some of [these coins] were eventually buried in coin hoards and not recovered by their owners. The owner may have died, or simply forgotten where they had put them. Alternatively, the coins may have been intended as permanent, sacred offerings to the gods.'

This particular coin had been found in 1849 'at Fenny Stratford, near Milton Keynes, England'. (The exact location is unknown or undisclosed.) After a morning spent in a labyrinth composed of a single, straight line, this fact, perhaps of no real interest, seemed all the more precious.

The train from Paddington Station slows down as it passes Osney cemetery and comes to a halt in Oxford Station three hundred metres north of the *omphalos* of Celtic Britain. That evening, I cycled home past the remnant of Osney Abbey, where the only reminders of Lludd's vat of mead were empty beer cans, then across the Wessex–Mercia border and up Cumnor Hill to Leys Cottage, which – thankfully, in view of the unconscious autobiography theory – lies a good kilometre and a half from the Oxford winter solstice line to Isca Dumnoniorum.

Outside, the only light was the crescent moon and the gleam of

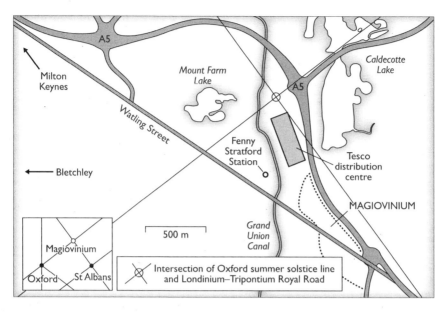

81. Magiovinium and the solar intersection

the excavators that had come to clear away the private woodland between the cottage and the farmer's field. The screen shimmered into life and populated itself with roads and place names. On the 1:25,000 Ordnance Survey map, Fenny Stratford, where the gold coin had been discovered, is helpfully labelled 'Magiovinium'. 'Great Something' ('*vinium*' has defied translation) was a small settlement on Watling Street – Roman, but with a Celtic name. Now, it lies in the south-eastern suburbs of Milton Keynes.

Ever since it was founded as a 'new town' in 1967, Milton Keynes has been a by-word for modernist banality. A Druid, however, might have felt more at home there than in central London. The designers of Milton Keynes were aficionados of the mystical paths known as ley lines, which were enjoying a revival in the late-1960s. At one stage, it was proposed that the entire town be organized along ley lines that would connect its brand-new roads, retail outlets and dwelling units to prehistoric sites such as Silbury Hill, Avebury and Stonehenge. 'Conventional wisdom prevailed', but not entirely: the three central thoroughfares of Milton Keynes – Silbury Boulevard, Avebury Boulevard and Midsummer Boulevard – are aligned so that the rising sun of the summer solstice shines through the middle of the shopping

centre and turns the glassy facade of the railway station into a blinding
wall of light.

I had not heard of Fenny Stratford before reading the description
of the coin in the British Museum, but I was familiar with Magiovinium
as the place where the summer solstice line from Oxford meets the
Royal Road from Londinium. In the area now covered by Caldecotte
Lake, on the site of a deserted medieval village, a Celtic field system,
Iron Age honey bees and a ditched enclosure have been found. The
original Celtic settlement must have been far more extensive than
the Roman town. The point of intersection lies between two lakes
on the edge of the former settlement. This watery domain may well
have been used by the inhabitants of Magiovinium for ritual deposition. A supermarket distribution centre, closed off by steel gates and
surrounded by feeder roads, occupies most of the site. Somewhere
under that tarmac blanket of amnesia – perhaps on that very spot –
for a reason that will never be known, the golden image of a sun god
was buried in the earth.

✿

For a twenty-first-century visitor to Celtic Middle Earth, the key
cartographic tools are the maps of the Ordnance Survey (the British
and the Irish), and the Institut Géographique National. In addition
to the modern maps of France, the IGN's superb public-access mashup
provides cadastral maps, the eighteenth-century Cassini *Carte de France*
and the nineteenth-century *Carte de l'État-major*. For archaeological
sites and finds, the first ports of call are the multi-volume *Carte
archéologique de la Gaule* (not yet online) and, for Britain, the records
of the Royal Commissions on the Ancient and Historical Monuments
of Scotland and Wales, and the National Monuments Record. Each
English county has a Historic Environment Record. Many can be
consulted online via the Heritage Gateway,* but some may still require
a visit to the archive in question.

The practical intricacies of charting a solar path are described at
various points in this book.† The basic problem is that of projection.
The shortest path between two points on a sphere is not the same as

---

* www.heritagegateway.org.uk/gateway/advanced_search.aspx
† See pp. 12–14, 125 and 227.

the path drawn by a straight line on a flat projection. When, several decades ago, I flew the short distance from Manchester to Dublin, the flight path made perfect sense: there was the Irish Sea and the coast of North Wales, just as it looked in the atlas. But when I first flew to America, expecting to see Ireland and then nothing but ocean until the Statue of Liberty, the pilot took a scenic route and descended into the United States over icy wastes which turned out to be Newfoundland and Nova Scotia. My imagined flight path was a rhumb line or line of constant bearing. The actual flight path was a Great Circle, which, in that case, is two hundred and nineteen kilometres shorter but demands a continual adjustment of the bearing.

Solar paths, and any pre-modern alignments or routes, are inevitably rhumb lines, which is why a straight line drawn on a road atlas or almost any other commonly used map will not be identical to a line produced by sundials, gromas and other antiquated equipment (fig. 82). By good fortune (and design), the projection currently used by Google Maps is a variety of Mercator projection. In Celtic latitudes, this is entirely acceptable for Druidic purposes. The angles and trajectories are those that an ancient surveyor would have derived, for example, from triangulation. (It is important to note that this applies only to large scales. When the maps are zoomed out to show areas the size of large countries, a different projection is used.) The bearings can be checked using the formula for calculating rhumb lines.* A comprehensive list of coordinates (to four decimal points) produced for the writing of this book is available at www.panmacmillan.com/theancientpaths. Several programs allow these coordinates to be plotted on a map.†

A certain amount of experimentation is required to determine an appropriate margin of error: variables include the length of a path, its point of origin, and the theoretical accuracy of the surveying method. It was Alexander Thom (1894–1985), a Scottish engineer, who introduced precise measurements to the study of prehistoric alignments. His painstaking work helped to give this mystic-muddled sphere some academic respectability. Ironically, though, it also introduced an incongruous degree of complexity. The problem is that

---

* For example: www.movable-type.co.uk/scripts/latlong.html

† In gpsvisualizer.com, the data should be preceded by the following header row: 'name,latitude,longitude'.

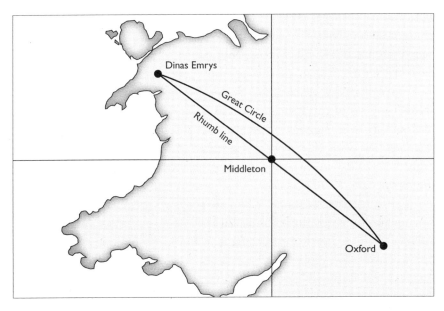

82. Rhumb line and Great Circle

If Lludd had possessed the technology available to a modern pilot, his flight path would have taken him and the dragons, not over the outskirts of Middleton, but over Downton Hall, one and a half kilometres to the north. The deviation on this Mercator map is exaggerated.

modern notions of exactitude are not those of an Iron Age or Roman surveyor. If an ancient road or temple is aligned on the solstice sun to within one-tenth of a degree, the match is almost certainly coincidental. On the other hand, if a margin of one degree or more is allowed, any number of sites could be included in the hypothetical pattern. Common sense suggests an occasional accommodation with physical reality, but it can never be said too often that a straight line drawn between a handful of points is not necessarily significant, especially if the line is traced in sleepwalking obliviousness to history, legend, archaeology and science.

☆

Any reader who has travelled this far in the book without taking shortcuts will certainly possess the patience necessary for visiting Iron Age sites. Some *oppida* are still major features of the landscape from Britain to the Danube Basin. A few even have visitor centres and exhibitions – Alesia, Bibracte, Castell Henllys, Ensérune, Glauberg, Hauterive-Neuchâtel, Heuneburg, Numantia and Parc Samara – but nearly all are deserted. 'Settlements of the ancient Celts' would be a perfect theme for a misanthrope's holiday. The remote and exposed locations of many *oppida* have preserved them from vandalism, and archaeologists of the recent past will find some almost pristine examples of pre-war signage. Sometimes, the only indication that the *oppidum* has been discovered is a stake and a plank of wood resembling a signpost in an *Astérix* comic, etched with the words '*Ancien site fortifié*' or '*Keltské oppidum*'.

Celtic treasures can be found in the national museums of most European countries, but also in local collections in small towns and villages. This scattering of artefacts is inconvenient for a researcher, but it makes the dramatically different population patterns of Iron Age Europe impossible to ignore. Here, too, persistence is required. The staff of one museum, which holds the unique and beautiful stone carvings from the Celtic shrine of Roquepertuse, were unaware of their whereabouts and even their existence until they were shown a photograph of the carvings in a book sold in the museum's own bookshop.

Since the solar network was based on celestial phenomena, a traveller to Middle Earth will naturally arrive in places where there seems to be nothing to see. In Britain, perhaps the most intriguingly uninteresting sites are the boundary intersections called tripoints (p. 219). Those that have a name – Three Shire Elms, No Man's Heath, etc. – are likely to be ancient. A typical tripoint is marked by a clump of ash and hawthorn or some other tenacious tree. Humanity is represented by a heap of discarded tyres and electrical appliances, though sometimes there are prehistoric mounds in the vicinity. Enormous crowds once gathered at these places to attend cockfights and boxing matches. Occasionally, there were reports of witches' covens and other suspicious activities. These illegal meetings may be the last recorded echoes of the inter-tribal assemblies of Celtic Britain.

In the spring of 2011, I visited some of these sites with a Welsh Hispanist from the University of Nottingham. An explorer of geomantic intersections may feel like an intruder and inevitably often is. Solar paths are not respecters of property, and it should be said that in cases of trespass, a magistrate or *juge d'instruction* is unlikely to accept the existence of a nodal point of Celtic Middle Earth as a mitigating factor.

The sacred tree of the Druids tends to live in communities of genetically similar specimens, and so the Three Shire Oak, which stands in derelict woodland on the Royal Road from Isca Dumnoniorum and on the borders of Leicestershire, Lincolnshire and Nottinghamshire, could well be the direct descendant of an Iron Age oak. 'Normanton Thorns', as the wood is called, shows what happens when woodland is neglected: it turns into an overgrown shrubbery in which native trees straggle towards the light like prisoners begging for food. Somewhere in the tangled depths, despite the failing light, a man was firing a shotgun at some woodpigeons. On its northern edge, the wood is hemmed in by a brutally illuminated business park. By squeezing along the security fence, it is just possible to reach the corner where three counties meet. An aged trunk had been protected with a picket fence. In the gathering gloom, Dr Roberts identified the tree by its sticky buds . . . Thanks to the arboreal ignorance of the council employee who had been sent to cordon it off, the Three Shire Oak had become the Three Shire Chestnut.

In such unpredictable ways, realities that have decayed into legends fade and change their form as they disappear. The woodland was as much a mystery to the anonymous fencer as a curiously patterned Celtic ornament to a Dark Age Pict.

The sun appears to accelerate as it descends to the horizon. The present breaks down into a succession of blurred moments, and the remote past acquires a solidity that it seemed to have lost. The Camelot theme park closed at the end of 2012 after almost three decades of existence. The Avalon Arena, the Mad Monastery and Merlin's School of Wizardry now belong to history. The place where 'Camelot' stands empty was once the edge of Martin Mere, the largest freshwater lake in England. A local legend claimed that this was the lake into whose waters, in what sounds like an act of ritual deposition, the sword Excalibur was thrown. In view of the unusual preponderance of nodal points in the environs of the vanished lake, this now looks more plausible than ever.

Chronology

BC

8th century	Hallstatt kingdoms in eastern Alps and middle Danube; Tartessian culture and language in south-western Iberia.
c. 680	Oldest dated features of Emain Macha (Navan Fort, Northern Ireland).
c. 600	Massalia founded by Greeks from Phocaea; '*Keltoi*' living on northern shores of Mediterranean.
6th century	Hill forts in Bohemia; Massalian trading posts on the Mediterranean; Lepontic (a Celtic language) spoken in northern Italy and Alps.
Late 6th century	'Princely residences' in Burgundy ('the Lady of Vix'), Marne, Rhineland; Massalian and Greek wine imported to central Gaul.
c. 500	Carthaginian navigators reach equatorial West Africa and North Atlantic coasts.
5th century	La Tène culture, from the Balkans to eastern Gaul; hill forts in southern Gaul, open settlements in the north.
Early 4th century	Gaulish migrations to northern Italy and to lands in and beyond the Hercynian Forest.
396	Destruction of settlement on site of future Mediolanum (Milan).
387	Celtic occupation of Rome.
350	Aristotle, *Meteorology*: *klimata* and zodiacal circle.
335	Celtic envoys meet Alexander the Great in Macedonia.
331	Lunar eclipse observed at Arbela, Syracuse and Carthage, perhaps also at Rhodes and Athens (international longitude experiment?).
c. 325	Voyage of Pytheas of Massalia.
310–260s	Belgic tribes arrive in northern Gaul from Germany and Central Europe.

c. 300	Euclid's *Elements*; invention of the dioptra; definition of meridians and parallels by Dicaearchus.
c. 280	Battle of Ribemont-sur-Ancre; Celts invade Illyricum, Pannonia, Macedonia; first coins minted in Gaul (principally Arvernian).
279	Celtic army plunders Delphi.
278	Gauls cross the Hellespont; Tolistobogii, Trocmii and Volcae Tectosages settle in Galatia.
250–41	Gauls recruited for Carthaginian army in Sicily.
c. 240	Eratosthenes calculates circumference of earth; invention of solstitial armillary sphere.
225	Battle of Telamon (Tuscany): defeat of Celtic coalition by Rome.
218	Hannibal marches from Spain to Italy; *September* – crossing of the Rhone; *November* – crossing of the Alps.
197	Eastern and southern Iberia divided into two Roman provinces, Hispania Citerior ('Nearer') and Ulterior ('Further').
196–189	Rome conquers Celtic northern Italy (later, the province of Gallia Cisalpina).
187	Completion of Via Aemilia.
182–133	Celtiberian Wars.
181	Massalia appeals to Rome for help against Ligurian pirates.
c. 180	*Oppida* in central Germany, Bohemia, Moravia, Hungary.
c. 175–50	Gundestrup Cauldron.
c. 150	Hipparchus calculates *klimata* and meridians; Antikythera Mechanism; Polybius travels through southern Gaul.
146	Fall of Carthage.
133	Siege and destruction of Numantia.
c. 130	German *oppida* (Basel, Berne, Breisach, Bad Neuheim, Manching, etc.).
125–121	Roman conquest of southern Gaul.
123	Roman garrison at Aquae Sextiae (Aix-en-Provence).
121	Defeat of Arverni (King Bituitos) and Allobroges; foundation of Roman province of Gallia Transalpina (later, Gallia Narbonensis).
c. 120–110	First Gaulish *oppida* (Besançon, Bibracte, Châteaumeillant, etc.); monetary union of Aedui, Lingones and Sequani; Boii *oppidum* at Bratislava.

118   Foundation of Narbo Martius (Narbonne); construction of Via Domitia.

113–101   Cimbri and Teutones invade Danube Basin, northern Italy, Gaul and northern Iberia.

106   Treasure of Tolosa (Toulouse) stolen by Roman proconsul.

102   Teutones defeated at Aquae Sextiae (Aix-en-Provence) by Gaius Marius.

Late 2nd century   First coins minted in Britain.

Early 1st century   Posidonius travels through Gaul; international trading ports in southern Britain.

c. 80–70   Collapse of *oppida* in southern Germany (Finsterlohr, Heidengraben, Heidetränk, Manching), and Rhineland (Fossé des Pandours, Donnersberg); German provinces of Inferior ('Lower') and Superior ('Upper').

c. 70   Earliest visible occupation of Alesia *oppidum*.

63   Diviciacus the Aeduan Druid asks Roman Senate for military aid.

62–61   Revolt of Allobroges crushed by Rome.

61   Gaius Julius Caesar governor of Gallia Transalpina.

58–51   Gallic War.

58   Helvetian migration; defeat of Helvetii and of German tribes by Caesar.

57   Defeat of Belgic tribes.

56   Defeat of Alpine and Atlantic tribes.

55   Expeditions to Britain and across the Rhine.

54   Second expedition to Britain.

53   Second crossing of the Rhine.

52   General uprising of Gaulish tribes; *Spring* – Siege of Avaricum (Bourges); battle of Lutetia (Paris); *August-September* – siege of Alesia (Alise-Sainte-Reine) and surrender of Vercingetorix.

51   *Autumn* – battle of Uxellodunum.

c. 50   Founding of Calleva (Silchester); Aylesford Bucket.

46   Revolt of Bellovaci.

44   Assassination of Caesar.

43   Foundation of Colonia Copia Felix Munatia, later Lugdunum (Lyon).

39–29   Revolts of Rhineland tribes and Morini.

c. 37   Celtic mercenaries in Judea.

27   Augustan Settlement at Narbonne organizes division of Gaul

north of Gallia Narbonensis into three provinces (Aquitania, Belgica, Lugdunensis); abandonment of Gaulish *oppida* continues.

c. 5   Birth of Jesus Christ.

AD

9   Battle of the Teutoburg Forest (German tribes massacre three Roman legions).

10   *1 August* – Birth of Claudius at Lugdunum (Lyon).

c. 20   Druidism outlawed by Tiberius.

21   Revolts of Aedui, led by Sacrovir, and Treveri, led by Florus; rumours of pan-Gallic and German uprising.

c. 30   Crucifixion of Jesus Christ.

43   Roman legions land on the coast of Cantium (Kent); Roman fortress at Camulodunum (Colchester).

48   Gauls from Gallia Comata admitted to the Senate.

51   Last stand of Caratacus in Wales.

c. 54   Druidism outlawed by Claudius.

60–61   Massacre of Druids on Mona (Anglesey); revolt of Iceni and allies led by Boudica: destruction of Camulodunum (Colchester), Londinium (London) and Verulamium (St Albans).

78   Surrender of Mona.

83 or 84   Battle of Mons Graupius.

122 – c. 126   Building of Hadrian's Wall.

142 – c. 154   Building of Antonine Wall.

252   Martyrdom of St Regina at Alesia (Alise-Sainte-Reine).

Mid-3rd century?   Martyrdom of St Alban at Verulamium (St Albans).

316   Birth of St Martin of Tours.

c. 387   Birth of St Patrick.

Early 5th century?   Roman withdrawal from Britain.

Mid-5th century?   Vortigern invites Saxons to Britain; Saxons defeated by Ambrosius Aurelianus.

c. 451   Birth of St Brigit.

Before 474   Arvernian aristocrats abandon 'Celtic speech' (Sidonius Apollinaris).

597   Gregorian mission to Britain; Augustine first Archbishop of Canterbury.

Notes

Abbreviation: *BG* = Caesar and Hirtius, *Commentarii de Bello Gallico*.

Note on portolan charts (see p. 147):

Portolan charts – mostly Portuguese, Spanish and Italian, from the thirteenth to sixteenth centuries – were cartographic equivalents of the ancient *periploi* (p. 22). They show what could be achieved, even at sea and with few more refinements than were available in the late Iron Age. The main innovation was the compass. This was not strictly necessary for a land survey and it introduced the complication of magnetic as opposed to true north.

The charts were not consciously based on a projection of the world, but the data (sailors' knowledge of distances and directions) naturally produced a proto-Mercator projection (Mercator's map dates from 1569), in which straight lines cross all meridians at the same angle and allow the navigator to follow the same bearing from start to finish.

Albino de Canepa's chart (Genoa, 1489), reproduced here in schematic form with five lines emphasized, is grossly distorted to the north of France but surprisingly accurate in other areas. It was probably pieced together from different maps, each one more or less consistent with itself, which would explain the northward rotation of Italy. The second map shows the five emphasized lines on a modern Mercator projection. The portolan charts gave bearings in increments equivalent to 11.25° (based on a compass rose divided into 32). The bearings in France and Iberia on Canepa's chart are skewed several degrees to the west but accurate to within one point of a 32-point compass.

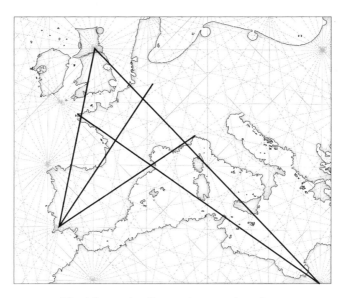

83. Albino de Canepa's portolan chart

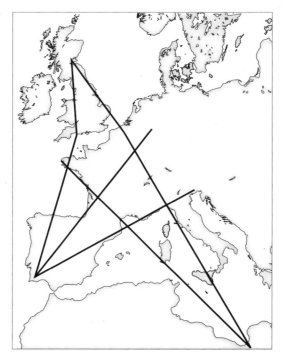

84. The portolan chart on a Mercator projection

Protohistory

x 'Note on Celtic origins': During the writing of this book, I was told
   that because my hair is dark and my parents Scottish, I must be Celtic.
   Hearing this, a German friend protested that the Celts were blond and
   came from the region of Bavaria. Another friend told me of a Spaniard
   whose red hair and freckles are thought to mark her out as a Celt.
   Many people still agree with Tacitus (early second century AD) that
   dark-skinned, curly-haired natives of western Britain and the Iberian
   Peninsula are ethnically Celtic. The ancient Celts themselves seem to
   have believed that they had no single origin. (See the map on p. 116.)
   Population movements suggested by genetic analyses may predate the
   appearance of Celtic culture by thousands of years (Cunliffe and Koch,
   110). The fact that Ireland was not noticeably invaded after the late
   Bronze Age and yet became Celtic (p. 169) is a reminder that, as an
   archaeological and historical term, 'Celtic' refers to the cultural and
   linguistic traits shared by the majority of the Iron Age inhabitants of
   western Europe, not to a particular ethnic group with a propensity for
   making war and a superhuman ability to populate half a continent
   within a few generations.
xii a professor of literature: Vadé (1972–74).
xii the Professor of Geography: Planhol, 15 and 24–25.
xiii heaving like a lung: Strabo, II, 4, 1 (perhaps referring to a type of
   jellyfish).
xiv 'ley lines': Watkins.
xvi 'a river called the Arar': *BG*, I, 12.
xvii 'They converse with few words': Diodorus Siculus, V, 31, 1.

1. The Road from the Ends of the Earth

3 'at the extreme west of Europe': Herodotus, II, 33; also IV, 49. On
   classical sources: Koch and Carey; Rankin.
5 One tale in particular: The account of Herakles' journey is based on
   the following: Ammianus Marcellinus, XV, 9, 6 (father of the Celts);
   Avienus, v. 322 (Sacred Promontory); Cassius Dio, XIII, 21
   (Bebruces); Diodorus Siculus, IV, 18, 5 (sea-monsters), IV, 19, 1–2
   (Alesia), IV, 19, 3–4 (Alps), V, 24, 2–3 (Alesia, Galates) and V, 26, 2
   (honeycombs); Dionysius of Halicarnassus, I, 41 (Spain to the Alps;
   building of cities and roads); Hesiod, 289–94 (Erytheia); Hyginus, I,
   2, 6 (Ligurians); Justinus, XXIV, 4 (Alps); Livy, V, 34 (Alps) and XXI,

37 (attributes the creation of a col to Hannibal: also Ammianus
Marcellinus, XV, 10, 11; Appianus, VII, 2; cf. Diodorus Siculus, IV,
19, 3); Lucian of Samosata, 'Herakles' (Ogmios); Mela, II, 76 (the
Crau); Nepos, *Hannibal*, III (Alps); Parthenius of Nicaea, XXX
(Celtine); Seneca (1984), 7 (Lyon); Silius Italicus, III, 420–40
(Bebruces, Pyrenea); Stephen of Byzantium, *Ethnika* (Nemausos,
Nîmes); Strabo, IV, 1, 7 (the Crau, which stretched as far north as
the Carpentras plain). On the Via Heraklea: Clavel, 419; Dellong, 95;
Duch; Knapp; Lugand and Bermond, 64; Plácido; Pseudo-Aristotle,
in Aristotle (1980). On Hercules: Benoît (1949 and 1965); Carrière;
Hofeneder, I, 82, 106 and 162; Moitrieux; Rawlings. Eustathius (V,
281) mentions two sons of Herakles, Celtus and Iber, progenitors of
the Celts and Iberians; also Dionysius of Halicarnassus, XIV, 1.

5   a tribe called the Andosini: Polybius, III, 35. 'Andosini' and
    'Andorra' may come from a Pyrenean Celtic god, Andossus, who was
    related to Hercules and Lugh: Benoît (1949), 114–15; Knapp, 111;
    Lajoye, 56.

5   a temple to Hercules: mentioned by Ephorus (c. 350 BC);
    contradicted in ignorance by Strabo (c. 7 BC), III, 1, 4. On ancient
    pilgrimage: Dillon; Fear.

7   Buccacircius: '*Ventus cercius . . . buccam implet*' (Gellius, II, 22, 29).
    Boucocers (Buccacircio) is the name of two sites in the Aude: Adams,
    227; Jullian, VI, 1, 1 n. 15; Nègre (1990–98), I, 1147. 'When he was
    living in Gaul, the divine Augustus had a temple built and dedicated
    to [the Mistral]': Seneca (1971–72), V, 17, 5.

9   Emain Macha: Warner, 31 (from *Annála Ríoghachta Éireann*).

10 Ogmios: Lucian of Samosata, 'Herakles'; Le Roux.

10 'come from remote regions': Pliny, XXI, 31 (57).

11 founded by a son of Herakles: Stephen of Byzantium (listed in
    Ethnika).

11 A cognitive psychologist: Boroditsky.

13 the Etruscans: Aveni and Romano; Frontinus (1971), 10–11.

14 Herakles was also a sun god: e.g. Macrobius, I, 20, 11; Porphyry, in
    Eusebius of Caesarea, III, 11.

14 pocket-sized votive wheels: e.g. over seventy thousand at La
    Villeneuve-au-Châtelot (Aube): Birkhan, 578.

14 'he measured the whole earth': Philostratus, V, 4.

15 'From Italy as far as the country of the Celts': Pseudo-Aristotle, in
    Aristotle (1980). On the road to the Hesperides and Herakles as a
    guide of dead souls: Wagenvoort, 115; also Knapp. Avienus (v. 322)
    applies the name 'Via Herculis' to the Sacred Promontory.

15 th[...]   443; Nickels
    et [...]
16 A[...]   ni (1989); Burl;
    Ja [...]   1.
16 th [...]   76 (from
    A[...]   'Solon', in
    P[...]   abo, IV, 1, 4;
    al[...]
16 A [...]   Cary; Cunliffe
    (1[...]
17 a [...]   :raklea (location
    ur [...]   *a*.
17 'o[...]
18 in [...]   plausibility of an
    in[...]
18 na[...]   on the same
    theme: Letters [...]   16), 534; Villar,
    180.
18 the temple of Melqart-Herakles: Fear, 319–20.
19 'a hero [Herakles]': Polybius, III, 48.
19 'the way had seemed long to no one': Livy, XXI, 30.
19 'unintelligible and meaningless sounds': Polybius, III, 36.
19 Roquemaure: e.g. Jullian, I, 11, 5 n. 82; Wickham, 30–32.
19 'marched up the bank': Polybius, III, 47.
20 the old 'Elephant' inn: Whymper, 52.
20 Hannibella: Hoyte.
20 the Col de Montgenèvre: Mahaney et al. suggest this col as
    Hannibal's 'intended path' (42); also Jullian, I, 11, 12 n. 219. On
    Mons Matrona: Ganet et al., 130–31. The Matrona is cited in
    Ammianus Marcellinus, XV, 10, 6, and in the anonymous *Itinerarium
    Burdigalense* (early fourth century).
21 Herculean sanctuary of Deneuvre: Hamm, 176–79.
22 *Ora Maritima* ('Sea Coasts'): Avienus; Saulcy.
22 '*Solis columna*': Avienus, v. 638.
22 Cassiterides or 'Tin Islands': see Ramin.

2. News of the Iron Age

23 the *horreum*: see Bromwich, 85–87.
24 gold jewellery: Diodorus Siculus, V, 27, 3.

24 undiluted wine: e.g. Athenaeus, IV, 36 (from Posidonius); Polyaenus, VIII, 25.

24 moustaches trailed in the soup: Diodorus Siculus, V, 28, 3.

24 the best cut of meat: Athenaeus, IV, 40 (from Posidonius).

24 throwing them into the river: *The Greek Anthology*, 9.125.

24 swallowed by the waves: Aristotle (2011), III, 1229 b; Aelian, XII, 23; see also Rankin, 56.

24 'raging with outlandish lust': Diodorus Siculus, V, 32, 7.

24 flabby Celtic youths: Strabo, IV, 4, 6.

24 slashed to ribbons with a sword: Strabo, IV, 4, 3.

24 Greek philosopher Posidonius: Strabo, IV, 4, 5.

25 the '*alces*': BG, VI, 27.

25 'because of our short stature': BG, II, 30.

25 St Jerome: Jerome, II, 7.

25 the dozen words that entered English: Charles-Edwards, 729–30.

25 lead curse-tablets: Delamarre (2003), 47, 332 and 334.

25 etched on spindle-whorls: Delamarre (2003), 335, 217, 133 and 331; see also Duval et al.

26 wheelwright of Blair Drummond: A. Harding, 165–67.

27 Marseille to Boulogne in thirty days: Diodorus Siculus, V, 22, 4.

27 chariots . . . found in graves: Verger; also Cunliffe (1999), 58–59.

27 their technology amazed the Romans: a list of Roman references in Napoléon III, II, 18 n. 5; see also Arrian of Nicomedia, *Tactics*, 37; Jullian, II, 7 nn. 64–65.

27 'la Dame de Vix': Egg and Franz-Lanord; Rolley.

28 'in about fifteen days': BG, II, 2.

29 entering or leaving a tribal territory: Jullian, II, 2, 7 and n. 94.

29 Roman roads can usually be distinguished: e.g. Chouquer (2005), 36; Jullian, II, 7, 3; Robert et al.; also Castellvi; Chevallier (1997); Gendron.

29 the Gaulish *oppidum* of Vermand: Fichtl (1994), 108 (with other examples); also Pichon (2002), 479.

30 used by the Romans: on Roman occupation of *oppida*: Todd, and p. 72 above.

31 'Gaul was now at peace': BG, VI, 44 and VII, 1.

31 'The report was conveyed': BG, VII, 3.

32 appetite for news: BG, IV, 5; also Diodorus Siculus, V, 28, 5.

33 'innumerable horns and trumpets': Polybius, II, 29.

35 a Gaulish word, '*equoranda*': Aeberhardt; Billy, 133–34; Cravayat; Dauzat and Rostaing; Delamarre (2003), 163–64; Gendron, 86–87; Jullian, II, 2 n. 95; Lebel (1937 and 1956); Nègre (1990–98), I,

195–96; Provost, *L'Indre-et-Loire*, 115; Roger; Vannérus; Vincent (1927 and 1937).

36 a 'sound-line': This is consistent with Gaulish word-formation: e.g. *'sonnocingos'* (sun-course) on the Coligny calendar.

36 *'per agros regionesque'*: *BG*, VII, 3; cf. VII, 46: *'recta regione'* ('in a straight line').

37 'Make straight in the desert a highway': Isaiah 40:3; also John 1:23. For Greek geometrical uses of *'euqunate'*: Mugler.

3. The Mediolanum Mystery, I

40 one of the commonest and oldest place names: Bayerri y Bertomeu et al.; Dauzat and Rostaing; Delamarre (2003), 220–21; Desbordes; Dowden, 274–75; Guyonvarc'h (1960 and 1961); Holder, II, 497–521; Longnon (1920–29); Nègre (1990–98), I, 189–90; Vincent (1937), 102–103.

40 must be a Latin term: Gasca Queirazza.

41 'a term of sacred geography': Delamarre (2003), 221.

41 The so-called Celtic cross: e.g. Rees, 36.

41 'the centre of the whole of Gaul': *BG*, VI, 13.

42 a small island in the Atlantic Ocean: Quatrefages, II, 296 (Montmeillan).

42 a headland near Carnac: Bougard. Other previously unrecognized Mediolana: Mions in the south-eastern suburbs of Lyon, whose inhabitants are called Miolands, and le Mayollant (formerly Meolanum), a collection of farm buildings further in the same direction.

43 Peutinger Map: Bibliotheca Augustana; Fortia d'Urban (1845); Talbert; Talbert et al. For other ancient 'itineraries': Fortia d'Urban (1845); Miller; Parthey et al.; Ptolemy (2000 and 2006).

44 In Vadé's reconstruction: Vadé (1972–74, 1976 and 2000).

44 'Unless the maps deceive us': Vadé (2000), 34.

45 mystery would be solved by archaeology: Guyonvarc'h (1961), 157.

45 the Mediolanum near Pontcharra: Faure-Brac, 302. The original source probably showed two separate routes to Lyon – a longer but easier route by Forum Segusiavum (Feurs), and the route by Mediolanum, which would have been on the eastern side of the Tarare Hill. Drivers changed horses near Pontcharra and the hamlet of Miollan (in this part of France, a recognizable mutation of 'Mediolanum').

46 the city of Saintes: Maurin et al., 61.

47 cartographic analysis: Vion, 69; also C. Marchand in Chouquer, ed., III, 68–70. A good example is Moislains (Somme).

4. The Mediolanum Mystery, II

49 'in summum venire non potuit': Trousset, 135.

50 about forty place names: Watson, 244–48.

50 the Greek 'nemos': 'Nemos' ('wood') is unknown in Gaulish. For a Gaulish speaker, a wood was a 'uidua' or a 'ceto'.

50 'altars horrible on massive stones upreared': Lucan, III, 399–411. (Tr. E. Ridley.)

51 Two terminal points were chosen: Bailey and Devereux; Woolliscroft, 155 (on the importance of Bar Hill).

52 the black-faced sheep: Reynolds, 189.

55 local groups of 'middle' places: e.g. in the Marne, the region to the east of Albi, the valley of the Isère, and the lands of the Gallaeci in north-western Spain.

55 A few had even been Mediolana themselves: Meilen, Switzerland (by Mittelberg); Melaine (below Mont Moyen, formerly 'Mons medianus'); Molien (by Monts Moyens); Montméal (Montemedio, Montmialon); Montmeillant, Ardennes (Monte Meliano); Montmélian, Oise (Mediolano Mon[te]); Montmélian, Seine-et-Marne (Monte Medio); Mont Milan, Côte-d'Or (by Montmoyen).

55 dubious chiselled stone: Harley and Woodward, 207. The Camp de César at the Butte Mauchamp lies west of Guignicourt.

55 a Greek unit of measurement: M. Guy, in Arcelin et al., 443.

56 patterning effects of catchment areas: on Bronze Age shrines as territorial markers: Delor, 99–100.

56 alignments of ditches and stones: on prehistoric alignments: Burl; Hoskin; Maravelia; Thom.

57 signs of cosmopolitan luxury: Provost et al. (1992), 78.

58 'Montes medii' and Mediolana place names: primarily from maps and the following: Amé; Bayerri y Bertomeu; C. de Beaurepaire; F. de Beaurepaire (1981 and 1986); Bouteiller; Boutiot; Boyer and Latouche; R. Boyer; Brun-Durand; Cappello and Tagliavini; Carré de Busserolle; Charrié; Chassaing; Chazaud; Clouzot; Dauzat and Rostaing; Deshayes; Dufour; Falc'hun and Tanguy; Gasca Queirazza; Gauchat; Germer-Durand; Goggi; Gourgues; Grässe; Gysseling; Haigneré; Hamlin and Cabrol; Hippeau; Jaccard; Jespers; Lambert;

Lecler; Lepage; Liénard; Longnon (1891 and 1920–29); Maître; Malsy; Marichal; Mastrelli Anzilotti; Matton; Menche de Loisne; Menéndez Pidal; Merlet; Nègre (1959 and 1990–98); Nicolaï; Olivieri (1962 and 1965); Perrenot; Pesche; Philipon; Pilot de Thorey; Poret; Quantin; Quilgars; Raymond; Rédet; Rigault; Rivet and Smith; Roland; J.-H. Roman; Rosenzweig; Roserot (1903 and 1924); Sabarthès; Smith; Soultrait; Soyer; Stein; Stoffel; Suter; E. Thomas; Vallée and Latouche; Villar; Vincent (1927 and 1937); Watson; Williamson.

59 its origin is obscure: e.g. Williamson, 46.

59 isolated finds: Brun and Mordant, 512.

59 the river Garonne: Giumlia-Mair, 105 (Greeks objects of the sixth and third centuries BC have been found along the Rhone and the Loire, but not the Garonne).

59 reluctant to colonize: e.g. Pilet-Lemière, 17 (Manche *département*).

60 directed heating-jets: Jope, 400; also Northover.

61 '*Ii regem Celtico dabant*': Livy, V, 34.

5. Down the Meridian

65 the Celtic god of light: on Celtic gods: e.g. Aldhouse-Green (1991); Brunaux (2000); Hodeneder; Jufer and Luginbühl; Jullian, II, 5.

65 waits for the tide to go out: Wagenvoort, 116.

65 the tidal island of Ictis: Diodorus Siculus, V, 22, 2; Pliny, IV, 16 (104).

66 Gold coin of the Aedui: Gorphe, 140–41.

67 nothing from the pre-Roman period: Pichon (2009), 29.

69 noticed geometrical patterns: Agache (1997), 557; also Agache (1961).

70 'the tribal capital': The same theory, based on coins: D. Bayard, in Ben Redjeb, 109.

71 'Roman' roads of northern France: The 'Roman' road north of Samarobriva points at the original capital of the Suessiones, not at their Roman capital (Soissons). It passes through a field called 'Danse des Fées' on the outskirts of Amiens. The straight section of road west of Samarobriva is included because of the field-names 'Chaussée' and 'Les Câtelets'.

72 'They worship above all': *BG*, VI, 17. Caesar's description is matched by the agnomen of the Irish Lugh: '*samildánach*'.

73 Promontorium Celticum: Pliny, IV, 20 (111).

74 St Martin's shrines: Dessertenne, 133 (on the saint's sunwise 'leaps'); also Hamerton, 59 (at Bibracte).

75 'hollow altars': Brunaux (2000), 94–95; also Brunaux (1986).
75 'a rather peculiar aesthetic effect': http://www.arbre-celtique.com/encyclopedie/sanctuaire-de-gournay-sur-aronde-937.htm.
76 Mont César: Woimant, 119.
76 site of a Celtic necropolis: Graves, 7.
76 Bratuspantium: BG, II, 13; also Forbes; Holmes, 400–402.
77 the capital of the . . . Parisii: Abert, 23–25 and 65–67.
77 'island in the river Sequana': BG, VII, 57.
77 an 'insula' rather than a peninsula: Abert, 25.
78 the name 'Merlin': on some 'Merlin' place names: Vadé (2008), 60–61.
79 municipal website: http://ot.chateaumeillant.free.fr/bienvenue.htm.
80 a gilded statue: Costello, 36.
81 African pool-diggers: Krausz, n. 20.
81 against fire and battering-rams: Colin, 115; Ralston, 76.
84 'the Pillar of the Sun': Avienus, vv. 638–39.

6. The Size of the World

87 Antikythera: Price; also Allen; Freeth; Moussas; Weinberg et al.
87 so many spectacular finds: Weinberg et al.
88 observations of the Metonic cycle: Kruta (2000), 348.
88 The exact purpose: Allen.
89 *horologium solarium*: Pliny, VII, 60 (213); also Gibbs, 10; Pattenden, 100.
90 the sky would fall in: Strabo, IV, 4, 4 and VII, 3, 8.
90 Aristotle had recently praised: Athenaeus, XIII, 576.
90 The traveller's name was Pytheas: see especially Cunliffe (2002); Roller, ch. 4; and notes below.
91 'where the starry light declines': Avienus, v. 199.
91 Euthymenes: Roller, 15–19.
91 the celestial pole: Hipparchos, quoting Pytheas (see Dicks); also Cunliffe (2002), 60.
91 Cap Croisette: Rawlins.
92 Corbilo: Strabo, IV, 2, 1.
92 Lampaul-Ploudalmézeau: Giot and Colbert de Beaulieu, 324–25.
92 bartering tokens: Giot and Colbert de Beaulieu, 330.
92 According to one source: Strabo, II, 4, 1.
92 calculated his latitude: Roller, 71.
93 'on which one can neither walk nor sail': Strabo, II, 4, 1.

93 'complete savages': Strabo, II, 5, 8.

93 'If judged by the science': Strabo, IV, 5, 5.

95 A scientifically produced map of the world: on ancient cartography: Beazley; Dilke; Harley and Woodward; Janni; Peterson; Talbert and Unger; Thomson; Wallis and Robinson.

95 Eratosthenes of Cyrene: Eratosthenes; Lelgemann; Russo, 68–69; Tavernor, 18–19.

96 caused by the moon: Aetios, from Pseudo-Galen: Cunliffe (2002), 102; Roller, 77.

97 The *oikoumene*: Borysthenes and the Pillars of Hercules are within 66 and 13 seconds of the exact times respectively.

98 zones of latitude called *klimata*: Ptolemy (2000), 9–10.

98 the Greek astronomer Hipparchos: Dicks, 253–55; Heath, II, 346.

99 Alexander's high-speed couriers: Pliny, II, 73 (181).

99 the dioptra: Hero of Alexandria (description of dioptra, late first century AD); see also Frontinus (1971); Heath, II, 256 and 345; Lewis; Trousset.

100 ten minutes in a twelve-hour period: Houston.

100 day lengths reported by Pliny: Pliny, VI, 39 (213–15, 217–18).

100 clockwork miracles: The Antikythera Mechanism might have measured longitude: Moussas.

101 Eudoxus of Kyzikos: Posidonius, III, 115–18; Roller, 107–14.

101 the 'Gorillai' tribe: Hanno; Roller, 132.

101 The people of Belerion: Diodorus Siculus, V, 22, 1.

101 Isles of the Blessed: Hesiod, 165–70; Konrad; Roller, 44–50.

102 the island of Corvo: Roller, 49–50.

102 'Persistent enquiries': *BG*, V, 12–13.

103 'the obstacle of the Cévennes': *BG*, VII, 56. Caesar had also decided to support Labienus. He probably crossed the Cévennes (*BG*, VII, 8) by the Col de la Chavade on the route of the modern N102, rather than by the Croix du Pal (the traditionally identified route, more in keeping with Caesar's exaggeration of the difficulties).

104 'ascertained fact': Tacitus, *Agricola*, 10.

104 'We do not have our enemy's knowledge': Tacitus, *Agricola*, 33.

104 'a scanty band': Tacitus, *Agricola*, 32.

105 sailing the unmapped seas: on seafaring Celts: Cunliffe (2002), 68–69, 91–92, 103–106; McGrail.

105 Veneti tribe: *BG*, III, 8.

106 Maps did exist: Tacitus, *Agricola*, 10; Pliny, III, 5 (43); Strabo, III, 1, 3.

7. *The Druidic Syllabus, I: Elementary*

107 They had all heard about Druids: on the Druids (in addition to
     references below): Aldhouse-Green (1997); Brunaux (2000);
     Hofeneder; Jullian, II, 4; Le Roux and Guyonvarc'h; Piggott; Ross;
     J. Webster.
107 leaning on his shield: Anon., 3, 2.
107 with tears in his eyes: *BG*, I, 20.
107 Wild Germans: *BG*, I, 31.
107 Trojan descent: see Braund.
108 the will of the gods: Diodorus Siculus, V, 31, 3.
108 the sacred mistletoe: Pliny, XVI, 95 (249).
108 'If there really are Druids . . .': Cicero (1923 and 2006), I, 41.
108 '*physiologia*': Cicero (1923 and 2006), I, 41; also Strabo, IV, 4, 4.
108 long white beards: Livy, V, 41; also Florus, I, 7, 14.
109 'a circuitous itinerary': *BG*, I, 41.
109 Some young people: *BG*, VI, 14.
109 under Druidic tuition for twenty years: *BG*, VI, 14.
109 Viridomarus had 'humble origins': *BG*, VII, 39.
109 Druids mentioned by the poet: Ausonius, V, 4 and 10
     ('Commemoratio Professorum Burdigalensium').
110 '[flocked] to the Druids': *BG*, VI, 13.
110 'in caves and secret woods': Mela, III, 15.
110 'Pythagoras himself': Hippolytus of Rome, I, 2.
110 Cabillonum: Rebourg et al. (1994), I, 127.
110 the roads around Autun: Rebourg (1998).
110 'the noblest progeny of the Gauls': Tacitus, *Annals*, III, 43.
111 outlawed by imperial decrees: summary in J. Webster, 11.
111 a scale map of the world: Talbert and Unger, 113.
111 teaching at Bayeux and Bordeaux: Ausonius, V, 4 and 10; Booth.
112 'You will never see': Timagenes, in Ammianus Marcellinus, XII, 9.
112 '*maximum et copiosissimum*': *BG*, I, 23.
113 an up-to-date description: J. Webster, 6–10.
113 'learn by heart': *BG*, VI, 14.
113 'cast letters to their relatives': Diodorus Siculus, V, 28, 6.
113–14 the Irish Dindsenchas: Pennick, 130.
114 'The Three Wives of Arthur': from *The Welsh Triads*.
114 'Gaul is divided into three parts': *BG*, I, 1.
114 'From the Pyrenees to the Garonne': Mela, III, 15.
114 'The Druids relate': Timagenes, in Ammianus Marcellinus, XV, 9,
     4–6.

116 *'Dysgogan derwydon'*: Ross, 430.

116 'They wish above all': *BG*, VI, 14; also Diodorus Siculus, V, 28, 6; Strabo, IV, 4, 4.

117 the only Druid teaching: Mela, III, 15.

117 'The Druids express their philosophy': Diogenes Laertius, I, 6.

117 a Welsh triad: Similarity first pointed out in *The Gentleman's Magazine*, January 1825, p. 8.

117 'Stranger,' he said: Lucian of Samosata, 'Herakles'.

8. The Druidic Syllabus, II: Advanced

119 'they perform none of their religious rites': Pliny, XVI, 95 (249). According to Maximus of Tyre, 'the Celtic image of Zeus is a lofty oak': Maximus of Tyre, 21 (oration 2; sometimes numbered 8 or 38).

119 'to hear the lofty oak': *Odyssey*, 14.326–28.

119 'discovered' (*'reperta'*) in Britain: *BG*, VI, 13.

120 'The Celtic Druids': Hippolytus of Rome, I, 2 and 22.

120 Celtic art: e.g. Buchsenschutz (2002) – especially article by M. Bacault and J.-L. Flouest; Jope; Kruta (2004); Lenerz-de Wilde (1977).

120 'for offerings should be rendered': Diodorus Siculus, V, 31, 4.

120 'conducted investigations': Timagenes, in Ammianus Marcellinus, XV, 9, 8.

121 fibrous qualities of wrought iron: Jope, 400.

123 The symbols are astronomical: Faintich; Fillioux.

123 the constellation of Ursa Major: The Celts would not have been alone in seeing the Great Bear as a horse: Gibbon.

123 'The Celt was a clever adaptor': Kilbride-Jones, 39.

123 he burst out laughing: Diodorus Siculus, XXII, 9, 4.

123 pink-granite basin: Almagro Gorbea and Gran Aymerich; Goudineau and Peyre, 40–44; Romero; R. White.

124 Druid mathematics: on ancient mathematics generally: Guillaumin; Heath; W. Richardson.

124 the Mont de Fer: P. Boyer, in Almagro Gorbea and Gran Aymerich, 252.

125 Gournay-sur-Aronde: Brunaux (1985–94).

126 unburned on the battlefield: Silius Italicus, III, 340–49.

127 'tight trousers akin to cycling shorts': Ritchie, 51.

127 British structural archaeologist: Carter.

127 a French archaeologist: Toupet.

128 Celtic subrectangular enclosures: Bittel et al.; Brunaux (1986 and 1991); Cunliffe (2005); Downs; Fauduet et al.; Wieland et al.

128 greater feats of engineering: Reynolds, 196.

129 'bound together in fellowships': Timagenes, in Ammianus Marcellinus, XV, 9, 8.

130 they turned to the right: Posidonius, in Athenaeus, IV, 36.

130 string construction of the ellipse: West, 710.

130 medicinal properties of plants: Pliny, XXIV, 62–63 (103–104).

130 instrument similar to the lyre: Timagenes, in Ammianus Marcellinus, XV, 9, 8.

131 settlement of debts: Mela, III, 15.

131 'Often, when two armies approach': Diodorus Siculus, V, 31, 5; also Strabo, IV, 4, 4; generally, Dio Chrysostom, Discourse XLIX, 7.

131 'Celtic women': Plutarch (1931), I, 6; Polyaenus, VII, 50.

131 The Druids discuss: *BG*, VI, 14.

131 '*Hi terrae mundique*': Mela, III, 15. On '*mundus*' as 'universe': Puhvel.

132 solar-lunar calendar: Le Contel and Verdier; Olmsted.

132 division of the inhabited world by Ephorus: Strabo, I, 2, 28.

9. Paths of the Gods

137 the mouth of the Borysthenes: 'Borysthenes' referred either to the river Dnieper or to a town near its mouth. It was mentioned both as a latitude and a longitude point: Pliny, VI, 39 (218); Strabo, I, 4, 4; also Roller, 80.

138 Celtiberian coins: Boutiot, iii. At 'La Muraille (or 'Les Murailles') du Diable', a thick dry-stone wall may once have belonged to a promontory fort: Ournac et al., 137.

138 Balbianas: Boutiot, 29.

139 'the hearth and metropolis': Diodorus Siculus, IV, 19, 2. Diodorus is sometimes said to have invented the fame of Alesia to flatter its destroyer, Julius Caesar, but since his *Bibliotheca Historica* ends in 60 BC and the details are consistent with Celtic legend, the reference to Caesar's victory is probably a later interpolation.

139 '*locus consecratus*': One of the oldest conundrums of Gaulish geography: e.g. Jullian, II, 4 n. 65. Caesar sites the 'sacred place' 'in the lands of the Carnutes – a region held to be the middle of the whole of Gaul' (*BG*, VI, 13). Knowing how long it took to reach Carnutia (the region of Chartres and Orléans) from the Alps and from the British Ocean, neither Caesar nor the Druids are likely to

have considered this the centre of Gaul. Perhaps the annual councils were hosted by different tribes, each capital being considered the symbolic centre of Gaul for the occasion, or perhaps a scribe substituted the Carnutes, mentioned earlier in Book VI, for the unfamiliar Mandubii of Alesia, who do not appear until Book VII. (There are no manuscripts of *De Bello Gallico* older than the ninth century.)

139 the Mandubii: on the tribe's cultural distinctness (revealed by pottery): P. Barral et al., in Garcia and Verdin, 282; Provost et al. (2009), 150.

140 The Fossé des Pandours: Fichtl and Adam; Flotté and Fuchs, 551–62.

141 whole-number ratio: on the Romans' use of rational tangents: A. Richardson.

142 Archimedes: Tavernor, 19.

143 capital of the Rediones: Leroux and Provost, 26 and 178. On hill forts of northern France: Wheeler and Richardson, and relevant volumes of *CAG*.

145 greater margins of error: The line from Namur passes just south of Trier or Trèves, which became the Treveri's Roman capital, and arrives at one of the biggest *oppida* in Europe, Heidengraben bei Grabenstetten. However, there is no sign that Trier was important in protohistory, and since Heidengraben covers more than sixteen hundred hectares, the coincidence is not especially remarkable.

145 cultural differences of 'Germanic' tribes: Caesar's notion of a Rhine frontier was contradicted by Cicero and Tacitus: Deyber, 30.

146 Sena, in the British sea: Mela, III, 40; also Strabo, IV, 4, 6 (quoting Posidonius).

147 long-distance land surveyors: Harley and Woodward, 214; Roth Congès, 330–49.

147 fuzziness of the shadow: The operation is described by Hyginus Gromaticus. Ancient Egyptians used a gnomon with a bifurcated tip for greater accuracy (Isler, with illustrations). The same function might have been performed by the spokes of a solar wheel or by a Gaulish precursor of the *'lanternes des morts'*, which survive primarily in the Limousin and Poitou-Charentes. 'Wheel towers' (perhaps including the original Tour Magne in Nîmes) existed in Gallo-Roman times, associated with a ceremony in which a flaming wheel was launched from a hilltop temple (see Momméja) – for example, at Vernemetis ('Great Sanctuary'), in the Gironde (but perhaps related to the imperial cult of Sol Invictus: e.g. Pettazzoni, 197).

147 portolan charts were so remarkably accurate: Harley and Woodward,
      385–86. On projections: Balletti; Boutoura.

147 directional error is less than two metres: Trousset, 139; also Lewis,
      245. On the thousand-kilometre-long Limes Tripolitanus: Goodchild
      and Perkins.

148 I-Hsing: Beer et al.

148 Some qanats: Stiros.

149 '[I came] from the Cover of the Sea': adapted from Pennick, 130.

149 twelve towns and four hundred villages: *BG*, I, 5.

150 'Writing tablets were found': *BG*, I, 29.

150 Scots who left their homeland: Devine.

150 the Gaulish diaspora: Livy, V, 33 ff.; Polybius, II, 17; also Diodorus
      Siculus, XIV, 113; Dionysius of Halicarnassus, XIII, 11; Pliny, XII, 2
      (5); Plutarch, 'Camillus', XV–XVII, in Plutarch (1914–26), II;
      Justinus, XXIV, 4. On the Celts in Italy: Chevallier (1983); Cunliffe
      (1992), 129–32; Cunliffe (1999), 75–78; Defente; Frey.

150 We have received the following account: Livy, V, 34 (also for
      Ambigatus and the crossing of the Alps).

152 the Tricastini's territory: Harley and Woodward, 222–24; Walbank,
      111.

153 Polybius gives a similar list: Polybius, II, 17.

153 Mezzomerico was once Mediomadrigo: Olivieri (1965), 218.

154 Tribal centres and the migration to Italy: Livy, V, 34–35; Polybius,
      II, 17; also Appianus, IV, 7; Athenaeus, VI, 25; Diodorus Siculus,
      XIV, 113; Florus, I, 7; Justinus, XXIV, 4; Pausanias, X, 19. At
      Évreux, the Saint-Michel hill is a probable *oppidum*. Angoulême is
      the likeliest site of a tribal centre in the region (J.-F. Buisson and J.
      Gomez de Soto, in Garcia and Verdin, 259). On *oppida* of the
      Ambarri: Buisson, 24, et passim. Mont Jovis: Chossenot et al. (2004),
      311. Mont Milan: Bonnet; Lhermet; Trintignac et al., 292. On
      south-eastern tribes: Barruol. *Oppida* in the far west: Galliou and
      Philippe; Galliou et al. *Oppida* in Normandy: Bernouis; Cliquet and
      Gauthier; Delacampagne; Rogeret.

156 'the remotest parts of Illyricum': Justinus, XXIV, 4.

156 Saint-Blaise: Benoît (1965); Gateau et al., 78 and 287–302; Trément.
      On Heraklea: Pliny, III, 4 (33). On ancient coastlines: Arnaud-
      Fassetta; Rothé et al., 716.

156 trading hub in the fifth century BC: Roure.

156 'fortified against the tribe of the Sallyes': Strabo, IV, 1, 5.

157 the excavator of Olbia: Coupry.

157 one of the three most important towns: Provost (1999), 30/2, 532. The others were Ugernum (Beaucaire) and Nemausos (Nîmes).

158 The Lingones, whose Gaulish capital: The Reims–Aosta line bisects the *oppidum* of Andemantunum (Langres) but meets the Châteaumeillant–Alesia line 1.5 kilometres to the north at the nineteenth-century Fort de la Pointe de Diamant, which controlled the valley of the Marne and the road to Chaumont: this could be an earlier tribal capital. Nothing remains of pre-Roman Langres (Joly; Thévenard et al.).

158 the Poenina was impassable: Strabo, IV, 6, 7.

159 'Because the region was scorching hot': Diodorus Siculus, XIV, 113, 3.

160 tribal centres of the Cenomani and the Carnutes: There are no clear signs of a pre-Roman *oppidum* at Le Mans (Bouvet et al., 61), nor at Orléans (Provost, *Le Loiret*, 84). Chartres was permanently occupied only from the time of the Roman conquest (Ollagnier and Joly, 114).

160 Five other tribes: Pollicini, 60–63, and Zanotto, 22 (Salassi); Polybius, II, 17 (Insubres); Olivieri (1965), 218 (Mediomatrici); Geoffrey of Monmouth: IX, 16 (Allobroges); Tacitus, *Annals*, XI, 23 (Veneti).

10. The Forest and Beyond

162 first recorded by Aristotle: Aristotle (1952 and 2000), I, 13.

162 The breadth of the forest: *BG*, VI, 25; Mela, III, 29.

162 'Impervious to the passage of time': Pliny, XVI, 2 (6).

163 'Folk of the Hercynian Forest': Pliny, III, 25 (148); Ptolemy (2006), II, 14.

163 'vague and secret paths': *BG*, VI, 34.

163 '*invia*' ('trackless'): Mela, III, 24.

164 'many myriads of warriors': Plutarch, 'Camillus', XV, in Plutarch (1914–26), II.

165 'The harmonious arrangement of the country': Strabo, IV, 1, 14.

165 'know nothing of road measurements': *BG*, VI, 25.

167 employed by Herod the Great: Josephus, 336 (*Antiquities of the Jews*, XV, 7, 3).

169 'driven from their homes': Timagenes, in Ammianus Marcellinus, XV, 9, 4.

169 'Where did they come from?': e.g. B. P. McEvoy and D. G. Bradley (on genetic analyses), in Cunliffe and Koch, 111.

170 'In days gone by': *BG*, VI, 24.

171 crossing the Hellespont: Polybius, IV, 46; also Memnon, 11.

171 Drunemeton: Strabo, XII, 5, 1; also Livy, XXXVIII, 16.

171 Delphi: Appianus, X, 1, 4; Justinus, XXIV, 6–8; Livy, XXXVIII, 48; Pausanias, X, 19–23; Strabo, IV, 1, 13.

172 The battle tactics of the Celts: Pausanias, X, 21.

172 Latter-day Titans: Callimachus, *Hymn to Delos*.

174 'It was the lakes': Strabo, IV, 1, 13 (from Posidonius); also Cassius Dio, XXVII, 90; Justinus, XXXII, 3.

174 'Many large rivers': Diodorus Siculus, V, 25, 3.

175 'a pool of standing water': Moret.

175 Pont des Demoiselles: Gaston Astre, quoted in Moret, 310.

11. Cities of Middle Earth

176 near the town of Biturrita: The place was called Vindal(i)um, according to Livy and Strabo. On Bituitos, see also Eutropius, IV, 22 (in Justinus); Florus, I, 37, 5; Orosius, V, 14; Valerius Maximus, IX, 6, 3. The solar intersection confirms the identification by, among others, Fortia d'Urban (1808), 52–63; see also D. and Y. Roman, ch. 5. Etymology: Nègre (1990–98), I, 197.

176 'Seeing such small numbers': Orosius, V, 14.

179 *oppidum* of Anseduna: Jannoray.

179 Marcus Fonteius: Cicero (2012), 13–15.

180 Louernios: Athenaeus, IV, 37; Strabo, IV, 2, 3.

180 tokens rather than treasures: on the history of Celtic coinage: Creighton; Cunliffe, ed.; Delestrée; Delestrée and Tache; Duval (1987).

182 'other hills of a similar height': *BG*, VII, 69.

184 'for the first time', says Caesar: *BG*, VII, 30.

185 coins found on the plateau of Gergovia: map based on information in Provost et al. (1994), 280–82; on *oppida* as centres of production and trade: Kruta (2006), 32–4; Wells, 'Resources', 225, and 'Trade', 240.

184 In 2004, a French archaeologist: Buchsenschutz (2004); on *oppida* superimposed on sanctuaries: Fichtl (2005), 154.

185 'the leaders of the Gauls': *BG*, VII, 1.

187 exactly the right place: The Druidic system thus reconciles opposing views of ancient cartography as representation and idealization: e.g. Janni, 66–69.

12. *The Gods Victorious*

188 the citadel of Namur: e.g. Napoléon III, II, 131–32 n. 1; other possible sites are the Montagne d'Hastedon in Namur, Huy (Mont Falhize), Lompret ('Camp romain') and Thuin (Bois du Grand Bon Dieu): see Roymans et al., 83–84.

188 traders who bought the Aduatuci: *BG*, II, 33.

188 'Upon receipt of Caesar's letters': *BG*, II, 35.

189 'the very great dangers': *BG*, III, 1.

189 a river called the Tamesis: *BG*, V, 18.

189 Varro Atacinus: Hollis, 165 (my translation).

189 'a copious letter': Cicero (1965), 113 (c. 1 July 54).

190 several letters at the same time: Plutarch (2011), 17.

190 treatise on the subject of analogy: Suetonius, 'Julius Caesar', 56.

190 mosaic squares: Suetonius, 'Julius Caesar', 46; also Goudineau (2000), 268.

190 Britain had been 'dealt with': Cicero (1965), 131 (between 24 October and 2 November 54).

190 a play called *Erigone*: Cicero (1988), 3.1.13; 3.5.7.

190 adding water to their wine: Cicero (2012), 4; quoted by Ammianus Marcellinus, XII, 4.

191 one hundred tons of wheat: Goudineau (2000), 249.

191 'to remedy the lack of corn': *BG*, V, 24.

191 'not long after those events': *BG*, V, 58.

191 'settle nearly all disputes': *BG*, VI, 13.

191 a certain 'Gutuater': *BG*, VIII, 38. (Manuscripts disagree on the spelling: a summary of the discussion in Lamoine, 358, n. 241.)

191 Sacrovir: Tacitus, *Annals*, III, 40–46.

192 'the power that fed the rebellion': Tacitus, *Annals*, XIV, 29.

192 'the custom of the Gauls': *BG*, IV, 19.

192 'The Suebi': *BG*, IV, 19.

193 The Gallic War and Gaulish strategy: on 'Champ-de-Bataille' (at the exact intersection of two solar paths): Thaurin, 285.

193 'But the enemy': *BG*, II, 27.

193 battle of the Sambre: Turquin.

194 'The rest of the multitude', *BG*, IV, 15.

194 massacre appalled Cato: Plutarch (2011), 22.

194 '*humani generis iniuria*': Pliny, VII, 25 (92).

194 Gaulish agriculture: Buchsenschutz (2004); Burnham, 130; Chouquer (2005), 46; Reynolds, 180–84.

195 The 39,200 killed: *BG*, VII, 28.

195 estimate given by Plutarch: Plutarch (2011), 14; also Appianus, IV, 2; Velleius Paterculus, II, 47.

195 slaves shipped to the American colonies: Goudineau (2000), 325.

195 its literal sense: 'depopulate': *BG*, VIII, 24.

195 'the race and name of the Nervii': *BG*, II, 28.

195 'their name and *stirps*': *BG*, VI, 34.

195 'a great multitude of wreckers': *BG*, III, 17.

196 'a young man of the highest ability': *BG*, VII, 4.

196 Ambassadors were sent: *BG*, VII, 4.

196 'fickleness' and 'eagerness for political change': *BG*, II, 1 and IV, 5.

196 'the finest of leaders': *BG*, VII, 21.

197 'a small sword hanging in a temple': Plutarch (2011), 26.

197 'The soldiers thought that they knew': *BG*, VII, 52.

197 'Having achieved what he intended': *BG*, VII, 47.

197 strangled in his cell: Cassius Dio, XL, 41.

197 'not even the whole earth': *BG*, VII, 29.

197 'it appears to defy military custom': Montaigne, II, 34.

198 'by popular vote': *BG*, VII, 63.

198 From Bibracte, following the same line: An ancient route between Bibracte and Alesia (Provost et al. (2009), 298) is now a marked itinerary: http://www.bibracte-alesia.com/un_itineraire_culturel_important.php

198 'Why . . . did the leader of all the Gauls': Montaigne, II, 34.

198 'the part of the hill that looks towards the rising sun': *BG*, VII, 69.

198 a levy of all the tribes: *BG*, VII, 75.

199 dressed in chainmail: Musée des Antiquités Nationales, 214; on Celtic dress: Lloyd-Morgan.

199 the civilian population was evacuated: Cassius Dio, XL, 40.

199 He rode in a circle: Plutarch (2011), 27; also Florus, I, 45, 26.

200 'a man of the utmost audacity': *BG*, VII, 5.

201 'to enter the province': *BG*, VIII, 32.

201 'very steep and rugged cliffs': *BG*, VIII, 33.

201 the Puy d'Issolud: Labrousse and Mercadier, 133–36. Attempts to identify the site: Champollion-Figeac; Holmes, 483–93; Jullian, III, 14 n. 137; etc.

202 A hamlet, first recorded in 1275: Courbin, 247.

202 the Bastard of Mauléon: Compayré, 325–26.

202 on the borders of the Cadurci and the Ruteni: The rebels left the *oppidum* to gather supplies 'from the territory of the Cadurci' (*BG*, VIII, 34). The *oppidum* itself was a dependency of Lucterius, who had previously recruited troops from the neighbouring Ruteni. The

site's only physical divergence from Hirtius's account is the width of land joining the *oppidum* to the outside world: 'almost 300 [Roman] feet'. The actual distance at Thuriès is 675 Roman feet. In almost vertical terrain, this could only have been an estimate.

202 'He reflected that . . .': *BG*, VIII, 45.

203 'They attributed the drying-up of the well': *BG*, VIII, 43.

204 his reputation for '*lenitas*': *BG*, VIII, 44.

204 'And the land, lying as it does': Diodorus Siculus, V, 25, 2.

208 a colossal statue of Mercury: Pliny, XXXIV, 18 (45–47); also Monceaux.

209 'for state purposes': *BG*, VI, 16.

209 The exodus from the *oppida*: e.g. Brun et al.; Colin; Fichtl (2005), ch. 5.

209 Solar orientation in Roman towns and forts: Magli; also Le Gall.

209 The road that enters Amiens: Bayard and Massy, 96.

210 The streets of Reims: The pre-Roman orientations varied: Chossenot et al. (2010), 62. The route to the British Ocean is described in Léman; see also Strabo, IV, 6, 11.

210 the Roman towns of Autun, Metz and Limoges: Rebourg et al. (1993), 24–25, and Provost et al. (1993), 63–65 (Autun); Flotté, 70–74 (Metz); Perrier et al., 87 (Limoges). Sometimes, as on the plateau of Langres (home of the pro-Roman Lingones), alignments were determined by geographical *force majeure*.

210 'Those who wish to make a more assiduous study': *BG*, VI, 13.

211 'infesting the roads': *BG*, VIII, 47; see also VIII, 23.

211 Defeated by the deified Caesar: Frontinus (1925 and 1990): *Strategemata*, II, 13, 11.

212 a certain Bretannos: Parthenius of Nicaea, XXX.

13. The Poetic Isles

215 'Their science crossed the ocean': Pliny, XXX, 4 (13).

215 a '*disciplina*': *BG*, VI, 13–14.

215 'The Britanni . . . fortify their tangled woods': *BG*, V, 21.

216 The name is often found: Delamarre (2003), 252; Delamarre (2007) ('Prito', etc.); Holder, II, 1046–47; Morris-Jones, 4–6; Rivet and Smith, 280–82. There was also a German or Belgic goddess called Pritona.

218 'old but not old fashioned': http://www.shropshiretourism.co.uk/whitchurch/.

218 The market town of Whitchurch: Brewer, 49; Rivet and Smith, 416 (identified with Mediolanum).

218 Mediobogdum: Shotter, 107; Smith, 383; cf. Rivet and Smith, 415.

220 the first Roman surveyors: Ferrar and Richardson, 15–16.

220 'which should run the whole length of the island': Geoffrey of Monmouth, III, 5.

223 so many hill forts: e.g. Cunliffe (1993 and 2005); Forde-Johnston.

224 in this telling of the tale, Merlin: Geoffrey of Monmouth, VIII, 2. (Explanation of the identification with Merlin: http://www. vortigernstudies.org.uk/artcit/caerdoward.htm.)

224 'a substantial ritual focus': Dodd, 7.

225 'Lludd and Llevelys': *The Mabinogion*, 128–33.

225 the *Historia Brittonum*: Nennius, 42.

229 intersection of three major tribal territories: Dodd, 11.

229 tribe of Oxubii: Pliny, III, 4 (35) and 5 (47); Polybius, XXXIII, 9–10; Strabo, IV, 1, 10.

229 a defensive enclosure or *oppidum*: Beckley and Radley, 17.

233 The causeway running the breadth of the kingdom: Other important forts (not shown): Twyn Cornicyll (Abertysswg), Coed y Bwnydd (Bettws Newydd) and Cholesbury Camp (Buckinghamshire). The line also bisects Stroud, Stanton Harcourt and Thame.

233 Belinus commanded another causeway: Geoffrey of Monmouth, III, 5.

234 'as though in accordance with some calculated plan': Strabo, IV, 1, 14.

14. The Four Royal Roads

236 tribe called the Weogora: Mills ('Worcester').

237 'of extremely slight interest': Beazley, II, 584.

238 the school of Autun: Eumenius, 20, 2 (c. AD 297); N. Lozovsky, in Talbert and Unger, 169–70.

238 the Four Royal Roads: Geoffrey of Monmouth, III, 5; Henry of Huntingdon, I, 7; Higden, I, 45; Robert of Gloucester, 7.

238 a rhetorical trope: Birkholz, 73.

238 'Two others he also made obliquely': Geoffrey of Monmouth, III, 5.

241 to within a few paces: As Oliver Rackham observes of the Fosse Way: quoted in Davies (2005), 40; see also Lewis, 226.

241 an extensive survey: Ferrar; Ferrar and Richardson; Jones and Mattingly, 94–95; also Davies (1998 and 2005). Roman roads in Britain: Margary.

242 the Celtic port of Durobrivae: On an exact bearing of 53.13°, the line meets Watling Street west of Rochester at Cobham Park Roman villa, a possible Iron Age site. On the bearing of the road: Lewis, 226. On the importance of Chichester in the first century BC: Jersey.

244 'Lyne me clepeth eke . . .': Robert of Gloucester, 7.

245 Calleva Atrebatum (Silchester): Fulford, Clarke and Taylor. For latest developments: http://blogs.reading.ac.uk/silchesterdig/. The south-west – north-east alignment of the temple in Insula XXXV is also very close to the British solstice angle: illustration from St John Hope in Frere and Fulford (2002), 168.

246 Molmutius, King of the Britons: Higden, I, 45.

246 'leave no loophole for quibbles': Geoffrey of Monmouth, III, 5.

248 almost featureless landscapes: Pryor, 372.

248 Iron Age tribal territories: on the association of dragons and other monsters with boundaries and borderlands: Semple, 114.

15. The End of Middle Earth

249 'I had horses, men, arms and wealth': Tacitus, *Annals*, XII, 37.

249 'Caratacus toured the city': Cassius Dio, LXI, 33.

250 'a citadel of perpetual tyranny': Tacitus, *Annals*, XIV, 31.

250 The invasion of AD 43: e.g. Frere and Fulford (2001); Salway, ch. 4; G. Webster (1981 and 1993).

251 'a particularly ferocious' people: Tacitus, *Annals*, XII, 33.

251 'luring' other tribes: Tacitus, *Annals*, XII, 39.

251 'those who dreaded': Tacitus, *Annals*, XII, 33.

252 'the haven of fugitives': Tacitus, *Annals*, XIV, 29.

252 Mona is the oblique focus: on the Boudican revolt as diversion: Lucas, 106; G. Webster in Aldhouse-Green (1996), 633.

252 'powerful population': Tacitus, *Annals*, XIV, 29.

253 'arduous and dangerous': Tacitus, *Agricola*, 18.

253 'Indignant at the thought': Cassius Dio, LX, 19.

253 'paralysed by fear': Tacitus, *Annals*, XIV, 30.

254 'a crucial error': La Bédoyère, 34.

254 an Iron Age settlement: Cunliffe (2005), 299.

254 '*lapis fatalis*': Giraldus Cambrensis (1868 and 1978), II, 9. Somewhere in the vicinity, there was once an oak-grove called Cell y Dewiniaid ('The Diviners' Cell') (Pennant, 176).

254 'in the lands of the Ordovices': Tacitus, *Annals*, XII, 33.

255 'find a fatherless boy': Geoffrey of Monmouth, VI, 19; Nennius, 40.

256 Caratacus 'piled up stones': Tacitus, *Annals*, XII, 33.

257 'utterly extinguished': Tacitus, *Annals*, XII, 39.

257 'amidst a hostile population': Tacitus, *Annals*, XIV, 33.

257 Poenius Postumus: Tacitus, *Annals*, XIV, 37.

257 a date of AD 60–61: Cunliffe (1993), 217–18; G. Webster (1993), 108.

258 'Secret conspiracies': Tacitus, *Annals*, XIV, 31.

258 strange occurrences: Tacitus, *Annals*, XIV, 32.

258 Boudica, queen of the Iceni: on Boudica: Aldhouse-Green (2006); Hingley and Unwin; G. Webster (1999).

258 Boudica's rabble-rousing speech: Tacitus, *Annals*, XIV, 35.

258 'possessed of greater intelligence': Cassius Dio, LXII, 2.

259 in a 'harsh voice': Cassius Dio, LXII, 2.

259 Wardy Hill: Hill and Horne.

259 ceremonial centre of Camulodunum: Dunnett and Reece.

260 Woolwich Power Station: Philp, 1 and 38–42.

260 'Constructed about 250 BC': Kent Archaeological Rescue Unit press release: http://cka.moon-demon.co.uk/woolwich.htm.

262 London-to-Hastings road: Leigh, 151–53 and 195–97.

263 They faced the Britons: Tacitus, *Annals*, XIV, 34.

263 'empty threats': Tacitus, *Annals*, XIV, 36.

263 Tripontium on Watling Street: Lucas, 108–10.

263 'terrain analysis techniques': Kaye.

263 'our soldiers': Tacitus, *Annals*, XIV, 37.

263 the Romans 'laid waste': Tacitus, *Annals*, XIV, 38.

263 Boudica survived the battle: Cassius Dio, LXII, 12.

264 enclosure of the Iceni at Thetford: Sealey, 42; also Gregory, I, 196–99 (from a suggestion of G. Webster).

264 'sued for peace': Tacitus, *Agricola*, 18.

264 'new peoples': Tacitus, *Agricola*, 22.

264 'Caledonian natives': Tacitus, *Agricola*, 25.

264 'a remedy for his grief': Tacitus, *Agricola*, 29.

264 'Still buoyant': Tacitus, *Agricola*, 29.

265 thirty contenders: Roman Scotland.

266 White Caterthun and Brown Caterthun: D. Harding, 91–92.

267 '*terminus Britanniae*': Tacitus, *Agricola*, 23, 27, 30 and 33.

267 'There are no nations beyond us': Tacitus, *Agricola*, 30.

267 'The flat country between': Tacitus, *Agricola*, 35.

267 'equipment, bodies': Tacitus, *Agricola*, 37.

267 'An enormous silence': Tacitus, *Agricola*, 38.

268 olive oil that was used as lamp fuel: Potter and Johns, 154.

16. Return of the Druids

269 a hardy race of Caledonians: Cassius Dio, LXXVII, 12; also Herodian, III, 14, 6.

269 'a grand and memorable exploit': Tacitus, *Agricola*, 28.

269 'red hair and long limbs': Tacitus, *Agricola*, 11.

272 'complete savages': Strabo, II, 5, 8.

272 'the livestock eat their fill': Mela, III, 43.

272 'a very tall lighthouse': Orosius, I, 2.

273 the deposed Irish chieftain: Tacitus, *Agricola*, 24.

273 'On a clear winter's evening': *Lebor Gabála Érenn*, I, 25.

273 'They landed on the "Fetid Shore" ': *Lebor Gabála Érenn*, V, 66.

273 Iberian-style defences: Raftery, 62.

273 a Barbary macaque: Raftery, 79.

274 the 'royal sites': Condit and Coyne; Newman; Raftery, 65.

274 Hill of Uisneach: see Schot.

274 The mighty burgh of Temra: Óengus the Culdee, 165, 177, 189, 193 and 205.

277 'annual scene of disgusting superstition': Hardy, 33.

277 'displays all the features': C. Newman: http://heritagecouncil.ie/unpublished_excavations/section10.html.

277 The earliest partition of Ireland: *Lebor Gabála Érenn*, II, 37.

278 the other 'Sacred Promontory': Freeman, 77–79.

278 Tartessian: Koch (2009); Cunliffe and Koch.

279 the 'victorious Brigit': Cogitosus (1987 and 1989); also Aldhouse-Green (1997), 134–36.

279 a circular hedge: Giraldus Cambrensis (1894), 34–36.

279 the Son of God: '*Mo druí . . . Mac Dé*' ('My druid . . . the Son of God'): Ross, 429.

279 Lucatmael: Byrne and Francis, 49.

279 '*professores*' teaching in Bordeaux: Ausonius, V, 4 and 10; Booth. Late sightings of Druids: Desforges, 302.

280 Pope Gregory I in c. 600: letter to Abbot Mellitus, in Bede, I, 30.

280 stones of the Picts: e.g. Murray; examples of 'neo-Celtic' art in souvenirs produced for Roman soldiers: Breeze.

280 two 'compass lines': In a random sample of fourteen, the average bearing of the right-hand rods of the Pictish 'compass' figures roughly corresponds to the summer solstice azimuth in AD 800 at the likely 'origin centre' of the carvings (Moray and Dornoch Firths).

281 the first Christian chapels: Deanesly; C. Thomas.

281 'Meanwhile, stiff with cold and frost': Gildas, 8.

281 St Regina: Boutry and Julia.

283 The early Christian sites: e.g. Blair; Brown; E. Evans; Redknap; Rees; C. Thomas; also from Bede; Geoffrey of Monmouth; Giraldus Cambrensis (1978); Nennius.

283 Hoards containing Christian artefacts: following C. Thomas, 103.

284 the native of a *nemeton*: Byrne and Francis, 22–23. On St Patrick as 'a super-Druid': Humphrey.

284 Pope Gregory had instructed: Bede, I, 30.

285 magpies used to gather: Leland, II, 44.

285 'fairy-paths', 'trods' or 'corpse roads': Pennick, 131.

286 Old Sarum: Hall, 4; the deer may be a later addition.

286 Myrfield: G. White, 2.

286 Mediocantus: Gregory of Tours, 1053.

286 struggles of slain animals: Diodorus Siculus, V, 31, 3.

286 'Honour the gods': Diogenes Laertius, I, 6.

286 'Death is but the middle': Lucan, I, 457–58 (on the Druids: *'longae . . . vitae / mors media est'*).

286 'Souls do not perish': *BG*, VI, 14.

287 guided by the blur of the Milky Way: Puel.

287 Christians removed his beard: Lancel, 307.

Epilogue: A Traveller's Guide to Middle Earth

289 Standish was a Roman road junction: Waddelove.

291 *'locus valde terribilis'*: from Genesis 28:17.

291 King Lucius of Britain: Flete, 63.

292 in magnified illustrations: e.g. Kruta (2004).

292 'at Fenny Stratford': The discoverer of the coin gave no other details: Sir John Evans, 50.

293 'Conventional wisdom prevailed': R. Hill, 85.

294 the area now covered by Caldecotte Lake: Zeepvat et al., and Milton Keynes Historic Environment Record.

Works Cited

Unless otherwise stated, the place of publication is either London or Paris.

Abbreviation:
CAG: *Carte archéologique de la Gaule* (Académie des Inscriptions et Belles-Lettres, 1988–2013).

Abert, Franck. *Les Hauts-de-Seine. CAG*, 92. 2005.
Adams, James N. *The Regional Diversification of Latin, 200 BC – AD 600*. Cambridge University Press, 2007.
Aeberhardt, André. 'L'Angoumois gallo-romain'. Thesis. Tours: Centre de recherches A. Piganiol, 1983.
Aelian. *Historical Miscellany*. Tr. N. G. Wilson. Cambridge, Mass.: Harvard University Press, 1997.
Agache, Roger. 'Vues aériennes et folklore de crop-marks circulaires au nord d'Amiens'. *Bulletin de la Société préhistorique de France*, LVIII, 3–4 (1961), pp. 224–36.
Agache, R. 'Repérage des sanctuaires gaulois et gallo-romains dans les campagnes du bassin de la Somme et ses abords'. *Comptes-rendus des séances de l'Académie des Inscriptions et Belles-Lettres*, CXLI, 2 (1997), pp. 551–66.
Aldhouse-Green, Miranda. *The Sun-Gods of Ancient Europe*. Batsford, 1991.
Aldhouse-Green, M. *Exploring the World of the Druids*. Thames & Hudson, 1997.
Aldhouse-Green, M. *Boudica Britannia: Rebel, War-leader and Queen*. Harlow: Pearson Longman, 2006.
Aldhouse-Green, M., ed. *The Celtic World*. Routledge, 1995; 1996.
Allen, Martin. 'The Antikythera Mechanism Research Project': http://www.antikythera-mechanism.gr/faq/general-questions/what-was-it-for
Almagro Gorbea, Martín and J. M. Gran Aymerich. 'Le Bassin

monumental du Mont Beuvray (Bibracte)'. *Monuments et mémoires de la Fondation Eugène Piot*, LXXI (1990), pp. 21–41.

Amé, Émile. *Dictionnaire topographique du département du Cantal.* Imprimerie Nationale, 1897.

Ammianus Marcellinus. *Römische Geschichte.* 4 vols. Ed. W. Seyfarth. Berlin: Akademie-Verlag, 1968–71.

Anon. 'Incerti Gratiarum Actio Constantino Augusto'. *In Praise of Later Roman Emperors: The Panegyrici Latini.* Ed. R. A. B. Mynors. Tr. C. E. V. Nixon and B. S. Rodgers. Berkeley: University of California Press, 1994. Pp. 264–87 and 585–93.

Appianus of Alexandria. *Roman History.* 4 vols. Ed. H. White. Heinemann, 1912–13.

Arcelin, Patrice, et al., eds. *Sur les pas des Grecs en Occident.* Lattes: A.D.A.M., 1994.

Aristotle. *Meteorologica.* Tr. H. D. P. Lee. Heinemann, 1952.

Aristotle. *Minor Works.* Tr. W. S. Hett. 1936; Cambridge, Mass.: Harvard University Press, 1980.

Aristotle. *Aristotle's Meteorology in the Arabico-Latin Tradition.* Ed. P. L. Schoonheim. Leiden: Brill, 2000.

Aristotle. *The Eudemian Ethics.* Ed. A. Kenny. Oxford University Press, 2011.

Arnaud-Fassetta, Gilles. 'Geomorphological Records of a "Flood-Dominated Regime" in the Rhone Delta'. *Geodinamica Acta*, XV (2002), pp. 79–92.

Arrian of Nicomedia. [On Tactics]. In *Extraits des auteurs grecs concernant la géographie et l'histoire des Gaules.* 6 vols. Ed. E. Cougny. Renouard, 1878–92. III, 363–67.

Athenaeus of Naucratis. *The Deipnosophists or Banquet of the Learned.* 3 vols. Tr. C. D. Yonge. Bohn, 1854.

Ausonius, Decimus Magnus. *The Works of Ausonius.* R. P. H. Green. Oxford: Clarendon Press, 1991.

Aveni, Anthony, ed. *World Archaeoastronomy: Selected Papers.* Cambridge University Press, 1989.

Aveni, A. and Giuliano Romano. 'Orientation and Etruscan Ritual'. *Antiquity*, LXVIII, 260 (1994), pp. 545–63.

Avienus, Rufus Festus. *Description de la terre.* Ed. E. Despois and E. Saviot. Panckoucke, 1843.

Avienus, R. F. *Rufi Festi Avieni Carmina.* Ed. A. Holder. Innsbruck: Wagner, 1887.

Avienus, R. F. *Ora maritima.* Ed. A. Berthelot. Champion, 1934.

Avienus, R. F. *Ora maritima: A Description of the Seacoast from Brittany to Marseilles*. Ed. J. P. Murphy. Chicago: Ares, 1977.

Bailey, G. B. and D. F. Devereux. 'The Eastern Terminus of the Antonine Wall: A Review'. *Proceedings of the Society of Antiquaries of Scotland*, CXVII (1987), pp. 93–104.

Balletti, Caterina. 'Georeference in the Analysis of the Geometric Content of Early Maps'. *e-Perimetron*, I, 1 (2006): http://www.e-perimetron.org/Vol_1_1/Balletti/Balletti.pdf

Barral, Philippe, et al., eds. *Alésia: fouilles et recherches franco-allemandes*. 3 vols. Académie des Inscriptions et Belles-Lettres, 2001.

Barruol, Guy. *Les Peuples préromains du sud-est de la Gaule*. Boccard, 1969.

Bayard, Didier and Jean-Luc Massy. 'Le Développement d'Amiens romain, du Ier siècle av. J. C. au IVe siècle ap. J. C'. *Revue archéologique de Picardie*, III, 3–4 (1984), pp. 89–112.

Bayerri y Bertomeu, Enrique, et al. *La Geografía histórico-toponímica de la España ibero-romana*. Tortosa: Dertosa, 1983.

Beaurepaire, Charles de. *Dictionnaire topographique du département de Seine-Maritime*. 2 vols. Bibliothèque Nationale, 1982–84.

Beaurepaire, François de. *Les Noms des communes et anciennes paroisses de l'Eure*. Picard, 1981.

Beaurepaire, F. de. *Les Noms des communes et anciennes paroisses de la Manche*. Picard, 1986.

Beazley, Charles Raymond. *The Dawn of Modern Geography*. 3 vols. John Murray, 1897–1906.

Beckley, Ruth and David Radley. 'Oxford Archaeological Plan. Resource Assessment 2011: The Iron Age. Draft'. Oxford City Council, 2011.

Bede, the Venerable. *Bede's Ecclesiastical History of England*. Tr. A. M. Sellar. Bell, 1907.

Beer, Arthur, et al. 'An Eighth-Century Meridian Line: I-Hsing's Chain of Gnomons and the Pre-history of the Metric System'. *Vistas in Astronomy*, IV, 4 (1961), pp. 3–28.

Ben Redjeb, Tahar. *La Somme*. CAG, 80/2. 2012.

Benoît, Fernand. 'La Légende d'Héraclès et la colonisation grecque dans le delta du Rhône'. *Lettres d'humanité*, VIII (1949), pp. 104–48.

Benoît, F. *Recherches sur l'hellénisation du Midi de la Gaule*. Aix-en-Provence: Ophrys, 1965.

Bernouis, Philippe. *L'Orne*. CAG, 61. 1999.

Bibliotheca Augustana. 'Tabula Peutingeriana': http://www.hs-augsburg.de/~harsch/Chronologia/Lspost03/Tabula/tab_intr.html

Billy, Pierre-Henri. 'Toponymie française et dialectologie gauloise'. In *Gaulois et celtique continental*. Ed. P.-Y. Lambert and G.-J. Pinault. Geneva: Droz, 2007.

Birkhan, Helmut. *Kelten: Versuch einer Gesamtdarstellung ihrer Kultur*. New ed. Vienna: Verlag der Österreichischen Akademie der Wissenschaften, 1997.

Birkholz, Daniel. *The King's Two Maps: Cartography and Culture in Thirteenth-Century England*. Routledge, 1967.

Bittel, Kurt, et al. *Die keltischen Viereckschanzen*. 2 vols. Stuttgart: Theiss, 1990.

Blair, John. *The Church in Anglo-Saxon Society*. Oxford University Press, 2005.

Bonnet, Oscar. 'Sur le camp romain de Mont-Milau [*sic*], près Langogne'. *Annales de la Société d'agriculture, sciences, arts et commerce du Puy*, XX (August 1855), pp. 524–29.

Booth, A. D. 'Notes on Ausonius' *Professores*'. *Phoenix*, XXXII, 3 (1978), pp. 235–49.

Boroditsky, Lera. 'How Language Shapes Thought'. *Scientific American*, February 2011, pp. 43–45.

Bougard, R. *Le Petit flambeau de la mer, ou le Véritable guide des pilotes côtiers*. Le Havre: Faure, 1763.

Bouteiller, Ernest de. *Dictionnaire topographique de l'ancien département de la Moselle*. Imprimerie Nationale, 1874.

Boutiot, Théophile. *Dictionnaire topographique du département de l'Aube*. Imprimerie Nationale, 1874.

Boutoura, Chryssoula. 'Assigning Map Projections to Portolan Maps'. *e-Perimetron*, I, 1 (2006): http://www.e-perimetron.org/Vol_1_1/Boutoura/1_1_Boutoura.pdf

Boutry, Philippe and Dominique Julia, eds. *Reine au Mont Auxois: le culte et le pèlerinage de sainte Reine des origines à nos jours*. Ville de Dijon, 1997.

Bouvet, Jean-Philippe, et al. *La Sarthe. CAG*, 72. 2002.

Boyer, Hippolyte and Robert Latouche. *Dictionnaire topographique du département du Cher*. Imprimerie Nationale, 1926.

Boyer, Roland. *Les Noms de lieux de la région du Mont-Blanc*. Montrouge: Boyer, 1979.

Braund, D. C. 'The Aedui, Troy, and the *Apocolocyntosis*'. *The Classical Quarterly*, new series, XXX, 2 (1980), pp. 420–25.

Breeze, David John, ed. *The First Souvenirs: Enamelled Vessels from*

Hadrian's Wall. Kendal: Cumberland and Westmorland Antiquarian and Archaeological Society, 2012.

Brewer, Richard J., ed. *Birthday of the Eagle: The Second Augustan Legion and the Roman Military Machine*. Cardiff: National Museums & Galleries of Wales, 2002.

Bromwich, James. *The Roman Remains of Southern France*. Routledge, 1993; 1996.

Brown, P. D. C. 'The Church at Richborough'. *Britannia*, II (1971), pp. 225–31.

Brun, Patrice and Claude Mordant, eds. *Le Groupe Rhin-Suisse-France orientale et la notion de civilisation des Champs d'Urnes*. Nemours: Musée de préhistoire d'Île-de-France, 1988.

Brun, P., et al. 'Le Processus d'urbanisation dans la vallée de l'Aisne'. In *Les Processus d'urbanisation à l'Âge du fer*. Glux-en-Glenne: Centre archéologique européen du Mont Beuvray, 2000.

Brunaux, Jean-Louis. *Gournay*. 3 vols. Errance, 1985–94.

Brunaux, J.-L. *Sanctuaires et rites*. Errance, 1986.

Brunaux, J.-L. *Les Religions gauloises*. New ed. Errance, 2000.

Brunaux, J.-L., ed. *Les Sanctuaires celtiques et leurs rapports avec le monde méditerranéen*. Errance, 1991.

Brun-Durand, Justin. *Dictionnaire topographique du département de la Drôme*. Imprimerie Nationale, 1891.

Buchsenschutz, Olivier, ed. *Décors, images et signes de l'Âge du Fer européen*. Tours: FERACF, 2002.

Buchsenschutz, O. 'Les Celtes et la formation de l'Empire romain', *Annales*, 59 (2004), pp. 337–61.

Buisson, André. *L'Ain*. *CAG*, 1. 1990.

Burl, Aubrey. *Prehistoric Astronomy and Ritual*. 2nd ed. Princes Risborough: Shire, 2005.

Burnham, Barry C. 'Celts and Romans: Towards a Romano-Celtic Society'. In M. Aldhouse-Green, ed. *The Celtic World*. Pp. 121–41.

Byrne, F. J. and Pádraig Francis. 'Two Lives of Saint Patrick: "Vita Secunda" and "Vita Quarta"'. *Journal of the Royal Society of Antiquaries of Ireland*, CXXIV (1994), pp. 5–117.

Caesar, Gaius Julius and Aulus Hirtius. *C. Iuli Caesaris commentariorum*. Ed. R. Du Pontet. 2 vols. Oxford: Clarendon Press, 1900–01.

Caesar and Hirtius. *Commentarii de Bello Gallico*. Ed. F. Kraner and W. Dittenberger. 17th ed. 3 vols. Berlin: Weidmann, 1913–20.

Caesar and Hirtius. *The Gallic War*. Tr. H. J. Edwards. 1917. Cambridge, Mass.: Harvard University Press, 1994.

Callimachus. *Hymns and Epigrams*. Ed. A. W. Mair. Rev. ed. Cambridge, Mass.: Harvard University Press, 1989.

Cappello, Teresa and Carlo Tagliavini. *Dizionario degli etnici e dei toponimi italiani*. Bologna: Pàtron, 1981.

Carré de Busserolle, Jacques Xavier. *Dictionnaire géographique, historique et biographique d'Indre-et-Loire et de l'ancienne province de Touraine*. 3 vols. Tours: Rouillé-Ladevèze, 1878–80.

Carrière, Jean-Claude. 'Heraclès de la Méditerranée à l'Océan'. In *Cité et territoire*. Ed. M. Clavel-Lévêque and R. Plana-Mallart. Les Belles Lettres, 1995.

Carter, Geoff. 'Systematic Irregularity: Why Almost Nothing in the Celtic World Was Square' (2009): http://structuralarchaeology.blogspot.co.uk/2009/03/24-systematic-irregularity-why-almost.html

Cary, Max. 'The Greeks and Ancient Trade with the Atlantic'. *Journal of Hellenic Studies*, XLIV (1924), pp. 166–79.

Cassius Dio Cocceianus. *Dio's Roman History*. Tr. E. Cary and H. B. Foster. 9 vols. Heinemann, 1914–27.

Castellvi, Georges. *Voies romaines du Rhône à l'Èbre*. Maison des Sciences de l'Homme, 1997.

Champollion-Figeac, Jacques-Joseph. *Nouvelles recherches sur la ville gauloise d''Uxellodunum' assiégée et prise par J. César*. Imprimerie Royale, 1820.

Charles-Edwards, Thomas. 'Language and Society Among the Insular Celts, AD 400–1000'. In M. Aldhouse-Green, ed. *The Celtic World*. Pp. 703–36.

Charrié, Pierre. *Dictionnaire topographique du département de l'Ardèche*. Guénégaud, 1979.

Chassaing, Augustin. *Dictionnaire topographique du département de la Haute-Loire*. Imprimerie Nationale, 1907.

Chazaud, Martial-Alphonse. *Dictionnaire des noms de lieux habités du département de l'Allier*. Moulins: Desrosiers, 1881.

Chevallier, Raymond. *La Romanisation de la Celtique du Pô*. Rome: École Française de Rome, 1983.

Chevallier, R. *Les Voies romaines*. New ed. Picard, 1997.

Chossenot, Raphaëlle, et al. *La Marne*. CAG, 51/1. 2004.

Chossenot, R., et al. *Reims*. CAG, 51/2. 2010.

Chouquer, Gérard, François Favory, et al. *Contribution à la recherche des cadastres antiques*. Les Belles Lettres, 1980.

Chouquer, G. 'L'Émergence de la planimétrie agraire à l'Âge de Fer'. In *Études rurales*, 175–76 (2005).

Chouquer, G., ed. *Les Formes du paysage*. 3 vols. Errance, 1996.

Cicero, Marcus Tullius. *De senectute, De amicitia, De divinatione*. Tr. W. A. Falconer. Heinemann, 1923.

Cicero. *Letters to Atticus*. Ed. D. R. Shackleton Bailey. Vol. II. Cambridge: Cambridge University Press, 1965.

Cicero. *Epistulae ad Quintum fratrem, Epistulae ad M. Brutum*. Ed. D. R. Shackleton Bailey. Stuttgart: Teubner, 1988.

Cicero. *Cicero on Divination: De divinatione, Book 1*. Ed. D. Wardle. Oxford: Clarendon Press, 2006.

Cicero. *Speeches on Behalf of Marcus Fonteius and Marcus Aemilius Scaurus*. Ed. A. R. Dyck. Oxford University Press, 2012.

Clavel, Monique. *Béziers et son territoire dans l'antiquité*. Les Belles Lettres, 1970.

Cliquet, Dominique and Nancy Gauthier. *L'Eure*. CAG, 27. 1993.

Clouzot, Henri. *Niort et sa banlieue: dictionnaire topographique et historique*. Niort: Société historique et scientifique des Deux-Sèvres, 1931.

Cogitosus, St. 'Cogitosus's *Life of St Brigit*'. Tr. S. Connolly and J.-M. Picard. *Journal of the Royal Society of Antiquaries of Ireland*, CXVII (1987), pp. 5–27.

Cogitosus, St. *Vita Prima Sanctae Brigitae*. Tr. S. Connolly. *Journal of the Royal Society of Antiquaries of Ireland*, CXIX (1989), pp. 5–49.

Colin, Anne. *Chronologie des oppida de Gaule*. Maison des Sciences de l'Homme, 1998.

Compayré, Clément. *Études historiques et documents inédits sur l'Albigeois, le Castrais et l'ancien diocèse de Lavaur*. Albi: Papailhiau, 1841.

Condit, Tom and Frank Coyne. *Knockainy Hill: A Ceremonial Landscape in County Limerick*. Bray: Archaeology Ireland, 2004.

Costello, Louisa Stuart. *A Pilgrimage to Auvergne, from Picardy to Le Velay*. 2 vols. Bentley, 1842.

Coupry, Jacques. 'Fouilles à Olbia (Hyères, Var)'. *Gallia*, XII, 1 (1954), pp. 3–33.

Courbin, Pierre. 'Méthodologie des fouilles de villages disparus en France'. *Annales*, XX, 2 (1965), pp. 243–56.

Cravayat, Paul. 'Un nouvel Equoranda de la Cité des Bituriges'. *Mémoires de l'Union des Sociétés savantes de Bourges*, VII (1958), pp. 7–17.

Creighton, John. 'Visions of Power: Imagery and Symbols in Late Iron Age Britain'. *Britannia*, XXVI (1995), pp. 285–301.

Cunliffe, Barry. *Greeks, Romans and Barbarians: Spheres of Interaction.* Batsford, 1988.

Cunliffe, B. *The Celtic World.* 1979; Constable, 1992.

Cunliffe, B. *Wessex to AD 1000.* Longman, 1993.

Cunliffe, B. *The Ancient Celts.* 1997; Penguin, 1999.

Cunliffe, B. *The Extraordinary Voyage of Pytheas the Greek.* 2001; Penguin, 2002.

Cunliffe, B. *Iron Age Communities in Britain.* 4th ed. Routledge, 2005.

Cunliffe, B., ed. *Coinage and Society in Britain and Gaul.* Council for British Archaeology, 1981.

Cunliffe, B. and John Koch, eds. *Celtic From the West: Alternative Perspectives From Archaeology, Genetics, Language and Literature.* Oxford: Oxbow, 2010.

Dauzat, Albert and Charles Rostaing. *Dictionnaire étymologique des noms de lieux en France.* 2nd ed. Guénégaud, 1978.

Davies, Hugh. 'Designing Roman Roads'. *Britannia*, XXIX (1998), pp. 1–16.

Davies, H. *Roads in Roman Britain.* Stroud: Tempus, 2005.

Deanesly, Margaret. *The Pre-Conquest Church in England.* 2nd ed. Black, 1963.

Defente, Virginie. *Les Celtes en Italie du Nord.* Rome: École Française de Rome, 2003.

Delacampagne, Florence. *Le Calvados. CAG*, 14. 1990.

Delamarre, Xavier. *Dictionnaire de la langue gauloise.* 2nd ed. Errance, 2003.

Delamarre, X. *Nomina celtica antiqua.* Errance, 2007.

Delestrée, Louis-Pol. *Monnayages et peuples gaulois du Nord-Ouest.* Errance, 1996.

Delestrée, L.-P. and Marcel Tache. *Nouvel atlas des monnaies gauloises.* Saint-Germain-en-Laye: Commios, 2002–04.

Dellong, Éric. *Narbonne et le narbonnais. CAG*, 11/1. 2002.

Delor, Jean-Paul. *L'Yonne. CAG*, 89. 2002.

Desbordes, Jean-Michel. 'Un problème de géographie historique: le Mediolanum chez les celtes'. *Revue archéologique du Centre de la France*, X, 3–4 (1971), pp. 187–201.

Desforges, A. 'Survivances: les sources païennes et les Pierres Pertuses christianisées du Morvan'. *Bulletin de la Société préhistorique française*, XV, 6 (1918), pp. 301–8.

Deshayes, Albert. *Dictionnaire des noms de lieux bretons.* Douarnenez: Chasse-marée / ArMen, 1999.

Dessertenne, Alain. *La Bourgogne de Saint Martin: histoire, monuments, légendes*. Yens-sur-Morges: Cabédita, 2007.

Devine, Thomas Martin. *To the Ends of the Earth: Scotland's Global Diaspora, 1750–2010*. Allen Lane, 2011.

Deyber, Alain. 'Les Frontières des peuples préromains dans l'Est de la Gaule à la fin de l'époque de la Tène'. In *Actes du colloque 'Frontières en Gaule'*. Ed. R. Chevallier. Université de Tours, 1981. Pp. 28–44.

Dicks, D. R., ed. *The Geographical Fragments of Hipparchus*. Athlone, 1960.

Dilke, O. A. W. *Greek and Roman Maps*. Thames & Hudson, 1985.

Dillon, Matthew. *Pilgrims and Pilgrimage in Ancient Greece*. Routledge, 1997.

Dio Chrysostom. *Dio Chrysostom*. 5 vols. Tr. J. W. Cohoon. Cambridge, Mass.: Harvard University Press, 1932–51.

Diodorus Siculus. *Diodorus of Sicily in Twelve Volumes*. Tr. C. H. Oldfather, et al. Heinemann, 1963–71.

Diogenes Laertius. *Lives of Eminent Philosophers*. Tr. R. D. Hicks. New ed. 2 vols. Heinemann, 1972.

Dionysius of Halicarnassus. *The Roman Antiquities of Dionysius of Halicarnassus*. 7 vols. Tr. E. Cary and E. Spelman. Heinemann, 1937–68.

Dodd, Anne, ed. *Oxford Before the University*. Oxford: Oxford Archaeology, 2003.

Dowden, Ken. *European Paganism*. Routledge, 2000.

Downs, Jane. 'The Shrine at Cadbury Castle: Belief Enshrined'. In A. Gwilt et al., eds. *Reconstructing Iron Age Societies*. Oxford: Oxbow Books, 1997.

Duch, G.-A. 'La Voie héracléenne, voie du mercure et du cinabre'. *Revue archéologique de l'Est*, XV (1964), pp. 123–31.

Dufour, Jean.-E. *Dictionnaire topographique du Forez et des paroisses du Lyonnais et du Beaujolais formant le département de la Loire*. Mâcon: Protat, 1946.

Dunnett, Rosalind and Richard Reece. 'The Excavation of the Roman Theatre at Gosbecks'. *Britannia*, II (1971), pp. 27–47.

Duval, Paul-Marie. *Monnaies gauloises et mythes celtiques*. Hermann, 1987.

Duval, P.-M., et al. *Recueil des inscriptions gauloises*. 4 vols. C.N.R.S., 1985.

Egg, Markus and A. Franz-Lanord. *Le Char de Vix*. Mainz: Verlag des Römisch-Germanischen Zentralmuseums, 1987.

Eratosthenes. *Diè geographischen Fragmente des Eratosthenes*. Ed. H. Berger. 1880; Amsterdam: Meridan, 1964.

Eratosthenes. *Eratosthenes' 'Geography': Fragments Collected and Translated.* Ed. D. Roller. Princeton University Press, 2010.

Eumenius. 'Eumenii pro Instaurandis Scholis'. In *Praise of Later Roman Emperors: The Panegyrici Latini.* Ed. R. A. B. Mynors. Tr. C. E. V. Nixon and B. S. Rodgers. Berkeley: University of California Press, 1994. Pp. 151–77 and 554–63.

Eusebius of Caesarea. Εὐσεβίου του Παμφίλου Εὐαγγελικῆς Προπαρασκευῆς λογοι ιε΄ (*Preparation for the Gospel*). 4 vols. Tr. E. H. Gifford. 1903.

Eustathius. [Commentary on Dionysius Periegetes]. In *Extraits des auteurs grecs concernant la géographie et l'histoire des Gaules.* 6 vols. Ed. E. Cougny. Renouard, 1878–92. I, 5–15.

Eutropius, Flavius. *See* Justinus.

Evans, Edith. *Early Medieval Ecclesiastical Sites in Southeast Wales.* Swansea: Glamorgan-Gwent Archaeological Trust, 2003.

Evans, James. *The History and Practice of Ancient Astronomy.* Oxford University Press, 1998.

Evans, Sir John. *The Coins of the Ancient Britons.* J. R. Smith, 1864.

Faintich, Marshall. *Astronomical Symbols on Ancient and Medieval Coins.* Jefferson: McFarland, 2008.

Falc'hun François and Bernard Tanguy. *Les Noms de lieux celtiques.* Geneva: Slatkine, 1982; Rennes: Éditions armoricaines, 1970; Bourg-Blanc, Plabennec: Éditions armoricaines, 1966.

Fauduet, Isabelle, et al. *Atlas des sanctuaires romano-celtiques de Gaule.* Errance, 1993.

Faure-Brac, Odile. *Le Rhône. CAG,* 69/1. 2006.

Fear, Andrew. 'A Journey to the End of the World'. In *Pilgrimage in Graeco-Roman and Early Christian Antiquity.* Ed. J. Elsner and I. Rutherford. Oxford University Press, 2005.

Ferrar, Michael J. 'From the Dee / Humber to the Solway / Tyne, AD 79: The Roman Disposition of Fortresses and Forts, and the Survey Technique Uncovered': http://www.cartographyunchained.com/rm1.html

Ferrar, M. J. and Alan Richardson. *The Roman Survey of Britain.* Oxford: Hedges, 2003.

Fichtl, Stephan. *Les Gaulois du Nord de la Gaule (150 – 20 av. J.-C.).* Errance, 1994.

Fichtl, S. *La Ville celtique. Les Oppida de 150 av. J.-C. à 15 ap. J.-C.* New ed. Errance, 2005.

Fichtl, S. and A. M. Adam. *L'Oppidum médiomatrique du Fossé des Pandours: rapport intermédiaire*. Strasbourg: Université Marc Bloch, 2004.

Fillioux, Antoine. *Nouvel essai d'interprétation et de classification des monnaies de la Gaule*. 2nd ed. Rollin et Feuardent, 1867.

Flete, John. *The History of Westminster Abbey*. C. 1450; Ed. J. A. Robinson. Cambridge University Press, 1909.

Florus, Lucius Annaeus. *Epitome of Roman History*. Tr. E. S. Forster. 1927. Heinemann, 1984.

Flotté, Pascal. *Metz*. CAG, 57/2. 2005.

Flotté, P. and Matthieu Fuchs. *Le Bas-Rhin*. CAG, 67/1. 2000.

Forbes, Henry. 'The Topography of Caesar's Last Campaign Against the Bellovaci'. *Geographical Journal*, LIX, 3 (March 1922), pp. 195–206.

Forde-Johnston, James. *Hillforts of the Iron Age in England and Wales*. Liverpool University Press, 1976.

Fortia d'Urban, Agricole-Joseph. *Antiquités et monumens du département de Vaucluse*. 2 parts. Déterville, 1808.

Fortia d'Urban, A.-J. *Recueil des itinéraires anciens, comprenant l'Itinéraire d'Antonin, la Table de Peutinger, et un choix des périples grecs*. Ed. B. Miller. Imprimerie Royale, 1845.

Freeman, Philip. *Ireland and the Classical World*. Austin: University of Texas, 2001.

Freeth, Tony. 'Decoding an Ancient Computer'. *Scientific American*, December 2009, pp. 76–83.

Frere, Sheppard and Michael Fulford. 'The Roman Invasion of A.D. 43'. *Britannia*, XXXII (2001), pp. 45–55.

Frere, S. and M. Fulford. 'The *Collegium Peregrinorum* at Silchester'. *Britannia*, XXXIII (2002), pp. 167–75.

Frey, Otto-Herman. 'The Celts in Italy'. In M. Aldhouse-Green, ed. *The Celtic World*. Pp. 515–32.

Frontinus, Sextus Julius. *The Stratagems, and The Aqueducts of Rome*. Tr. C. E. Bennett, et al. Heinemann, 1925.

Frontinus, S. J. 'De limitibus'. In *Corpus agrimensorum romanorum*. Ed. C. Thulin. 1913; Stuttgart: Teubner, 1971.

Frontinus, S. J. *Iuli Frontini Strategemata*. Ed. R. I. Ireland. Leipzig: Teubner, 1990.

Fulford, Michael, A. Clarke and F. Taylor. *Silchester Insula IX: The 'Town Life' Project, 2009–2010*. University of Reading, 2010.

Galliou, Patrick and Éric Philippe. *Le Finistère*. CAG, 29. New ed. 2010.

Galliou, P., et al. *Le Morbihan*. CAG, 56. 2009.

Ganet, Isabelle, et al. *Les Hautes-Alpes. CAG*, 5. 1995.

Garcia, D. and F. Verdin, eds. *Territoires celtiques: espaces ethniques et territoires des agglomérations protohistoriques d'Europe occidentale.* Errance, 2002.

Gasca Queirazza, Giuliano. *Dizionario di toponomastica.* Turin: UTET, 1990; 1995.

Gateau, Fabienne, et al. *L'Étang de Berre. CAG*, 13/1. 1996.

Gauchat, Louis. '*Medius* et ses dérivés romands'. *Vox Romanica*, II (1937), pp. 34–46.

Gellius, Aulus. *The Attic Nights of Aulus Gellius.* 3 vols. Tr. J. C. Rolfe. 1927; Cambridge, Mass.: Harvard University Press, 1961.

Gendron, Stéphane. *La Toponymie des voies romaines et médiévales.* Errance, 2006.

Geoffrey of Monmouth. *Historia Regum Britanniae.* Ed. J. Hammer. Cambridge, Mass.: Mediaeval Academy of America, 1951.

Geoffrey of Monmouth. *The History of the Kings of Britain.* Ed. M. D. Reeve and N. Wright. Woodbridge: Boydell, 2007.

Germer-Durand, Eugène. *Dictionnaire topographique du département du Gard.* Imprimerie Impériale, 1868.

Gibbon, William B. 'Asiatic Parallels in North American Star Lore: Ursa Major'. *Journal of American Folklore*, LXXVII, 305 (1964), pp. 236–50.

Gibbs, Sharon. *Greek and Roman Sundials.* New Haven, Conn.: Yale University Press, 1976.

Gildas. *The Ruin of Britain* [*De Excidio et Conquestu Britanniae*], *and Other Works.* Ed. M. Winterbottom. Phillimore, 1978.

Giot, P.-R. and J.-B. Colbert de Beaulieu. 'Un statère d'or de Cyrénaïque découvert sur une plage bretonne et la route atlantique de l'étain'. *Bulletin de la Société préhistorique de France*, LVIII, 5–6 (1961), pp. 324–31.

Giraldus Cambrensis (Gerald of Wales). *Giraldi Cambrensis Opera.* Ed. J. F. Dimock. Vol. VI. *Itinerarium Kambriae et Descriptio Kambriae.* Longmans, 1868.

Giraldus Cambrensis. *The Topography of Ireland: Its Miracles and Wonders.* In *The Historical Works of Giraldus Cambrensis.* Ed. T. Wright. Bell, 1894.

Giraldus Cambrensis. *The Journey Through Wales and The Description of Wales.* Tr. L. Thorpe. Penguin, 1978.

Giumlia-Mair, Alessandra and Fulvia Lo Schiavo, eds. *Le Problème de l'étain.* Oxford: Archaeopress, 2003.

Goggi, Clelio. *Toponomastica ligure dell'antica e della nuova Liguria*. Genoa: Bozzi, 1967.

Goodchild, Richard George and John Bryan Ward Perkins. 'The Limes Tripolitanus in the Light of Recent Discoveries'. *Journal of Roman Studies*, XXXIX, 1–2 (1949), pp. 81–95.

Gorphe, Jacques. *Le Trésor de Tayac*. Les Chevau-légers, 2009.

Goudineau, Christian. *César et la Gaule*. New ed. Errance, 2000.

Goudineau, C. and Christian Peyre. *Bibracte et les Éduens*. Errance, 1993.

Gourgues, Alexis-Joseph-Dominique de. *Dictionnaire topographique du département de la Dordogne*. Imprimerie Nationale, 1873.

Grässe, Johann Georg Theodor and Friedrich Benedict. *Orbis Latinus: Lexikon lateinischer geographischer Namen des Mittelalters und der Neuzeit*. 3 vols. Ed. H. and S. C. Plechl. Braunschweig: Klinkhardt & Biermann, 1972.

Graves, Louis. *Notice archéologique sur le département de l'Oise*. Beauvais: Desjardins, 1839.

The Greek Anthology. 5 vols. Tr. W. R. Paton. 1916–18. Cambridge, Mass.: Harvard University Press, 1993.

Gregory, Tony. *Excavations in Thetford, 1980–1982: Fison Way*. 2 vols. Dereham: Norfolk Museum Service, 1991.

Gregory of Tours. *Sancti Georgii Florentii Gregorii, episcopi Turonensis: Opera omnia*. Ed. T. Ruinart. Migne, 1849.

Guillaumin, Jean-Yves. *Mathématiques dans l'antiquité*. Université de Saint-Étienne, 1992.

Guyonvarc'h, Christian-Joseph. 'Vocabulaire vieux-celtique'. *Ogam*, XII (1960), pp. 403–4 and 531–32.

Guyonvarc'h, C.-J. 'Mediolanum Biturigum: deux éléments de vocabulaire religieux et de géographie sacrée'. *Ogam*, XIII (1961), pp. 137–58.

Gysseling, Maurits. *Toponymisch Woordenboek van België, Nederland, Luxemburg, Noord-Frankrijk en West-Duitsland, voor 1226*. Brussels: Belgisch Interuniversitair Centrum voor Neerlandistiek, 1960.

Haigneré, Daniel. *Dictionnaire topographique de la France . . . arrondissement de Boulogne-sur-Mer*. Boulogne-sur-Mer: Aigre, 1881.

Hall, Rev. Peter. *A Brief History of Old and New Sarum*. Salisbury: Brodie, 1834.

Hamerton, Philip Gilbert. *The Mount: Narrative of a Visit to the Site of a Gaulish City on Mount Beuvray*. Seeley, 1897.

Hamlin, Frank and André Cabrol. *Les Noms de lieux du département de l'Hérault*. Nîmes: Lacour, 1988.

Hamm, Gilles. *La Meurthe-et-Moselle. CAG*, 54. 2004.

Hanno. *Periplus, or Circumnavigation of Africa*. Ed. A. N. Oikonomides, et al. 3rd ed. Chicago: Ares, 1995.

Harding, Anthony F. *European Societies in the Bronze Age*. Cambridge University Press, 2000.

Harding, Dennis W. *The Iron Age in Northern Britain: Celts and Romans, Natives and Invaders*. Routledge, 2004.

Hardy, Philip Dixon. *The Holy Wells of Ireland*. Dublin: Hardy, 1836.

Harley, John Brian and David Woodward, eds. *The History of Cartography*. Vol. I. University of Chicago Press, 1987.

Heath, Thomas. *A History of Greek Mathematics*. 2 vols. Oxford: Clarendon Press, 1921.

Henry of Huntingdon. *Historia Anglorum (History of the English People)*. Ed. D. E. Greenway. Oxford: Clarendon Press, 1996.

Hero of Alexandria. *Heronis Alexandrini opera quae supersunt omnia*. Ed. W. Schmidt. 5 vols. Stuttgart: Teubner, 1899–1914.

Herodian. *Herodian of Antioch's History of the Roman Empire*. Tr. E. C. Echols. Berkeley: University of California Press, 1961.

Herodotus. *Herodotus*. Tr. A. D. Godley. New ed. 4 vols. Heinemann, 1982.

Herodotus. *Herodotus*. Tr. D. Grene. University of Chicago Press, 1987.

Hesiod. *Theogony, and Works and Days*. Ed. M. L. West. Oxford University Press, 1988.

Higden, Ranulf. *Polychronicon Ranulphi Higden monachi Cestrensis*. 9 vols. Ed. C. Babington. Longman, 1865–86.

Hill, J. D. and L. Horne. 'The Iron Age and Early Roman Pottery'. In Christopher Evans, et al., eds. *Power and Island Communities: Excavations at the Wardy Hill Ringwork, Coveney, Ely*. Cambridge Archaeological Unit, 2003.

Hill, Rosemary. *Stonehenge*. Profile, 2008.

Hingley, Richard and Christina Unwin. *Boudica: Iron Age Warrior Queen*. Hambledon, 2005.

Hippeau, Célestin. *Dictionnaire topographique du département du Calvados*. Imprimerie Nationale, 1883.

Hippolytus of Rome. *Philosophumena, or The Refutation of All Heresies*. Tr. F. Legge. 2 vols. SPCK, 1921.

Hofeneder, Andreas. *Die Religion der Kelten in den antiken literarischen Zeugnissen*. 3 vols. Vienna: Verlag der Österreichischen Akademie der Wissenschaften, 2005.

Holder, Alfred. *Alt-celtischer Sprachschatz*. 3 vols. Leipzig: Teubner, 1896–1913.

Hollis, Adrian Swayne. *Fragments of Roman Poetry, c. 60 BC – AD 20.* Oxford University Press, 2007.

Holmes, Thomas Rice. *Caesar's Conquest of Gaul*. 2nd ed. Oxford: Clarendon Press, 1911.

Hoskin, Michael. *Tombs, Temples and their Orientations*. Bognor Regis: Ocarina, 2001.

Houston, George W. 'The State of the Art: Current Work in the Technology of Ancient Rome'. *The Classical Journal*, LXXXV, 1 (1989), pp. 63–80.

Hoyte, John. *Trunk Road for Hannibal*. Bles, 1960.

Humphrey, Lauren. 'Saint Patrick and the Druids: A Window into Seventh-Century Irish Church Politics'. Thesis. University of Michigan, 2009.

Hyginus, Gaius Julius. *L'Astronomie*. Ed. A. Le Boeuffle. Les Belles Lettres, 1983.

Hyginus Gromaticus. *Hygin: l'œuvre gromatique: corpus agrimensorum Romanorum*. Tr. O. Behrends. Luxembourg: Office des Publications officielles des Communautés européennes, 2000.

Isler, Martin. 'The Gnomon in Egyptian Antiquity'. *Journal of the American Research Center in Egypt*, XXVIII (1991), pp. 155–85.

Jaccard, Henri. *Essai de toponymie: origine des noms de lieux habités et des lieux-dits de la Suisse romande*. Lausanne: Bridel, 1906.

Janni, Pietro. *La Mappa e il periploi: cartografia antica e spazio odologico*. Rome: Bretschneider, 1984.

Jannoray, Jean. *Ensérune: contribution à l'étude des civilisations pré-romaines de la Gaule méridionale*. Boccard, 1955.

Jerome, St. *The Principal Works of St. Jerome*. Tr. W. H. Fremantle. Oxford: Parker, 1893.

Jersey, Philip de. 'Exotic Celtic Coinage'. *Oxford Journal of Archaeology*, XVIII, 2 (1999), pp. 189–216.

Jespers, Jean-Jacques. *Dictionnaire des noms de lieux en Wallonie et à Bruxelles*. Brussels: Racine, 2005.

Joly, Martine. *Langres*. CAG, 52/2. 2001.

Jones, Barri and D. J. Mattingly. *An Atlas of Roman Britain*. Oxford: Blackwell, 1990.

Jope, Martin. 'The Social Implications of Celtic Art, 600 BC to AD 600'. In M. Aldhouse-Green, ed. *The Celtic World*. Pp. 376–410.

Josephus, Flavius. *The Work of Flavius Josephus*. Tr. W. Whiston. Halifax: Milner, 1850.

Jufer, Nicole and T. Luginbühl. *Les Dieux gaulois: répertoire des noms de divinités celtiques connus par l'épigraphie, les textes antiques et la toponymie*. Errance, 2001.

Jullian, Camille. *Histoire de la Gaule*. 8 vols. Hachette, 1908–26.

Justinus, Marcus Junianus. 'Epitome of *The Philippic History* of Pompeius Trogus'. In *Justin, Cornelius Nepos, and Eutropius*. Tr. J. S. Watson. Bohn, 1853.

Kaye, Steve. 'Finding the Site of Boudica's Last Battle: An Approach Via Terrain Analysis' (2010): http://www.bandaarcgeophysics.co.uk/Boudica/Boudica-terrain-analysis.pdf.

Kelley, David H. and E. F. Milone. *Exploring Ancient Skies: A Survey of Ancient and Cultural Astronomy*. 2nd ed. New York: Springer, 2011.

Kendall, David George. and F. R. Hodson, eds. *The Place of Astronomy in the Ancient World*. Oxford University Press, 1974.

Kilbride-Jones, Howard E. *Celtic Craftsmanship in Bronze*. Croom Helm, 1980.

Knapp, Robert. 'La *Via Heraclea* en el Occidente: mito, arqueología, propaganda, historia'. *Emerita*, LIV, 1 (1986), pp. 103–22.

Koch, John. *Tartessian: Celtic in the South-West at the Dawn of History*. Aberystwyth: Celtic Studies Publications, 2009.

Koch, J. and John Carey, eds. *The Celtic Heroic Age: Literary Sources for Ancient Celtic Europe and Early Ireland and Wales*. 4th ed. Aberystwyth: Celtic Studies Publications, 2003.

Konrad, C. F. *Plutarch's Sertorius: A Historical Commentary*. Chapel Hill: University of North Carolina Press, 1994.

Krausz, Sophie. 'La Topographie et les fortifications celtiques de l'oppidum biturige de Châteaumeillant-Mediolanum (Cher)'. *Revue archéologique du Centre de la France*, XLV–XLVI (2006–2007): http://racf.revues.org/632.

Kruta, Venceslas. *Les Celtes: histoire et dictionnaire*. Laffont, 2000.

Kruta, V. *Celts: History and Civilization*. Hachette, 2004. (Photographs by Dario Bertuzzi, Werner Forman and Erich Lessing.)

Kruta, V. *Celtes, belges, boiens, rèmes, volques*. Mariemont: Musée royal de Mariemont, 2006.

La Bédoyère, Guy de. *Roman Britain: A New History*. Thames & Hudson, 2006; 2010.

Labrousse, Michel and Guy Mercadier. *Le Lot*. *CAG*, 46. 1990.

Lajoye, Patrick. 'Lug, Caradoc, Budoc'. *Ollodagos*, XIX, 1 (2005), pp. 51–116.

Lambert, Émile. *Dictionnaire topographique du département de l'Oise*. Amiens: Musée de Picardie, 1982.

Lamoine, Laurent. *Le Pouvoir local en Gaule romaine*. Clermont-Ferrand: Presses universitaires Blaise-Pascal, 2009.

Lancel, Serge. *Saint Augustine*. Tr. A. Nevill. SCM Press, 2002.

Lebel, Paul. 'Où en est le problème d'Equoranda?' *Romania*, LXIII (1937), pp. 145–203.

Lebel, P. *Principes et méthodes d'hydronymie française*. Les Belles Lettres, 1956.

Lebor Gabála Érenn: The Book of the Taking of Ireland [The Book of Invasions]. 6 vols. Ed. R. A. S. Macalister. Dublin: Irish Texts Society, 1938–2009.

Lecler, André. *Dictionnaire historique et géographique de la Haute-Vienne*. 2 vols. Marseille: Laffitte, 1976.

Le Contel, Jean-Michel and Paul Verdier. *Un calendrier celtique*. Errance, 1997.

Le Gall, Joël. 'Les Romains et l'orientation solaire'. *Mélanges de l'École Française de Rome. Antiquité*, LXXXVII, 1 (1975), pp. 287–320.

Leigh, Samuel. *Leigh's New Pocket Road-Book of England and Wales*. 4th ed. Leigh, 1833.

Leland, John. *The Itinerary of John Leland the Antiquary*. 9 vols. Ed. T. Hearne. Oxford University Press, 1710–12.

Lelgemann, Dieter. 'On the Ancient Determination of the Meridian Arc Length by Eratosthenes of Kyrene' (2004): http://www.fig.net/pub/athens/papers/wshs1/wshs1_1_lelgemann.pdf.

Léman, P. 'La Voie de l'Océan: la branche orientale'. In *Actes du colloque, 'Du Léman à l'Océan'. Caesarodunum*, 10 (1975), pp. 102–8.

Lenerz-de Wilde, Majolic. *Zirkelornamentik in der Kunst der Latènezeit*. Munich: Beck, 1977.

Lenerz-de Wilde, M. 'The Celts in Spain'. In M. Aldhouse-Green, ed. *The Celtic World*. Pp. 533–51.

Lepage, Henri. *Dictionnaire topographique du département de la Meurthe*. Imprimerie Impériale, 1862.

Le Roux, Françoise. 'Le Dieu celtique aux liens, de l'Ogmios de Lucien à l'Ogmios de Dürer'. *Ogam*, XII (1960), pp. 209–34.

Le Roux, F. and C. Guyonvarc'h. *Les Druides*. 2nd ed. Rennes: Ogam-Celticum, 1978.

Leroux, Gilles and Alain Provost. *L'Ille-et-Vilaine*. *CAG*, 35. 1990.

Lewis, Michael J. T. *Surveying Instruments of Greece and Rome*. Cambridge University Press, 2001.

Lhermet, J. *Autour du Mont-Milan*. Aurillac: Lescure, 1922.

Liénard, Félix. *Dictionnaire topographique du département de la Meuse*. Imprimerie Nationale, 1872.

Livy (Titus Livius). *History of Rome*. Ed. B. O. Foster, et al. 14 vols. Heinemann, 1919–59.

Livy. *The Early History of Rome: Books I-V of The History of Rome from its Foundation*. Tr. A. de Sélincourt. Penguin, 1960.

Livy. *The Rise of Rome: Books One to Five*. Tr. T. J. Luce. Oxford University Press, 1998; 2008.

Lloyd-Morgan, Glenys. 'Appearance, Life and Leisure'. In M. Aldhouse-Green, ed. *The Celtic World*. Pp. 95–120.

Longnon, Auguste. *Dictionnaire topographique du département de la Marne*. Imprimerie Nationale, 1891.

Longnon, A. *Les Noms de lieu de la France*. Champion, 1920–29.

Lucan. *The Pharsalia of Lucan*. Tr. E. Ridley. 2nd ed. Longmans. 1905.

Lucan. *Civil War [Pharsalia]*. Tr. J. D. Duff. 1928; Cambridge, Mass.: Harvard University Press, 2006.

Lucas, Jack. *Tripontium: The Discovery and Excavation of a Roman Settlement on the Watling Street near Rugby*. Lutterworth: Irene Glendinning, 1997.

Lucian of Samosata. *Lucian*. 8 vols. Tr. A. M. Harmon, et al. 1913–67; Heinemann, 1961–79.

Lugand, Marc and Louri Bermond. *Agde et le Bassin de Thau*. *CAG*, 34/2. 2001.

The Mabinogion. Tr. J. Gantz. Penguin, 1976.

Macrobius, Ambrosius Aurelius Theodosius. *Saturnalia*. 3 vols. Ed. R. A. Kaster. Cambridge, Mass.: Harvard University Press, 2011.

Magli, Giulio. 'On the Orientation of Roman Towns in Italy'. *Oxford Journal of Archaeology*, XXVII, 1 (2008), pp. 63–71.

Mahaney, William, et al. 'Hannibal's Trek Across the Alps: Geomorphological Analysis of Sites of Geoarchaeological Interest'. *Mediterranean Archaeology and Archaeometry*, VIII, 2 (2008), pp. 39–54.

Maître, Léon-Auguste. *Dictionnaire topographique du département de la Mayenne*. Imprimerie Nationale, 1878.

Malsy, Jean-Claude. *Dictionnaire des noms de lieu du département de l'Aisne*. 3 vols. Champaubert: Société Française d'Onomastique, 1999–2001.

Maravelia, Amanda-Alice. *Ad astra per aspera et per ludum: European Archaeoastronomy and the Orientation of Monuments in the Mediterranean Basin*. Oxford: Archaeopress, 2003.

Margary, Ivan D. *Roman Roads in Britain*. 3rd ed. Baker, 1973.

Marichal, Paul-Georges-François-Joseph. *Dictionnaire topographique du département des Vosges*. Imprimerie Nationale, 1941.

Mastrelli Anzilotti, Giulia. *Toponomastica trentina*. Trento: Servizio Beni librari e archivistici, 2003.

Matton, Auguste. *Dictionnaire topographique du département de l'Aisne*. Imprimerie Nationale, 1871.

Maurin, Louis, et al. *Saintes*. CAG, 17/2. 2007.

Maximus of Tyre. *The Philosophical Orations*. Tr. M. B. Trapp. Oxford: Clarendon Press, 1997.

McGrail, Sean. 'Celtic Seafaring and Transport'. In M. Aldhouse-Green, ed. *The Celtic World*. Pp. 254–81.

Mela, Pomponius. *Pomponius Mela's Description of the World*. Ed. F. E. Romer. Ann Arbor: University of Michigan Press, 1998.

Memnon. [History of Heracleia]. No. 434 in *Die Fragmente der griechischen Historiker*. Ed. F. Jacoby. Part 3. Leiden: Brill, 1955.

Menche de Loisne, Auguste-Charles-Henri. *Dictionnaire topographique du département du Pas-de-Calais*. Imprimerie Nationale, 1907.

Menéndez Pidal, Ramón. *Toponimia prerrománica hispana*. Madrid: Gredos, 1952.

Merlet, Luc. *Dictionnaire topographique du département d'Eure-et-Loir*. Imprimerie Impériale, 1861.

Miller, Konrad. *Itineraria romana*. Stuttgart: Strecker und Schröder, 1916.

Mills, Anthony David. *A Dictionary of British Place-Names*. 1998. Rev. ed. Oxford University Press, 2003.

Moitrieux, Gérard. *Hercules in Gallia*. Boccard, 2002.

Momméja, Jules. *L'Oppidum des Nitiobriges*. Caen: Delesques, 1903.

Monceaux, Paul. 'Le Grand temple du Puy-de-Dôme'. *Revue historique*, XXXV (1887), pp. 1–28; XXXVI (1888), pp. 241–78.

Montaigne, Michel de. *Les Essais*. Ed. J. Balsamo et al. Gallimard, 2007.

Moret, Pierre. 'Tolosa, 106–47 av. J.-C.: topographie et histoire'. *Pallas*, LXXVI (2008), pp. 295–329.

Morris-Jones, John. *A Welsh Grammar, Historical and Comparative*. Oxford: Clarendon Press, 1913.

Moussas, Xenophon. 'The Antikythera Mechanism: Astronomy,

Mathematics and Technology Embedded in the First Mechanical Universe' (2011): http://www.astro.unipd.it/insap6/INSAP6_web. pdf.

Mugler, Charles. *Dictionnaire historique de la terminologie géométrique des Grecs*. 2 vols. Klincksieck, 1958–59.

Murray, Gordon. 'The Declining Pictish Symbol: A Reappraisal'. *Proceedings of the Society of Antiquaries of Scotland*, CXVI (1986), pp. 223–53.

Musée des Antiquités Nationales. *Vercingétorix et Alésia*. Réunion des Musées Nationaux, 1994.

Napoléon III. *Histoire de Jules César*. 2 vols. Plon, 1865–66.

Nègre, Ernest. *Les Noms de lieux du Tarn*. 2nd ed. Artrey, 1959.

Nègre, E. *Toponymie générale de la France*. 4 vols. Geneva: Droz, 1990–98.

Nennius [?]. *The Historia Brittonum*. Ed. D. N. Dumville. Cambridge: Brewer, 1985.

Nepos, Cornelius. *Cornelius Nepos*. Tr. J. C. Rolfe. 1929. Cambridge, Mass.: Harvard University Press, 1984.

Newman, Conor, et al. *Tara: An Archaeological Survey*. Dublin: Royal Irish Academy, 1997.

Nickels, André, et al. 'La Nécropole du premier Âge du fer d'Agde'. *Mélanges de l'École Française de Rome. Antiquité*, XCIII, 1 (1981), pp. 89–125.

Nicolaï, Alexandre. *Les Noms de lieux de la Gironde*. Bordeaux: Féret, 1938.

Northover, Peter. 'The Technology of Metalwork: Bronze and Gold'. In M. Aldhouse-Green, ed. *The Celtic World*. Pp. 285–309.

Óengus the Culdee, St. *Félire Óengusso Céli dé. The Martyrology of Oengus the Culdee*. Ed. W. Stokes. Harrison and Sons, 1905.

Olivieri, Dante. *Toponomastica veneta*. 2nd ed. Venice: Istituto per la collaborazione culturale, 1962.

Olivieri, D. *Dizionario di toponomastica piemontese*. Brescia: Paideia, 1965.

Ollagnier, Anne and Dominique Joly. *L'Eure-et-Loir*. CAG, 28. 1994.

Olmsted, Garrett. *The Gaulish Calendar*. Bonn: Habelt, 1992.

Orosius, Paulus. *Orosius: Seven Books of History Against the Pagans*. Ed. A. T. Fear. Liverpool University Press, 2010.

Ournac, Perrine, et al. *L'Aude*. CAG, 11/2. 2009.

Parthenius of Nicaea. *The Poetical Fragments and the 'Erōtika pathēmata'*. Ed. J. L. Lightfoot. Oxford: Clarendon Press, 1999.

Parthey, Gustav, et al., eds. *Ravennatis Anonymi Cosmographia*. Berolini: F. Nicolai, 1860.

Pattenden, Philip. 'A Late Sundial at Aphrodisias'. *Journal of Hellenic Studies*, CI (1981), pp. 101–12.

Pausanias. *Description of Greece*. 5 vols. Tr. W. H. S. Jones, et al. Heinemann, 1918–35.

Pennant, Thomas. *The Journey to Snowdon*. Vol. II of *A Tour in Wales*. Hughes, 1783.

Pennick, Nigel. *Celtic Sacred Landscapes*. Thames & Hudson, 1996.

Perrenot, T. *La Toponymie burgonde*. Payot, 1942.

Perrier, Jean, et al. *La Haute-Vienne. CAG*, 87. 1993.

Pesche, Julien-Rémy. *Dictionnaire topographique, historique et statistique de la Sarthe*. Mayenne: Floch, 1974.

Peterson, John. 'Some Computer Tools for Investigating Ancient Cadastres' (2009): http://www.uea.ac.uk/~jwmp/compmethods/cmintro.html.

Pettazzoni, Raffaele. *The All-Knowing God*. Methuen, 1956.

Philipon, Édouard. *Dictionnaire topographique du département de l'Ain*. Imprimerie Nationale, 1911.

Philostratus, Lucius Flavius. *Life of Apollonius*. In *Philostratorum et Callistrati opera*. Ed. A. Westermann. Didot, 1849.

Philp, Brian. *Woolwich Power Station Site, S. E. London (Formerly Kent)*. Dover: Kent Archaeological Rescue Unit, 2010.

Pichon, Blaise. *L'Aisne. CAG*, 2. 2002.

Pichon, B. *Amiens. CAG*, 80/1. 2009.

Piggott, Stuart. *The Druids*. Thames & Hudson, 1968; 1975.

Pilet-Lemière, Jacqueline, et al. *La Manche. CAG*, 50. 1989.

Pilot de Thorey, Emmanuel. *Dictionnaire topographique du département de l'Isère*. Romans: Imprimerie Jeanne-d'Arc, 1921.

Plácido, Daniel. 'Le Vie di Ercole nell'estremo Occidente'. In *Ercole in Occidente*. Ed. A. Mastrocinque. Trento: Labirinti, 1993. Pp. 63–80.

Planhol, Xavier de. *An Historical Geography of France*. Tr. J. Lloyd. Cambridge University Press, 1994.

Pliny the Elder. *Natural History*. 10 vols. Tr. H. Rackham, et al. Heinemann, 1938–63.

Plutarch. *Parallel Lives*. 11 vols. Ed. B. Perrin. Heinemann, 1914–26.

Plutarch. 'De Mulierum Virtutibus'. In *Plutarch's Moralia*. Vol. III. Tr. F. C. Babbitt, et al. Cambridge, Mass.: Harvard University Press, 1931.

Plutarch. *Caesar*. Ed. C. B. R. Pelling. Oxford University Press, 2011.

Pollicini, Angelo. *Archeologia in Valle d'Aosta*. Aosta: Assessorat du Tourisme, Urbanisme et Biens Culturels, 1988.

Polyaenus. *Polyaenus's Stratagems of War*. Tr. R. Shepherd. George Nicol, 1793.

Polybius. *The Histories*. 6 vols. Tr. W. R. Paton. Cambridge, Mass.: Harvard University Press, 1954.

Polybius. *Histoires*. Vols I–VIII and X. Tr. P. Pédech, et al. Les Belles Lettres, 1969–95.

Poret, Bénigne-Ernest. *Dictionnaire topographique du département de l'Eure*. Imprimerie Nationale, 1877.

Posidonius. *Posidonius*. 3 vols. Ed. L. Edelstein and I. G. Kidd. Cambridge University Press, 1972–99.

Potter, Timothy W. and Catherine Johns. *Roman Britain*. British Museum Press, 1992.

Price, Derek J. de Solla. *Gears from the Greeks: The Antikythera Mechanism*. 1974; New York: Science History Publications, 1975.

Provost, Michel. *L'Indre-et-Loire*. CAG, 37. 1988.

Provost, M. *Le Loiret*. CAG, 45. 1988.

Provost, M., et al. *Le Cher*. CAG, 18. 1992.

Provost, M., et al. *Autun: atlas des vestiges gallo-romains*. CAG, 71/2. 1993.

Provost, M., et al. *Le Puy-de-Dôme*. CAG, 63/2. 1994.

Provost, M., et al. *Le Gard*. CAG, 30/2 and 30/3. 1999.

Provost, M., et al. *La Côte-d'Or. Alésia*. CAG, 21/1. 2009.

Pryor, Francis. *The Making of the British Landscape*. Allen Lane, 2010.

Ptolemy. *Ptolemy's Geography: An Annotated Translation of the Theoretical Chapters*. Ed. J. Lennart-Berggren and A. Jones. Princeton University Press, 2000.

Ptolemy. *Klaudios Ptolemaios Handbuch der Geographie: griechisch-deutsch*. 2 vols. Ed. A. Stückelberger, et al. Basel: Schwabe, 2006.

Puel, François. 'La Voie lactée indique-t-elle le Chemin de Compostelle?' *SaintJacquesInfo*, 2012: http://lodel.irevues.inist.fr/saintjacquesinfo/index.php?page=index_2.

Puhvel, Jaan. 'The Origins of Greek *Kosmos* and Latin *Mundus*'. *American Journal of Philology*, XCVII, 2 (1979), pp. 154–67.

Quantin, Mathieu-Maximilien. *Dictionnaire topographique du département de l'Yonne*. Imprimerie Impériale, 1862.

Quatrefages, Armand de. *The Rambles of a Naturalist on the Coasts of France, Spain and Sicily*. Tr. E. C. Otté. 2 vols. Longman, 1857.

Quilgars, Henri. *Dictionnaire topographique du département de la Loire-Inférieure*. Nantes: Durance, 1906.

Raftery, Barry. *Pagan Celtic Ireland: The Enigma of the Irish Iron Age*. Thames & Hudson, 1994.

Ralston, Ian. 'Fortifications and Defence'. In M. Aldhouse-Green, ed. *The Celtic World*. Pp. 59–81.

Ramin, Jacques. *Le Problème des Cassitérides et les sources de l'étain occidental*. Picard, 1965.

Rankin, Herbert D. *Celts and the Classical World*. 1987; Routledge, 1996.

Rawlings, Louis. *Herakles and Hercules: Exploring a Graeco-Roman Divinity*. Swansea: Classical Press of Wales, 2005.

Rawlins, Dennis. 'Pytheas' Solstice Observation Locates Him'. *DIO*, XVI (December 2009), pp. 11–17.

Raymond, Paul. *Dictionnaire topographique du département des Basses-Pyrénées*. Imprimerie Impériale, 1863.

Rebourg. Alain. 'L'Urbanisme d'Augustodunum (Autun, Saône-et-Loire)'. *Gallia*, LV (1998), pp. 141–236.

Rebourg, A., et al. *Autun*. CAG, 71/1. 1993.

Rebourg. A., et al. *Saône-et-Loire*. 2 vols. CAG, 71/3 and 71/4. 1994.

Rédet, Louis. *Dictionnaire topographique du département de la Vienne*. Imprimerie Nationale, 1881.

Redknap, Mark. 'Early Christianity and Its Monuments'. In M. Aldhouse-Green, ed. *The Celtic World*. Pp. 737–78.

Rees, Elizabeth. *Celtic Saints: Passionate Wanderers*. Thames & Hudson, 2000.

Reynolds, Peter J. 'Rural Life and Farming'. In M. Aldhouse-Green, ed. *The Celtic World*. Pp. 176–209.

Richardson, Alan. 'The Orientation of Roman Camps and Forts'. *Oxford Journal of Archaeology*, XXIV, 4 (2005), pp. 415–26.

Richardson, William. *Numbering and Measuring in the Classical World*. 2nd ed. Bristol: Phoenix Press, 2004.

Rico, Christian. *Pyrénées romaines*. Madrid: Casa de Velázquez, 1997.

Rigault, Jean. *Dictionnaire topographique du département de Saône-et-Loire*. CTHS, 2008.

Ritchie, J. N. G. and W. F. 'The Army, Weapons and Fighting'. In M. Aldhouse-Green, ed. *The Celtic World*. Pp. 37–58.

Rivet, Albert Lionel Frederick and Colin Smith. *The Place-Names of Roman Britain*. Batsford, 1979.

Robert, Sandrine, et al. *Dynamique et résilience des réseaux routiers et parcellaires en région Île-de-France*. geoPratiq, 2006–11: http://pratiq.tge-adonis.fr/Observatoire/Projects?ID=101.

Robert of Gloucester. *Robert of Gloucester's Chronicle*. 2 vols. Ed. T. Hearne. Samuel Bagster, 1810.

Roger, Lucien. 'Chaussées Brunehaut, Pires, Piges, Equoranda'. *Zeitschrift für französische Sprache und Literatur*, LXIII (1940), pp. 166–75.

Rogeret, Isabelle, et al. *La Seine-Maritime*. CAG, 76. 1998.

Roland, C. G. *Toponymie namuroise*. Brussels: Schepens, 1899–1903.

Roller, Duane. *Through the Pillars of Herakles: Graeco-Roman Exploration of the Atlantic*. Routledge, 2006.

Rolley, Claude, ed. *La Tombe princière de Vix*. 2 vols. Picard, 2003.

Roman, Danièle et Yves. *La Gaule et ses mythes historiques: de Pythéas à Vercingétorix*. L'Harmattan, 1999.

Roman, Joseph-Hippolyte. *Dictionnaire topographique du département des Hautes-Alpes*. Imprimerie Nationale, 1884.

Roman Scotland. 'Mons Graupius Identified: The Hunt for Ancient Scotland's Great Clash of Arms' (2009): http://www.romanscotland.org.uk/pages/campaigns/mons_graupius/contents.asp.

Romero, Anne-Marie. *Bibracte: archéologie d'une ville gauloise*. Glux-en-Glenne: Bibracte – Centre archéologique européen, 2006.

Rosenzweig, Louis-Theophile. *Dictionnaire topographique du département du Morbihan*. Imprimerie Impériale, 1870.

Roserot, Alphonse. *Dictionnaire topographique du département de la Haute-Marne*. Imprimerie Nationale, 1903.

Roserot, A. *Dictionnaire topographique du département de la Côte-d'Or*. Imprimerie Nationale, 1924.

Ross, Anne. 'Ritual and the Druids'. In M. Aldhouse-Green, ed. *The Celtic World*. Pp. 423–44.

Roth Congès, Anne. 'Modalités pratiques d'implantation des cadastres romains'. *Mélanges de l'École Française de Rome. Antiquité*, CVIII, 1 (1996), pp. 299–422.

Rothé, Marie-Pierre and Henri Tréziny. *Marseille et ses alentours*. CAG, 13/3. 2005.

Rothé, M.-P., et al. *Arles, Crau, Camargue*. CAG, 13/5. 2008.

Roure, Réjane. 'Nouvelles données sur l'occupation protohistorique de Beaucaire (Gard)'. *Documents d'archéologie méridionale*, XXV (2002), pp. 171–214.

Roymans, Nico, Guido Creemers and Simone Scheers, eds. *Late Iron Age*

Gold Hoards from the Low Countries and the Caesarian Conquest of Northern Gaul. Amsterdam University Press, 2012.

Russo, Lucio. *The Forgotten Revolution: How Science Was Born in 300 BC*. Tr. S. Levy. Berlin: Springer, 2004.

Sabarthès, Antoine. *Dictionnaire topographique du département de l'Aude*. Imprimerie Nationale, 1912.

Salway, Peter. *Roman Britain*. Oxford University Press, 1998.

Saulcy, Félicien de. 'Étude topographique sur *l'Ora Maritima* de Rufus Festus Avienus'. *Revue archéologique*, XV (1867), pp. 54–62 and 81–98.

Schot, Roseanne. 'Uisneach Midi a medón Érenn: A Prehistoric "Cult" Centre and "Royal Site" in Co. Westmeath'. *Journal of Irish Archaeology*, XV (2006), pp. 39–71.

Sealey, Paul R. *The Boudican Revolt Against Rome*. Princes Risborough: Shire, 1997; 2004.

Semple, Sarah. 'A Fear of the Past: The Place of the Prehistoric Burial Mound in the Ideology of Middle and Later Anglo-Saxon England'. *World Archaeology*, XXX, 1 (1998), pp. 109–26.

Seneca, Lucius Annaeus. *Naturales Quaestiones*. 2 vols. Ed. T. H. Corcoran. Cambridge, Mass.: Harvard University Press, 1971–72.

Seneca, L. A. *Apocolocyntosis*. Ed. P. T. Eden. Cambridge University Press, 1984.

Shotter, David. *Romans and Britons in North-West England*. Lancaster: Centre for North-West Regional Studies, 1993.

Silius Italicus, Tiberius Catius. *Punica*. 2 vols. Tr. J. D. Duff. 1934. Heinemann, 1983–89.

Smith, Ian G. 'Some Roman Place-Names in Lancashire and Cumbria'. *Britannia*, XXVIII (1997), pp. 372–83.

Soultrait, Georges. *Dictionnaire topographique du département de la Nièvre*. Imprimerie Impériale, 1865.

Soyer, Jacques. *Les Noms de lieux du Loiret*. Roanne: Horvath, 1979.

Stein, Henri. *Dictionnaire topographique du département de Seine-et-Marne*. Imprimerie Nationale, 1954.

Stephen of Byzantium. *Stephanus Byzantinus*. 4 vols. Ed. L. Holstenius, et al. Leipzig: Kühn, 1825.

Stephen of Byzantium. *Stephani Byzantii Ethnica*. 2 vols. Ed. M. Billerbeck, et al. Berolini: W. de Gruyter, 2006–11.

Stiros, Stathis C. 'Accurate Measurements with Primitive Instruments'. *Journal of Archaeological Science*, XXX, 8 (2006), pp. 1058–64.

Stoffel, Georg. *Dictionnaire topographique du département du Haut-Rhin*. 2nd ed. Mulhouse: Bader, 1876.

Strabo. *The Geography of Strabo*. 8 vols. Tr. H. L. Jones and J. R. S. Sterrett. Heinemann, 1954–61.

Suetonius. *Suetonius*. 2 vols. Rev. ed. Tr. J. C. Rolfe. Cambridge, Mass.: Harvard University Press, 1997–98.

Suter, Henry. 'Noms de lieux de Suisse romande, Savoie et environs' (2009): http://henrysuter.ch/glossaires/toponymes.html.

Tacitus, Cornelius. *Tacitus in Five Volumes*. 1914–37. Cambridge, Mass.: Harvard University Press, 1968–70.

Talbert, Richard. 'Peutinger Map Names and Features': http://www.cambridge.org/us/talbert/talbertdatabase/prm.html#toc.

Talbert, R. and R. Unger, eds. *Cartography in Antiquity and the Middle Ages*. Leiden: Brill, 2008.

Talbert, R., et al. *Rome's World: The Peutinger Map Reconsidered*. Cambridge University Press, 2010.

Tavernor, Robert. *Smoot's Ear: The Measure of Humanity*. New Haven, Conn.: Yale University Press, 2007.

Thaurin, J.-M. 'Mémoire sur les antiquités découvertes à Neubourg et dans les paroisses voisines'. *Recueil des travaux de la Société libre d'agriculture, sciences, arts et belles-lettres de l'Eure*, 3rd series, IV (1855–56), pp. 266–86.

Thévenard, Jean-Jacques, et al. *La Haute-Marne*. CAG, 52/1. 1996.

Thom, Alexander. *Megalithic Lunar Observatories*. Oxford University Press, 1971.

Thomas, Charles. *Christianity in Roman Britain to AD 500*. Batsford, 1981.

Thomas, Eugène. *Dictionnaire topographique du département de l'Hérault*. Imprimerie Impériale, 1865.

Thomson, J. Oliver. *History of Ancient Geography*. Cambridge University Press, 1948.

Todd, Malcolm. '*Oppida* and the Roman Army'. *Oxford Journal of Archaeology*, IV, 2 (1985), pp. 187–99.

Toupet, Christophe, et al. 'Vers une géométrie des enclos quadrangulaires celtiques à partir du cas des enclos de Bruyère-sur-Oise (Val-d'Oise)'. *Bulletin du Vexin Français*, 36 (2004), pp. 5–19.

Trément, Frédéric. *Archéologie d'un paysage: les Étangs de Saint-Blaise, Bouches-du-Rhône*. Maison des Sciences de l'Homme, 1999.

Trintignac, Alain, et al. *La Lozère*. CAG, 48. New ed. 2012.

Trousset, Pol. 'Les Bornes du Bled Segui: nouveaux aperçus sur la centuriation romaine du Sud tunisien'. *Antiquités africaines*, XII (1978), pp. 125–77.

Turquin, Pierre. 'La Bataille de la Selle (du Sabis) en l'an 57 avant J.-C'. *Études classiques*, XXIII (1955), pp. 113–56.

Vadé, Yves. 'Le Système des Mediolanum en Gaule'. *Archéocivilisation*. New series, 11–13 (1972–74), pp. 87–109.

Vadé, Y. 'Le Problème des Mediolanum'. In Centre de recherches A. Piganiol. *Le Vicus gallo-romain*. Université de Tours, 1976. Pp. 50–58.

Vadé, Y. 'Nouvelles recherches sur les Mediolanum gaulois'. *Mythologie française*, 201 (2000), pp. 2–35.

Vadé, Y. *Pour un tombeau de Merlin*. Corti, 2008.

Valerius Maximus. *Memorable Deeds and Sayings*. Ed. D. Wardle. Oxford: Clarendon Press, 1998.

Vallée, Eugène and Raymond Latouche. *Dictionnaire topographique du département de la Sarthe*. 2 vols. Imprimerie Nationale, 1950–52.

Vannérus, Jules. 'Noms de lieu du type "equoranda" '. *Bulletin de la Commission Royale de toponymie et de dialectologie*, IX (1935), pp. 129–63.

Velleius Paterculus. *Compendium of Roman History*. Tr. F. W. Shipley. 1924. Cambridge, Mass.: Harvard University Press, 1979.

Verger, Stéphane. *Les Tombes à char de la Tène ancienne en Champagne*. 3 vols. Dijon: Université de Bourgogne, 1994.

Villar, Francisco. *Estudios de celtibérico y de toponomia prerromana*. Ediciones Universidad Salamanca, 1995.

Vincent, Augustine-Berthe. *Les Noms de lieux de la Belgique*. Brussels: Librairie générale, 1927.

Vincent, A.-B. *Toponymie de la France*. Brussels: Librairie générale, 1937.

Vion, Éric. 'L'Analyse archéologique des réseaux routiers: une rupture méthodologique, des réponses nouvelles'. In *Paysages découverts: histoire, géographie et archéologie du territoire en Suisse romande*. Vol. I. Lausanne: Groupe romand d'archéologie du territoire, 1989. Pp. 67–99.

Waddelove, E. 'The Location of Roman "Coccium"?'. *Britannia*, XXXII (2001), pp. 299–304.

Wagenvoort, Hendrik. 'The Journey of the Souls of the Dead to the Isles of the Blessed'. *Mnemosyne*, XXIV, 2 (1971), pp. 113–61.

Walbank, Frank. *Selected Papers: Studies in Greek and Roman History and Historiography*. Cambridge University Press, 1985.

Wallis, Helen and A. H. Robinson. *Cartographical Innovations: An International Handbook of Mapping Terms to 1900.* Tring: Map Collector Publications, 1987.

Warner, Richard. 'The "Prehistoric" Irish Annals: Fable or History?' *Archaeology Ireland*, IV, 1 (1990), pp. 30–33.

Watkins, Alfred. *The Old Straight Track: Its Mounds, Beacons, Moats, Sites, and Mark Stones.* Methuen, 1925.

Watson, William J. *The History of the Celtic Place-Names of Scotland.* Edinburgh: Birlinn, 1993; 2011.

Webster, Graham. *Rome Against Caratacus.* Batsford, 1981.

Webster, G. *The Roman Invasion of Britain.* New ed. Batsford, 1993.

Webster, G. *Boudica: The British Revolt Against Rome, AD 60.* Rev. ed. Routledge, 1993; 1999.

Webster, G. 'The Celtic Britons Under Rome'. In M. Aldhouse-Green, ed. *The Celtic World.* Pp. 623–35.

Webster, Jane. 'At the End of the World: Druidic and Other Revitalization Movements in Post-Conquest Gaul and Britain'. *Britannia*, XXX (1999), pp. 1–20.

Weinberg, Gladys Davidson, et al. 'The Antikythera Shipwreck Reconsidered'. *Transactions of the American Philosophical Society*, LV, 3 (1965), pp. 3–48.

Wells, Peter S. 'Resources and Industry'. In M. Aldhouse-Green, ed. *The Celtic World.* Pp. 213–29.

Wells, P. S. 'Trade and Exchange'. In M. Aldhouse-Green, ed. *The Celtic World.* Pp. 230–43.

West, William Kyer, 'Problems in the Cultural History of the Ellipse'. *Technology and Culture*, XIX, 4 (1978), pp. 709–12.

Wheeler, Mortimer and K. M. Richardson. *Hill Forts of Northern France.* Oxford: Printed at the University Press for the Society of Antiquaries, 1957.

White, Gleeson. *The Cathedral Church of Salisbury: A Description of Its Fabric and A Brief History of the See of Sarum.* Bell, 1901.

White, Raymond. 'Determining the Orientation of le Bassin monumental de Bibracte' (1991): http://revistas.ucm.es/index.php/CMPL/article/view/CMPL9191220275A/30086.

Whymper, Edward. *Escalades dans les Alpes de 1860 à 1869.* Tr. A. Joanne. Hachette, 1873.

Wickham, Henry L., et al. *A Dissertation on the Passage of Hannibal Over the Alps.* Oxford: Parker, 1820.

Wieland, Günther, et al. *Keltische Viereckschanzen: einem Rätsel auf der Spur.* Stuttgart: Theiss, 1999.

Williamson, May G. 'The Non-Celtic Place-Names of the Scottish Border Counties'. Thesis. University of Edinburgh, 1942. Rep. by Scottish Place-Name Society: http://www.spns.org.uk/MayWilliamsonComplete.pdf.

Woimant, Georges-Pierre. *L'Oise. CAG*, 60. 1995.

Woolliscroft, D. J. 'Signalling and the Design of the Antonine Wall'. *Britannia*, XXVII (1996), pp. 153–77.

Zanotto, Andrea. *Valle d'Aosta antica e archeologica.* Aosta: Musumeci, 1986.

Zeepvat, R. J., et al. 'A Roman Coin Manufacturing Hoard from "Magiovinium", Fenny Stratford, Bucks'. *Britannia*, XXV (1994), pp. 1–19.

General Index

Aduatuci / Atuatuci tribe 25, 155, 188–9, 194

Aedui tribe or federation xvi, 66, 84, 111–13, 114, 198, 199
   migration 152, 153, 159
   relations with Rome 107–8, 196, 210

Agache, Roger 69

Agesinates tribe 140

Agricola, Gnaeus Julius 104–6, 253, 264, 266, 267–8, 269, 270, 273

agriculture xv, 8, 12, 149, 180, 191, 194

Agrippina the Younger 249

Alban, Saint 237

Alexander the Great 96, 99, 100

Allobroges tribe 160, 176

Ambarri tribe 152, 160

Ambiani tribe 56, 72, 160

Ambigatus, king of the Celts 151

Ambrosius (Emrys) Aurelianus 224, 256, 291

Amphitryon 115

Ananes / Anani tribe 158

Andosini tribe 5

Andossus, god 306

Antikythera Mechanism 87–9, 95, 100

Antoninus Pius, emperor 50, 52

Apollo, god 172, 179, 291

Aquitanian tribes 114, 194

Archimedes 142

Aristotle 90, 91, 132, 133, 140, 143, 162

Armorican tribes 191

Arnold, Matthew ix

art, Celtic see La Tène

Arthur, king of the Britons 223–4, 256, 289–90

Arverni tribe or federation 84, 107, 180, 182, 202, 208
   defeat by Rome 176–7, 187, 192
   in Gallic War 31, 32, 196, 197
   migration 152, 159

Arvii tribe 143, 155

Astérix 29, 82, 297

astronomy 16, 88–9, 96, 98–100, 101, 105–6, 108, 121, 123, 129, 131, 147, 148

Atacini tribe 138–9, 155

Atrebates tribe
   British 211, 216, 229, 245
   Gaulish 155, 211, 216

Attila the Hun 185

augury see divination

Augustan Settlement 207

Augustus, emperor 110

Aulerci federation 152, 159
   see also Cenomani; Eburovices

Ausci tribe 114

Ausetani tribe 155

Ausonius, Decimus Magnus 109, 279

Avienus, Rufus Festus 22

Aylesford Bucket 121, 123, 124, 245, 247, 292

azimuth 13, 14, 327

Babylonians 88, 91, 96, 131, 142

bards xv, 9, 74, 130, 169, 216, 220, 255, 256, 272

Battersea Shield 245, 247

Geographical Index

Acknowledgements

I am grateful to Margaret (many times over) and to all my other first readers: Kate Harvey and Starling Lawrence; Gill Coleridge and Melanie Jackson; Nicholas Blake and Kris Doyle; Stephen Roberts; and my guide to ancient Greek, Gerald Sgroi. Thanks also to Paul Baggaley, Nick Brown, Wilf Dickie, Stephen Edwards, Camilla Elworthy, Ryan Harrington, Sam Humphreys, Sophie Jonathan, Cara Jones, Laurence Laluyaux, Drake McFeely, Elizabeth Riley, Peter Straus, Isabelle Taudière and Katie Tooke, and to the following institutions: the Bibliothèque Nationale de France, the British Library, the British Museum, the Centre archéologique européen (Bibracte), Cumbria Woodlands, the Hunterian Museum (Glasgow), the Mairie de Paris, the Musée d'Archéologie méditerranéenne (Marseille), the Musée d'archéologie nationale (Saint-Germain-en-Laye), the Musée Émile Chenon (Châteaumeillant), the National Museum in Prague, the National Museum of Denmark, the National Museum of Scotland, Parc Samara, Stanfords map shop, Tullie House Museum (Carlisle), and, in Oxford, the Ashmolean Museum, the Bodleian Library, Exeter College, Linacre College, the Sackler Library, the Social Science Library, the Taylor Institution Library, the Vere Harmsworth Library and the Oxford University Parks.

Permissions Acknowledgements